Nation-Building and Foreign Policy in India

An Identity-Strategy Conflict

Tobias F. Engelmeier

FOUNDATION®
BOOKS

Delhi • Bangalore • Mumbai • Kolkata • Chennai
• Hyderabad • Pune

Published by
Cambridge University Press India Pvt. Ltd.
under the imprint of Foundation Books
Cambridge House, 4381/4 Ansari Road, Daryaganj, **New Delhi** 110 002

Cambridge University Press India Pvt. Ltd.
C-22, C-Block, Brigade M.M., K.R. Road, Jayanagar, **Bangalore** 560 070
Plot No. 80, Service Industries, Shirvane, Sector-I, Nerul, **Navi Mumbai** 400 706
10, Raja Subodh Mullick Square, 2nd Floor, **Kolkata** 700 013
21/1 (New No. 49), 1st Floor, Model School Road, Thousand Lights, **Chennai** 600 006
House No. 3-5-874/6/4, (Near Apollo Hospital), Hyderguda, **Hyderabad** 500 029
Agarwal Pride, 'A' Wing, 1308 Kasba Peth, Near Surya Hospital, **Pune** 411 011

First Published 2009
Transferred to digital printing 2011

ISBN 978-81-7596-635-2

Published by Manas Saikia for Cambridge University Press India Pvt. Ltd.
and printed at India by Bhavish Graphic, Chenni

Contents

List of Figures

Preface

This book is likely to generate as much controversy in India as George Tanham's monograph 'Indian Strategic Thought: An Interpretive Essay' did in 1992. However, in this case the author's approach is more empathetic to India. His argument is that there is an inflection and a duality in Indian foreign policy that makes India less inclined than most other countries to evaluate and justify its foreign policy purely in terms of its national interest and power considerations or even to distinguish clearly between ideal and interest, between pious hope and reality. In the International Institute for Strategic Studies and CITI India Global Forum held in Delhi on 18–20 April 2008, attention was focussed on the fact that it is a unique development in the history of the last three centuries that the emergent India is not looked upon as a threatening factor in the present day international system. One wonders whether the analysis in this book will provide a satisfactory answer to the question why India's emergence is considered benign.

In the author's view, India is still a nation in formation – nation defined in the classical sense. He is full of admiration for Gandhi and Nehru for the way they handled the nation-building process during the freedom struggle. This vast entity with such diversity of religions, languages and ethnicities could not have been welded into a nation without adopting secularism, tolerance and inclusiveness as a basic approach and invoking syncretic civilisational memories and values. Since these approaches and values were basic to Indian nation-building, the Indian leadership tended to extend them into international relations. Mainstream Indian nationalism was free of chauvinism and considered itself a part of the progress towards one world. India talked of enlightened national interest in harmony with the national interests of other nations. The author has analysed at length whether these values were developed by Gandhi and Nehru purely as ideals or pragmatic necessities compelled by the imperatives of Indian nation-building. While Gandhi did not assume office, Nehru was Prime Minister and Foreign Minister for seventeen years. He had to deal with the real world and compromise with reality. Hence, the duality in Indian foreign policy. For the author, India is a unique case which sets it apart from other nations which tend to focus entirely on national interests.

The author is of the view that today, sixty years after Independence, though the belief in India's moral greatness is less voiced and more implicit, it still exists among the strategic community. So also a belief in its political greatness, especially in the light of recent high economic growth. Recognition and external affirmation are today sought more for political achievements than moral greatness. The conflation of ideals and interests, between ends and means, has become less strong. The author's assertion of the uniqueness of the Indian foreign policy is based on his comparison of India with countries of similar capabilities and their behaviour in the international system. He believes that India has behaved with a great deal of restraint. He attributes India's problems with its neighbours to their imperative needs to develop their national identities on values different from those of India and their attempts to take advantage of India's tensions with China and the United States of America (USA).

His admiration for Gandhi and Nehru does not lead him to overlook their critics. He traces the evolution of both *Hindutva* and the Muslim League's 'two nation' theory and concludes, the survival and evolution of the Indian nation state would not have been successful in the absence of the Gandhi-Nehru approach, their vision and policies and their emphasis on non-violence. He accepts that Nehru's successors did not have his stature nor could they play the role he did in nation-building. Yet, in his view, the Nehruvian values of secularism, tolerance and all inclusiveness continue to form the basis of Indian national identity. Towards the end, he draws attention to the ongoing debate in the country about the foreign and strategic policy India should pursue.

Many of the interpretations and conclusions of the author are bound to be disputed as happened in the case of Tanham's monograph. But such a debate will be healthy. There has been a widely held view that foreign policy is an extension of domestic policy though that view conflicts with the actual experience with countries which are democratic at home and very aggressive in their foreign policies. The author has chosen a unique case of a multireligious, multilingual and multiethnic entity with one of the largest populations in the world, still developing as a cohesive nation state with potential for aggression vis-à-vis its external environment, nevertheless observing restraint. He has tried to reinforce his case about the uniqueness of this development with enormous theoretical research on the influence of culture and identity on a nation's foreign policy and external behaviour.

In India, politicians and political parties are extremely adept in playing realpolitik in domestic politics. Parochial party interests generally prevail over democratic norms. Yet the country, in its foreign policy, has been very restrained and is considered a nonthreatening factor in the international balance of power. This paradox between the domestic politics and foreign policy needs to be analysed and this book makes a useful contribution in that regard.

Obviously, the argument that India is still a nation under formation whose identity is being formed is bound to be challenged by many. A section of our strategic community considers Nehru naïve and thinks that he compromised Indian interests and security. The debate on these issues have been heating up in the country after the Shakti tests were carried out, India's globalisation process speeded up and the international community as a whole has signalled its readiness to welcome India in the emerging balance of power system. This book is the perspective of a scholar from the European Union which is itself in the process of cohering into a multinational, multireligious and multilingual entity. In today's world, the European Union (EU) is recognised as the most liberal and most restrained among the great powers. Is there a parallelism between evolving India and an evolving EU in respect to their attitudes towards the rest of the world?

K Subrahmanyam

Glossary of Terms

BJP	Bharatiya Janata Party
INC	Indian National Congress
NDA	National Democratic Alliance
UPA	United Progressive Alliance
RSS	Rashtriya Swayamsevak Sangh
INA	Indian National Army
NPT	Non-Proliferation Treaty
CBMs	Confidence Building Measures
POI	Person of Indian Origin
NRI	Non-Resident Indian

1

Introduction – Identity, Values and Indian Foreign Policy

'There is far too much tendency today to... not try to understand the psychological backgrounds of other countries, with the result that in spite of complete knowledge of political and economic data they completely fail to understand each other. This is because understanding is something much more than memorising facts of history and geography. Ultimately understanding comes from a certain emotional appreciation of other people, of how an individual or nation functions.'

(Jawaharlal Nehru[1])

Although a national identity may be an elusive element of the foreign policy equation, it is crucially important when analysing any country's behaviour, to look at the intellectual and organisational environment from which the decision-makers come and in which they take their decisions. In as far as it causes a long-term, persistent and significant idiosyncrasy in the foreign policy of an individual country, it has to be factored into the analysis.

How is a nation's foreign policy – an essentially rational, strategic task – influenced by a nation's internal identity dynamics? And, inversely, how do the issues and challenges that underpin foreign policy affect and shape the collective identity of the nation? In general terms, it can be assumed that whenever foreign policy is not exclusively concerned with foreign policy objectives, but – incidentally or purposely – is part of a different or larger political process such as the consolidation of a national identity, foreign policy behaviour is inflected away from what

[1]In an address to the Indian consular corps entitled 'The Occident and the Orient' (Nehru, J., 2003, Vol. 2, p. 245)

most international relations theories would predict. When such an inflection is substantial, it is necessary to make sense of it by understanding its nature (of what type is the inflection?) and logic (what is its inner dynamic and how does it affect foreign policy decision-making?).

A mutually constitutive relationship between foreign policy and national identity exists to a greater or lesser extent in all countries. Elites may make conscious use of this relationship for specific ends. Governments lacking democratic legitimacy may, for instance, be tempted to create a domestic consensus through emotional foreign policy issues. The use of the plight of the Palestinians by the Syrian or Egyptian governments is an example. Also, governments of unstable nations or nations-in-the-making may want to use foreign policy in order to stabilise or unify. The Franco-German war of 1870–1871, which paved the way for German unification, comes to mind. Foreign Policy has the potential – and sometimes even purpose – to make people 'rally around the flag' (think of any popular war, such as initially, USA's 'War on Terror'), as much as it has the potential to bring national divisions and fault-lines into focus (think of any unpopular war, such as that of the USA in Vietnam).

Inversely, national identity tends to spread into foreign policy. Often, a national identity is linked to a specific world view and corresponding beliefs. Nations based on values they believe to be universal, moreover, tend to have a particular desire to spread them. The French Revolutionary armies' credo, the French 'mission civilisatrice', the British 'white man's burden' and the US-American 'Manifest Destiny', Wilson's Fourteen Points and Nehru's five points of peaceful coexistence (Panchsheel[2]), the ideological bipolarity of the Cold War, and the self-imposed military restraint of modern German and Japanese foreign policies had or have significantly identity or value-based motivations. Often, values get entangled in considerations of interests, sometimes leaving little less than a hollow shell. At other times, however, values lead countries to act even against their own interests. This can be so, because in the realm of politics, values are a priori. While they may be in tune with the national interest (a non-violent approach may, in a particular situation, also be

[2]These principles where contained in the joint communiqué by Chinese Prime Minister Zhou Enlai and the Indian Prime Minister Jawaharlal Nehru in 1954. Subsequently, they have been frequently voiced, especially by Nehru and have become integrated into a number of further international documents. They are – 1. Mutual respect for each other's territorial integrity and sovereignty; 2. Mutual non-aggression; 3. Mutual non-interference in each other's affairs; 4. Equality and mutual benefit; 5. Peaceful coexistence.

a prudent approach), and while the national interest may be thought of as the only, ultimate value to which all other values are means, they conceptually come before a consideration of interest. They are linked to an identity. So-called values, which are merely conditional to achieving a specific end, for example, non-violence as a strategic choice of a weak state, are strictly speaking not values, but merely prudent or naïve components of a strategy.

Values and interests interact in a highly complex manner, producing synergy or contradiction. It is very difficult to distinguish values and interests in any given foreign policy decision. For one, the motivation structure of political actors is intricate and often hidden from public view. Secondly, many political actors possess an astonishing capacity for double-standards. Thirdly, values and interests are often consciously conflated for political gains. One way of dealing with this problem is to view value-rhetoric as always no more than a fig-leaf for interest politics and to focus entirely on the rational nature of actors and states. This implies that the analyst of foreign policy can decode the 'real' motivation underlying the stated motivations. Undoubtedly, one should be very skeptical with the justifications political actors give for their own actions. However, to conclude that all political actors are always cynically camouflaging a naked national interest when they take recourse to, 'value language' is going too far. There are enormous grey zones between what is thought and what is said, between what is said and what is done, between what is done and how it affects reality, and between the effect and the perception of the effect.

Within these grey zones, it is likely that some leaders may genuinely believe in the moral dimension of their foreign policy. That does not necessarily mean that a country will in fact always act morally by its own standards or by universal standards (if such standards exist), or be perceived as doing so by other, often rival, countries. Nevertheless, there exists a relationship between a state's view of itself and its national identity as reflected in its rhetoric, on the one hand, and its actual behaviour, on the other. Attitudes, beliefs, or identity, all influence decision and policy-making at various levels – from the perception and evaluation of situations to the choice of effective and legitimate responses to them and the way success and failure are evaluated, to name just a few. For example, nations with a universalist value identity may well find it more difficult and consider it less legitimate to pursue their specific national interest in all forcefulness than nations based on a chauvinist identity.

India, as will be shown, is an ideal case study for understanding the relationship between foreign policy and national identity. Foreign policy is important to any new state because it helps it to reaffirm its independence and to articulate its identity. At the same time, foreign policy is not likely to be critical for an under-developed new state, whose preferred focus is domestic. Thus, as long as the new state faces no direct external threat, foreign policy 'tends to be some kind of residual category, dominated not only by domestic politics, but also by rhetorical and ideological preoccupations' (Rothstein). It may thus be used to achieve symbolic and psychological domestic goals, 'to create a degree of identity with the nation, to affirm a new status and to enhance the sense of national unity' (Rothstein, 1976). This link between nation-building and foreign policy is reinforced by dominant, often charismatic leaders (such as Nehru), a lack of experience, strategy and know-how, few bureaucratic pressures, few interest groups with a stake in foreign policy, and a populace for whom foreign matters are remote and abstract. If a leader manages to enshrine his ideas by crafting a public consensus, they are more likely to outlast him than if he merely bases them on his personal popularity and power.

The specific Indian process of identity formation provides a crucial insight into what is a striking duality in Indian foreign policy between a realist pursuit of its national interests, on one hand, and an idealist pursuit of system-level goals, on the other. Realism is neither subordinate to idealism, nor is idealism necessarily subordinate to realism. There is a genuine duality which, at times, produces a dilemma. This duality – or, more precisely, the inflection towards an uncommon, idealist element – can best be explained neither by reference to cultural uniqueness, as nationalist leaders have claimed, nor by reference to individual leaders' preferences, but by understanding the specific dynamics of India's nationalism and highly complex project of nation-building. Idealism in Indian foreign policy can be understood as serving a nation-building purpose – and it is, in turn, the expression of a specific type of nationalism. The challenges and choices of an ambitious and precarious Indian national project made an active identity politics necessary. The idealist element in foreign policy is to be understood with regard to this specific Indian dynamic of nation-building. Given that the grooves for India's national identity have been set many years ago, in the era of Gandhi and Nehru, we can compare the relationship between identity and foreign policy as it originally appeared during their times, with recently collected data (in 2005–2006). This comparison allows a glimpse at those aspects of the national identity that have become deeply internalised and can be expected to continue to play an important role in Indian foreign policy.

Figure 1.1 shows that, if Indian foreign policy were the product only of realism based on a consideration of national-interest and unit-level goals, it would have an uninflected foreign policy. Indian foreign policy, however, displays a duality or an ambiguity. It is not only the product of realism, but also of idealism, of values and system-level goals. The duality caused the foreign policy to be inflected away from 'Indian foreign policy, (without inflection)' to 'Indian foreign policy actual'. The focus here is on understanding the inflection and the nature and direction of the inflection, namely the idealist element, (as in diagram) not on the realist element, which also exists and provides the second pole for the duality.

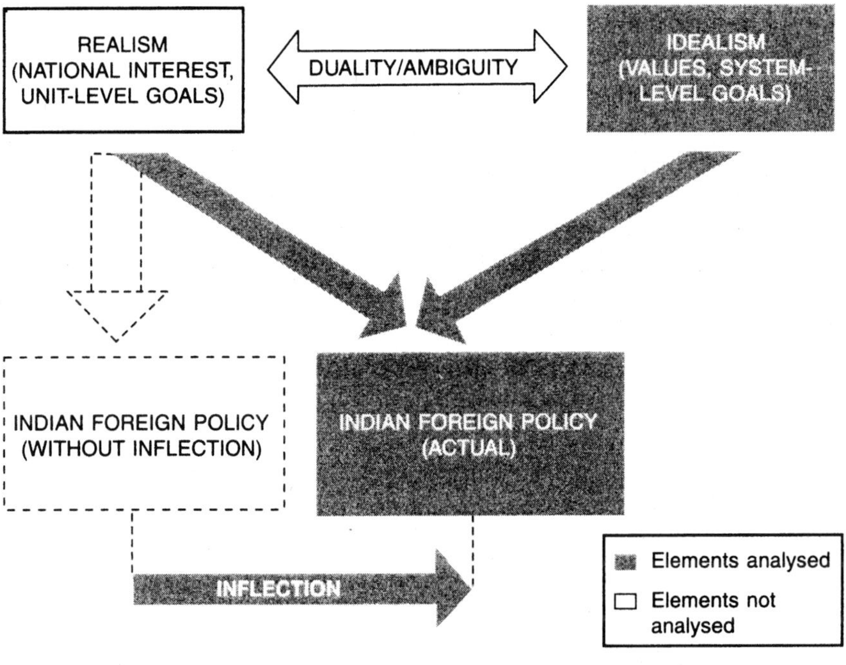

Figure 1.1: The Focus of the Analysis

The above representation of Indian foreign policy as a function of the two elements, realism and idealism, is of course, an abstraction. Reality is far more complex. Firstly, Indian foreign policy has fluctuated significantly between the two poles. At times, hegemonic aspirations were on the rise alongside a greater focus on the military, as in the 1970's; at others, Indian policy was marked more by diplomacy and restraint, as in the early 1990's. More often, idealism, soft power and hard power approaches were used simultaneously, in varying combinations. Fluctuations are caused, for example, by changes in the international environment, by specific security and diplomatic constellations, by the preferences and personal styles of individual leaders, or by domestic tactical considerations and constraints. However, there remains an underlying idealist inflection, not simply a tactical one, appearing only at times, but a systemic, long-term one.

Secondly, the two poles in Figure 1.1 are represented in a zero-sum-situation – as one is becoming less important, the other is becoming more prominent – in direct correlation. In reality, their relationship is much more interdependent and difficult to determine. As stated earlier, it is difficult to separate ideal from interest when understanding a political actor's motivations. Besides, the effects of actions cannot entirely be controlled by the actor, nor can they be exactly predicted. Thus, it often happens that a policy designed to serve the national interest, actually undermines it; and that a policy chosen for idealist reasons, actually turns out to be very much in the national interest.

The inflection and the duality mean that India is less inclined than most other countries to evaluate and justify its foreign policy purely in terms of its national interest and power considerations, or even to distinguish clearly between ideal and interest, between pious hope and reality. Why has India shuttled uneasily between interests and values, between unit-level and system-level goals, and between cool power-political calculation and statements of identity? Why is Indian foreign policy not 'normal'[3] (Mitra, 2003)? The schematic account of the idealist inflection can be traced in reality only with difficulty, relying to some extent on overall judgments, educated guesses and contextual interpretations. There are, however, indicators of it.

For an argument attempting to identify and explain a duality, it is all the more important to be unambiguous about the terminology. The overall framework used here is based on a dichotomy between realism and idealism, as well as between strategy and identity. These are widely used concepts with often disparate meanings and hence are in need of definition.

[3]'Normal' is posited in inverted commas, because it is a theoretical abstraction, much like the 'equilibrium' in economic theory. It means a rational, strategic pursuit of national interests without limitations such as considerations of values or identity.

To E. H. Carr, idealism – he calls it utopianism[4] – is a belief in the possibility of transforming society by an act of will. It fails to duly appreciate the constraints placed upon actors by material reality. Thus, it must fail. The realists, on the other hand, understand their environment as the product of a long chain of causality which cannot be changed at will. Carr relates idealism to a belief in the pre-eminence of ethical considerations and realism to a pre-eminence of politics (Carr,1946).

While realism in the political context can thus be understood as dealing strictly with what is, idealism, on the other hand, is dealing with what could be. An idealist is therefore likely to argue that the future, the potential reality is the more important reality than the existing one. One of the most eloquent descriptions of idealism is provided by Friedell – an 'ideal', he writes, is 'something that is and is not... it is our shining counter-pole, the platonic other half we are searching for both indefatigably and always in vain throughout our entire journey on earth' (Friedell). His argument is interesting – 'Who makes reality?' The realist only tries to catch up with a reality, which is always in flux, in a 'state of agony'. His reality is a 'post-dated' fiction, comparable to the light of a star that may no longer exist. Reality is in a constant process of being shaped by men of imagination (Friedell,1927). Idealism by this description is value-free. It is a description of a reality waiting to be materialised, a transcendental reality that is nevertheless more actual than the fleeting moment. Gandhi made a similar point, but with a subtle difference – 'To believe that what has not occurred in history will not occur at all is to argue disbelief in the dignity of man' (Gandhi,1997). The crucial word is 'dignity'. It can be understood to refer to human beings as creators, as actors; it furthermore, in the context of Gandhi's thought and actions, can be understood to imply a moral quality.

Idealism, as it is used here, rests on two assumptions – that human agency is relevant and that there is a possibility of progress through it. This progress is (this is where idealism is most clearly demarcated from realism in the realm of the political) not only possible theoretically but within our power to achieve in the foreseeable future. In international politics, this idealism has an effect on ends as well as means. In terms of ends, it delineates a foreign policy which pursues system-level goals, if necessary at the expense of direct national interests, in the conviction that

---

[4]It is admittedly difficult, if not impossible to distinguish between idealism and utopianism (as much as it is difficult, if not impossible to distinguish between realism and fatalism).

they will – in the long run – serve everybody's interests, including one's own. By taking on system-level responsibilities for stability and progress, such a policy supplants the realist assertion that human nature and the international condition is fixed with a belief in purposive human (national) agency. In terms of means, idealism is the application of an ethical dimension to foreign policy which is not necessarily shared by others, nor is it necessarily expected from others – it is a conscious, unilateral restriction of the potential foreign policy options beyond what is the international norm[5].

Realism, here, is taken to be a strict focus on the existing environment, on the structural realism of an incorrigibly anarchic self-help system that provides a 'norm' for political behaviour based on power, conceptions of security and rational, interest-oriented action. The idealist element in Indian foreign policy is a significant deviation from this norm. It is a concern with a better, potential environment and with system-level goals. What 'better' means, is derived from values.

Realism is linked to strategy, a cerebral exercise concerned with the means to achieve given ends; idealism is linked to identity, an emotional, constitutive view of the self from which ends may be derived. The two ancient Asian master strategists and firm realists, the Indian Kautilya and the Chinese Sun Tzu, make clear that identity and strategy are to be kept apart. Whatever the desired ends, any strategy to reach them must deal with reality in an impassioned, rational manner. Deception and war are as much a part of the toolbox as are loyalty and restraint. Strategy is concerned with the most effective means given a particular situation and specific ends. Kautilya elaborates on methods of foreign policy by which the king can 'bind other rulers by the chains of his intellect and can play with them as he pleases' (Kautilya, 1992). To Sun Tzu, strategy is regressive ad infinitum. It is superior foresight, the ability to do 'what is difficult, while it is easy... what is great, while it is small' (translator's introduction – Sun Tzu, 1988). This requires a dispassionate assessment of situations, an inner detachment.

Identity is not concerned with means and the realm of action – but rather with being. Here, identity is used in the sense of a national identity,

[5]Idealism thus defined is, therefore, only one specific form in which ideational factors may impact on state behaviour and significantly inflect rational choice models. Other ideational factors are, for instance, ideologies of supremacy, expansion or isolationism, or historical fears and enmities. Ideational factors can be linked to cultural identity in as far as they are carried by a significant group of people and have a certain degree of consistency over time.

as in Anderson's 'imagined community' (Anderson, 1991). Identity will impact on strategy. The chess game cannot be abstracted from the chess players. Compound identities (here, national identities) have a more complex effect on strategies (here, national strategies). The effect is determined not only by the type and strength of the identity, but also by its inner mechanisms and the identity formation process. If an identity can produce ends solely from a consideration of the national interest, there is no immediate conflict with a strategy based on a realist assessment of the environment and designed to achieve the given ends. Such an identity, based solely on a common interest and the successful pursuit of it is, however, of limited community building power. A stable national identity will hold people together not only in relation to a common goal, but at a deeper level, around a shared belief in the inherent nature and purpose of the community, thus making it independent of political expediencies. If identity introduces idealist (or other ideational) considerations into the foreign policy process, there is a duality between what is and what could be, between realism and idealism (or other ideas). Identity may then come to rival strategy and produce an inflection as in the case of India.

1.1 India's Idealism–Realism Duality Observed

While it is an exaggeration to attribute to India a 'perverse delight in being called a soft state' (Kanwal, 2005), it is fair to wonder why it has often decided to engage in politics that are not explicable by reference to an internationally valid realism. It seems that, since the time of Nehru, there has been a continuing struggle between what Dixit called 'two contradictory trends' in Indian foreign policy thinking, with unusual, idealistic motivations on one hand and 'normal', interest-based motivations on the other. Dixit argues that these contradictory trends have always existed at the 'subconscious level'. In modern times, these trends surfaced and presumably became more conscious as the 'origins' of the 'ethos and motivations' of India's foreign policy in the 'thought processes of the leaders of our renaissance in the late eighteenth and in the nineteenth centuries and in those of the national freedom movement' (Dixit, 2003). Marcus Kim speaks of the same duality in terms of the two opposing cultural characteristics of 'dharma and political pragmatism'. He argues that they have been 'an intrinsic and often conflicting part of the Indian strategic culture' (Kim, 2004). Stephen Cohen, one of the most balanced and incisive outside observers of Indian foreign policy, has described

Indian strategic thinking as 'both idealist and realist, Gandhian and Machiavellian' (Cohen, 2001). K. Subrahmanyam has argued that there is 'an implied assumption that, having won freedom through a non-violent struggle... this nation has an obligation to conduct its international security policies with less violence than is normally adopted by other nations'. Many Indians tend to believe, he continues, 'that India's role in international affairs had a moral content'. (Subrahmanyam, 1985)

In Dixit's argument, the duality (the idealist inflection) was carried into the foreign policy domain of a newly independent India by its two greatest modern leaders, namely, Mahatma Gandhi and Jawaharlal Nehru. Gandhi continues to define 'the normative and moral terms of reference' within which India's foreign policy is conceptualised. His influence led to a disregard of interest-based strategic thinking and in some ways 'resulted in India failing to cope with the realities of international politics' (Dixit). Influenced by Gandhi, he describes Nehru as having had 'an idealistic approach to foreign policy'. However, in the course of his tenure as Prime Minister, he was forced to progressively adjust and accept the realities of international politics (Dixit, 2003). G.S. Bajpai admired Nehru's foreign policy for it had the 'distinction' of 'combining idealism with national interest' (Bajpai, 1977). According to Cohen, Nehru has set the tone for Indian foreign policy to come by anticipating and reflecting a 'hawkish-dovish, aggressive-moderate, forceful-diplomatic, moralistic-realist' approach to foreign policy (Cohen, 2001). The subsequent search for a 'golden mean' between an idealist 'vision of an eventual peaceful world and possessions of the wherewithal to defend itself in the interim', Bertsch writes, 'has troubled [India's] conscience for decades' (Bertsch, Gahlaut, et al., 1999).

Analysts of Indian foreign policy have written much about the duality between idealism and realism – usually interpreted as an idiosyncrasy or irregularity. They approach it from varying perspectives. Depending usually on what they consider to be the 'right' conduct of international affairs and the nature of India's national interests, the focus is either on the lack of realism (and the emotional, ad hocist or non-strategic interferences with the proper conduct of foreign policy), or on the purity or utility of the ethical elements. It thus provides the starting point to either criticise or extol the policy process. Nehru, who is usually regarded as the originator of the idealist element as well as of the duality, is often at the centre of such debates.

Tharoor, mixing mild criticism with admiration, argues that Indian foreign policy under Nehru was conducted not as professionally as it could have been because Nehru was fundamentally disinterested in matters of defense and security. He had an 'Olympian disdain for "power politics"'. Foreign policy and the repeated articulation of the ideals underlying it was an expression of India's national values, that is to say, of his own values (Tharoor). Nehru's India 'did not speak in terms of nation-state rivalry or patriotic chauvinism... it sought an altogether loftier place on the world stage' (Tharoor, 2003). Other observers are far less lenient in their assessment of Nehru's idealism. Kapur excoriates it as injurious folly. By rejecting the 'classical approach to diplomacy and war... which sets the problem of war and conflict as the central question' and instead projecting a globalist and utopian view 'that stressed peace and harmony among states and nations', he did significant harm to India's interests (Kapur). What is more, his idealism was fundamentally unethical. It 'betrayed' the people of India, who trusted him, 'through a series of failed policies' (Kapur, 2004). Prakash also deeply deplores that an over-simplification of Gandhian values has led to an 'idealistic world-view amongst our post-independence leadership' (Prakash, 2005). Chaulia, on the other hand, lauds Nehru for the same thing he is criticised for by Kapur – a fundamentally value-driven foreign policy, opposed to any form of realpolitik (which, according to Chaulia, had previously 'betrayed the people of the world'). Instead, Nehru (in Chaulia's view correctly) asserted that 'the ends should be people and the only justifiable means should be peace' (Chaulia, 2002). Interestingly, with respect to the Bharatiya Janata Party (BJP), where Chaulia sees continuity, Kapur sees a radical break in foreign policy. For Chaulia, Nehru's idealism remains the backbone of Indian foreign policy, whereas for Kapur, the BJP has finally brought a much needed and radical change. Cohen takes an intermediate position, he perceives a current Indian strategic community in which many still hold on to the general principles established by Nehru, but accept that as circumstances have changed, Indian policy must also change (Cohen, 2001).

The former Canadian ambassador Escott Reid, in a personal history of disenchantment with Nehru, criticises not only the utility of Nehru's idealism but questions the very existence of it. He argues that Nehru's vainglorious, pompous and impetuous moral grandstanding without strategy contradicted both – ideal and interests (Reid, 1981)[6]. Raju Thomas

[6]In the preface to 'Envoy to Nehru', Reid writes that 'often governments are criticised for pursuing foreign policies based on national self-interest. I am coming more and more to believe that more often the valid basis for criticism is that the foreign policy is not based on national self-interest but on irritation, resentment, anger... There is much in this book to support this thesis.' (Reid, E., 1981, p. x).

and Aspy Rana, by contrast, believe that the idealism was quite real – and very useful, politically (Rana, 1976; Thomas, 2004; Rana, 2005). Critique of the duality is especially strong with regard to the 1962 Indo–Chinese War. Neville Maxwell has suggested that India shares a large part of the responsibility for the war, precisely because it disastrously combined realism and idealism – or rather naiveté (Maxwell, 1970). D.K. Palit, among many others, suggested that, had Nehru been less idealistic and more realistic in his assessment of China, the 1962 war and the resounding defeat of the Indian army could have been avoided (Palit, 1991).

The argument about Nehru seamlessly passes into an argument about the duality, the role, capabilities and responsibilities of India today. Khilnani, for example, believes that India with its unique cultural background and social make-up can achieve a unique and powerful synthesis between the idealist and realist elements in its foreign policy, much like the one attempted by Nehru (Khilnani, 2005). Kumaraswamy, on the other hand, condemns the hovering between idealist aspirations and realist instincts. Whilst enabling India to take the 'moral high ground', it in fact only results in 'India pushing itself into a corner' (Kumaraswamy, 2004).

Most Indian foreign policy literature proposes that the duality and the inflection due to the idealist element has become less prominent in recent years (Dixit, 2003; Mohan, 2003). 'Fortuitously', Mitra noted, 'Indian policy has gravitated towards placing her interests in the international arena with the right combination of structural realism and national identity' (Mitra, 2005). It has gravitated towards a stronger verbalisation of the national interest and away from, what Mitra has called the 'classical idealism', marked by 'the primacy of norms and laws over materialist interests' under Nehru (Mitra, 2001). Albeit smaller, an inflection still remains – 'Rather than being self-consciously aloof', India's current foreign policy is still 'drawing on national identity (culture and ideology) and liberal values of peace and plurality' (Mitra, 2005). And India will probably continue to display an idealist inflection as it moves towards the future. Its central foreign policy identity is likely to remain stable at the core – 'there is a recognisably Indian worldview and a recognisably Indian way of dealing with the world' (Cohen, 2001).

1.2 Tracing the Duality

'Idealism', Nehru once said, 'is nothing but the realism of tomorrow' (Nehru, 1961). In this view, reality is not an exogenous immobile structure, but the product of our conscious actions, of our will and our choices; it can be shaped by imaginative vision and bold action. That is not all, however; the view also implies that the future can be better than the past. It is optimistic. The mindset underlying Nehru's Panchsheel posits an ideal world, composed of countries interested in peacefully maintaining the status quo and settling just national interests and concerns by dialogue, international law and mediation. India, not compromising on its moral credibility and freedom of action by alliance to either of the two great power blocs, would play a pivotal role in this set-up – a role justified by its honest system-level concerns and by its moral and civilisational greatness. This role would be accepted as natural and legitimate by others (Cohen, 2001; Mitra, 2005). India would seek to play an active role in global politics to promote peace (Misra, 1982). At the same time, however, Nehru was pragmatic enough to defend India's interests – by force, if necessary. He realised that there was a fundamental difference between the 'realism of tomorrow' and the realism of today, between an effort to change the system and survival in the existing system, between the direction of change and the capacity for change. Thus, the realpolitik of Kashmir, Goa or Hungary stood alongside Panchsheel, *Bhai-bhai-ism* and highbrow global diplomacy.

1.2.1 *Pakistan, China and the United Nations*

Most scholars agree on Nehru's seminal influence on Indian foreign policy discourse in general and the existence of an idealist element in particular (for example, Appadorai, 1971; Nanda, 1976; Kulke, and Rothermund, 1998; Cohen, 2001; Dixit, 2003; Mitra, 2003; Khilnani, 2005). The trend set by Nehru continued after his death. India's involvements in Bangladesh as well as Sri Lanka have been justified or condemned as both, humanitarian as well as power-political interventions. Forceful, even brutal choices in Kashmir, Punjab or the North East Frontier Region as well as (at times) determined attempts at South Asian regional hegemony (the Indira Doctrine, Cohen, 2001) stand alongside longstanding Indian support for the Tibetans[7], Palestinians or for Ho Chi Minh in the face of Great Power opposition, and such lofty proclamations as the Gujral Doctrine[8]. In Shimla, following the 1971 war, at the height

[7]After fleeing Tibet, the Dalai Lama was allowed to set up a government in exile in Dharamshala, India. Nehru initially discouraged the Dalai Lama from seeking refuge in India for fear that it would disrupt relations with China which it did (Gopal, S., 1993, p. 228).

[8]These are some excerpts from Prime Minister I.K. Gujral's speech – '...Independence for us did not signify only the new-found freedom to control our own

of Indian regional dominance and from a position of strength, Indira Gandhi (arguably the most power-politically inclined of the Indian Prime Ministers) agreed to a settlement with Pakistan marked by the renunciation of strategic advantages gained during the war. The BJP conducted both, 'Bus Diplomacy' and nuclear tests.

Since its independence, India has been a firm supporter of the United Nations (UN) and international co-operation. In fact, the text of the Indian Constitution explicitly demands of the national leadership not only to take care of the national interest, but also to 'endeavour to promote international peace and security', to 'maintain just and honourable relations between nations', to 'foster respect for international law and treaty obligations in the dealings with other peoples' and to 'encourage settlement of international disputes by arbitration'[9]. India has been highly supportive of the UN, both, diplomatically as well as with troop contributions. It has historically been one of the major troop contributors in a large number of UN missions around the globe[10], often taking a leading role (for instance, in Korea in the 1950s and in Somalia in the 1990s). It has been at the forefront of the UN struggles against colonisation and apartheid, and for disarmament.

At the same time, however, India – despite having first referred the issue to the UN – today firmly opposes any attempt at finding a solution to the Kashmir conflict by way of international mediation. The UN-resolution on Kashmir, demanding a popular vote on the future of the state is being disregarded[11]; instead, an all-party resolution of the Lok

---

destinies. More importantly, it represented an obligation and a call to duty to stand up firmly for what was right and just. By upholding what was right and just, we, in essence, upheld and reinforced our own independence… The principles of truth and non-violence, of tolerance and justice, which guided India's freedom struggle, also inspired the vision and subsequent development of India as a free society, and shaped its foreign policy…'. The 'Gujral Doctrine' is encompassed in a commitment to peaceful, cooperative relations and non-interference, as well as, a commitment to non-reciprocity. This is the genuinely novel element, transcending the idea of raison d'etat – '…with its neighbours like Bangladesh, Bhutan, Maldives, Nepal and Sri Lanka, India does not ask for reciprocity, but gives and accommodates what it can in good faith and trust…' (Gujral, I. K., 1997). Curiously Pakistan is not mentioned as a beneficiary of the Gujral Doctrine.

[9]The Constitution of India, § 51, (a) – (d), on http://www.constitution.org/cons/india/const (accessed on 7 March, 2005).

[10]See the information provided by the UN Department of Peace Keeping Operations on http://www.un.org/Depts/dpko (accessed on 29 August, 2007).

[11]UN Resolution 47 (1948), Section B – Plebiscite. See, especially point 7, stating that 'the Government of India should undertake that there will be established in Jammu and Kashmir a Plebiscite Administration to hold a plebiscite as soon as possible on the

Sabha in 1995 voted unanimously to affirm Kashmir as an integral part of Indian territory and as India's internal problem. The Kashmir-issue, one of the most intractable global conflicts over the last 60 years, has taken on a complex dynamic of its own and needs to be analysed within a very specific framework. The initial Indian approach is nevertheless indicative of the idealist inflection. 'Strikingly', Ray argues, India in 1947 stopped the victorious armed forces 'shortly before a final triumph', to refer the case to the UN[12]. There followed years of 'conjectural realist gamesmanship'. In the following years, it insulated its developmental strategies for the region from the 'structural corollaries of the realist paradigm'. India continued on a relatively low defense budget and kept the professional armed forces under strict institutional control, severely limiting its military capabilities (Ray, 2004). In January 1948, despite the fact that fighting in Kashmir was still fierce, the Indian government decided, on Gandhi's recommendation, to transfer previously withheld funds to the government of Pakistan (ca. GBP 30 million, due to Pakistan as part of the assets of the British Raj). In Gandhi's mind – and the Indian government under Nehru eventually came to accept his reasoning – the fight with Pakistan in Kashmir (which India needed to win by force) and the fair distribution of the partition assets were unrelated issues[13] (Gopal, 1993). The idea of transferring money to a military adversary – for whatever reason – is entirely opposed to *raison d'etat.*

Over the course of the last 60 years, the idealist element has survived a number of realist 'shocks', such as the 1962 Indo-Chinese war, the USS Enterprise incident during the 1971-war with Pakistan, or the collapse of India's most important strategic partner, the Soviet Union, in 1991. While it was evolving, adapting to new circumstances, even ripening over the years, it appears to have survived as an essential and vital phenomenon in the minds of the political leadership. This was amply demonstrated when, in March 2003, the Indian Lok Sabha passed a unanimous resolution condemning the invasion of Iraq by a US-led coalition. Iraq was a long-time partner of India, but the USA was the key to India's new security

---

question of the accession of the State to India or Pakistan', http://www.un.org/documents/sc/res/1948/scres48 (accessed on 1 December, 2006).

[12]Another factor leading to an abortion of the effort was that Sheikh Abdullah cautioned Nehru against moving further into parts of Kashmir over which he had no control.

[13]Gandhi's call for proceeding justly with regard to the funds, together with his fast to end Hindu-Muslim violence were the immediate cause for his assassination by a Hindu fanatic on 30 January, 1948.

strategy. In order to show India's general willingness to support the USA, the BJP-lead coalition government was planning to send troops to Iraq. During a heated debate on the issue, however, the government had to backtrack, as many of the Nehruvian moralistic policy reflexes resurfaced. Priya Ranjan Dasmunshi, for instance, a Congress MP and one of the central figures in the debate, argued for India's duty to condemn the aggression on the grounds that 'we are a country of a billion people, which preaches, right from the days of the Buddha and Mahatma Gandhi, the message of peace' (Government of India 2003). Just over two years later, in July 2005, India was ready to strike a highly pragmatic nuclear deal with the same country it had previously condemned on moral grounds.

In 2006, the Indian Prime Minister Manmohan Singh, declared that –

> '...the philosophy of "non-alignment" was based on the principle that we were aligned only with our values and our enlightened national interests... Non-alignment was... always an expression of our enlightened national interest and, I dare say, will remain so... While the instruments of policy and the tactics and strategy we adopt may change with time, the values in which they are embedded are universal and will remain true for all time' (Singh, 2006).

India does not merely have a national interest – India has an 'enlightened' national interest (Nehru called it 'intelligent self-interest', or 'practical idealism'[14]). That implies prudence, far-sightedness and restraint. It also implies system-level concerns[15] and the readiness to include in decisions, a consideration of the welfare of other nations – from a position of strength – as a benign hegemon in South Asia and an equal partner in the international concert of great powers (Mitra, 2003).

---

[14]As quoted in Khilnani (2005) and Chaulia (2002).

[15]In a speech in 2005, Manmohan Singh explained that 'if there is an 'idea of India' that the world should remember us by and regard us for, it is the idea of an inclusive and open society, a multicultural, multiethnic, multilingual society'. India has an 'obligation to history and to mankind to show that pluralism works'. It can help other nations in their own progress towards building functioning liberal-democratic societies. However – and this is a key difference compared with Nehru, India is aware of the limitations of its influence and will give advice only when asked (Singh, M. 2005b). In another speech in Mumbai, he repeated India's claim to moral and political greatness – 'I am convinced that the twenty-first century will be an Indian century. The world will once again look at us with regard and respect, not just for the economic progress we make, but for the democratic values we cherish and uphold and the principles of pluralism and inclusiveness we have come to represent, which is India's heritage.' (Basu, P. K., Chellaney, B. et al. 2005, p.vii).

The terminology is reminiscent of the 'enlightened despot' of eighteenth century Europe who uses his unlimited power benevolently in the interest of his subjects, based on humanist values and a belief in progress. The idealist inflection is encapsulated in these very words – 'enlightened national interest'. Like so many of his predecessors, Manmohan Singh also advocated (with respect to terrorism, at the UN general assembly) a 'global response', a 'meaningful consensus' in order to 'succeed in creating a world that truly manifests the ideal of the United Nations... we must now give it substance and credibility, avoiding selective approaches and political expediency' (Mitra, 2005). By political expediency, Singh presumably refers to the national interest. Even the structure of the Common Minimum Programme (CMP) of the United Progressive Alliance (UPA) government in a way exemplifies the idealist inflection. It clearly differentiates between the agenda point 'Defense, Internal Security', dealing with the armed forces, with nuclear weapons and the struggle against terrorism, on the one hand, and the agenda point 'Foreign Policy', focussing on diplomacy, bilateral and multilateral conflict- and trade-related dialogue, on the other. In his interpretative essay on Indian strategic thought, George Tanham notes that India wants to be a world power – with nuclear missile capabilities, a blue water navy and a strong military-industrial complex. However, the 'paramount goal' is 'recognition as a great nation (rather than as a superpower)' (Tanham, 1992).

1.2.2 *The Nuclear Issue*

Nowhere has the idealism–realism duality and the inflection been more pronounced than in the field of nuclear weapons. Perkovich argues that the theories of structural realism, rational choice and nuclear deterrence –

> '...cannot explain why and how India's policy developed from 1947-1964. Nor can they explain why India waited thirty-four years after China's first nuclear weapons test to declare that it had countervailing nuclear weapons' (Perkovich, 2001).

Of course, India's nuclear quest has not simply been a just pursuit of a civillian technology or an imposed, merely defensive and fundamentally disliked military technology, as Indian conventional wisdom suggests. Power political considerations existed from the beginning, when Nehru decided to create the groundwork for a future nuclear option. At the same time, however, 'moral considerations have had an unusually material impact on Indian policy' (Perkovich). Later, nationalist and tactical-political considerations have been important in India's decision to become a nuclear weapons state. On the whole, domestic factors have been at least as important during India's nuclear quest as balance of power factors (Perkovich, 2001). K. Subrahmanyam in a newspaper article for the Indian Express on 29 May, 2008 described his personal experience with Rajiv Gandhi, who eventually took the decision of building a nuclear deterrent in 1988–1989 –

> 'It was obvious that Rajiv Gandhi was against going nuclear. In 1986... he joined Mikhail Gorbachev in issuing the Delhi declaration on a nuclear-weapon free, non-violent world. He persisted in this policy though Pakistan had publicly boasted about its nuclear weapon and threatened India during Operation Brasstacks. Rajiv Gandhi persisted in his action plan for disarmament to the UN General Assembly on 9 June, 1988... He offered that India would not go nuclear if the world accepted his phased disarmament plan... Rajiv Gandhi's pleas were totally ignored. After another eight or nine months of agonising, he put India's security and interests ahead of all other considerations and directed the weaponisation of the Indian nuclear programme' (Subrahmanyam, K., 2008).

Today, India has a nuclear programme but lacks a strategy of what to do with it (Cohen, 2001; Perkovich, 2001; Tellis, 2001; Basrur, 2005; Mitra, 2005). India is proud of having 'the bomb', and wants to have a credible nuclear deterrent, it accepts it as a symbol of power and status – yet it feels oddly ashamed of it as a weapon. Tellis refers to India's 'singular view of nuclear weapons as "pure deterrents" rather than as war-fighting instruments' (Tellis, 2001). India and China have both departed significantly from the traditional nuclear weapons doctrines of the US, Russia, the United Kingdom and France, by unilaterally making No-First-Use declarations. In rhetorical terms, India's 'singular view' has led to awkward verbal capers. The description of the 1974 nuclear weapons test as a 'peaceful nuclear explosion' is a grotesque euphemism. With more than a hint of self-righteousness and with an unequivocal reference to the duality, it was called 'Smiling Buddha'[16]. Then, there is the recurring linkage between nuclear weapons and nuclear disarmament, the idea of advancing a nuclear-free world by way of becoming a nuclear power (Subrahmanyam, 2005) and the ambiguous concept of 'credible minimum deterrence' (Basrur, 2005).

In practical terms, there has always been a significant ambivalence in the Indian nuclear status. Far from being the product of strategic

---

[16]The Pokhran-II tests in 1998 were given the much more straightforward name 'Operation Shakti' – Shakti meaning 'strength' or 'power'.

brilliance, this ambivalence was the result of uneasiness, a lack of strategic clarity and the underlying idealist inflection. It has been manifest in Indian decision-making from the beginning. Nehru, who was firmly opposed to nuclear weapons on ideological grounds, nevertheless laid the foundations of a broad programme of nuclear research. It did not openly aim at the bomb, but gave Indian leaders the scientific know-how to do so later. He furthermore refused to unilaterally disavow the nuclear option, lest it could be used later as a bargaining chip. In 1964–1965, following the Chinese nuclear test and after unsuccessful approaches to the USA and the Soviet Union for nuclear guarantees, it would have been most natural for India to set up an unambiguous, dynamic nuclear weapons programme of its own. India, however, hesitated. At the same time, it declined to sign the non-proliferation treaty (NPT) put forward by the Soviet Union and the USA. The reasons for this decision are many and the treaty continues to be hotly debated in India. A principled rejection of the institutionalised inequality between the nuclear 'haves' and 'have-nots' is almost invariably voiced (Nizamani, 2000). This stance has cost India dearly, especially in its relationship with the USA.

From 1974 onwards, India was a semi-nuclear power. Indira Gandhi was, however, 'shy' about openly exercising the nuclear option (Subrahmanyam). During the Janata government of Morarji Desai (1977–1979), India even temporarily renounced all further nuclear ambitions. In a statement to the UN, Desai declared India's intention 'not to manufacture or acquire nuclear weapons even if the rest of the world did so'. He abjured 'nuclear explosions even for peaceful purposes' (Perkovich). It is not clear, to what extent India at that time was aware of the Pakistani nuclear programme, initiated in 1972. In the 1980s and 1990s, the unequivocal renunciation of nuclear weapons was given up again in favour of a continuation of ambiguity; the status eventually became institutionalised in the 'recessed deterrent' strategy of threatening with a bomb without actually having it, but being capable of fabricating it at short notice (on India's nuclear quest, Perkovich, 2001; Tellis, 2001; Subrahmanyam, 2005). Later, in 1998, the BJP-led National Democratic Alliance (NDA) government made the bomb 'into a symbol of Indian nationhood' and, paradoxically, into 'an act of peaceful resistance to international bullying' over the NPT (Mitra, 2005). It did not, however, dispel the precarious uncertainty about India's nuclear programme by giving it a clear doctrine or by integrating the nuclear force fully with the military. The subsequent UPA government largely reiterates this duality. It seeks to maintain a credible threat and at the same time 'take a leadership role in promoting universal, nuclear disarmament and working for a nuclear weapons-free world' (UPA 2004). Cohen, who attributes to India a very different 'strategic style' and 'civilisational tradition' (Cohen) as compared to the USA, describes the thinking of the Indian foreign policy community thus –

> 'India would acquire nuclear weapons in order to pressure the nuclear "haves" to disarm and to protect itself against nuclear blackmail. Indians could thus have their cake and eat it: the Indian nuclear bomb would be an instrument of resistance to the blackmail tactics of the nuclear weapons states, while affirming India's concern with the welfare of all nations. The Indian programme could be justified on the grounds of morality and realpolitik, idealism and self-interest' (Cohen, 2001).

An example of this reasoning has been given by K. Subrahmanyam. He argues that it is better to safeguard one's own interests and to continue the campaign for disarmament as an active global player instead of being a 'lonely plaintive petitioner'. To build nuclear weapons whilst arguing for their renunciation 'in a world which mindlessly legitimised the weapon', are 'not mutually exclusive propositions' (Subrahmanyam, 2005).

From the outside, such an argument may appear to be a circuitous attempt to place a highly implausible fig-leaf on a policy designed to serve naked national interest, prestige and ego. However, there is more to it. Generations of Indian policy-makers and analysts have struggled with the moral implications of the nuclear question in a way unknown in other countries (Basrur, 1998). The idealist element is more than mere rhetoric. It is creating an ambiguity in policy-making.

1.2.3 *Restraint*

The idealist inflection is not only found in what is done, but also in what is not done. Restraint can be indicative of interest politics – India only very slowly decided to condemn the Soviet Union for crushing the popular uprising in Hungary in 1956. It also did not make too much of a fuss about the Soviet invasion of Afghanistan after 1979. In 1962, India accepted an unfavourable ceasefire with China simply because it had no choice to do otherwise. Often, however, restraint is indicative of the idealist strand. This restraint is not always absolute. It may be relative – relative to India's capabilities of wielding power, and relative to the actions of other, comparable countries. It is almost impossible to pin down exactly where, in individual cases, value-based restraint comes in –

as opposed to, say, prudence, fear or mere inability. In order to understand the restraint one has to look at the picture from a certain distance.

India is a status-quo power in Asia (Cohen, 2001; Subrahmanyam, 2005). It reclaims certain territories in Kashmir and the North East Provinces under Pakistani and Chinese control, as its own. Other than that, despite its overwhelming position of power in South Asia, and despite potential historical grievances (the partition was more or less forced on the Indian National Congress [INC] prior to the British pull-out in 1947), India has not laid claim to other South Asian territories. India has accepted partition and by-and-large accepts the sovereignty of the smaller states around its rim[17]. It has not occupied Bangladesh, Nepal or Sri Lanka, despite these countries' instability and despite very concrete opportunities of doing so (such as temporary troop deployments). Nor has India initiated the wars with Pakistan. Even when attacked by Pakistan, India has not sought territorial gains from a war[18]. The only offensive action taken by India was the large scale mobilisation of its armed forces during Operation Brasstacks in 1986–1987. This maneuver came close to, but did not lead to actual conflict. There is a certain restraint in Indian external military relations, which is in need of explanation[19].

Restraint in choosing war as an instrument is one matter. A different one is restraint in fighting wars and insurgencies. Subrahmanyam notes that 'terrorism in India is being handled with far greater restraint and quiet heroism on the part of the people than analogous acts in the Western world' (Subrahmanyam). This gives politicians room for maneuver, facilitating, for example, military restraint in dealing with insurgencies. This, according to Rajagopalan is the result of India's (implicit) counterinsurgency doctrine, which 'stresses the impossibility of military victory against guerrillas, emphasises the political resolution of insurgencies and places severe limitations on the use of force in counterinsurgency operations' (Rajagopalan; Subrahmanyam, 2005).

---

[17]The exception is Sikkim. It has a strategically vital geographic location between China/Tibet and India. After Sikkim rejected becoming part of the new Indian Union in 1947, Nehru drew it close through a treaty of association in 1955. In 1975, following riots, India was quick to seize the opportunity of integrating it fully into the union.

[18]At the Shimla agreement with Pakistan in 1972, India returned vast territories conquered during the 1971 war, as well as 91,000 prisoners of war as an act of goodwill, without a tangible quid pro quo. It did not, for instance, receive in return the Pakistani occupied part of Kashmir or even an official transformation of the Line of Control into an international frontier in return.

[19]At the same time, India has been and still is engaged in several war-like situations within its own borders.

Operationally, this meant that punitive actions such as village burning (a policy followed earlier by the British in the Indian frontier regions) and the use of heavy military equipment such as artillery and air-power were largely renounced, despite complaints by Indian army officers who considered such means militarily necessary (Rajagopalan, 2000).

A similar restraint (already under a nuclear shadow) in international relations was shown at Kargil, where the Indian forces pushed the invading insurgents back to the Line of Control, and no further, despite the tactical expediency[20] of an expanded battle-field for which preparations had been made (Sagan, 2001). Whilst it has arguably often been in India's interest to favour stability over change, allowing it to focus on the vast internal problems it faces, the strong status-quo orientation of a state with such a powerful regional position reflects the underlying mindset of a strategic community 'unable or unwilling to face up to the challenges and opportunities of a dynamic security environment' (Mitra, 2003).

A comparison with China may be of help to understand this point. China, which started from a similar starting point of poverty, backwardness and civil war after the Second World War, has been much more ruthless in expanding its power and staking its claims. Recent studies have suggested that China has a realist strategic culture (Johnston; Swaine, and Tellis, 2000; Scobell, 2002). Johnston even argues that there is a preference for the use of force to resolve disputes (Johnston, 1995a). How do China's strategic choices compare to India's? First of all, China has developed nuclear weapons as fast as possible (first atomic bomb tested in 1964, first hydrogen bomb tested in 1967). It felt threatened by the nuclear superpowers, the USA as well as the Soviet Union, having been engaged in conflict with both (full scale war with the US-led UN force in Korea in 1950–1951, border skirmishes in Mongolia with the Soviets in 1969). India, which felt threatened by a nuclear China as well as a nuclear USA (Indo-Chinese war in 1962, Enterprise incident in 1971), did not build a credible nuclear deterrent until many years later, in 1998, despite having the potential to do so at least since 1974. China, like India, has a no-first use doctrine. However, there have been public remarks by senior Chinese officials to the contrary. The last one was made by Major General Zhu Chenghu, Dean of the National Defense University, in July 2006. He warned that China could destroy hundreds of American cities if the two countries clashed over Taiwan. He said, 'We

[20]It should be remembered that tactical expediency during war translates into soldiers' lives.

Chinese will prepare ourselves for the destruction of all of the cities east of Xian. Of course, the Americans will have to be prepared that hundreds of cities will be destroyed by the Chinese' (Watts, 2006). Zhu's remarks were formally disavowed by the Chinese government. Nevertheless, the psychological-political damage was done. The 2006 annual report of the US Secretary of Defense on Chinese military capabilities submitted to the US Congress, came to the conclusion that Zhu's remarks 'show that the circle of military and civilian national security professionals discussing the value of China's "no first use" nuclear policy is broader than previously assessed' (Government of the United States 2006). Without holding a country responsible for one lunatic, it is nevertheless noteworthy to recall that, during a meeting in Beijing in October 1954, Mao explained the Chinese view of a nuclear war to a bewildered Nehru – its harm would be limited, because even if it killed 300 million people in China there would still be enough left to rebuild a glorious civilisation (Inder Malhotra in, Subrahmanyam, 2005). Apart from presenting a worrisome nuclear posture, China has been engaged in proliferation of nuclear technology. It helped Pakistan significantly in the development of its nuclear arsenal (bombs and delivery systems), directly harming India's interests. India refrains from doing the same with, for example, Vietnam. Rajesh Basrur rightly observed a 'persistence of restraint, stability and minimalism in India's nuclear policy' (Basrur, 2001).

In terms of military strategy, China has traditionally sought to control its periphery (Korea, Mongolia, Central Asia, Tibet, Nepal, Myanmar, Vietnam, Swaine and Tellis, 2000). Since the 1940's, it has – in contrast to India – taken an active role in a number of conflicts – the war against the UN in Korea in 1950, the occupation of Tibet in 1950–1951, wars with Taiwan in 1954 and 1958, an attack on India in 1962 and on Vietnam in 1979. Threats of war are regularly directed at Taiwan (and, by implication, at the USA, which guarantees Taiwan's status). The last major incident took place in 1996, when President Clinton sent the US navy into Taiwan straight in response to offensive Chinese missile tests. China rejects many of its current borders as impositions by outsiders, mainly European imperialists. India accepts the boundaries of 1947. While India is status-quo oriented, China is revisionist. Further-more, the ruthlessness and brutality of the destruction of Tibetan culture is not comparable to Indian atrocities in the tribal areas of the North East or in Kashmir – there is no mass scale relocation of Hindu Indians to the vale of Kashmir as there is of Han Chinese in Tibet in an attempt to alter the demographic and cultural basis. Destruction and violence against the general population are not political strategies, but individual excesses of war and many Indian soldiers are in prison for crimes committed during such operations. In general, the Indian strategy has been to attempt to co-opt secessionist movements into the system by making them part of it.

To repeat, India is no saint among nations. It pursues its interests, uses its power levers, has nuclear weapons and is ready to use military force against internal and external threats. It is not disinclined, for instance, to deal with a repressive Iranian regime or with the brutal military junta in Burma to ensure that its interests are protected. Relatively speaking, however, there is an unusual restraint with respect to the use of force and a readiness to incorporate system-level goals into foreign policy. India stridently contests the universal relevance of the realist approach to international affairs (Ray, 2004). It likes to think of itself as a 'benevolent nation'. In the Indian Ocean region, which it regards as its own strategic backyard, it 'aspires to serve as a friendly regional peacekeeper', a *primus inter pares* without hegemonic ambitions (Tanham). This is a departure from the Indira Doctrine. In global politics, many senior Indian policy makers still 'insist that India's claim to world leadership must be based on moral and spiritual values', while others stress the need for hard power to generate influence in the first place (Tanham, 1992). India is sometimes prepared to forego immediate, concrete benefits for potential, future benefits. This may be called rationalism, idealism or utopianism. In any case, it is an inflection.

1.3 The Identity Process and Indian Foreign Policy

In order to understand the inflection in Indian foreign policy, the dynamic of the national identity process has to be understood as a whole (Figure 1.2). It starts with the challenges and choices of Indian nation-building from the 1920s until the 1960s, when Gandhi and Nehru laid down the architectural blueprint for the Indian nation. The challenges of Indian nation-building limited the options available for the leaders to choose from, but choices were nevertheless made. There was both significant need for as well as room for maneuver. This will be discussed in Chapter 4.

The choices were institutionalised through ideological politics, or nationalism. Agents (especially Gandhi, Nehru) created a specific Indian political identity to give the new nation a stable emotional backbone. This is discussed in Chapter 5.

The ideological politics impacted on the political community. In foreign policy, this community is the strategic community, which has a

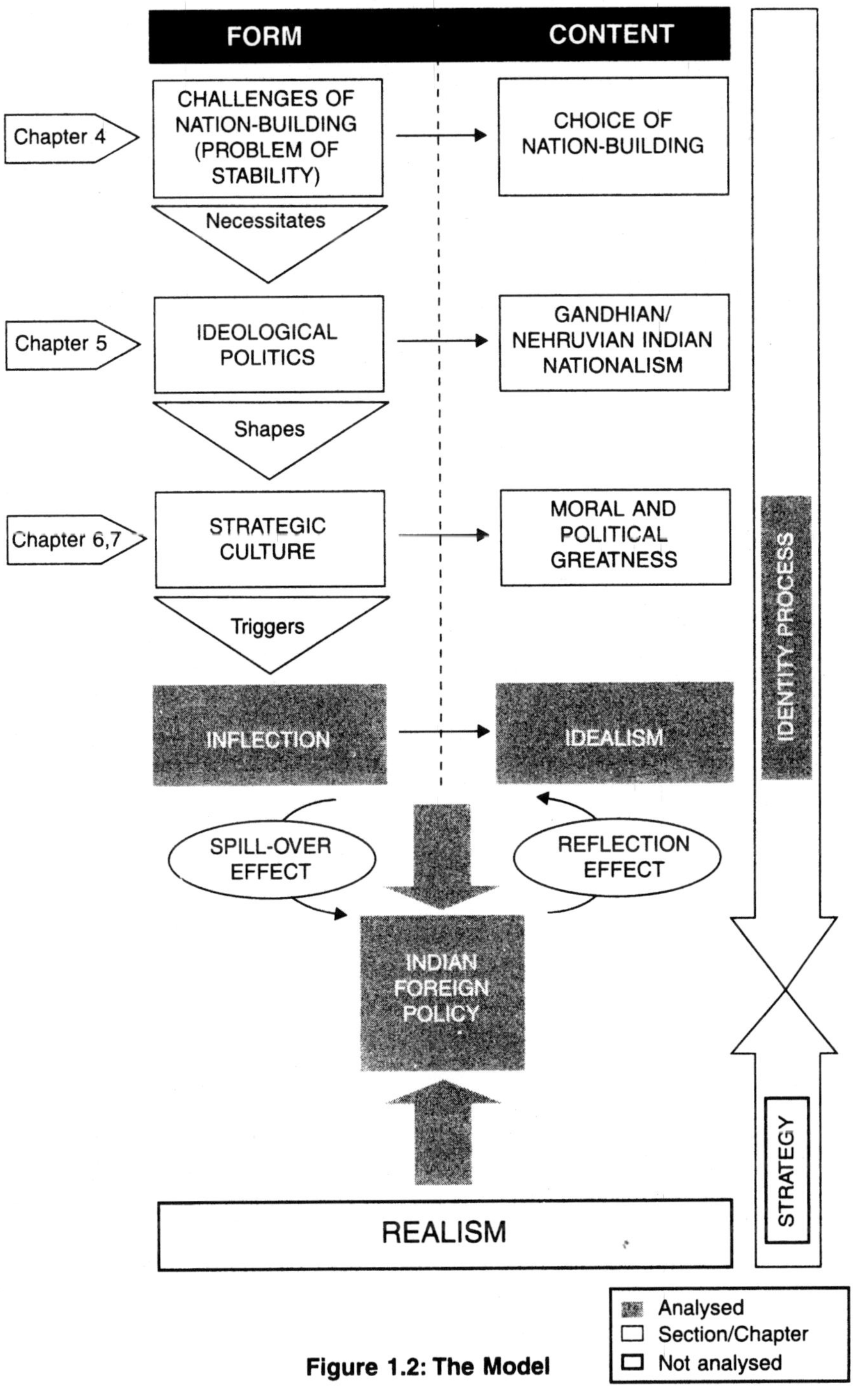

Figure 1.2: The Model

strategic culture – a way of looking at the world and a reference for decision-making. The link between nation-building and foreign policy is a dual one. On the one hand, there is an unconscious 'spill-over' from the former to the latter, on the other hand, there is a conscious reflection of the former through the latter. This is discussed in Chapter 6 (for Nehruvian foreign policy) and in Chapter 7 (for contemporary Indian foreign policy).

According to realist, systemic theories of international relations, state behaviour in the international arena is determined by the pursuit of national interests and a state's capabilities as defined by relative power (Carr, 1946; Morgenthau, 1963; Waltz, 1979; Bull, 1995). Strategy is – in a paradigmatic sense – formulated in a detached, rational manner and serves the sole purpose of securing the national interest, whatever that may be (preservation of the status-quo, changing the status-quo, enabling economic growth, limiting security threats, etc.). To Waltz, a theory of international relations ceases to be systemic when individual states' characteristics are relevant to the explanation (Waltz, 1996). Where domestic political issues play a significant role, foreign policy can be regarded as suboptimal, as it differs from the policy that decision-makers would prefer if domestic considerations were not a constraint (Fearon, 1998). Domestic political concerns produce goals which may rival pure foreign policy goals.

Indian foreign policy needs to be contextualised. It is fulfilling a dual purpose – that of improving external security and that of enhancing an integrative national identity. The idealist inflection of Indian foreign policy can thus become intelligible. Mitra made this point – '...while all states are members of the international system, the use to which they put international politics varies from one context to another. Western nation-states, products of a long process of nation-building, industrialisation and state-formation, seek the promotion of national interest through their strategic initiatives. Post-colonial state-nations, engaged in the process of nation-creation, are more complex in their rhetoric. For these actors, international politics, in addition to being used as an instrument of national interest, also plays a symbolic role in the building of a national profile' (Mitra, 2003).

India has opted for a national profile based on universal values. This choice of national profile must be understood with reference to the specific experience of India's independence movement and in the context of the particular complexity of the Indian national project. Foreign policy becomes part of the nation-building process in two ways – it is consciously used as a national mirror to reflect Indian identity back to Indians themselves and it is unconsciously affected by the spill-over of identity into the field of foreign policy.

The idealist inflection is a type of exceptionalism[21], a belief that India has a special destiny and moral purpose in history, and is driven by a set of values that are universally valid, but most poignantly developed in India. Such an exceptionalism is not the natural expression of a cultural predisposition, but rather the product of a specific national project. Its key purpose is to build a nation, to craft an abstract pan-Indian national identity in order to bridge the unparalleled religious, ethnic, linguistic, social and economic diversity of the subcontinent[22]. The identity is not primarily the result of a postcolonial struggle with Western modernity. Despite some (post) colonial insecurities, the civilisation of the Indian subcontinent is far too rooted in its own age-old history and traditions to be swept off its feet by a temporary historical phenomenon. It is, rather, the conscious and pragmatic political project of an elite, implemented at the formative stage of the new Indian nation state. India's nationalism, in the absence of primordial or modern-economic unity, is thus a case of what Kedourie has termed by 'ideological politics' (Kedourie, 1993).

The identity thus created has two co-constitutive components – a sense of moral greatness and a sense of political greatness. Moral greatness is expressed in a belief that India is a 'civilisationally blessed, responsible and peaceful state'. Other countries 'must become cognizant of the moral quality of Indian foreign and strategic policy' (Cohen). This quality is based on the notion that internally, India has shown a unique capacity to accommodate diversity, while externally it has a predominantly pacific tradition of cultural and social rather than military expansion. India thus has 'something to offer' to the world. There is a sense of mission accompanied by a tendency to moralise and lecture other nations (Cohen, 2001).

---

[21]Exceptionalism as a term has often been used with reference to the USA. It can mean two things. Either an observer (e.g. an economist) perceives an anomaly in terms of the behaviour of a particular group (e.g. US investment decisions) and describes this as an instance of exceptionalism. This can be called objective exceptionalism. Alternatively, a group (e.g. the US political class) understands itself as carrying an exceptional duty (e.g. to spread democracy). This can be called subjective exceptionalism. Here, the second, subjective meaning is used, although the Indian foreign policy duality can also be called an objective exceptionalism from the observer's point of view.

[22]The nation-building project, of course, incorporated other key fields, too, such as economic growth and the stabilisation of democratic structures and institutions.

This sense of moral greatness among the politically mobilised in India comes in conjunction with a sense of political greatness or importance. India not only has a message, it also has the capacity to effectuate a global impact. Indians often compare themselves to China and stress that as an ancient Asian civilisation they cannot be subsumed under the Western cultural influence. They understand themselves 'to be distinct and great and have a set of fundamental premises and assumptions, and a particular way of ordering both their own societies and guiding relations with the outside world' (Cohen). Indian officials see themselves as representing not only a state, but an entire civilisation with certain intrinsic qualities, towards which other nationalities should be respectful (Cohen, 2001). The discourse of civilisation is critical for the construction of an Indian identity as a modern nation state. The West, Malik argues, does not take sufficient note of the 'sense of national destiny' that drives India's ambitions (Malik). When Indian elites speak of restoring their country's rightful place in the world –

> '...they give expression to a concept of "pre-eminence" or "centrality" in Asia and the wider world that prevailed before the European colonisation of Asia. This concept reflects their perception that the founders of regional cultural patterns, their rightful place is at the apex of world hierarchy' (Malik, J. M. 2004)[23].

The problem with ideological politics, as far as foreign policy is concerned, is that the identity conjured up and a foreign policy strategy may come into conflict. Whereas identity is an emotive force, generating internal stability and simplicity through a sense of belonging, strategy is the product of reason and requires flexibility and nuance in application. Even if they do not clash at first, they may fall out of sync in time, because they have different life cycles. An identity is (and should be) 'sticky'. A strategy should be changing with changing internal and external parameters, such as the state's power base and the distribution of power in the international system. During Nehru's period in office as Prime Minister of a young nation, the Indian national identity as a secular, pluralist, non-violent and great state and the foreign policy strategy of non-alignment and Panchsheel were pretty much in tune. Nehru, furthermore, understood that when – in specific situations – they were not, there had to be some flexibility with regard to foreign policy. India's forceful response to the insurgency in Kashmir in 1947, which

---

[23]Malik makes the same assertion about China.

even Gandhi approved of, demonstrated this. However, Nehru himself, as well as his successors, was not always able to differentiate clearly between interest and ideals as stemming from identity – hence, the duality. To an extent, this failure is natural – in a world where actors' identities and beliefs are not entirely separate from their rhetoric and actions, the identity–strategy dilemma is the price to pay for a value-based national identity.

The post BJP-India (after 2004), makes a very good point of contrast and comparison for analysing the identity–strategy relationship. In terms of identity, the BJP stood for a different national project, one not based on supra-religious, supra-traditional values, but one based on a Hindu culture. In terms of strategy, moreover, India exploded a nuclear weapons device in 1998 – the ultimate instrument of violence. India has, over the years, become more realist in its foreign policy. However, while it is approaching the Rubicon (beyond which lies the realm of strictly national-interest-based foreign policy), it has not yet crossed it, as C. Raja Mohan suggested (Mohan, 2003). And perhaps, it never will. Values are still very much a part of the thinking of the foreign policy elite today. The Nehruvian national project has taken root. Other factors, foremost, India's economic growth and integration into the global economy, and the correlating new global energy and trade interests, but also the economic growth of the entire region, as well as the changing security landscape driven by an ever more powerful Chinese neighbour, are more responsible for the shift than ideological changes. In terms of the national project, India is still a highly imperilled nation. However, economic stake-holding, growth and the participation in the growth by a new middle class, offers an incentive to identify with the whole. The new economic stake-holders are the same group (sociologically speaking, the politically aware, on a national level) to which the previous ideological messages had been addressed to. Thus, while India as a whole is not necessarily more stable today, the need to generate stability through using ideological politics in foreign policy has become less, while the cost for ideological politics in foreign policy – the identity–strategy dilemma – has increased.

This analysis aims to contribute to a growing body of literature on the strategic behaviour of one of the future key international players. With its independence in 1947, India immediately became one of the most important nations with a population second only to China's. Despite this, and despite the enormous international standing of figures such as Gandhi and Nehru, significant Indian diaspora communities and the global influence of South Asian culture, India has, for a long time, been neglected by international strategic thinkers. There are a number of reasons for this. India's poverty and perceived weakness as a state quickly placed it in the development aid sections of diplomacy. The attempt by Indian leaders to take their country out of the global power political and economic equations of the Cold War era, with policies of non-alignment and economic autarky, detached it from many of the global strategic issues, which focussed the attention of the Cold War powers. Furthermore, the notorious 'Hindu rate of growth' ensured that India's power base did not fundamentally change over decades.

In the Post-Cold War era, none of these reasons hold any longer. India is extremely dynamic economically. It is the world's leading supplier of outsourcing services and has thus in some ways become the back office of the global economy. Whether aligned or not, it is inescapably a part of what is likely to be the most complex security environment of the next decades – the new Asian Great Game which India plays with a powerful USA, a booming China and a resource-rich Russia. It is also, together with Pakistan, part of what is arguably the most dangerous security relationship of the day. The Kargil war in 2000 was fought between two nuclear weapon states. Relations today are far from stable. While India is still struggling with crippling poverty, it is nevertheless set to become one of the world's leading economies and powers.

Despite this strategic importance and despite the fact that India, as a secular, liberal society and the world's largest democracy shares fundamental political values, relations with Europe and the USA have been difficult. They were marked by distrust and misunderstandings. The controversies over the non-proliferation treaty are the most poignant recent examples. India presents a great opportunity for the West – and a great challenge. It is willing to play a responsible part in global affairs. It shares many political and social values with the West. However, it is also a proud country, which demands to be treated with respect, as an independent member of the club of great powers.

India requires a more insightful treatment than it has been given by many Western politicians and academics in the past. This task is all the more necessary in view of India's rapid growth. International relations theory since the Second World War has been strongly influenced by the realist paradigms of US academics concentrating on the confrontation with the Soviet Union and after the end of the Cold War, on the meaning and functioning of unipolarity. Realism has not been applied very successfully to India. This is part of the reason for the misunderstandings and irritations. In an emerging multipolar world, in which India can be expected to take up a key position, these shortcomings have to be remedied. An important element of an improved understanding of India is to understand the country's identity and internal dynamics. This book aspires to contribute to such an understanding.

2

Reason and Culture

Much of the criticism as well as the endorsement of Indian foreign policy has been concentrated on issues of goal formulation rather than goal achievement – on what should be done with foreign policy, rather than on how the goals are best approached. Indian foreign policy discourse has a history of profound uneasiness and a long struggle with the concept of national interest. Authors who sought to explain this uneasiness from a realist point of view, have attributed it either to a superior strategic insight or to conscious smoke-screening. They would see the idealist inflection not as substantial in its own right, but as a residual consideration, subordinated to the national interest. Authors who believed the uneasiness to be substantial and pre-rational, on the other hand, have often looked for historical and cultural explanations.

Figure 2.1 shows four alternative approaches to understanding the idealist inflection in Indian foreign policy.

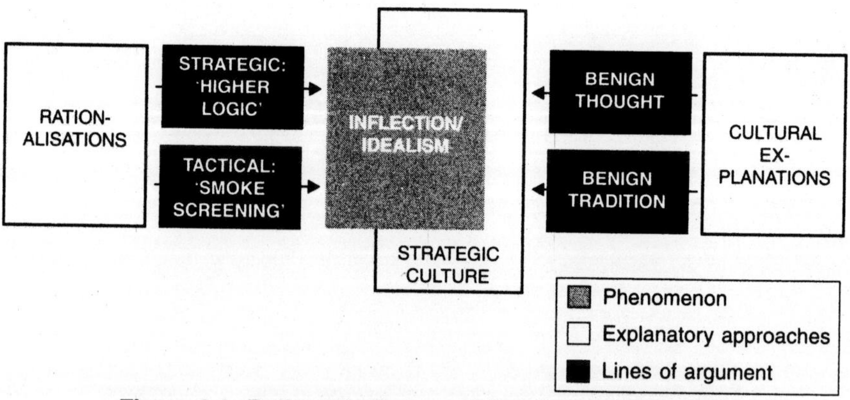

Figure 2.1: Rationalisations and Cultural Explanations

2.1 The Inflection as Chimera

Can the idealist element in Indian foreign policy be regarded as substantial? There are a number of arguments suggesting that it may not be. Looking beneath the surface of heated debate over the role and utility of idealist elements in Indian foreign policy, these arguments challenge the debate as such, suggesting that what appears as a duality or as an inflection is, in fact, normal (prudent or naïve) realpolitik. There are two main objections to the duality – one may be termed 'superior insight', and the second may be called 'smoke-screening'. The difference is in the substantiality of the component that may at first sight appear to be idealism. The first objection calls into question the duality on the grounds that what seems like idealism is, in reality, nothing but a sophisticated form of realism (a pseudo-idealist 'master plan'). The second objection calls into question the duality by arguing that what seems like idealism is, in reality, realist rhetorical obfuscation or mere pompousness (a bigot or naïve moralistic reflex). While the first line of argument tends to be admiring of Nehru's strategic skill and far-sighted idealism as a form of 'higher' realism or at least acknowledges the benefit of a benign philosophy of the weak; the second line of argument tends to be less admiring of Nehru's tactical use of moral language as a cover-up for 'basic' realism. Both objections illuminate aspects of India's strategic idiosyncrasy, but they cannot sufficiently explain the Indian inflection away from normal foreign policy making.

2.1.1 *Superior Insight – Strategic Idealism as 'Higher' Realism*

Is the idealist inflection merely realism on a higher plane? Was Nehru smarter than his critics and successors, who misunderstood the depth of his thought and took him too literally? Raju Thomas, for example, argues that Indian 'moralpolitik', as bequeathed by Nehru, is in India's interest as much as it is in the world's interest. 'A return to Nehru's policy of non-alignment overseas and Gandhi's philosophy of non-violence at home would best ensure India's external and internal security and advance the prospect of a less violent world' (Thomas). While not discounting the idealist element altogether, he nevertheless believes that 'underlying Nehru's concept of non-alignment was an element of hard-headed realism'. It allowed India to distance itself from the threat of war, the lower defense budgets made available more funds for investment in infrastructure and the resulting military weakness was not opposed to India's influence in the world (Thomas, 2004).

Aspy Rana, one of the leading scholars of Nehru and of Indian foreign policy, has put forward a powerful and very interesting argument to the effect that Nehru had a realist strategy superior to the 'simple' and unmitigated realism of most other states. Panchsheel and non-alignment were designed to further India's national interest in the international arena in a highly imaginative manner (Rana). According to Rana, Nehru established in India a foreign policy tradition that attempted a 'complex reconciliation between unit-level national-security goals, and larger normative system-level concerns'. These are two ends of a spectrum 'more often irreconcilably at odds with each other' (Rana). He writes that –

> 'it has become somewhat customary, especially after 1962, to be dismissive of Nehru on the ground that he was impossibly idealist in a world which required a much surer grasp of realism. If idealism and realism are counter-posed in this simplistic way, we shall never arrive at a just reckoning of Nehru's place in the history of international relations. A more apposite juxtaposition of realism with idealism, on the other hand, is likely to yield a juster estimate of his place in history' (Rana, 2005).

'In a way, Nehru has become a victim of his own success and popularity. His moral overall design was taken for too long as an end in itself, rather than as a means to achieve national security' (Rana).

Rana's analysis of Nehru's foreign policy is very insightful and carefully argued. However, the terminology is unclear. Philosophically speaking, it may be true that idealism and realism cannot ultimately be separated. In practical, political and analytical terms, they should not be conflated, however. Rana quotes Martin Wight, who said that 'realism can be a good thing – it all depends whether it means the abandonment of high ideals or of foolish expectations' (Rana, 1998). The quote sets the main theme in Rana's argument, namely, the belief that a qualitatively refined pursuit of the national interest would imply a 'qualitative improve-ment of the international system', and that 'the greater realism lies in searching for the cure, rather than in helplessly accepting the brutal reality of the disease without deciphering its hidden causations' (Rana, 2005).

The problem with such arguments is that the distinction between ideal and interest is blurred. The two concepts are conflated. In reality, however, real (substantial) idealism and system-level goals, standing as national goals side-by-side with the goal of serving the national interest, produce a duality. Any rival goal to that of the national interest is a potential infringement on it. In practice, there may well, at times, be considerable overlap and certain benefits of an idealist approach. However, when system-level goals and national-goals happen to diverge, a state has to decide for one or the other – for the real benefit of now or the potential benefit arising from a changed system in the future. The value of the latter proposition depends largely on the system-shaping power of the nation and the likelihood of converting the potential future benefit into a real one. India has not been a powerful nation. The United States, by far the most powerful nation today, may have the power to influence the system, but even they do not have the power to shape the system as they like, as the current failure to democratise the Middle East shows. Substantial idealism requires a concession in terms of the national interest. If, however, idealism is merely expedient and subservient to the national interest, it would either be a cynical philosophy of the weak or mere smoke-screening.

Rothstein has put forward an argument for idealism as a philosophy of the weak. It is, in his view, clearly a means to a realist end and as such not a substantial but a residual quality of Indian foreign policy. Non-aligned restraint, he proposes, naturally appeals to the weaker members of a bipolar international system, who may thus find themselves the object of competition and not the victims of war. India's idealist element is, thus, a tactical response to a particular power situation. The response would be different, if there was a desperate need for foreign aid and assistance in the face of a stronger opponent, as was the case with Taiwan (theatened by China, supported by the USA), Cuba (USA, Soviet Union) or Pakistan (India, China) (Rothstein, 1968). Small powers, he argued, are, furthermore, prone to fall victim to the illusion that a lack of power is somehow equated with an inherently moral behaviour. 'Nehru's desire to establish a zone of peace – implicitly a morally superior zone – between the great power blocs was the latest version of this presumption'. Nehru's behaviour, Rothstein believes with Neville Maxwell or Escott Reid, is essentially marked by 'moral hypocrisy', by the self-righteous glorification of weakness (Rothstein, 1976).

There is certainly some truth to the claim that Indian idealism is really a philosophy of the weak[24]. India was (and still is) a status-quo power, in part because it is instable domestically and there is little excess capacity

[24]It is worth noting that Gandhi, who was aware of the limitations of Indian power, nevertheless rejected the argument that passive resistance is a 'splendid weapon of the weak'. He calls this a 'gross ignorance' and declares that 'passive resistance, that is, soul force, is matchless. It is superior to the force of arms'. To use passive resistance is to be courageous and strong, not to be weak (Gandhi, M., 1997, p. 93). To Gandhi, who equated self-mastery with national independence, individual mental strength and national strength are concurrent

for foreign adventures. Its most pressing concern has been, and still is, to generate the governance and economic growth necessary to lift its millions out of poverty. India has, in the past, not focussed on military power. Mitra argues that India's relative power is today still far lower than its size and technical capabilities would suggest. Indian governments face severe limitations on mobilising their economy and people for war. The reasons are, on the one hand, India's low per capita income, and on the other, the fact that India is 'an intensely politicised society and contentious democracy' (Mitra, 2005). The structure of the Indian state (long, isolated contentious borders, internal conflicts), the structure of the Indian polity (a federal, democratic system made up of states with very different concerns and interests), the structure of Indian politics (elected governments made-up of broad people's parties and/or coalitions), and, one might add, the structure of the Indian nation (diverse, with significant centrifugal tendencies), limit India's potential power.

Can we conclude that India is benign or value driven because of its weakness? That would be premature. Firstly, even strong countries may have moral aspirations and even weak countries may use values out of conviction. There is a possible, but not a necessary connection between weakness and morals. Secondly, federalism and democracy may be weakening India's potential power. However, it must not be forgotten that federalism and democracy are not given, but are themselves the products of choice and values. Thirdly, while facing economic limitations, Nehru was, in spite of the democratic setup, more powerful in the arena of politics, and especially in foreign policy, than most other rulers, democratically elected or not. If any leader could have mobilised power like his contemporaries Mao or Stalin did (to their people's intense suffering), it would have been him. Fourthly, a look at the depressive history of conflict in Africa shows that neither poverty nor instability necessarily prevents countries from pursuing expansionist, militaristic and often suicidal policies. There is thus at least a high degree of reasonableness and restraint in India's choice of resource allocation and its status-quoist foreign policy. Fifthly, relatively weaker countries may consider it to be in their interest to seek military power and play an aggressive international role (for example Iran), as much as stronger countries may consider it to be in their interest to show restraint (for example the Soviet Union during the breakup of communist

(Gandhi, M., 1997, pp. 26–30). He admits that it is an everyman's weapon which even the physically weak may use, nevertheless, it is very powerful – 'its very glance withers the enemy' (Gandhi, M., 1997, p. 94).

Europe). Whilst it would presumably be better for weak countries to have an international legal-ethical superstructure, in the absence of one, they cannot afford to disregard the instruments of (relative) military power. Thus, whilst small and weak countries may be particularly supportive of the UN and other international regimes, there is, to my knowledge, no evidence that they are less prone to resort to violence in solving conflicts. Sixthly, despite India's development needs and precarious political texture, it is doubtful whether it is really a 'weak' country. China demonstrated the effect sheer masses of soldiers can have in the face of a technologically vastly superior opponent during the Korean War. India is one of the world's largest countries with an enormous reservoir of people and above-average natural and industrial resources. Togo is weak. India is only poor and instable. Without going as far as saying that backwardness was an excuse rather than an imperative for a value-component in foreign policy, it seems like India did have a choice and could have pursued more assertive policies. A look at relative defense spending may illustrate the point. Indian defense spending in the past was approximately 3 per cent of the national income. This compares unfavourably with India's regional rivals, Pakistan and China, who spent 6.5 per cent and 5.3 per cent, respectively (figures for 1998, Cohen, 2001). These neighbours are not much more stable, nor can they be considered wealthy (although China is becoming significantly wealthier). They, like India, have enormous and pressing domestic tasks – and yet they allocate a higher proportion of their national income to the military and pursue revisionist and assertive foreign policies.

2.1.2 *Smoke-screening – Tactical Idealism as 'Basic' Realism*

Some analysts, far from regarding the idealist element as high strategy or expedient philosophy of the weak, believe that it is merely a verbal smoke-screen, a convenient way of selling realist policies. Karnad, for instance, believes that Nehru's idealist rhetoric was a useful (even ingenious) obfuscation of a strongly realist policy. It was a superb tactical maneuver (Karnad, 2002). Kumaraswamy, equally questions the substantiality of the idealist elements (but nevertheless holds it accountable for a number of Indian policy mistakes). He argued that 'by ignoring or condoning a number of actions taken by the Soviet Union, India severely undermined its claims to idealism in international relations'. India's hegemonic behaviour in South Asia (e.g. Nepal and Bangladesh) shows double standards concerning the involvement of outside powers (Kumaraswamy). The nuclear issue, however, is the prime example – Nehru's public anti-nuclear posture was 'primarily meant for external consumption'. While allowing for nuclear ambiguity, 'Nehru and his successors adopted a realist attitude vis-à-vis the nuclear bomb, perhaps as a "necessary evil"'. Later on, Rajiv Gandhi's 'much publicised... disarmament initiative of 1986' went hand in hand with 'definite moves towards weaponisation' (Kumaraswamy, 2004).

The smoke-screening argument is, however, most often proposed by other members of the international community and especially by India's strategic rivals. Here, Indian moral grand-standing is viewed with ridicule, suspicion or hostility as plain naïveté, moral pride, sanctimonious hypocrisy or obfuscation. Only rarely is it met with admiration or respect. Depending on one's perspective, Mitra observes, India may appear 'either as a "regional bully" or the "regional push-over"'. India, in turn, 'Janus-like, often proves both speculations to be right, appearing in the process to be either mystical-moral, or utterly devoid of principle or doctrine' (Mitra, 2005). The assessment is, of course, determined among other things by observing the country's particular position and interests, which in turn depend to a large degree on geopolitical location as well as on historic, diplomatic and power-political relationships. The smaller South Asian neighbours, confronted with India's size and might, as well as with India's regional ambitions, are usually unwilling to accept the idealist element as anything more than a smoke-screen of meaningless rhetoric, contradicted by India's everyday behaviour in the region's many conflicts and hotspots. Without going as far as Gohar Ayub Khan, a former Pakistani Foreign Minister, who described India as a 'habitual aggressor and hegemon', or former Pakistani Chief of Staff General Karamat, who regards New Delhi as being dominated by 'militant nationalists' and 'rabid anti-Muslims' (Talbott, 2004), the Pakistani view of India is quite the opposite of that of Indian politicians – India appears as an aspiring hegemon and rival using all power-political and diplomatic tools at its disposal to achieve goals which are profoundly antagonistic. The moral language does not correspond to reality.

Pakistan's perspective on India is up close and determined by rivalry. The USA has a much more detacted perspective on India. Here, the picture becomes more blurred. India and the USA rarely felt good about each other. The relationship between the two great moralisers on the international scene was a difficult one for most of the years following India's independence. Talbott was amazed at his counterpart Jaswant Singh's belief in the 'innate rationality' of Indian civilisation (Talbott) and the self-righteous argument that the 'disharmony between India and the rest of the globe is that India has moved from being totally moralistic to being a little more realistic' (Talbott). However, the USA expects some substance in the moralist rhetoric. Clinton, Talbott remembers, had been taken aback by the Indian nuclear test on precisely these grounds, saying that it betrayed 'the ideals of non-violent democratic freedom and independence at the heart of Gandhi's struggle' (Talbott, 2004). Previous US governments were equally puzzled by India's ambiguities. Dennis Kux describes how, under Eisenhower, relations between New Delhi and Washington were highly strained –

> 'For many Americans, Krishna Menon, now a fixture at the United Nations, had become a symbol of India – a country that preached non-alignment and high moral principles in international affairs but hypocritically favoured the Communists and cold-bloodedly pursued its interests in Kashmir' (Kux, D. 1994).

Under Kennedy, things were hardly any better, reaching a low point during the Nixon administration (Kux, 1994), when Kissinger famously scoffed at India's 'assumption of almost hereditary moral superiority' (Talbott, 2004).

With regard to the argument of smoke-screening, two questions arise – one logical, one empirical. The logical question is – what would be the potential benefit of a moral smoke-screen? Will other countries be fooled by it? It is doubtful that India has the media-management skills that would be needed for effective smoke-screening (Subrahmanyam, 2005). As mentioned earlier, India's neighbours are very skeptical of its ambitions. The USA also finds the moral language more irritating than assuring. Moreover, a mere moral smoke-screen without any behaviour to back it up is not credible over a sustained period of time. It could lead to diplomatic ambiguity (and to hedging by others) or to diplomatic self-entanglements (of which other countries would profit more than India). Why then, would there be a desire to use moralistic language? Does it reflect an underlying attitude? The fact that the language was used fairly consistently across time and space, spanning parties and generations, suggests that it is linked to a larger cultural framework. However, is this cultural framework one that favours mere grandstanding and moral pompousness – or is it something more substantial?

The empirical question is, did India ever act against its national interest in the name of values? If value-laden rhetoric is merely a smoke-screen, either consciously employed to cover-up realist designs, or simply the product of grandstanding for its own sake, the answer would probably be, no. If that was the case, however, why are so many Indian commentators lamenting an idealism they consider naïve and adverse to India's interests? General V.P. Malik, for instance, cites a number of instances in which India has acted against its national interest for reasons of a (in his opinion, entirely misplaced) value approach to foreign policy – referring the Jammu and Kashmir issue to the UN Security Council at a point in time when India was winning that war (1947); granting a 'suzerainty' to China over Tibet without any quid pro quo[25]; return of the strategically important Haji Pir Pass to Pakistan after the 1965 war; returning 91,000 prisoners without making Pakistan agree to a permanent solution in Jammu and Kashmir at the time of signing the Shimla Agreement in 1972 and dithering for 24 years between the testing of a nuclear device in 1974 and manufacturing nuclear weapons in 1998 (Malik, 2002). Kanwal adds to this list the restraint of Indian security forces in not following Kashmiri insurgents across the Line of Control where their bases are and the restraint of the Indian Border Security Forces to provocations by the Bangladeshi army (Kanwal, 2005).

While India certainly has been pursuing realist, interest-based and even hegemonic policies, it has also at other times acted according to an idealist parameter. From the perspective of a weaker neighbour, such as Pakistan, naturally the realist traits are most prominent; at the same time, from the Indian perspective, in matters closer home and core security interests, pragmatic realism is more likely to prevail over idealism (Tanham, 1992). The duality exists, albeit in an asymmetric way.

2.2 The Inflection as Character

> *'The Ramayana and the Mahabharata were woven into the texture of millions of lives in every generation for thousands of years. I have often wondered if our race forgot the Buddha, the Upanishads and the great epics, what then will it be like! It would be uprooted and would lose its basic characteristics which have clung to it and given it distinction throughout these long ages. India would cease to be India...'*
>
> (Nehru, 2003)

Is there such a thing as a historically consistent, meaningful 'national culture' and a particular view of the world characterising a country's motivations, hopes, fears and choices? People have always sought to differentiate between themselves and others, between insiders and outsiders. Such considerations naturally lead to classifications and stereotypes. Almost everyone thinks and works with such prejudices on a daily basis, consciously

[25]Mao claimed Tibet as an integral part of China and the matter was presented as a strictly domestic issue. Nehru vaguely accepted the Chinese claim but strongly advised against the use of force.

or unconsciously. However, when put to test, they are elusive. It is very difficult to draw useful conclusions from them.

During the Enlightenment in Europe, it became fashionable to characterise nations according to the 'rational' ramifications of their society. Voltaire, for example, distinguished people who are living in a state of civilisation and those living in a state of barbarism. Hume, a rationalist and empiricist to the bone, discarded the idea of deriving a theory of 'national character' from 'physical causes'. Instead, he argued that there are so-called 'moral causes' shaping the character of a people. By moral causes, he meant conditions pertaining to the political framework – type of government, size of territory, longevity and stability of the state, etc. (Hume, 1998). In nineteenth century Europe, the issue of culture, of the social make-up and normative basis, gradually drew more attention and triggered efforts to characterise different cultures. The German sociologist Alfred Weber eventually made a clear distinction between 'civilisation' – a material, practical measure of a people's way of life – and 'Kultur' – as a set of values and ideas (Weber, 1935). Does such a culture provide a recognisable worldview?

Fernand Braudel believes that it does. In his *History of Civilisations* (in French, more revealingly entitled *Grammaire des Civilisations*), he traces the 'lives' of countries and civilisations, the 'psychological and spiritual attitudes of peoples' (Braudel). He speaks of a 'mentality', a framework of reference, 'dictating attitudes, guiding choices, confirming prejudices and directing actions' (Braudel). People have a 'psychological history', the result of distilled tradition, giving it a 'collective personality' of permanent features – an abstract, but essential 'diagrammatic form' (Braudel, 1995).

There are two main problems with this 'diagrammatic form' of a national character. The problems are general, but become particularly visible in the context of India. The first problem is that a national character stipulates a cultural consistency over time which may or may not exist. A national character may change considerably over time. Hume, who himself was prone to argue in national stereotypes, nonetheless acknowledged that –

> '...the manners of a people change very considerably from one age to another; either by great alterations in their government, by the mixtures of new people, or by that inconstancy, to which all human affairs are subject' (Hume, 1998).

Secondly, and more importantly, it stipulates what Singh called a 'unity of history'. Can one really weave one conclusive narrative out of the different threads of life running through a country? Will the result be precise enough to matter?

Despite these difficulties, a number of recent studies have looked at culture, broadly or narrowly defined, in trying to explain India's strategic idiosyncrasies (Larus, 1979; Tanham, 1992; Rosen, 1996; Latham, 1997; Singh, 1999b; Basrur, 2001; Bakshi, 2002; Kim, 2004)[26]. Such an approach is not unwarranted – understanding culture is an essential factor in understanding behaviour. Furthermore, in the Indian case, the traditional, cultural element in life is significant. India is an intensely religious and traditional society. Consequently, modern India has an obvious cultural peculiarity, the density and strength of which attracts and overwhelms millions of foreign visitors each year, who can witness (especially in the rural areas) a very idiosyncratic and distinct society. There is something akin to an Indian 'way of life'. In such issues as family relations, religiosity, medicine or food, for example, India has an approach which can by-and-large be recognised as different from that of other large civilisational entities, such as 'The West', or 'China' (Kakar and Kakar, 2006). This led Weiner to assert that 'contemporary Indians are more akin to their ancestors than they are to other contemporaries' (Weiner, 1984).

Historically, India's culture could pass through generations largely undisrupted. Without serious breaks, the evolution of Indian civilisation can be traced as far back as the earliest known times of literary and urban life. This is unique. The antique civilisations of Babylon and Egypt are long gone. The ancient civilisation of China as well as the younger European civilisation was uprooted by the violent spasms of modernity. They took serious damage during disastrous self-immolations under fascist or communist rule, which brought the monstrosities of a Cultural Revolution, a Great Leap Forward, a Holocaust, and mass-scale modern warfare. The people of India were largely spared a similar uprooting. Partition violence showed the potentially devastating power of modern ideas in India, but it did not grip the entire subcontinent. Indian politicians and leaders, furthermore, from Vivekananda, through Gandhi and Nehru, all the way to recent governments, tirelessly stress the cultural consistency and uniqueness of India.

Culturally based studies of Indian foreign policy usually take their cue from here. They sometimes, following Nehru's storyline, trace a benign element in Indian culture. At other times they contrast a tradition of idealism with a tradition of realism. Often, they justify an argument on Indian strategic culture with reference to past individuals, such as Ashoka

---

[26]For an assessment of strategic culture from a military perspective, see the study by former officer V. R. Raghavan (Raghavan, V. R., 2005).

or texts, such as the *Arthashastra*. However, they rarely clarify the link between historical moments and contemporary popular ways of life; or that between popular ways of life and elitist political culture[27].

One line of argument holds that strategic culture per se is absent or underdeveloped in India and that a defensive posture arises from an inability of the Indian strategic elite to look after the national interest professionally[28]. By this argument, India does not have a culture suitable for the processes of military-strategic thinking and decision-making (Tanham, 1992). There is a good case for a lack of military-strategic thought in Indian foreign policy making. Analysts involved in the decision-making processes in one way or other, have been particularly worried by this (Kapila, 2003; Kanwal, 2005; Subrahmanyam). The Indian nuclear explosion, in combination with the absence of a clear nuclear doctrine and the Kargil war, have recently given the issue an acute significance (Singh, 1999a; Kumaraswamy, 2004; Subrahmanyam, 2005). Reforms are now underway[29].

Some, who deplore the military-strategic inability, look primarily at institutional inadequacies (Subrahmanyam, 2005). Others, however, try to understand the problem including the institutional inadequacies from a larger historical and cultural perspective. The latter authors are looking at such issues as the divisive effect of the caste system (Gordon, 1995; Rosen, 1996) or India's historic failure to organise state power efficiently to avoid back-breaking invasions and the subsequent 'emasculation of state power' (Singh, 1999b). Tanham lists three cultural-historical reasons for India's lack of strategic planning. (1) India has rarely been unified territorially and hence Indians have not learned to think in terms of overall national defense planning. (2) The Hindu concept of time as eternal and cyclical as well as (3) the Hindu view of the world as an unknowable mystery discourage planning as such (Tanham, 1992). Counter-arguments are often also proposed in cultural terms – Bakshi asserts that there is an ancient Indian way of war and strategy (a 'Weltanschauung') as derived from the Mahabharata (Bakshi, 2002). Kim stresses the strategic tradition founded on Kautilya's *Arthashastra* (Kim, 2004).

---

[27]A notable exception is Myron Weiner (Weiner, M., 1965a).

[28]C. Raja Mohan has spoken about an institutionalised 'Indo-pessimism' with an 'ingrained risk-aversion' and a mindset of 'thinking small' (Mohan, C. R., 2005, p. 32).

[29]'Reforming the National Security System: Recommendations of the Group of Ministers' by the Group of Ministers (http://mod.nic.in/newadditions/rcontents.htm, accessed on 6 December, 2006); the Kargil Review Committee Report (http://www.fas.org/news/india/2000/25indi1.htm, accessed on 6 December, 2006) (For an organisation chart of the security management as recommended by the Group of Ministers, Mitra, S. K., 2003, p. 408).

Tanham has put forward what is perhaps the most influential account of Indian strategic culture (Tanham, 1992). He paints with a very broad brush, viewing Indian foreign policy behaviour as being highly contradictory, proud, even imperialistic, moralistic, hypocritical, fiercely independent, demanding recognition as a great power, but lacking the resources, institutions and organisational will to put their designs into effect. Indians, he argues, do not understand the difference between a great country and a great power. Nehru's Panchsheel, in conjunction with the policy of non-alignment, can be said to have been a coherent strategic doctrine at the height of the Cold War. However, by laying down ethical rules for engagement rather than goals, it can also be considered profoundly a-strategic in nature. Furthermore, Tanham argues that the very idea of devising a purely rational, interest-oriented strategy had a disturbingly Western ring to the Indian leadership. It was thought that it would be leading India down the wrong path, the path that had led Europe, within half a century, into two world wars and was then leading towards a third, potentially apocalyptic confrontation between the Soviet Union and the USA. Therefore, there may have initially been something like an institutional dislike of strategy. At the same time, the fact that India has been a status-quo country after independence, may have limited the urgency of developing a strategy. Tanham believes that India's 'defensive posture' has, at least in part, been the result of this lack of strategic planning.

By itself, however, a lack of strategy will not explain a 'defensive posture', as Tanham suggests (Tanham, 1992). It could equally, as North Korea demonstrates, produce a 'loose-cannon posture'. Strategic blindness and a lack of understanding of the security environment could lead to errors on both sides – excessive restraint as well as excessive aggression. Arguments reaching the conclusion that India behaves in a restrained way as a result of an underdeveloped culture of strategic thought, thus – implicitly or explicitly – refer back to larger cultural-historical explanations supplying the actual meaning of a lack of strategic thinking in the Indian context. At this point, their reasoning converges with that of analysts who, while not troubled primarily by a lack of strategic capabilities, explore India's past in order to explain idiosyncrasies in strategic choices such as restraint (the idealist element) or inconsistency (duality).

In such analyses it is often noted that India possesses a strategic culture – as in a culture of realism (embodied, for instance, in the *Arthashastras*). At the same time, however, there is also a culture of idealism (embodied, for instance, in great Indian spiritual leaders from the Buddha to Gandhi). These are Dixit's 'contradictory trends' (Dixit, 2003) – he regards India's foreign policy as being driven by (it is unclear, whether generally, allegorically or more precisely, historically) two traditions of thought – that of Kautilya, who 'believed that politics was mostly a non-moral or amoral phenomenon', and that of Ashoka, who 'was influenced by the teachings of Lord Buddha'. For Dixit, the duality is a quasi-cultural phenomenon. Realism, which has roots in Indian history, is rivalled by a strong, benign or tolerant trait, epitomised and brought to contemporary expression in the foreign policy of post-independence India (Dixit, 2003). Kim has a similar line of argument. To him, 'the origins of India's strategic thought' are extant in India's cultural and ideational resources, and 'many of these have been in existence for millennia' (Kim). Especially the traditions exemplified by Kautilya (realist) and Gandhi (idealist) have influenced Indian politics 'for almost three millennia'. The ideas have thereby become 'an integral part of the cultural context of Indian political and strategic thinking' (Kim, 2004). Bozeman searches in Kautilya's *Arthashastra* and in Buddhist thought for the sources of Indian foreign policy (Bozeman, 1994). Baljit Singh believes that 'political thinking in India, past as well as present, is deeply and overwhelmingly rooted in the native thought of that country'. Even the modern influence of 'occidental ideas', this 'most articulate challenge', ultimately 'failed on the bedrock of classical Hindu thought' (Singh). Singh describes Nehru's foreign policy as being based on the 'age-old Indian tradition of coexistence between different, often opposing sections and communities' (Singh) and praises Gandhi for having rediscovered 'the age-old and acceptable Indian tool – the uncommon common sense of self restraint and non-violence, ingrained into the thinking of Indians from the times of the Vedas and Buddha' (Singh, 1964). Andrew Latham argued, from an opposite point of view, that Indian security culture discourages confidence-building measures (CBMs), because 'such measures operate on a premise that is directly contrary to the Kautilyan paradigm' (Latham, 1997).

Culturalist approaches are attractive in part because of the simplicity a stereotypical approach brings with it. In the West, there has been a tendency to idealise, demonise, romanticise or otherwise categorise Indian culture (Inden, 1990). Colonial anthropology has attributed to India an essentially a-strategic, spiritual character, to which independent India's declaration of Panchsheel appears at first sight to have given institutional form (Singh, 1999b; Mitra, 2005). Such arguments rest on the tripartite assumption that, firstly, Indian thought (and the associated culture) is, to a significant extent, benign or idealist in content, that, secondly, these thoughts actually impacted on society so as to create a significantly benign tradition, and, thirdly, these arguments assume that there is a consistent historical trend, that contemporary Indian strategic thought and practice is influenced by (or at least stands in a tradition of) certain texts, some of which date back thousands of years. No part of these assumptions, as will be demonstrated here, is entirely convincing.

2.2.1 *The Myth of Benign Thought*

> *'Maybe India will give us, in return for conquest, pretension and exploitation, the gentleness and forbearance of the mature spirit, the quiet contentment of the disimpassioned soul, the calm of the understanding mind and will teach us a unifying, pacifying love for all of life.'*
>
> (Will Durant[30])

It is undeniable that India brought forth a number of great thinkers and world historical figures, such as the Buddha, Mahavira, Ashoka, Akbar, and Gandhi, who are associated with a tolerant, non-violent life and had a significant influence in India as well as outside India. Whilst Indians struggled, like everyone else, with the realities of everyday life, with the question of how power and wealth are to be distributed and with the problem of human vices, the assumption often is, that they did not give in to worldly imperatives as easily as others did – that there is an otherworldly quality to the Indian mind, a preoccupation with individual salvation through renunciation, non-violence and tolerance, that the religious traditions of thought are esoteric and apolitical[31].

Brown argues that Indian thought is special in that it refuses to be compartmentalised. In the Western tradition, private ethics, political theory and strategy are fields often thought about and discussed independently of each other. In India, they are part of an 'integrated system of reasoning which poses and interprets the very problem of human existence' (Brown,

---

[30]The American philosopher and historian Will Durant wrote this as part of his extensive 'Story of Civilisation' in 1935 (Durant, W., 1965). He was an avid admirer of Mahatma Gandhi, whose freedom struggle he evaluated in a short book called 'The Case for India' (Durant, W., 1930).

[31]In a 1957 study on American views of China and India, Harold Isaacs found that while Americans revered Gandhi and admired Nehru, their image of India as a whole was split. Of the 181 interviewees, about half (92) mentioned moral qualities. Of them, half thought of India in terms of 'spiritual, high-minded, moral', positive categories (44) and half thought of them in terms of 'holier-than-thou, hypocritical', negative categories (Isaacs, H. R., 1958, p. 324). The primary associations Americans had with Indians were of misery and oppression. American images of India at the time were, however, as Isaacs clarified, based on very limited and recent information and determined primarily by foreign policy differences between the US and India after the Second World War.

1953). Ultimately, the key problem of human existence is existence itself. Consequently, India has an unsurpassed tradition of esoteric and spiritual thought, to which the idea of non-violence is central. Zimmer called this the 'philosophy of the infinite'. By his categorisation, it includes – Jain and Buddhist philosophy, Brahmanism (which includes the Vedas, the Upanishads, the Bhagavad Gita, and Vedanta), Sankhya/Yoga and Tantra (Zimmer, 1969).

However, India also has a strong realist intellectual tradition. It can already be found in the great ancient epics, which in turn are based on yet earlier Vedic scriptures. In the Mahabharata, even the divine hero and protagonist of the Bhagavad Gita, Lord Krishna, is ready to use pragmatic wit and judicious deceit in order to advance the cause of *dharma*. The 'Santiparvan' book of the Mahabharata, set against a gory scene of the destruction and death of a generation of warriors, lays out some of 'the most cold-blooded realism in the history of political theory' (Brown, 1953). The great, wise warlord Bishma, lying on his bed of arrows, imparts his advice on good rule to the righteous Yudhishtira, who will become king[32]. The two spheres of personal ethics (Yudhishtira) and good rule (Bishma) meet, but they only partially overlap. The king, Bishma expounds, 'should be honest; but he must know the ways of the world, how to fight fire with fire'. Stating one of the key ethical justifications for a realist pursuit of the national interest, the king, 'on whom his people rely', must, furthermore, 'never hesitate to be ruthless with his enemies. It must not be beneath him to use treachery, fire and poison against them'. He should rule with *dharma*, 'but with adharma, too' (Menon, 2004).

In traditional Hindu political thought the Dharmashastras are treatises on law and political theory (of which the 'Code of Manu' is the most prominent). They set out the just and divine rule and the ethical conduct associated with it (Brown, 1953; Zimmer). The Arthashastras, on the other hand, dealt with utility, property and power in national and international politics. They make up a body of writing which Heinrich Zimmer has called the 'philosophy of success', based on a 'cynical realism and sophistication that is the very life-sap and flavour of the ancient Indian style of political theory and casuistry' (Zimmer, 1969).

Kautilya's *Arthashastra*, a treatise exclusively concerned with political advice, is perhaps the most brilliant example of the 'philosophy of success'. Often compared with Machiavelli's *'The Prince'*, it is highly practical and

---

[32]K. Subrahmanyam chose this scene as the cover illustration for his book 'Shedding Shibboleths', as a reminder of India's great strategic and realist intellectual heritage (Subrahmanyam, K., 2005).

unencumbered by moral considerations. For example, Kautilya treats the central question of war and peace from a purely instrumentalist point of view – 'when the degree of progress is the same in pursuing peace and waging war, peace is to be preferred' – not for ethical reasons, but rather, quite pragmatically, 'for, in war, there are many disadvantages, such as the loss of troops, expenditure, and absence from home' (Kautilya). War is to be preferred when the expected gains outweigh the expected costs. Kings should – by-and-large – behave justly; but they should do so because it is – by-and-large – in their interest. When this is not the case, all other instruments, just or unjust, should be at their disposal (Kautilya, 1992).

The *Arthashastra* brashly and unscrupulously espouses success as the true end and measure of statesmanship and restates, highly systematically –

> '...the cold wisdom that India has traditionally rendered in its celebrated fables – where mice can survive the presence of cats only by dint of constant vigilance, resourcefulness, and treachery, and where little fish are the natural nourishment of big fish' (Bozeman, 1994).

International relations, in Kautilya's writings, were concerned only with national interest, the most pressing of which was political survival. In order not to be overwhelmed, a king must seek to balance-off the surrounding states against each other in an elaborate system of alliances, of which his own state is to be the epicentre. In a fish-eat-fish world, the neighbour is always the potential enemy and the neighbour's neighbour the enemy's enemy, and thus a potential partner (Brown, 1953; Mukherjee, 1976; Naga, 1997). It is perhaps noteworthy that one of the great modern champions of realpolitik, Otto von Bismarck, would use precisely this theory of *Mandalas* to great effect in order to secure the position of a newly unified Germany within a finely balanced nineteenth century European system of powers. His maxim was to always be allied with at least two of the other four great powers, and France, the 'Kautilyan neighbour' was to be isolated (Fuller, 1967).

Beyond this realistic and pragmatic approach to international relations, however, there always loomed an ideal, a 'compensatory dream' that ultimately peace and harmony should replace the world of war (Zimmer, 1969). And –

> '...while no hope was held out by theorists that this peaceful pattern should ever become transferred to the larger field of nations, people continued to hold fast to an ancient mythical ideal which represents a universal world-wide

empire and enduring tranquility under the Chakravartin, a just and virtuous world monarch' (Bozeman, 1994).

The early Vedic or even pre-Vedic figure of the Chakravartin came to be associated with the Buddha and his moral code of non-violence. When the great emperor Ashoka, ruler over most of India, converted to Buddhism, he sought to embody this Chakravartin-rule. Thus, Buddhist morality (non-violence) became for a while 'the mainspring of Indian foreign policy' (Bozeman, 1994). In his foreword to 'The White Umbrella', Ramaswami Aiyar, writes that 'despite certain Machiavellian forms of diplomacy recommended with respect to international relations', these were primarily considered low expedients in comparison with the 'high ideals of the royal *Dharma*' (Brown). Brown argues that the theory of *Artha* is embedded into a theory of *Dharma*, which takes 'theoretical precedence' and that this 'reaffirms the *Dharma* concept as the ultimate basis of Indian political thought' (Brown). A thought, in which 'the moral behaviour of the ruler may be taken as a cornerstone' (Brown). The great bracket holding together a consistent Indian (Hindu) heritage of political thought is the pervasive belief that 'the problem of government is the ethical problem of the individual projected onto the field of state' (Brown, 1953).

If that is the case, what does it tell us about the Indian tradition of thought concerning international relations? Not too much. The Arthashastras were certainly among the earliest specialised works on pragmatic politics to be found anywhere[33]. The fact that they were, as strategic texts, incorporated into a wider ethical philosophy is, however, not surprising. Few thinkers anywhere have considered power or even survival to be an ultimate end in itself. They would have had to posit, as Hobbes has famously done (in an age of devastating civil wars all across Europe) that survival is already all we can hope for in a world where life is otherwise 'solitary, poore, nasty, brutish, and short' (Hobbes, 1991). Almost invariably, a notion of the 'good life' and the 'right life' looms behind a 'philosophy of success'. Machiavelli was not only thc author of *The Prince*, but also of the liberal 'Discourses' (Machiavelli, 1970). When Clausewitz called war a continuation of politics by other means, he did not mean that there was no qualitative difference between politics and war, but that war only made sense with respect to a precise political goal (Clausewitz, 2003). Mere

[33]Most scholars believe that Kautilya's *Arthashastra* was written in the fourth century BC (Mabbett, I. W., 1964). Comparable to it is Sun Tzu's *The Art of War*, written in the sixth century BC.

strategy without the slightest value-judgment is a fiction. It is the norm, rather than the exception that philosophies of success are embedded in an ethical framework. Most arguments deducing an Indian strategic approach from an Indian way of thinking do not make a sufficient effort to show how it differs from non-Indian ways of thought (Rosen, 1996).

The main problem with the assumption of benign thought, however, is that the Indian heritage contains 'every known theory of government and temporal power' (Brown, 1953). Even if that is an exaggeration and some theories, such as that of what constitutes human rights and a just society are missing (Paz, 1997), the Indian civilisation has, over the last four thousand years, brought forth so many different theories and responses to the dilemmas of life, that it cannot be limited to a particular strand (Weiner, 1984). The Vedic texts already espouse high ideals as well as highly pragmatic advice. The Mahabharata knows the characters of Yudhishtira, Duryodhana and Bhishma – the just, the ruthless and the pragmatic. Each one has his moment of praise and condemnation. There is the Buddha preaching to people to withdraw from the material world and there is Kautilya teaching people how to survive in the material world; there is the charmingly humane, down to earth wit of the *Karmasutra* and the powerful, ethical wit of Gandhi. India, like China or Europe, has produced far too many thoughts to be reducible to an idealist (or a realist) intellectual pattern.

2.2.2 *The Myth of a Benign Tradition*

The East bow'd low before the blast,
In patient, deep disdain.
She let the legions thunder past,
And plunged in thought again.

(Matthew Arnold[34])

Does India lack the 'martial imperial instincts' found elsewhere (Malik, 2002)? Is it true that, 'as the land of Buddha and Gandhi, India always yearned for peace' (Kondapi, 1951)? When the British classified the Sikhs, Marathas and Rajputs as martial races, they suggested that the other Indians were fundamentally 'weak in constitution, clerical in mentality and servile in attitude', as Macaulay said of the Bengalis (Som, 2004). Max Weber contrasted the Indian 'most highly anti-rational world of universal magic' with the realist and materialist Protestant ethic (Weber, 1958). Indians often bought into this characterisation in one way or another. Radhakrishnan, for instance, argues that, as a result of four millennia of venerating gurus

[34] 'Obermann Once More', Stanza 28.

instead of soldiers, statesmen, scientists, poets or philosophers, India suffers from a severe lack of pragmatism. It does not appreciate sufficiently 'the importance of wealth and power to give expression to the spirit' (Radhakrishnan, 1974).

The psychologist and humanist philosopher Erich Fromm compared the approach to religion and truth dominant in the West (Europe and North America) with that dominant in the East (India and China). In the West, logic is based on the Aristotelian non-paradox system. In the East, in Taoist, Buddhist or Brahmin thought, logic and truth are fundamentally paradox. He argues that paradox thinking stresses right action over right thought. This produces tolerance and 'an effort at self-modification'. The Aristotelian, Western standpoint, however, favours dogma and the illusory clarity of science, thus producing the Catholic Church and the atom bomb. Whereas violence is endemic in the 'thinking' tradition, seeking a right/wrong distinction, it is not aroused in the paradox tradition creating a mysterious grey area within which humans interact non-aggressively (Fromm, 2002).

When Gandhi contrasts ancient Indian civilisation with modern European civilisation, he demands of Indians to reject the latter. Modern civilisation, he writes, 'takes note neither of morality (*niti*) nor of religion (*dharma*)'. Modern Europeans 'appear to be half mad' (Gandhi, 1997). Gandhi believed that, while all peoples have the potential for a non-violent, moral civilisation, they have in the past been corrupted by their rulers. This is quite understandable, since 'kings will always use their kingly weapons. To use force is bred in them'. In general, however, people resent force. The question is – how will the people respond to their rulers' demands? They will either follow the path of 'body-force' or that of 'soul-force'. If they follow the former, both rulers and ruled 'become like so many mad men'. If they decide to learn and practice 'soul-force', however, 'the commands of rulers do not go beyond the point of their swords'. India, according to Gandhi, is a special case, because it is a rare example of a nation following the latter path. It has 'generally used passive resistance in all departments of life' (Gandhi). It has a propensity to use soul-force; 'brute force is not natural to the Indian soil' (Gandhi, 1997). Gandhi has given credibility to his interpretation of Indian culture in his own life and actions. Thus, Saunders could assert that in Gandhi –

> 'India's age-long search for God finds a new and wonderful expression, and her great idealism, proclaiming all down the ages that... hatred cannot be cast out except by love, comes to a practical application on an immense scale.

> Never before in history have these principles of India's ancient *Rishis* been applied in the sphere of politics, or the Sermon on the Mount been made to work on an imperial scale' (Saunders, 1931).

Only in Asia, could such great power be wielded by 'one so poor and simple' (Saunders, 1931).

Amartya Sen, in a collection of essays on Indian history, culture and identity (which reflect his own humanist ideals more than the real India) traces a unique, highly tolerant 'argumentative tradition'. Indian society has unusual absorptive powers, an inclusive character, and a broad, open identity. It is characterised by heterodoxy, tolerance and a specific type of secularism which accommodates religiosity in the public sphere rather than excluding it, but does not let it become political (Sen, 2005).

In terms of international politics, Indian cultural tolerance is often said to have led to a rejection of imperialism. Such an argument may be religiously based, emphasising the nature of Hinduism. Where Muslim, Christian or secular cultures take recourse to conflict in order to settle cultural spheres of influence, Hinduism feels no need to proselytise or expand. Instead of drawing clear cultural and political boundaries, it slowly and relentlessly absorbs, reformulates and digests foreign gods, cultures, languages and beliefs 'like an enormous metaphysical boa' (Paz). Indian cultural history is not a chronological succession, but an enormous 'superimposition' (Paz, 1997). India is the land in which the status of the priest exceeds (at least in theory) that of the king and warrior. The argument for Indian restraint may also be historically based – whenever Indian influence reached outside the confines of the motherland, like it did with the Chola traders in South East Asia, it did so peacefully, not militarily[35]. Trade routes enabled Indian ideas, thought and religion to travel and flourish in other countries. Thus did Buddhism reach Central and Eastern Asia and Indian scientific knowledge reached Muslim and Christian lands.

Europe, by contrast, has a bloody tradition of inflicting war and suffering on far away peoples – the Crusades, the destruction of the Pre-Columbian peoples, the global slave trade, the imperialism, peaking in the nineteenth century, and the two world wars are only the more striking examples of a history steeped in human blood. Islamic civilisation was inaugurated by a run of conquests which only the Mongols could rival.

---

[35]Former prime minister I.K. Gujral, for instance, stated the widely used argument that '...none of those who are neighbours in the Indian subcontinent, from Iran in the west to Burma and Indo-China in the east, have ever had reason to accuse India of having invaded their territory or exhibited any hostile designs against them'. (Gujral, I. K., 2004, p. 4).

With regard to China, Swaine and Tellis argue that, despite the pacifist views of Confucius and Mencius which have, at times, influenced statecraft –

> '...a cursory examination of the security behaviour of the Chinese state suggests that Chinese rulers have frequently resorted to violence to attain the national security objectives. In fact, one could argue that the use of force has been endemic in Chinese history' (Swaine, and Tellis, 2000).

China has, furthermore, lead a number of major campaigns against its periphery (Swaine, and Tellis, 2000). According to Johnston, there is a Confucian-pacifist and an imperialist-realist tradition of strategic culture in China – the second being dominant (Johnston,1995a).

The fact that Indian rulers did not venture beyond the subcontinent (very generously defined as including tracts of Afghanistan) with armies and fleets to conquer or subdue other peoples, may, however, have more to do with a lack of unity, central authority and thus power, than with benign cultural predispositions. Within the continent, Indian rulers fought almost incessantly (Tanham, 1992). The Mahabharata and the Arthashastras are representative of an age of warfare, a 'reflection of India's long history of practically continuous war, strife, and division' (Bozeman, 1994). Bozeman even suggests that the Indian cultural setting was particularly prone to engender warfare.

In ancient India, kings did not have the same godlike status as, for example, the Chinese Emperor or Egyptian Pharaoh, or even the divinely sanctioned European monarchs. They had to legitimise themselves through good governance, which mainly meant establishing law and order. They were the enforcers of *dharma*, but not the source of it, nor even the main interpreters of it. The Brahmins superseded the kings in moral and religious authority. Furthermore, in the case of India, which was for most of its history a landscape scattered with rival kingdoms, kings always had to be vigilant and ready to defend their position vis-à-vis rival kings – 'In the resultant Indian jungle of competing bids for power, war was accepted as a continuance of policy and the ultimate arbiter of conflicting claims' (Bozeman, 1994).

Indian history is, thus, by no means a peaceful one. Indian culture and politics can also not be described as predominantly spiritual, idealist or non-violent. First of all, current Indian domestic politics has significant Machiavellian traits –

> 'Our politicians display extraordinary skills in strategic realpolitik in domestic politics, where different parties anarchically interact in total defiance of democratic norms laid down by the Constitution' (Subrahmanyam, 2005).

A look at the political scene in Bihar, for example, would convince most observers that Indian politics is a particularly amoral undertaking. Furthermore, one of the many paradoxes and contradictions confronting observers of India, Brass notes, 'is the competing imagery of violence and non-violence'. This, he continues, is symbolised in two recurrent representations of India – one is that of the saintly Gandhi, fasting against violence. The other is that of the bloody riots that occurred as a result of partition immediately before and after independence (Brass). According to Brass, 'Hindu-Muslim pogroms (rather than simply "riots") have been endemic in India since independence' (Brass). Violence is so persistent that it deserves the adjective 'endemic' (Brass). Riots have become 'an anticipated form of collective action', at least as much as the great peaceful movements of non-cooperation and civil disobedience (Brass, 2003). Bayly and Gaborieau argue that Hindu–Muslim communal violence has a pre-modern history reaching as far back as 1700 and 1000 respectively (Bayly, 1985; Gaborieau, 1985). While leaders such as Gandhi could propagate peaceful tactics and reach the people, the history of communal violence demonstrates that other leaders could just as well take recourse to violent tactics, which also resonated with Indians.

Katharina and Sudhir Kakar write that the Indian civilisation has its own, distinctive worldview. This is a construct of ideas designed to explain the goals of human existence and the path to be taken to reach those goals. This framework provides answers for fundamental questions arising from human existence, such as, among others, the question of what is good and what is evil. The key Indian character trait the Kakars identify is a 'pronounced ethical relativism' (Kakar, and Kakar), deeply embedded in the Indian psyche. There is no one truth or one right action. Right and wrong are relative to a context. This depends on *desa* (the culture), *kala* (the historical epoch), *shrama* (the personal exertion) and *guna* (the inborn character traits). These four dimensions leave plenty of room for interpretation. Furthermore, there is no single text or church to offer guidance. If, however, there is no objective yardstick to determine truth, right or wrong, one has no choice but to tolerate the other. 'The roots of the much vaunted Hindu tolerance may, thus, be found in this contextual way of thinking' (Kakar, and Kakar, 2006).

However – and here the Kakars make a crucial point – a contextual way of thinking may equally blur the understanding of wrong. Tolerance could result from it, but also indifference to violence. As an example, they cite discussions with both Hindu and Muslims perpetrators of communal violence, finding that the Hindus were much less clear about the rights and wrongs of their actions than the Muslims (Kakar, and Kakar, 2006). In as far as tolerance in India is culturally rooted, it is a form of, what Jyotirmaya Sharma calls 'repressive' tolerance, a tolerance based on disinterest[36]. It has a theological precedent – the 'superhuman disinterest that Krishna preaches has another face – the indifference to the suffering of others' (Paz, 1997). There is no concept of pity and charity in the Christian sense, no 'love thy neighbour' in a world in which human worth is still widely considered relative to a person's position within a rigidly hierarchical caste system. Violence against members of other religions, other castes, against women and children, is unfortunately a part of everyday Indian life. A thousand years ago, the Muslim traveller Alberuni, already observed the 'repressive' tolerance. He noted that –

> '...on the whole, there is very little disputing about theological topics among themselves; at most, they fight with words, but they will never stake their soul or body or their property in religious controversy. On the contrary, all their fanaticism is directed against those who do not belong to them – against the foreigners. They call them 'mleccha', i.e. impure, and forbid having any connection with them... because, thereby they think they would be polluted' (Alberuni, 1964)[37].

Thus, the enormous achievement of making a multicultural society work and restrain religious conflict, an achievement which is undeniable despite all the problems and violence that persists, is not the natural product of 'a genuinely 'composite' culture founded on an active and mutual respect among practitioners of different religions' as 'nationalists fondly liked to suppose'. Instead, it is the product of specific policies and a 'routine indifference, a back-to-back neglect, which on occasions like religious festivals could be bloodily dispensed with' (Khilnani, 1998). The idealistic, non-violent and tolerant element in Indian foreign policy is, thus, not a natural quality of the Indian culture.

2.2.3 *The Inconclusiveness of India's Past*

It would bc foolish to arguc that contemporary India is not related to the Indias of the past and that 'Indian culture' is nonexistent. However, to

---

[36]Personal interview with the author (2006)

[37]Alberuni, born in AD 973, was a Muslim scholar from Khiva (today Uzbekistan). He followed the conquering Muslim king Mahmud of Ghazi into India. There, he wrote down what he learned and experienced, producing one of the most famous reports on traditional Hindu life and beliefs by an outsider. Similar reports about India have been written by the Greek historian Megasthenes (3rd century BC) and the Chinese Buddhist pilgrim Huen Tsang (7th century AD).

determine what exactly it entails, how it impacts on people's thoughts and behaviour and how it affects the decision-making of the strategic elite with respect to foreign policy is a daunting task. Can we really say, as Kim does, looking back at the reign of Emperor Ashoka (who may be regarded as an early incarnation of Indian duality) more than two thousand years ago, that he became 'a part of India's moral strength' (Kim, 2004)? May we conclude that Jesus, with his path-breaking Sermon on the Mount (much admired by Gandhi), has become part of Europe's moral strength? No – such an overly simplistic culturalism is not useful. To argue that the Indian government today makes a decision because of anything Ashoka or Kautilya or Akbar did centuries ago or because of holy texts written even longer ago, would be misleading. The fact that one can find many instances of benign thoughts and traditions in India's long history cannot by itself explain anything more than the fact that there were many instances of violence. One would have to make sense and evaluate an enormous panoptic of Indian culture, and one would have to do so objectively.

Indian thoughts and traditions are, however, many. They reinforce and contradict each other, co-exist and overlap (Sen, 2006). The result is many different imaginable Indias – a vast reservoir of cultural building blocks that can be used almost at will by elites to incite the masses both to non-violence as well as to communal rioting, to justify Panchsheel as much as realpolitik. The sheer complexity of India is described colourfully by Shashi Tharoor –

> 'How can one approach this land of snow peaks and tropical jungles, with seventeen major languages and twenty-two thousand distinct dialects (including some spoken by more people than speak Danish or Norwegian), inhabited in the last decade of the twentieth century by nearly 940 million individuals of every ethnic extraction known to humanity? How does one come to terms with a country whose population is 51 per cent illiterate, but which has educated the world's second largest pool of trained scientists and engineers, whose teeming cities overflow while four out of five Indians scratch a living from the soil? What is the clue to understanding a country rife with despair and disrepair, which nonetheless moved a Mughal emperor to declaim, 'If on earth there be paradise of bliss, it is this, it is this, it is this ...?' How does one gauge a culture that elevated nonviolence to an effective moral principle, but whose freedom was born in blood and whose independence still soaks in it? How does one explain a land where peasant organisations and suspicious officials attempt to close down Kentucky Fried Chicken as a threat to the nation, where a former Prime Minister bitterly criticises the sale of Pepsi-Cola in a country where villagers don't have clean drinking water, and which yet invents a greater

quantity of sophisticated software for US computer manufacturers than any other country in the world? How can one portray the present, let alone the future, of an ageless civilisation that was the birthplace of four major religions, a dozen different traditions of classical dance, eighty-five political parties, and three hundred ways of cooking the potato?' (Tharoor, 1989).

In all this diversity, there is a notion of cultural Indianness – but it is intangible, unconscious and politically indeterminate. To deduce an idealist or a realist strategic impulse from this would be to oversimplify, making spurious use of historical arguments (Basrur, 2001). The working out of tradition is manifold and depends very much on context. Neither literature nor society justify the conclusion that the political values which enter the Indian foreign policy discourse, spring from some perennial and natural benignity in thought or practice.

That is not to say, however, that there is no Indian strategic culture. There is one – but it is not defined by ancient tradition. It is defined, rather by the modern imagining of the Indian nation, by what nationalists have interpreted and institutionalised as Indian political culture. From a diverse cultural legacy, a certain view of Indian culture was constructed by way of emphasis, selection, and interpretation. Strategic culture is the product of the dynamics created by nationalism. Nationalism in turn references aspects of traditional culture.

Figure 2.2 shows the two unsatisfactory approaches and the third one, that is based on the national identity formation process. Theories which

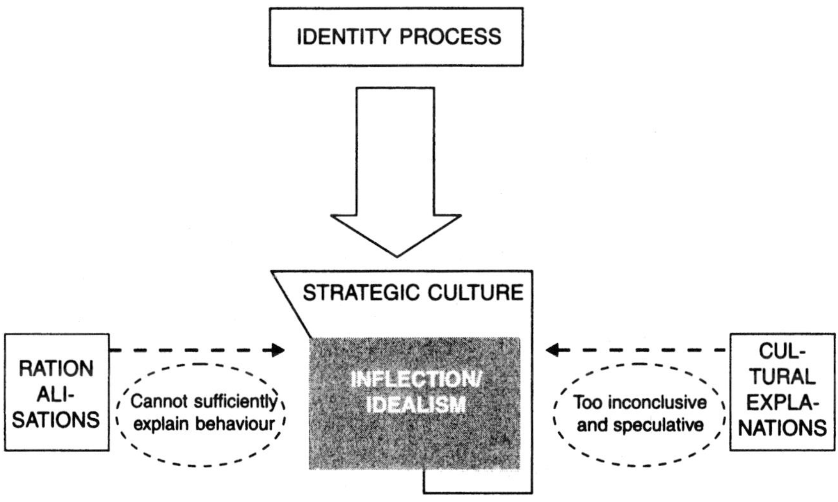

Figure 2.2: The Identity Process as Independent Variable

seek to rationalise the idealist inflection either as 'higher logic' or as 'smoke-screening' may in certain instances be useful, but cannot fully explain Indian foreign policy behaviour. Theories which seek to explain the duality with reference to Indian cultural history in thought and tradition, on the other hand, are too speculative. Neither approach can provide a convincing overall argument for the idealist inflection. An approach based on the identity process can. In accepting the reality of the idealist inflection and in using strategic culture as an intermediary element, it is similar to the culturalist approach. However, in focussing on the process of creating a modern political identity it can provide a less speculative, more coherent explanation for the idealist inflection in Indian foreign policy.

3

Nation-Building and International Relations Theory

The duality in Indian foreign policy is the result of an inflection away from the 'norm'. This norm, for the purpose of conceptual clarity, is considered to be the structural realist model for international relations in which states are conceptualised as units without significant internal dynamic, following the imperatives of a universal rationality. Realism, by-and-large, provides a good guideline for understanding foreign policies of states. However, deviations from this norm can be found in many state-actors. Issues of identity, value or belief, and also institutional dynamics, domestic political calculations or individual and group emotions, frequently interfere with the rational decision-making processes. In India, the deviation is particularly noteworthy, both for its strength as well as its persistence over time. In order to make sense of the phenomenon in international relations theory, the concept of strategic culture is useful. It has the advantage of addressing irregularities and idiosyncrasies.

As explained in the last chapter, strategic culture and the idealist inflection is insufficiently understood with direct reference to cultural building-blocs from Indian thought and tradition. It can be best understood as a product of the precarious and ambitious identity formation process of the new nation. What is needed, therefore, is a second theoretical framework within which the Indian national identity can be located in terms of stability. The assumption being that identity can generate political stability and that the less natural a common identity, the more precarious the nation-building process and hence the more urgent the need for ideological politics which will, in turn, impact on strategic culture and foreign policy.

3.1 Realism, Culture and their Limits

Some analysts of international relations argue that a state's strategy is the product of the international system. Postures can be more or less deduced from it. In an anarchic system, which lacks a central regulating authority, interstate relations are determined fundamentally by power structures. As there is no structure or higher authority through which differences and grievances can be addressed and resolved, and since there is no outside guarantor of a state's security, it is a 'self-help system' populated by –

> '...rational self-seeking actors resolutely if not exclusively concerned with relative gains because they must function in an anarchical environment in which their security and well-being ultimately rest on their ability to mobilise their own resources against external threats' (Krasner, 1992).

Broadly speaking, this may be done in two ways – through alliances (external balancing) or through the development of a state's own power-base (internal balancing). Power itself can become manifest in a number of different ways, but ultimately military power is the key currency (Jones and Miller, 1995). According to Kenneth Waltz, 'balance of power politics prevail whenever two, and only two, conditions are met – that the order be anarchic and that it be populated by units wishing to survive' (Waltz, 1979). This view, which leaves little room for systemic change and political choice, is termed 'structural realism'. It has significant clout among scholars of international relations, especially in the USA. Its key merits are the parsimony and rational clarity of its structure, and the propensity to describe probable scenarios and actions[38], as well as its applicability to a wide range of problems in the field. It is the Platonic 'idea' of international relations – a universal, constant pattern transcending the fog of war in all its particular manifestations[39].

The strength of the theory is, however, also a weakness – it presents a stereotypical ('ideal') mechanism, flattening out national strategic idiosyncrasies – all states, at all times, in all places proceed in the same predefined manner (Gilpin, 1981; Mearsheimer, 1990; Rengger, 1992; Waltz, 1995). They define the same goal – survival, identify the same

---

[38]'The theoretical strategy', Donelly explained, 'is to make the fewest assumptions possible and use the smallest imaginable number of explanatory variables. Structural realists self-consciously sacrifice richness and depth for a simple, rigorous theory that holds widely across time and space' (Donnelly, J., 2000, p.107).

[39]John Herz called it 'the very geometry of human conflict... the basic pattern for all narratives of human conflict' (Herz, J. H., 1950, p.20).

threats – power imbalances, come up with similar answers – internal or external balancing, and divide their resources accordingly – primarily towards military strength. Deviations from this norm happen all the time. Eventually, the implosion of the Soviet Union and the end of the Cold War, a major turning point in world history which almost all theorists – including the dominant realists – failed to predict, has led to an intense scrutiny of universal structural explanatory models (Lebow and Risse-Kappen, 1995; Katzenstein, 1996b; Glenn, Howlett, et al. 2004).

Even before this turning point, however, there were a number of scholars who believed that a universal rationalist meta-theory should be complemented (and at times substituted) by an understanding of the make-up of individual states (Singer, 1961). Waltz denies such a necessity. 'If changes in international outcomes are linked to changes in actors', he asks, 'how can one account for similarities of outcome that persist or recur even as actors vary?' (Waltz, 1979). The answer to such a question can only be that the outcomes are not as uniform as they may seem – no two international competitions, wars, negotiations, alliances, treaties, organisations and even states, are really the same. Differences are, in fact, substantial. In Waltz' theory, the differences will eventually even out in the big picture. To an extent, the problem thus becomes a chronological one. Waltz admits this. He argues that structural realism is 'better at saying what will happen than in saying when it will happen'. His theory cannot predict state behaviour, because it deals with the 'pressures of structures on states and not with how states will respond to the pressures'. Structural realism is then functioning like the always elusive, yet magnetically attracting 'equilibrium' in economic theory. It predicts that a balance of power disrupted will 'one day' be restored (Waltz, 2000). It can 'explain certain big and important things' (Waltz, 1998) – but it cannot explain how and when an individual state responds to them. Critics of structural realism go further than that. They question the content – does this theory describe the pressures correctly and does it really predict 'natural' responses? They also question the logic behind it, the heavy reliance on structure – do states really respond in ways similar enough to validate a universal theory? How important is an understanding of agency and of the individual characteristics of states[40]?

---

[40]The debate over the primacy of structure or agency in explaining behaviour can be found in sociological scholarship as well as in scholarship on international society (IR). Anthony Giddens' 'structuration theory' is a key work, proposing that the structure/agency dichotomy is reconciled in a constant and mutually affecting interaction between an evolving actor and an evolving structure (Giddens, A.,1984).

The liberal school questions the anarchical nature of international relations and hence the capacity of structural realist approaches to describe, understand and predict the behaviour of states in the international system[41]. The key areas of contention are – the use of force (more restricted), the roles of diplomacy, of companies and international institutions (important and not merely derivative), the understanding of power (should be more broadly defined), domestic politics (society and economics exert constraints), cooperation (is likely to occur), and social ideas (have an influence allowing for purposive change) (Keohane, and Nye, 1977; Hanrieder, 1978; Keohane, 1986; Rosecrance, 1986). However, liberal thinkers are, by and large, not too concerned with national idiosyncrasies[42]. This may sometimes simply be because some liberals are not so concerned with the state as a key actor in international relations (Held, 1989). More often, it is because – as in structural realist thinking – national interests are taken as a given, an exogenous and independent variable in the analysis (Legro,1996).

Some key traditional realists, on the other hand, have paid attention to them (Kennan, 1947; Morgenthau, 1963; Kennan, 1993)[43]. Far from being uniform and easily predictable, the argument goes, a number of international, regional, national and intra-national specifics impact on a state's strategy. Morgenthau, who bases his thought on a universal (pessimistic) view of man and a realist paradigm, nevertheless calls the existence of a national character 'an undeniable truth, without which all history would be a riddle' (Morgenthau). To him, it is crucial for making the past actions of states intelligible, as well as for predicting their future behaviour. He cites Coleridge's 'invisible spirit', which 'breathes through a whole people, and is participated by all, though not by all alike', giving 'colour and character both to their virtues and vices'. Morgenthau concurs, calling it 'incontestable' that 'certain qualities of intellect and character occur more frequently and

---

[41]Fukuyama, for instance, attacks the very root of realist thought by stipulating that the (Hegelian) desire for recognition is a more fundamental human trait than the (Hobbesian) desire for self-preservation (Fukuyama, F., 1992).

[42]There are, of course, exceptions – Fukuyama discusses the idea of social capital and trust in economic success with some degree of national differentiation. He defines trust as 'a product of preexisting communities of shared moral codes or values' (Fukuyama, F. 1995, p.336). See also, the work of Keohane, Nye and Jervis (Keohane, R. O., 1984; Nye, J. S., 1987; Jervis, R., 1988).

[43]Other realists, such as Schelling or Kahn, on the other hand, worked with a timeless rationality and abstract, game theoretical models, consciously disregarding national history, politics or culture (Kahn, H., 1960; Schelling, T. C., 1960).

are more highly valued in one nation than in another' (Morgenthau). The observer of the international scene must take national character into account, 'however difficult it may be to assess correctly so elusive and intangible a factor. Failure to do so will lead to errors in judgment and policies...' Only thus can one make sense, for example, of the decisions and capabilities of Germany, the Soviets and the USA during the Second World War (Morgenthau, 1963).

Morgenthau, however, remains firmly within a discussion of means (power) rather than ends. The specific ethical principles and goals formulated within a national context are not of primary concern to him. Like Machiavelli in his council to the prince, he is concerned with how a state (given its own idiosyncrasies and those of others around it) can best achieve its goals – whatever they may be[44]. For instance, whilst Morgenthau addresses the case in which the ideals of peace and international law are subject to an instrumental ideology of securing the status-quo (used by a country seeking the preservation of its current level of power), he does not theorise on the ideal of peace and international law as an end in itself, or on other worthy ends of foreign policy (Morgenthau, 1963). Raymond Aron, who shares Morgenthau's realist views on the nature of the international system and his belief in the importance of understanding the idiosyncratic patterns of behaviour of actors[45], takes up the cue where Morgenthau leaves it –

> 'Security, power, glory, ideas, are essentially heterogeneous objectives which can be reduced to a single term only by distorting the human meaning of diplomatic-strategic action. If the rivalry of states is comparable to a game, what is 'at stake' cannot be designated by a single concept' (Aron, R., 1968).

Realists, however, rarely ventured deeper into the study of what is 'at stake', and how it may be evaluated and determined by different states,

---

[44]'Since we are not concerned here with the ultimate goals of international politics, we shall deal with ethical and legal principles and biological necessities only in so far as they perform the function of ideologies'. By 'ideologies', he refers to Karl Mannheim's purely instrumental idea of 'particular ideology' (Morgenthau, H. J. 1963, p.88). In an earlier work, Morgenthau argued that, since the defining characteristic of politics is the use of power to dominate others, morality and reason are subordinate qualities, instrumental for attaining and justifying power – 'Nations are "peace-loving" under certain conditions and are warlike under others' (Morgenthau, H. J., 1946, p.66).

[45]He refers to this phenomenon, which needs to be understood in conjunction with the paradigms of the historical epoch as well as the material constraints, as the 'styles of being and behaving' (Aron, R., 1968, p.279).

presumably because it would distance the analysis from a general theory of international interaction based on the universal concept of power.

Constructivists do just that. Taking up Cynthia Weber's categorisation of international relations theories as rival 'myths', providing apparent truths while withholding from view the a priori assumptions which enable a theory to function in the first place, it can be said that (neo)realism, with its focus on structure, withholds from view the authors of the structure. Wendt, then, asks the 'obvious' question – 'who is the author of international anarchy? And he gives us his answer – socially constructed states' (Weber, 2005). Refusing to take rational self-interest for granted, the so-called constructivists are deeply concerned with how interests are shaped; they take a more sociological (identity-driven) rather than economic (ratio-driven) approach (Onuf, 1989; Wendt, 1992; 1994; Guzzini, and Leander, 2006). Pure, perfect anarchy is a fictional and abstract idea (in the same way as a 'state of nature' or an absolutely free market is) –

> 'Anarchic structure explains little by itself; what matters is the identities and interests that states bring to their interactions and the subsequent impact of the latter on the former... Anarchy is what states make of it' (Wendt, A. 1994)[46].

The state remains the key unit of analysis, but it is not taken as an undifferentiated and essentially robotic unit. The states, as well as the system they act in, are not fixed realities existing a priori, but the products of intersubjectively constructed relations (Wendt, 1994). The international structure and the agents within it are, therefore, not observed along independent levels of analysis but are essentially co-constituting. Social structures, he argues, have an 'inherently discursive dimension in the sense that they are inseparable from the reasons and self-understanding that agents bring to their actions'. On the unit-level, the implication of this co-constituting model is that game theory cannot sufficiently explain state behaviour. One has to develop a theory of state preferences and 'self-understandings' (Wendt, 1987). Wendt's focus is on the relationship between representations of material reality and material reality itself, and on the interpretation and signification by individual actors, who then act on the basis of the meanings that objects have for them. 'A gun in the hands of a friend is a different thing from one in the hands of an enemy'. Meanings, such as enmity, are socially constructed (Wendt, 1996). Wendt

---

[46]'Anarchy is what states make of it' is what Weber describes as the founding 'myth' of constructivism. It is the counterpart to the realist myth that 'international anarchy is the permissive cause of war' (Weber, 2005, pp. 60–61).

is interested in identity formation in the international context and posits that strategies cannot simply be pre-supposed, based on a posited material 'reality'. He says little, however, about how identity influences a state's behaviour prior to the intersubjective process taking place in the international arena or about the internal motivations and dynamics of a state.

3.1.1 *Internal Dynamics and Agency*

The element of agency in generating a political (strategic) culture has been looked at before; mostly, however, at the level of particular interests within the state. Klein, for instance, analysed US strategic culture in light of the military-industrial-complex and the desire of some elements in society to stimulate overtly aggressive foreign policies (Klein, 1989). Luckham similarly argued that elements of Western society have created an 'armaments culture' to suit their interests (Luckham, 1994). The influence of the military and its particular interests can also be strong in countries which rely on the military for nation-building purposes (and often as guardians of secular national values), such as Turkey or Pakistan. In other countries religious institutions provide the state with an identity focus and internal cohesion at the cost of an uninfringed pursuit of their particular interests. Examples are the Catholic Church in Franco's Spain, in Ireland or Poland, or the Shiite clergy in Iran.

In times of domestic crisis, moreover, politicians in authoritarian as well as democratic countries have a tendency to deflect attention away from the domestic scene and use polarising foreign policy issues to generate emotions and rally everyone 'around the flag' (which usually means 'behind the government'). Of course, such a diversionary manoeuvre works best if people are genuinely convinced of the importance of the foreign policy issue and the correctness of the government's approach. There are many examples of domestic crises followed by sudden, populist foreign policies. Some recent ones are – the Argentine attack on the Falkland Islands during a time of political instability in 1982, US air strikes on Sudan and Afghanistan (ordered 21 August, 1998) during the height of President Clinton's Lewinsky scandal (public confession of misconduct on 17 August, 1998) or the political reaction to the Danish Mohammed Caricatures in 2005 and 2006 by non-democratic governments seeking popular support in Saudi-Arabia, Egypt, Libya and Syria. There are many other instances in which domestic considerations limit, prescribe or define options available to foreign policy makers.

Foreign policy can, however, also be used to advance non-particular political goals, such as national integration and identity formation. For some countries, international wars have been used not only to make independence or unity possible within the international power system, but also to create the internal unity of the entity that is to become an independent actor in the first place. In 1870, North and South Germany united to fight a common enemy – France. William I was crowned emperor of a unified Germany by the potentates present in Versailles, the site of their common victory. The founding myth of the Swiss federation is the struggle against the Habsburgs, the William Tell legend and the mythological Rütli-Schwur of 1307. The United States first became united in the process of a common war of all New England colonies against British rule between 1775 and 1783. The victorious general, George Washington, was to become the first President. Struggles against groups considered foreigners and invaders have considerable potential to stir a people's imagination and arouse feelings of mutual identity by virtue of negative definition against the outside element. The potential can be translated into political currency through propagandistic myth-making to serve an identity building purpose.

This is frequently the case with struggles that have a legendary, heroic story-telling quality. Such struggles are often victorious ones, such as the British battles against a succession of threatening European hegemons from the Spain of Phillip II (sinking of the Armada in 1588), to Napoleon's France (Trafalgar in 1805 and Waterloo in 1815) and Hitler's Germany (Battle of Britain in 1940). The Soviet defeat of the invading German armies in the 'Great Patriotic War' of 1941–45, or the victories over colonisers at the hands of great liberators across the colonised world from Latin America (San Martin and Simon Bolivar) to Asia (Ho Chi Minh). They may also be glorified defeats, such as the Jewish war against Roman occupation, culminating in the siege of Masada (AD 70–73) or the Serbian defeat by the advancing Ottomans on the Kosovo field in 1389. It may also – and very potently – be an ongoing struggle against foreign occupation or interference such as in Palestine, Afghanistan or Iraq. The foreign policy of wars, battles, and struggles, with its dramaturgic power, heroes and villains, sacrifice and glory, goes well with national identity formation. Sometimes the link is accidental, more often it is purposely exploited by political entrepreneurs.

Although wars seem to be particularly susceptible to nation-building by creating a sharp distinction between 'us' and 'them', political declarations and actions with a universal moral appeal can also be potent identity-shapers – they give a sense of great moral standing and responsibility, and thereby a national mission in international politics. Foreign policy remains a stage for nation-building, but now national identity shapes foreign policy more than being shaped by it. In some cases revolutions are domestic affairs, but often they stand for values with a universal message and appeal and have significant implications, opponents and 'others' on the international scene – in recent years, this was often a cynical, immoral 'old' Europe. An example is the US Declaration of Independence of 1776 ('We hold these truths to be self-evident...')[47] or the French Declaration of the Rights of Man and of the Citizen of 1789[48]. Both documents marked a starting point for foreign policy with an air of exceptionalism. The Russian Revolution of 1917, driven by Lenin's interpretation of communism, was initially considered to be the beginning of a worldwide revolution ushering in a new age[49]. Communism as a universal ideology, like liberalism, had an inherent missionary drive.

These examples show how an agent-driven ideology may affect foreign policy. Nationalism is such an ideology. Different types of nationalism (cultural, ethnic, civic, etc.) will likely impact differently on foreign policy – and will in turn be affected differently by foreign policies. Thus, the type of national-project to be analysed – here the Indian one – needs to be understood in its particular manifestation first.

The starting point is that India is not a 'natural' nation, with a readily available linguistic, cultural, historic, or other common denominator. India is at best a very vaguely defined civilisational entity, comparable perhaps to 'Europe'. For reasons that will be discussed later, it did not develop a bottom-up national identity shared by a large group of people. On the contrary, the national project was top-down. It involved the extremely challenging task of marking a vanishing point of emotional focus for hundreds of millions of people with different religions, languages and traditions.

In a way, the task is comparable to that of the 'United States' of America which built and continues to build a nation out of people with highly diverse origins – first Europeans (English, Germans, Scandinavians, French, Spanish, Greeks, Italians, Irish, East-Europeans, and Russians, Catholics, Protestants, Orthodox Christians and Jews), then Africans (they

---

[47]Available online at Project Gutenberg *http://www.gutenberg.org/files/16780/16780-pdf.pdf* (accessed on 19th March, 2007).

[48]Full text available online at *http://www.hrcr.org/docs/frenchdec.html* (accessed on 19th March, 2007).

[49]This is ironic, because even in Russia, the revolution was little more than a coup d'etat.

were there from the beginning, but became incorporated into the national project only later), Latin Americans, Asians[50]. English became the main language, but it was initially rivalled by German and is today increasingly rivalled by Spanish. Christianity is the strongest religion, but it is highly fragmented in many churches and sects. Had the political leaders chosen to rally people around linguistic, religious or cultural identities, the result would not have been a United States of America, but at best a federation of states, comparable to the European Union. Instead, the new American nation was built around abstract values and myths, such as the rights of man, the 'American way of life', the land of unlimited opportunity for individuals, or a peculiar mixture of a Calvinistic belief in destiny (e.g. 'Manifest Destiny') and an Enlightenment belief in material and human progress. The USA and India have similar mechanisms of linking a comparably value-based identity with foreign policy.

Such a comparison is, of course, only an indicator. India and the USA differ fundamentally in many ways. The most important difference in terms of the national project is that the USA was an immigrant country, a 'melting pot', in which people showed a certain readiness to exchange their primordial identities in favour of a new one. In India, of course, the situation is entirely different – cultural, ethnic and linguistic groups are mostly geographically separated. They are far from leaving behind their regional identity. An Indian national identity has to envelop and encompass these regional identities. This has implications for the types of values nationalism can be built on. For example, pluralism and tolerance among groups is stressed in place of individual rights and freedoms. Secularism has a different meaning in India than it has in the USA – religion is not so much excluded from the public sphere but rather tolerated (Bhargava, 2005; Bilgrami, 2005; Sen, 2005). To some extent, the European Union may be a better comparison, but it would be premature to gauge the effects of a European common identity on a European foreign policy.

Cultural nationalisms may also affect foreign policy (and vice versa) – think of France's policy of Francité, Russian Pan Slavism or Iranian relations with Shi'a groups outside its borders. However, value nationalisms do so in a different way. This is the core argument put forward here. Firstly, it is more difficult for a value-based community to openly follow the national interest irrespective of considerations relating to the shared political values. The capacity for schizophrenia is limited – what is right and important inside the country, will not be wrong or irrelevant outside it.

[50]Native Americans are, until today, not really part of the national project.

There is some 'spill-over' linking beliefs and behaviour. This is the strategic culture argument. Secondly, foreign policy behaviour and the recognition or reception it receives in the international scene reflects and constructs the identity of the state. Foreign policy can become an important and conscious arena of nation-building (even for rival national projects). This is Wendt's argument, modified from a system-centered approach to an agent-centered approach. The need for recognition and for conscious identity- (value-) based foreign policies will be larger, the more fragile the national identity. It is fragile, if the national project has not yet taken root, or is challenged by rival regional or supra-regional national projects. The reflexive spill-over effect, on the other hand, will be stronger, the more entrenched the national identity is in the strategic community.

Decision-makers themselves may have already ingested an identity or they may be consciously catering to or manipulating an existing identity for political reasons. In reality, there is a spectrum along which a society, even a person moves, reaching from active, conscious identity-building to actions unconsciously shaped by identity. Both dynamics may become increasingly conflated as identity takes shape and individual policy makers within the state will shift status from 'producers' of identity to 'consumers' of identity. This raises the question, as to how far elites are able to rise above strategic cultural constraints or become socialised within the myths they are instrumental in creating (Johnston, 1995b). Snyder, for example, discusses a 'blow-back' or 'echo-effect', whereby elites start to believe their own lies and fall prey to the cultural symbols they helped create (Snyder, 1984). Kupchan notes how great powers may pursue strategies contrary to their interest if elites are entrapped in a strategic culture of their own making (Kupchan,1994).

National identity formation and unity cannot only be advanced by using foreign policy. Other elements, such as economic policy and other domestic political issues are also very important. However, foreign policy has the advantage of clearly working with an 'us'/'them' framework. Moreover, if the national project is particularly frail, all resources at hand, including foreign policy, are expected to be used to advance the national project. At the same time, it is worth recalling that the theory does also not suggest that the internal dynamic of the national project, as expressed in the strategic culture, is the only way to understand Indian foreign policy at all times. It is a necessary, not a sufficient or comprehensive explanation of India's behaviour in the international arena. It can explain the idealist inflection in Indian foreign policy.

3.1.2 *The Problem of Culture*

'Culture' – whether as a framework for individual motivations, as the strategic culture of a group or in its broader historical meaning – poses a significant challenge to international relations. While 'only the most dogmatic materialist would deny the importance of the dominant ideas in the minds of those who think and act strategically' (Rosen, 1996) and while excluding cultural factors from analysis would lead to grave errors in judgment and policy (as Morgenthau wrote), including it as an identifiable and useful variable is very difficult indeed. It defies precise definition and clear-cut explanations. Positivist social scientists, interested in observable, quantifiable data, understandably tend to find culture a frustrating and unattractive ingredient in theory and often relegate it to a residual variable of last resort (Poore, 2004). However (returning once more to Morgenthau), making culture a secondary, often overlooked variable, because it poses methodological problems is leading us towards the fallacy of believing that only what we can understand precisely (and measure) determines what actually is. Such thinking would indeed lead to grave errors in judgment and policy. It is difficult to envisage strategists as not embedded in a cultural or political context (Gray, 1999). At the same time, however, the limitations of culture as a parameter have to be understood.

Firstly, there is the issue of the levels of analysis. Waltz argued that a theory 'at one level of generality cannot answer questions about matters at a different level of generality' (Waltz, 1979). Whilst the issue may not be as categorical in the field of culture where it may, at times, be possible to explain very specific occurrences with reference to broad cultural trends, it is usually better to maintain commensurability between the independent and the dependent variable. Culture as civilisation, for example, can thus be applied to large scale theories of the rise and fall of nations or even parts of the world (Spengler, 1919; Friedell, 1927; Kennedy, 1989; Braudel, 1995), while culture in a more precise context, such as the decision-making culture of an institution such as the military, can be applied to more precise theories, such as nuclear strategy (Snyder, 1977). To explain, for instance, why the German army continued to fight the battle for Stalingrad even after all hope was lost, it may make more sense to understand the dominant culture within the German army during that time period rather than to look at the broader German civic culture.

Secondly, certain situations may be more culture-sensitive than others, so that 'exogenous conditions' may determine 'when and how a strategic culture becomes dominant' (Poore, 2004). This is the case, for example, when issues are touched which are close to a people's identity. In times of domestic crisis or conflict, patriotism and identity politics are often enforced in order to induce people to 'rally around the flag'. There may be foreign policy issues, furthermore, which the politicians and population of a state can hardly assess dispassionately. Kashmir is such an issue for India and Pakistan, Palestine for many Muslim states, Kosovo for Serbia, and Israel for Germany. There may also be topics which arouse an identity-driven response. They are usually related to identity through religion, values or history. Sino-Japanese relations are marred by history schoolbooks. Relations between Poland and Germany are made difficult by (among other things) the ineffective but provocative activities of German refugee organisations.

Thirdly, it needs to be clarified whose culture we are speaking about. States are not necessarily culturally monolithic entities. There are different levels of cultures and subcultures. Often, they are overlapping and mutually influencing (Krause, 1997; Gray, 1999). Within one state, there may be different, even rival strategic cultures (Johnston, 1995a). Furthermore, some groups and agents may be more strongly affected by culture than others. Thus, one has to be precise about whose culture one refers to – that of the direct decision-makers, the opinion-shaping social elites, the wider politically active segment in society, or everybody? Moreover, should culture be regarded as a political, institutional or social phenomenon (Kupchan, 1994)? In order to avoid an amorphous independent variable and an *'atomised research agenda'* (Hoffman, and Longhurst, 1999), culture has to be understood at some aggregate level. As stated above, which classification of culture is chosen ultimately depends on what is to be explained by it. A broader understanding of culture may be advisable in some cases, whereas a closer look at specific subcultures and their interaction may be better in others.

A fourth issue is that of change. If culture is taken as an independent variable, it should have a certain degree of stability. Cultures, however, are always in flux (Aberbach, Chesney, et al., 1975). The question is, then, how fast does a specific culture change? Thus –

> '...while it could be viewed as self-defeating for a strategic culture advocate to argue that culture is constantly changing... it might be conceded that it is important not to be too deterministic – cultures evolve and take on new meanings over time.' (Poore, 2004).

What is the correct chronological point of reference when using culture? The older a reference point is, the more it has to be pervasive and recurrent in order to be a credible determinant of contemporary culture. To extrapolate the behaviour of modern India from the activities of the Buddha or that of modern European states from the life and ideas of St Augustine would be misleading because the Buddhist tradition has been significantly diminished in India by Hindu and Muslim traditions whilst in Europe religious traditions as a whole have taken a backseat in political discourse. It may be appropriate, however, to look at the manifestation of Christianity at a particular time period and place (Europe in the sixteenth and seventeenth centuries, the USA since 9/11) in order to explain the actions of leaders under its influence (Charles, US President George W. Bush and the Neocons). Equally, it may be useful to look at the influence of the Buddha on Gandhi, and through Gandhi on India. Vietnam's or Afghanistan's fierce resistance to foreign influence, on the other hand, has a historical pedigree reaching back centuries. It is a recurring and pervasive characteristic. If specific elements of culture are not constant over time, it may become important to understand what factors induce them to change – endogenous or exogenous ones, man made or environmental, are they products of conscious action or best understood intersubjectively?

The fifth and most important question that culture raises for international relations is, what is the relationship between culture and actual behaviour? Johnston argued that the two have too often been tacitly conflated (Johnston, 1995b). While most authors would agree that 'the overall effect of culture is to predispose collectivities towards certain actions and policies rather than others' (Duffield, 1999), just how this happens, remains difficult to calibrate. Does culture simply provide tendencies, a context for decision-making and a meaning for material factors, rather than precise determinants of decisions, as Gray argues (Gray, 1986)? Or does it, as Krause and Latham argued, shape 'policy reflexes', the 'understanding of what constitutes "normal", "appropriate", or "desirable" practices and responses' (Krause, and Latham, 1997). Or does it inform concrete decisions, directly (Kier, 1996)?

The answer to this question depends on whether we can single out the cultural elements of a decision vis-à-vis the non-cultural variables. That is a challenging task. Understanding actions is essentially the problem of understanding motivations, we have to look into the decision-makers' minds. Culture can affect a decision at many different levels. At the ontological level, culture influences who we believe we are and what we consider to be important and worthy goals. At the cognitive level, culture may predetermine what phenomena we can take note of and conceptualise in the first place and what we categorise as important enough to merit further consideration. At the analytical level, culture is likely to affect the way we interpret and prioritise a given phenomenon. It helps us shape our opinion about facts, which may be a more important measure than the facts themselves (Angell, 1951). At the decision-making level, culture influences our understanding of what means are possible, useful, legitimate, and justified. At the implementation level, culture may determine with what resolution we put decisions into effect and at the interpretative level, culture may influence what we classify as success and failure and what we learn from our experiences. These issues are difficult enough to understand with respect to actual actions. However, they will be much more difficult to understand with respect to what is not thought of, considered and done.

Another problem is that decision-makers are usually unwilling to lay bare their process of reasoning. It is common for agents to 'sell' their actions, i.e. not to be honest about their reasons for doing something. Decision-makers often explain a decision with a particular domestic or international audience in mind. An idealist choice may thus be portrayed as realist and interest oriented, if the decision-maker is, for example, trying to sell it to a skeptical populace faced with the prospect of having to give up concrete benefits. Inversely, a realist choice may be embroidered in idealist language, for example, in order to make it more palatable to other states. Furthermore, an action (or inaction) may be the product of a mixed process, supported by some on cultural grounds and by others on rational grounds, with opinions converging by chance. Lastly, one may reasonably ask in how far any actor is himself really aware of his own motivations, and in how far he is driven by emotions, desires, fears or his subconscious – each of which may in turn have a cultural element or not. This is the still largely uncharted field of the human psyche. Some path-breaking studies have attempted to understand history through a psychological analysis of key actors (Erikson, 1958; 1969). The result is that cultural and rational elements are usually intricately conflated in the minds of individual decision-makers, political elites and the broader public.

If a cultural element is to be filtered out, understanding the motivations is, however, only one dimension along which behaviour needs to be analysed. A second dimension is given by the inflections that invariably drive a wedge between the reasoning of the decision-makers (from which a cultural trend is to be extrapolated), the actual decision and the implementation of the decision. Decision-makers do not act in a vacuum. There may be lobbies and pressure groups pushing certain topics at the expense of others at the ontological and cognitive levels. There may be a problem of imperfect information at the analytical and again at the interpretative level and there may be bureaucratic decision-making, corruption or simply chance and a human touch at the decision-making and implementation levels. It is, subsequently, extremely difficult to reconstruct a cultural pattern from a given behaviour.

Is it better then, to argue the other way round, from an understanding of culture to a prediction of behaviour? The answer is, no. The problems with understanding motivations persist. If cultural expressions and meanings are analysed (striking rhetoric, symbols, beliefs, etc.) in order to predict behaviour, it still needs to be demonstrated how culture affects behaviour. In order to make that connection, however, it would again be necessary to deconstruct the motivations behind an action in order to find out how strong the influence of cultural elements vis-à-vis rational elements or chance is.

What people say is not the same as what they believe; what they believe is not the same as what they do; and what they do is not the same as what actually happens. The final outcome of a policy decision may be entirely unpredictable. In strategic culture theory, scholars have grappled with this problem from both sides of the equation, deductively arguing from behaviour, and inductively arguing from culture. The argument has been led exemplarily by Johnston and Gray (Gray, 1986; Johnston, 1995b; Gray, 1999; Johnston, 1999).

3.1.3 *Deductive vis-a-vis Inductive Approach*

Johnston prefers an empirical, deductive research agenda with a limited understanding of strategic culture as the mindset of strategic decision-makers. This, he believes, allows for testable hypotheses and recovers strategic culture from a realm of mere speculation. The relationship between 'big C culture' as well as (small c) strategic culture and behaviour, to him is unknown unless put to the test. The test, he admits, is difficult and fraught with assumptions and ambiguities. It is, however, our best bet (Johnston). Gray, on the other hand, believes that Johnston's work 'rests upon a misunderstanding of the nature, character and working of strategic culture' (Gray, 1999). In his view, it is futile to separate strategic culture from the wider ('big C') culture, it is impossible to establish ideas and beliefs as an independent variable separate from behaviour (as the dependent variable). The attempt to make strategic culture scientifically tangible through a rigorous methodology is illusory and flawed. He believes that strategic culture provides a context for understanding, rather than an explanatory causality for behaviour. Johnston, on the other hand, regards contextual explanations as 'gross generalisations', 'untestable, unfalsifiable, and frankly, smack of the old, discredited, essentialising, national character studies of the past' (Johnston, 1999).

Johnston provides what is possibly the most thorough attempt to solve the methodological difficulties of cultural explanations for strategic behaviour (Poore, 2004). Without addressing all the challenges culture poses, he focusses on two issues. First, it must be established whether strategic culture exists across time and across actors within a society as a dominant variable in decision-making. Secondly, it must be established whether strategic culture affects actual behaviour or at the very least can be shown to limit the options considered. This can best be done by tracing strategic culture 'from its sources, through the socialisation process, to the values and assumptions held by particular decision-makers.' (Johnston, 1995b).

Initially, Johnston suggests, it has to be decided what the objects to be analysed are. There are many possible objects, but the most useful, in his view, are – writings, debates, thoughts and words from 'culture bearing units' (such as strategists, military leaders, security elites), weapons designs, media images of war, military ceremonies and military literature (Johnston, 1995b). If the preference rankings are congruent across these objects of analysis and across time, then strategic culture can, in his view, be considered a significant factor.

In order to pin down a strategic culture, Johnston suggests the use of Axelrod's cognitive mapping – uncovering the causal mechanisms of a person with respect to a particular policy and then extrapolating from this structure the 'deeper causal arguments that may be obscured by the surface logics and perfunctory language' (Axelrod, 1976; Johnston). Furthermore, symbol analysis could be of help. Elder and Cobb have suggested that symbols are important elements of a political culture, because they give 'definition to a political community, indexing common understanding and relatively stable patterns of reference' (Elder, and Cobb, 1983). Johnston suggests that a good way to make sense of symbols is to look at the use of value laden, symbolic vocabulary with a behavioural meaning such as 'deterrence' or 'diplomacy' (Johnston). Johnston believes that through a corroboration of such elements one can arrive at a scientific understanding of strategic culture and avoid the sui generis and incommensurable explanations Desch deplores (Desch, 1998). Johnston also argues that understanding cultural phenomena, such as the shared process of identity formation (Johnston, 1995b) can take strategic culture scholarship further than general statements concerning culture, such as – it is a property of collectivities, not individuals; there may be profound cultural differences between collectivities; they change only slowly, if at all (Duffield, 1999).

To overcome the ambiguities culture carries with it, Johnston demands a positivist approach. He stresses the need to supply a theory of strategic culture with sufficient methodological sophistication to fulfill the criteria of comparability, testability and falsifiability. He believes that this demand is in line with a desire by the current generation of strategic culture researchers to solve earlier terminological and methodological shortcomings (Johnston, 1995b). Elizabeth Kier, for instance, tries to avoid the methodological difficulties by retaining a clear focus on a specific, manageable group for which empirical evidence can be gathered and analysed. She has undertaken to assess the influence of a specific, limited relationship, namely that between French organisational culture and military doctrine, in a defined period of time, the interwar years from 1918 to 1938. The 'political-military subculture' is partly defined by wider national culture and partly defined by its own powerful assimilation processes (Kier). She challenges the view that military organisations inherently tend towards offensive doctrines (Kier, 1996). Jeffrey Legro takes a similarly restricted approach – he looks at the subculture of the military in order to understand an inadvertent escalation in the Second World War. He argues that organisational culture provides a better explanation for the phenomenon than rationalist theories (Legro, 1994).

The empirical, deductive method appears to be 'scientific', falsifiable and thereby also potentially generalisable. However, it still is sui generis and fraught with difficulties. Every organisational (strategic) culture has to be examined in itself in order to enable an understanding of the inherent assimilation processes at work. There may be some mechanisms that can be generalised, such as group pressure, communication issues or a readiness of actors to exploit identities for political gain, but the content of the organisational culture is essentially idiosyncratic. Thus, it may be asked to what extent the 'scientific' approach is really a tautology. Is organisational culture not ultimately derived from behaviour? (Where else should the idiosyncratic element be uncovered?) If that is the case – how can it also be used to explain behaviour? Independent and dependent variables are at best, to use Wendt's terminology, intersubjective.

The deductive approach, of course, does not pretend to make intelligible the elusive and (possibly) immeasurable 'invisible spirit' that provides a nation as a whole with 'qualities of intellect and character' (Coleridge/ Morgenthau). However, the issue cannot be entirely avoided, if the organisational culture of the unit under observation (such as the military, or the civilian-military decision-makers) is in any way connected to the larger cultural framework. Poore suggests that it may be useful to focus on the sociological factors influencing civilian policy-makers, before assessing how they interact with the military establishment. 'Having done this, it may then be possible to establish when it is appropriate to consider the impact of organisational culture at a purely military level' (Poore, 2004). However, would that not require an understanding of the mechanisms of culture in a more general sense, bringing back all the imprecision and ambiguity of the approach through the back door?

The alternative is to work with a broader conception of strategic culture right from the start, as Berger has done. He sets out to explain an empirical anomaly in the realist framework. The approach he offers is to look at the historical experiences, national identities and domestic-institutional context in order to explain why Japan and Germany are 'profoundly ambivalent about any increase in military power' (Berger, 1998). The analysis thus becomes less measurable and more encompassing, again. It also becomes more inductive. The precise relationship between his wider concept of strategic culture and an approach to military power can only be sketched.

The analysis here does not follow the path of narrow, precise strategic culture research, as exemplified by Kier or Legro, because it is not useful for understanding long-term, encompassing foreign policy trends. Nor does it look at regional strategic cultures as Ball has done (Ball, 1993), nor at the broad effect of global cultural norms on state behaviour as do, for example, Finnemore, Price and Tannenwald (Finnemore, 1996; Price, and Tannenwald, 1996).

Strategic culture here is used in Berger's and Johnston's sense as a national cultural trend. The focus is on the state as the main actor and on the cultural factors that shape its strategic behaviour. However, Johnston's deductive 'scientific' method will not be used. As the motivation problem of cultural explanations, addressed above, demonstrated, it would be overly confident to promise a precise map of decision-making processes. Furthermore, the deductive approach is faced with the tautological trap of explaining behaviour through behaviour. This, it seems, is almost impossible to avoid.

The Indian strategic context will here be approached using logical induction, rather than empirical deduction. Johnston's take on culture as a dynamic phenomenon that needs to be understood in terms of its own mechanisms and logic will be combined with Gray's assertion that strategic culture can be a guide to general understanding rather than an explication of actions. In order to avoid Johnston's criticism of Gray's approach as both blunt and stereotypical, the view of culture will not be based on intangible meta-phenomena in the collective consciousness, derived from such things as religion or historical experience. Instead, it will be based on the much more tangible and rationally traceable dynamic of the nation-building process in India. The necessities and choices of the nation-building process provide an identity that is not separate from foreign policy decisions. They can explain an inflection from the norm.

The motivational problem and the tautological trap may be evaded, if strategic culture is understood in its own terms in a particular situation, explained through its own dynamics and taken as important information making the mindset of a strategic community intelligible. To an extent, this is evasive action – avoiding a problem by not touching it. It is, in my view, however, the best approach, because it respects the importance of cultural factors while avoiding an oversimplification of the motivational grey area within which it operates. The proposed theory is not sui generis if a similar internal cultural dynamic is logical and observable in another state-actor. It is then logically reasonable (rather than empirically provable) that behaviour will have parallels. It will be falsifiable if the theory can be shown to have flaws or can be shown not to apply. The task at hand is, then, to understand the internal dynamic of a strategic culture triggered by the national identity formation process.

3.1.4 *Internal Dynamic as Explanatory Variable*

It would be very difficult to assess the effect of a broadly defined strategic culture on specific policy choices. Here, instead, an attempt is made to provide a framework for understanding an underlying trend in Indian foreign policy. Following Waltz' explanation for the way structural realism can be put to use (Waltz, 2000), the theory here holds that, given the material conditions and the specific strategic culture, a state is expected to react in certain ways sooner or later.

The framework has legitimacy not through its empirical testability, but, much like the arguments of structural realists, by virtue of a rational train of thought based on specific, reasonable assumptions. The internal dynamic of the Indian national project can reasonably be expected to make its mark in the field of foreign policy. Data, such as explanations for and interpretations of choices by the strategic community make a link between identity and behaviour possible. Indian foreign policy can be understood within this framework. There is no proof that it is the right and only framework. That would be an unreasonable proposition for any theory. Without ever entirely understanding motivations, common sense suggests that agents within states and states as a whole should be understood as having complex motivational structures.

A good approach to make the effect of culture on strategic thinking intelligible is to avoid the explaining of behaviour through behaviour by excluding it as a variable in the definition of strategic culture itself (Johnston, 1995a). If the 'attitudes', 'beliefs' or 'habitual behaviour' of a strategic community can be understood independently of their strategic actions, they can then be applied to an understanding of strategic actions. Johnston used Chinese history as a stable parameter to derive a Chinese strategic culture which could then be applied to foreign policy as a dependent variable. However, the definition of strategic culture used here, is more akin to Gray's broad and more amorphous one – it is the cultural context within which analysis, decision-making and actions are embedded, or, to use Gray's neologism – in which agents are 'encultured' (Gray, 1999). Indian nationalism, and the inherent dynamic it created, is used to derive a strategic culture composed of a set of collective, enduring attitudes, assumptions, beliefs and values. This is then applied to an understanding of Indian foreign policy as an equally broad dependent variable.

There are a number of assumptions underlying this approach. Firstly, decision-makers are to some extent 'encultured' and their identity matters to them. Secondly, they have only a limited capacity to free themselves from their cultural and ideological environment when evaluating foreign policy choices[51]. The exact nature of the link remains undefined. Thirdly, they care at least partly about the overall welfare of the state (in this case, the success of the national project)[52]. Fourthly, the foreign policy of a nation state has a constitutive effect on the people who matter for nation-building purposes (those, who are politically aware on a national rather than regional and local level, presumably from the urban middle and upper classes). People associate themselves with their foreign policy, it matters to them and they take pride in it. Fifthly, whilst national and strategic cultures may be

[51]Gandhi, who was admittedly extraordinary in his capacity to align beliefs with actions, stated that, 'One cannot be nonviolent and friendly in ones family and even inside the nation and practice violence and hatred in international dealings' (Kripalani, J. B., 1981, p.23).

[52]Some nationalisms may be projects of elites hoping to profit from them. However, a successful, constructive, long-term and top-down national project will require that short term, sectarian interests are prevented from sabotaging the overall success.

in flux, they nevertheless have sufficient longevity to be used in explanations of strategic behaviour. These assumptions are not more daring than those of rational actor theories, such as, for example, actors are not influenced significantly by culture; actors have an understanding of a somewhat objective national interest, can prioritise among rival tasks and act accordingly. There are no significant distortions through, for example, lack of information, bureaucratic mechanisms, individual or group interests.

The proposed relationship between identity and foreign policy would be weakened if it could be shown that any of the assumptions are unfounded, that, for example, very few opinion-shaping people in India take an interest in foreign policy, that the national-project in India is not based on values or has been popularly rooted from the beginning. The theory would also be undermined if there would be a consistent violation of the values used for nation-building in the explanations of and justifications for foreign policy.

Figure 3.1 visualises the approach taken. The deductive empirical approach to an understanding of the strategic culture and ultimately the inflection in foreign policy is discarded. The motivational problem and the tautological problem make case studies and quantitative analyses highly problematic. An inductive approach is instead taken. This approach also has problems, but these can be addressed. The precise link between strategic culture and foreign policy ultimately remains a black box. However, if the dynamic influencing the strategic culture can be made intelligible, then the effect on foreign policy can be broadly traced.

3.1.5 *The Strategic Community in India*

Who are the carriers of the strategic culture? It is here the strategic community, consisting of the foreign policy opinion-shapers. Conceptually, it can be thought of as an intermediary between the decision-making process and the interested public. While the decisions themselves are typically made by no more than a handful of individuals at any one point of time, the interested public comprises the entire politically aware and mobilised section of the Indian population. This is predominantly the Indian urban middle and upper class, a rapidly expanding group, which, depending on the issue and the definition, currently includes anything between 10 and 250 million people (Varma, 1998; Das, 2002). It does not include the segments of society living local, traditional lives untouched by international issues, those too poor or uneducated to form an opinion and those lacking even a basic interest in foreign policy. The strategic elite stand between the two groups. It creates the intellectual atmosphere within which decisions are

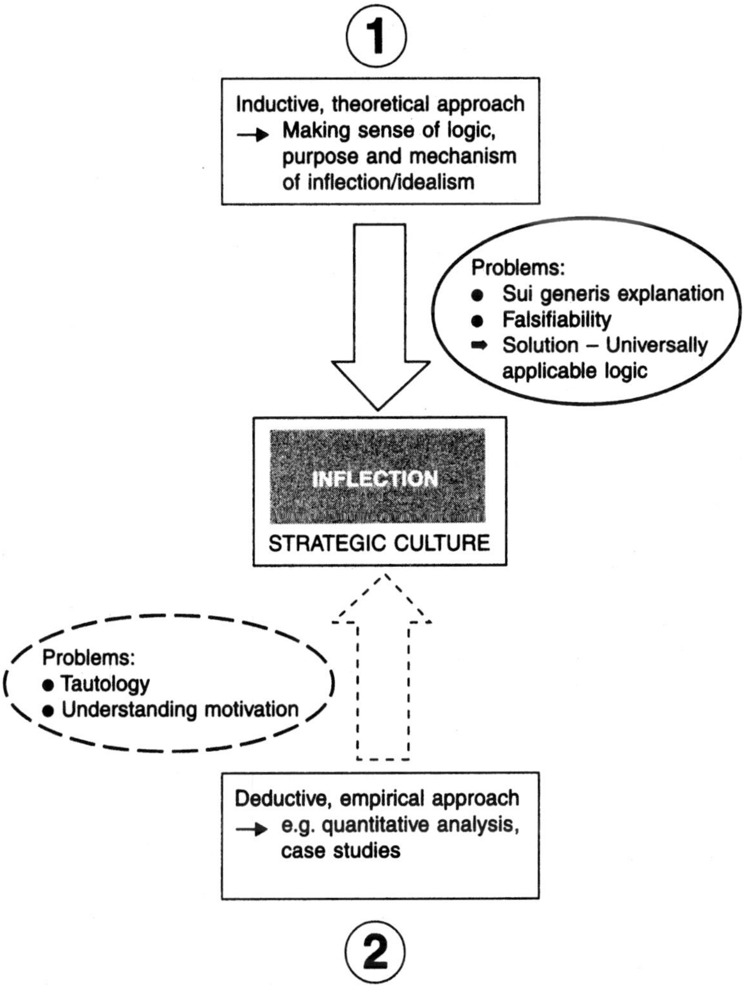

Figure 3.1: Inductive vs. Deductive Approach

taken. At times, it mediates upwards from the broader public to the decision-makers, informing and shaping policy choices. At other times, it mediates downwards, evaluating, criticising or explaining policies or policy choices. The strategic elite embody the Indian strategic worldview and the Indian strategic culture.

For an understanding of the early Indian strategic community, one can reasonably focus on two individuals. Mahatma Gandhi was the key nationalist leader during the struggle for independence. Jawaharlal Nehru, strongly influenced by Gandhi but by no means a mere disciple, was the towering figure in the formative years of the new state. It may be a simplification to argue that in many ways Nehru was the strategic elite from independence in 1947 until the Indo-China war in 1962. It is, however, a useful and workable simplification. Nehru's pre-eminence was such that few diversions from his worldview found expression in Indian foreign policy. Already before independence, Nehru was the leading Indian voice on foreign policy issues. He had 'no serious rivals within the Congress Party on international questions'. Gandhi's concerns were primarily domestic, so 'he was content to leave the field of foreign affairs entirely to his protégé' (Tharoor). After independence, of course, Nehru's role in foreign policy as a Prime Minister cum Foreign Minister was pivotal – so much so that Nehru's policies were India's (Maxwell, 1974; Tharoor, 2003). His legacy remained highly influential even after his death. Kumaraswamy, by no means uncritical of Nehru, summarises his role as follows –

> 'Since the early 1920's, Jawaharlal Nehru remained the undisputed architect, articulator, and practitioner of Indian foreign policy. His virtual monopoly in defining India's place among the comity of nations not only lasted for over 40 years, but continued to dominate Indian foreign policy even after his death in 1964.' (Kumaraswamy, 2004).

The reasons for Nehru's singular position were many. His charismatic leadership in India as well as on the stages of international diplomacy, his knowledge of world affairs, his didactic and rhetoric abilities, and the absence of serious rivals in a young democracy (especially after Sardar Vallabhbhai Patel's death in 1950), in which foreign affairs as a whole were the preserve of a small elite and far detached from the lives and interests of most Indians, are among them. For this reason, it was, until fairly recently, possible to speak of 'the' Indian strategic perspective, centered in New Delhi and 'dominated by Jawaharlal Nehru's view of India and the world' (Cohen, 2001; Singh, 2006).

In 2005–2006, however, the situation was different. The strategic community has significantly broadened. The education system has generated a large 'new generation' of strategic thinkers 'across a range of ideologies' (Cohen). The media, furthermore, has taken on a very diverse and powerful role, drawing in larger parts of the population. This is especially the case, when it comes to emotionally charged issues such as Kashmir. The Kargil War in 1999 thus became 'India's first televised war, rousing nationalist fervour throughout the country' (Cohen, 2004b). An increase in public interest in strategic matters further expanded the group of professional analysts and writers. Cohen traces several intellectual groups through this expanded strategic community. One is, of course, the group of traditional Nehruvians. Another group, which Cohen does not explicitly set apart, is that of the Gandhians who reject violence as a means in foreign policy. Former Prime Minister Morarji Desai, who sought to base India's foreign policy on 'Gandhian moral principles' (Dixit, 2004), was the most prominent advocate of this view. This group is relatively small today, but by no means irrelevant. The 'militant Nehruvians' are a third group. They were best exemplified by Indira Gandhi. This approach shares 'many assumptions about the greatness of India and the imbalances in the international system but differed from Nehru in the use of force'. While dismissing Nehru's visions as idealistic, it focussed on the threats of a perceived reality (Cohen). A fourth group, Cohen identifies, is that of the 'realists and revivalists'. It is mainly found in the environment of the BJP. Jaswant Singh, former Foreign Minister and author of *Defending India*, is a key spokesperson. Also sharing Nehru's belief in India as a great and unique civilisation, the focus is, however, on liberal economic development as the main source of national power. The USA is regarded as a key strategic partner (Cohen). Despite a stronger realist element in his thinking, however, Singh shuns straight realpolitik and advocates a balance between idealism and self-interest (Singh, 1999b). The 'revivalists' are linked to the Rashtriya Swayamsevak Sangh (RSS), a Hindu nationalist organisation with ties to the BJP. It stresses, even more than the BJP or Nehruvians, a 'culture-driven view of the world in which India represents one of humankind's supreme civilisational accomplishments'. Indian culture is portrayed as essentially non-aggressive (Cohen, 2001). Naunihal Singh reproduces Cohen's description in his account of the Indian strategic community (Singh, 2006).

Amidst the new diversity, Cohen detects three overarching trends. The first trend is the rise of a new generation with strongly domestic priorities, focussing on the generation of economic opportunities (Cohen). The second trend is a rise of regional perspectives, with an interest-based approach relevant to a particular region. These regional perspectives differ significantly in their set of priorities – while the Pakistan/Kashmir problem is what Punjabis will likely worry about most, in Tamil Nadu it would be the civil war in Sri Lanka (Cohen, 2001). The third trend is that the groups are not strictly demarcated. Pure Nehruvians, Gandhians or Hindutva civilisationalists are seldom found (Bajpai, 1998).

Today, the, narrowly defined, strategic community consists of at least a couple of hundred individuals based predominantly (but not exclusively) in New Delhi. Compared to the size of India, geographically as well as demographically, this is still a relatively small group, of which a representative sample can be taken. It consists of bureaucrats, members of the armed forces, politicians, diplomats, journalists, academics and members of think tanks. Although the 'revolving-doors' are still rusty when it comes to positions of political power (Subrahmanyam, 2005), the strategic community is intellectually interlocked. It very actively engages, discusses and publicly voices its views in books, over TV or through the print media, thus shaping the strategic outlook.

3.2 National Identity and its Dynamic

The duality and the idealist inflection in Indian foreign policy is linked to the process of national identity formation. Strategic culture is the intermediary element upon which the identity process impacts and which, in turn, produces the idealist inflection. As shown in Figure 3.2, the identity process impacts on strategic culture through ideological politics. Ideological politics in turn is linked to the challenges and choices of nation-building in India and to the underlying problem of creating a stable nation state by

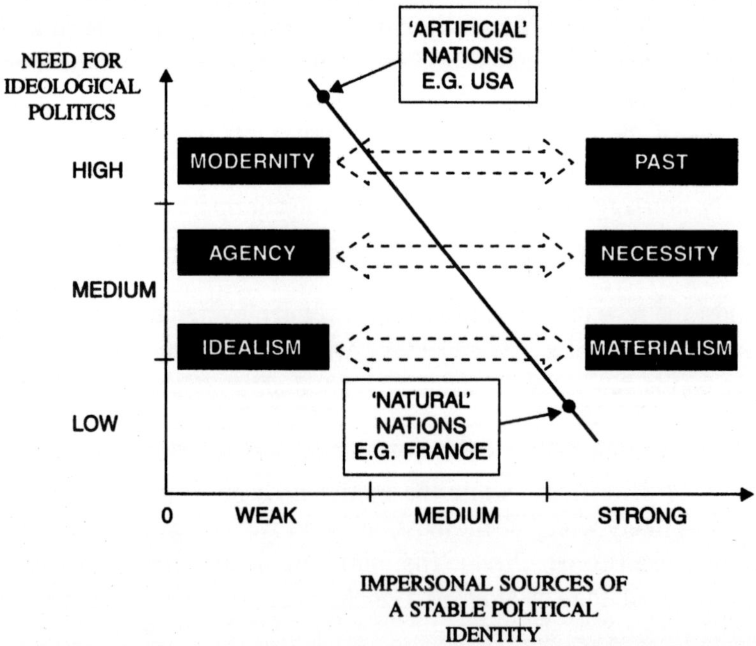

Figure 3.2: Stable Identities and the Need for Ideological Politics

giving it a strong political identity. It is, therefore, imperative to understand both the challenges of nation-building in India (and the problem of stability) as well as its choices in detail. They determine the type and the role of ideological politics (nationalism) in the country. The idealist inflection in Indian foreign policy derives its momentum from here. Nationalism, however, is far from being a simple concept and the link with ideological politics is not a given. The relationship between ideological politics and the formation of the modern nation, furthermore, touches upon a number of crucial philosophical issues that are elaborated on here not only for their direct relevance regarding a classification of types of nationalism, but also for their relevance with respect to the overall process of history, including the question of agency in foreign policy.

Over the last 200 years, nationalism has arguably been one of the most potent political forces worldwide. As a key focal point of political expression and identity, it has been instrumental both in the shaping and unmaking of states, as well as in a number of wars and revolutions along the way. Nationalism works in favour of a system of nation states and against the idea of empires. There is widespread consensus among scholars today that nationalism, whilst potentially appealing to pre-modern sentiments or structures, is itself a distinctly modern historical phenomenon (Hutchinson, and Smith, 1994). By-and-large, however, there is much more controversy than agreement with regard to the slippery and unwieldy subject of nationalism. Gellner recognised this problem, but nevertheless argued for an overall theory of nationalism. In his early work *Thought and Change*, he laid out a plan to separate the 'quite spurious "national" and "natural" justifications and explanations of nationalism' from an underlying pattern and the 'genuine, time- and context-bound roots of it' (Gellner, 1964). He believed, as self-respecting political scientists should, that an underlying pattern must exist, for –

> '…if nationalism is a general phenomenon, covering a whole variety of nations, quite obviously it cannot be explained by the reasons operating internally within each national movement… specifically related to each nation and its culture.' Such internal reasons '…cannot apply generally, otherwise there could hardly be rival nationalisms. So the general explanation cannot be internal to the circumstances' (Gellner, 1997).

Although there is considerable disagreement over what exactly this pattern is and how universally it can be applied, Gellner's argument may be correct when limiting a discussion of nationalism to the European experience in the nineteenth century (as Gellner mostly does).

However, viewed over time and space, nationalism is extraordinarily difficult to grasp in an essentialist way. While, on the one hand, there can be no doubt that it exists as a useful category of understanding, on the other hand, not only the 'specific reasons', but also the broader conditions to which Gellner applies his 'general theory' have changed since nationalism made its first appearances. Like open-source software, it appears to have acquired a life of its own, evolving and taking on new forms as history progresses. Thus, both, the circumstances within which nationalism as such can flourish, as well as the idea of what nationalism actually constitutes, have varied in different situations. Smith, therefore, criticises Gellner's endeavour to derive a general theory of nationalism from the postulates of modernity – 'For myself, no such theory is possible' (Gellner and Smith, 1996).

For the purpose of this argument, an argument that deals with an ancient Asian culture in the twentieth century, rather than a nineteenth century European situation, Gellner's 'one-theory-approach' is not helpful. When using nationalism as an independent variable in the Indian context, it makes more sense to think about it in terms of what Wittgenstein famously called 'family-resemblances', an identity not in fact, but by association. It is a concept that can be meaningful despite having blurred edges, which can be open to new varieties without having to be altered (Wittgenstein, 1974; Baker, and Hacker, 2005). This is not to say that there are no parallels among specific nationalisms and no frameworks within which nationalism can be conceptualised. However, any two nationalisms can potentially be very different – related in their mechanisms only through other 'family members'. Since there is no single, constant blueprint, what is required is an analysis of nationalism in a specific context, or, an understanding of a specific nationalism.

There are three main dimensions relevant for the purpose of this argument on India, which will be looked into, here – firstly, what drives nationalism? Is nationalism a product of modern ideas such as the enlightenment and romanticism, or is it the product of the material conditions modernity happened to produce? Is it a root cause in its own right, or is it a catalyst? Secondly, is nationalism necessary or contingent? Is history – whether idealist or materialist – bound to produce nationalism? Is there a role for human agency? Thirdly, what is the role of the past? Is nationalism based on a popular primordial connection or is it solely a product of modernity?

These questions are best answered in a specific case, here, the case of India. The answers, however, have general implications. A national project that is idealist rather than materialist, agent driven rather than driven by circumstances, and revolutionary rather than evolutionary in the connection to its past, will lack natural stability. This lack of stability will have to be compensated by ideological politics. Ideological politics, in turn, unfolds a dynamic that will impact on foreign policy.

Before going into the details, two issues may need prior clarification. Firstly, what is the justification for choosing – as I do – a specific set of thinkers, rather than others? Secondly, what is the relevance of European thinkers to an Indian problem? The answer to the first question is that among a large host of writers on nationalism, those were chosen who can be regarded as leaders of the key schools of thought. They establish their views most clearly and show what is at stake along the three dimensions under review. The scholars are – Ernest Gellner, Elie Kedourie, Anthony Smith and Paul Brass. On the philosophical level, in which the discussion of nationalism is enveloped, the focus is on German thinkers of the nineteenth century, especially on Georg Wilhelm Friedrich Hegel and Karl Marx. The reason is that, as Benedetto Croce argued, the 'historicist revolution' of the time, in many ways the intellectual ancestor of studies of nationalism, was, if not entirely German by origin, a predominantly German development (Croce,1941). There is, furthermore, an important link between German romanticism, historicism and nationalism. This will be discussed here. The answer to the second question is, to begin with, that the origin of an idea does not necessarily say anything about either its value or its applicability. What is more, nationalism, like a number of other ideologies of the eighteenth, nineteenth and twentieth centuries such as socialism or democracy, has spread from Europe to other countries, where it was applied and adapted. The leaders of the National Movement in India were themselves profoundly influenced by European ideas. However, the Indian application of nationalism has been original. In the way in which nationalism is treated here, there is significant room for and even a focus on tracing India's specifics. Indeed the key question is – what precisely is the nature of Indian nationalism? The framework for the discussion of nationalism should be considered with these comments in mind.

3.2.1 *Idealism vis-a-vis Materialism*

In general, the dichotomy between idealist and materialist conceptions of the world has been at the very root of many philosophical and theological discourses throughout history. The issue was discussed usually with respect to the ontological status of the world or of God. In the nineteenth century, two German philosophers, G.W.F. Hegel and Karl Marx, spurned by a then omnipresent belief in progress, gave this old debate a new twist and applied it to the field of social science. They juxtaposed the idealist and the materialist point of view, respectively, with the utmost clarity in their bold philosophies of world history. Both gave competing views of how history happens, how societies change and why they change.

Nationalism as a political phenomenon is intricately linked to the very idea of history. A linear 'world history' – as opposed to static or cyclical 'histories', biographies, annals or simply 'stories' – is a profoundly modern conceptualisation of the world. In Europe, since the enlightenment (as the idealist momentum) and the industrial revolution (as the materialist momentum), change happened much faster than ever before. People could experience it within their lifetimes. Old certainties and conservative 'stabilisers' like religion or the monarchies lost power and influence over people's lives. Many turned towards history for purpose and direction – and in such a rapidly advancing, linear history, the ideas of progress and nostalgia became paramount (Anderson, 1991; Kedourie, 1993; Hutchinson, and Smith, 1994). Nationalism, as a product of or an interpretation of modern history, dovetails modern history as such.

In theories of nationalism, there is a fundamental divide between those thinkers who profess to an idealist view of history and believe that nationalism is a product of the mind and therefore often an elite enterprise, and those who subscribe to a more materialist view of history and subsequently believe that social and economic changes have been more important factors in creating nationalism.

The Philosophical Framework – Phenomenological vis-a-vis Materialist History

To Hegel, it is not nature or geography or economics or any other aspect of material reality that propels mankind along its path of progress. It is the mind, the ever evolving consciousness. Consciousness experiences the external world and interacts with it. It usually interacts with other consciousnesses; but even when it interacts with material reality, the origin and the result of the interaction are tied to the ideal, not the real world. The world is no more than a bouncing board for the mind. As Theodor W. Adorno explains –

> 'it is precisely through absolute idealism, which permits nothing to remain outside the subject, now expanded to become infinite, but instead sweeps everything along with it into the current of immanence, that the opposition

between mere matter and a consciousness that bestows form and meaning is extinguished' (Adorno, 1993).

Consequently, in laying out his theory, Hegel takes pure will as a starting point[53]. He understood historical change or progress as taking place in and through human consciousness. His world history is thus, written from a purely phenomenological point of view. This is one end point of the ontological spectrum; the other end point is given by Marx' materialism.

Marx, famously, claimed that in Hegel's philosophy the truth was turned on its head. In principle, he likes the idea of dialectical historical progress through a dynamic inherent in the relationship between thesis and antithesis, but the focus must be on material reality and not on the mind[54]. Of course, Marx did not deny the existence and even importance of ideas, in the same way that Hegel did not deny the existence and even importance of the material world, but to Marx, the driver of change and progress is the inherent dynamic of the material (economic) world. Whereas in Hegel, reason has a history, in Marx, history has a reason. For Marx, Bertrand Russell explains –

> '...matter, not spirit is the driving force... This means that, for Marx, the driving force is really man's relation to matter, of which the most important part is his mode of production. In this way Marx' materialism, in practice becomes economics. The politics, religion, philosophy, and the art of any epoch in human history are, according to Marx, an outcome of its methods of production, and, to a lesser extent, of distribution' (Russell, 1996).

This approach came to be known as historical materialism. In 'The Communist Manifesto', Marx and Engels give an example of how it works. They explain how the bourgeoisie is, by its capitalist nature, bent on an ever-increasing industrial production. This necessarily brings forth an ever

---

[53]In his Philosophy of Right, he explains that 'the basis (Boden) of right is the realm of spirit in general and its precise location and point of departure is the will; the will is free, so that freedom constitutes its substance and destiny (Bestimmung) and the system of right is the realm of actualised freedom, the world of spirit produced from within itself as a second nature' (Hegel, G. W. F., 1991, § 4, p.35).

[54]He made this difference between his approach and Hegel's clear in his postface to the second German edition of Capital, Volume I – 'My dialectic method is, in its foundations, not only different from the Hegelian, but exactly opposite to it. For Hegel, the process of thinking, which he even transforms into an independent subject, under the name of 'the Idea', is the creator of the real world, and the real world is only the external appearance of 'the Idea'. With me, the reverse is true – the ideal is nothing but the material world reflected by the mind of man, and translated into forms of thought' (Marx, K., 1976, p.102).

larger, progresively homogenous and organised proletariat which is becoming more and more aware of its class identity as well as of its exploitation. Capitalism, by its very own aggressively competitive nature, is bound to propel the development of a unified, antagonistic proletariat. Therefore, they conclude, capitalist society 'cuts from under its feet the very foundation on which the bourgeoisie produces and appropriates products'. The bourgeoisie thus produces, above all, 'its own gravediggers' (Marx, and Engels, 1998). It is a law of unintended consequences.

While both Hegel and Marx are fundamentally interested in how social and political change happens, neither of them has theorised on nationalism which was powerfully acting out its potential right under their noses. Hegel does mention 'patriotism', but for him, patriotism is not directed towards a particular cultural community or nation. Instead, it is, quite generally, the understanding by the individual (i.e. reason not passion) that the community as such is essential (useful) for it[55]. In Hegel's thought, the state is the central unit of political organisation. However, because the state derives its right of existence not only from the reason of the partaking individuals, but also from its natural position within a larger teleological pattern (Hegel's 'Weltgeist'), it does not require the internal, emotional (extra-rational) glue of a national identity.

For Marx, nationalism did not play an important role. He appears to have underrated it. There are only few passages in his writings where nationalism or patriotism is mentioned, and if they are, they are marginal to his thought. From his work on 'The Eighteenth Brumaire of Luis Bonaparte', for example, it can be inferred that he considers patriotism to be an artificial and 'melodramatic' sentiment (Marx, 1996). Marx, of course, was much more interested in social classes as political units and in their inter-nationalism which Alan Gilbert called the 'hallmark of his political activity' (Gilbert, 1978).

The underlying reason why neither Hegel nor Marx looked thoroughly into the phenomenon of nationalism may, however, quite simply be a personal one – neither of them was particularly sympathetic to the sentiments

[55]'Patriotism', he explains in his 'Philosophy of Right', 'is frequently understood to mean a willingness to perform extraordinary sacrifices and actions. But in essence, it is that disposition which, in the normal conditions and circumstances of life, habitually knows that the community is the substantial basis and end.... Furthermore, if we take this disposition to be something which can originate independently (*für sich*) and arise out of subjective representations (Vorstellungen) and thoughts, we are confusing it with opinion; for in this interpretation, it is deprived of its true ground, i.e. objective reality' (Hegel, G. W. F., 1991, § 268, pp.288–289).

of the mass middle class and subsequently neither of them may have been willing to attribute a significant role to 'its' ideology within their respective political theories. Therefore, while the two thinkers can be seen as representing opposite poles in their approach to understanding human political development – the idealist, more metaphysical Hegelian approach, on the one hand, and the materialist, more empirical, (pseudo)scientific Marxian approach on the other – they left a glaring gap, which other scholars filled, using Hegel's and Marx' parameters.

Theories of Nationalism – Is Nationalism Driver or Catalyst?

Nationalism, although a highly potent political force since at least the late eighteenth century, was only slowly recognised as a phenomenon worthy of in-depth political analysis. It only became the subject of historical enquiry sometime in the middle of the nineteenth century. A thorough social scientific analysis was outstanding until the early twentieth century. Sustained investigations of nationalism as an academic topic in its own right had to wait until after the First World War and it is really only since the 1960s, after the wave of anti-colonial and ethnic nationalisms, that the subject has begun to be thoroughly investigated by scholars from several disciplines (Hutchinson, and Smith). When nationalism did finally come under intense investigation, the old idealist-materialist dichotomy of the Hegelian-Marxian discussion of historical change resurfaced. The key representatives are Elie Kedourie, who emphasises the power of ideas, and Ernest Gellner, 'who turns Kedourie on his head' (Hutchinson, and Smith, 1994) much like Marx had done with Hegel. Gellner believes that nationalism is a product of the material need of modern societies for cultural homogeneity. Kedourie thinks of it as 'ideological politics' driven by political entrepreneurs.

Gellner defines nationalism as a 'political principle which maintains that similarity of culture is the basic social bond' (Gellner) and – ontologically speaking – as a 'phenomenon of Gesellschaft using the idiom of Gemeinschaft' (Gellner, 1997). It is a catalyst for the momentous changes modernity creates in societies and for the new demands it places on it and not a romantic elite invention. Nationalism is the amalgamation of the more or less conscious, interest-based strategies of many members of a particular region to successfully partake in the modern economy and society –

> 'It is the consequence of the mobility and anonymity of modern society and of the semantic non-physical nature of work that mastery of such a culture and

acceptability in it is the most valuable possession man has. It is a pre-condition of all other privilege and participation. This automatically makes him into a nationalist because if there is non-congruence between the culture in which he is operating and the culture of the surrounding economic, political and educational bureaucracies, then he is in trouble' (Gellner, and Smith, 1996).

In 'Nationalism', Gellner mentions a fourth point, in addition to anonymity, mobility and the semantic nature of work, to characterise modern industrialised society – the break-up of traditional social ties and the subsequent atomisation of individuals (Gellner). Modernity thereby produces magnetic fields of standard, codified, literacy-linked 'high idioms', in which businesses of all kind are conducted. Persons who are not masters of the idiom are reduced to the status of 'humiliated second-class members' (Gellner, 1996). With time, the process brings forth a new, shared 'high culture', which in turn is the foundation of the nation-to-be (Gellner, 1997). Nationalism, to Gellner, is thus the result of the enormous social convulsions industrialisation produced in the nineteenth and twentieth centuries and not a root cause for change in its own right.

Kedourie takes the opposite point of view. To him, nationalism is not a natural historical occurrence or the necessary by-product of modernity. He believes that it is artificial – not an objective force, but a subjective idea. National identity is the political reflection of a particular intellectual mindset which impacts on the material reality through the power of ideas (Kedourie). He traces the development of nationalism as an idea through modern Europe where and when it emerged as the product of a fusion of the Kantian enlightenment ideal of autonomy with the romantic notion of cultural uniqueness. Kedourie, therefore, defines nationalism as an invented 'doctrine' (Kedourie) and not as a 'phenomenon' as Gellner does. The doctrine holds that the nation – whatever it may be – is the only legitimate political sovereign. The doctrine of nationalism fills the political vacuum left behind by the delegitimisation of the old political system both in principle (through a number of theories stressing individual autonomy) and in practice (through the French Revolution) (Kedourie, 1993). Nationalism and democracy, thus, initially (and mostly only theoretically) went hand in hand.

Kedourie starts his analysis with Kant. His conception of morality stipulates autonomy. Morality is not derived externally, from God or from an ominous 'natural law'. Instead it is the product of an individual's own judgment and conscience. The individual thereby becomes 'the very centre, the arbiter, the sovereign of the universe' (Kedourie). Politics, which is no longer embedded in a stable metasystem, thus becomes an incessant, individual moral struggle, in which 'the autonomous man is a stern activist, a perpetually tormented soul'. A politics fashioned in his image, is a politics where 'struggle per se is a necessary feature' (Kedourie). This Kantian concept was subsequently given a decisive twist by a number of German romantic thinkers. Under their influence, 'the whole' (the *Volk*) came to be seen as being more important than its constitutive parts (the individuals). Autonomy became an attribute of the community, which also appropriated such concepts as 'historical agency' and 'meaningful life'[56]. Herder then made the case for a 'natural' division of the world into nations, and Fichte added a very problematic element of cultural purity (Kedourie). Kedourie holds that this romantic notion of a nation is inherently violent, because it is based on the mistaken conception that nations have natural frontiers. They do not. More often, they overlap and intermix. Fichte's purity often has to be purchased with blood (Kedourie, 1993).

Gellner criticises Kedourie's 'intellectualist' theory of nationalism as misleading (Gellner, 1997). He cannot see how one idea can have so profound an effect –

> 'There is something bizarre in the suggestion that a force so widespread and pervasive, a flame that springs up so strongly and spontaneously in so many disconnected places, and which needs so very little fanning to become a devouring forest blaze, should spring from nothing more than some extremely abstruse lubrications of philosophers. For better or worse, our ideas seldom have quite such power' (Gellner, 1983).

He freely admits that his treatment of nationalism lacks references to the history of nationalist ideas or to the contributions and nuances of particular nationalist thinkers. Gellner does not discount the possibility that ideology can have an effect on history. Christianity and Marxism, for instance, were powerful concepts. He simply argues that this was not the case with nationalism (Gellner). Nationalist thinkers did not make much difference for two reasons. Firstly, they were not original thinkers, but gave expression to what was obvious to many. Thus, they were replaceable – 'If one of them had fallen, others would have stepped into his place'. Secondly, there is no substance in their thought. Their doctrines are 'hardly worth

---

[56]An empathic appeal by Schleiermacher, which Kedourie cites, demonstrates this new thinking – 'Where is the devotion to this new existence that man has conceived, a will to sacrifice the old individual soul rather than lose the state, a readiness to set one's life at stake rather than see the fatherland perish? Where is foresight keeping close watch lest the country be seduced and its spirit corrupted? Where find the individual character each state should have, and the acts that reveal it?' (Kedourie, E., 1993, p.34).

analysing' (Gellner). To Gellner, the power of 'an arbitrary idea, thrown up by the play of European intellectual fancy at the turn of the eighteenth and nineteenth centuries' (Gellner) was simply not substantial and convincing enough to be able to move so many people on a grand scale. On the same grounds, Gellner rejects the idea put forward by K.W. Deutsch, who stresses the crucial role new means of communication played in the unfolding of nationalism by disseminating the nationalist message (Deutsch, 1966). To Gellner, this is 'altogether the wrong way to see it'. It is not the content of the transmission (the idea) that matters, but rather the fact that there existed such a thing as a national media transmitting to a national audience, in the first place (Gellner). In general, Gellner asserts (in a language very much reminiscent of Marx) that 'nationalist ideology suffers from pervasive false consciousness. Its myths invert reality' (Gellner, 1983).

In response, Kedourie points out that nationalism as an idea came prior to the economic and social phenomenon of industrialisation. The idea was articulated in Germany at a time when there was as yet hardly any industrialisation and 'by writers who themselves were not aware that they were reacting to or supplying a necessary requisite for industrialisation' (Kedourie, 1993). Furthermore, he points out a chronological/geographical inconsistency in Gellner's link between industrialisation and nationalism. Some countries, like Germany, Italy or Japan, developed the most feverish peaks of nationalism only decades after their first industrialisation. At the same time, in other countries, where industrialism appeared early and progressed rapidly, such as in Great Britain and the USA, 'nationalism is unknown'. Kedourie continues –

> 'The theory and the evidence thus unfortunately pull in different directions. These various products of the sociological temptation seem then, to have in common what may be called Monsieur Jourdain's syndrome. Like the hero of Molière's comedy whom the learned doctors taught that he had been really speaking prose all his life, nationalism is declared to be, 'in reality' and quite unbeknown to itself, either an expression of bourgeois self-interest, or an industrial lubricant, or a reflection of deep subterranean movements slowly maturing through centuries and millennia. But Monsieur Jourdain, we remember, was a figure of fun' (Kedourie, 1993).

The issue Gellner and Kedourie are at odds over, is whether nationalism is a driver for political change or simply a political catalyst for economic and social changes? It is impossible to decide one way or the other in the absence of clear definitions (Kedourie, for example, seems to have a virulent, extremer form of nationalism in mind than Gellner, who seems to think of nationalism in broader, more moderate terms). Both writers' theories cannot explain the full range of nationalisms that history has witnessed. Kedourie cannot explain, for example, why, in the nineteenth century, nationalism was more successful in some countries (namely, industrialised or modern societies) than in others (namely, agrarian or pre-modern societies). Gellner, on the other hand, underestimates the power of ideas and of individual leaders. When discarding nationalist ideas as simplistic and therefore powerless, he confuses his own critical reasoning ability with that of the masses. The intellectual quality of a theory is not necessarily the key to its success. At times, the contrary is the case and simplistic, polemical theories (and nationalism often tends towards the simplistic and polemical) have more momentum than complicated or differentiated ones. Moreover, ideas do not need to convince everyone – it may be sufficient if an idea acquires a following among a group just large enough to gain control of public opinion or of political decision-making mechanisms. Ideological revolutions, for instance, may well be driven by a small group[57].

Given the view of nationalism as 'family resemblances', there may well be some types of nationalism which are better explained by Gellner's materialist arguments, and some which are better described by Kedourie's idealist arguments. The sources from which a particular nationalism springs and the way in which it grows, have important effects on the nationalism itself as well as on the nation it creates. A nationalist movement which is a brainchild, an *idée fixe* that seeks to impose the national boundaries onto ground realities which may not be ready for it, is much more likely to create conflict than a nationalism which builds on a pre-existing social cohesion. A second consequence of nationalism as an idea is that it is not per se self-evident. It is frailer than a nationalism based on hard facts, such as a cultural-linguistic community. Since there is no such thing as an a priori (natural) nation, the nation always needs to be created. The further material conditions go in the creation of magnetic identity fields, the easier the task

---

[57]Theda Skopcol makes this point – 'Some Revolutions – i.e. revolutions from above – which have had outcomes and consequences that seem quite revolutionary from a Marxist perspective, have not actually been made by class forces or through class struggles; instead, bureaucratic-military political elites have reorganised states and used state power to effect socio-economic structural transformations'. As examples, she gives the Meiji Restoration in Japan in 1868 and the Revolution in Turkey in 1921 (Skocpol, T. 1994, pp.123–125). Jonathan Schell argues in a similar fashion when he describes the Russian Revolutions in 1905 and 1917 as elite undertakings (Schell, J. 2005).

for the nationalist. Sometimes nationalists succeed in creating a state for the nation before the task of creating the nation itself is completed. In such circumstances, the nation state will acquire the difficult task of consolidating itself by creating a cohesive identity (Rotberg, 2004).

3.2.2 *Necessity vs. Agency*

> *'There is a disputation that will continue till mankind is raised from the dead, between the necessitarians and the partisans of free will'*
>
> (Rumi[58])

It is obvious that nobody can act entirely freely, without any constraints. We are constrained by our limited capacities such as, for example, intelligence, strength, stamina, but also, at a second level, our will power, our education, or our character. We are constrained by external conditions, such as laws, money or other people's actions. We may also even be constrained by forces entirely outside of human control, such as, for example, genes, human nature, God, fate/chance or historical teleology. There is little argument that complete freedom of action is impossible. The question is – in how far do these constraints merely inhibit our freedom of action, and in how far do they actually determine our actions? Is there any space left for individual free agency? The question of what 'freedom' actually means is philosophically very intricate. It is not of direct concern, here. Of concern is, whether or not there exist factors outside of human control, which are not only powerful influences, but are actually determining the course of history. More precisely, the question is whether history has an inner logic or is shaped by actors. For as long as there is an omnipotent 'higher' logic, humans ultimately do not have the power to shape the world they live in (Van Inwagen, 1983).

The Philosophical Framework – Determinism vis-a-vis Free Will

The idealist-materialist argument as it is led by Kedourie and Gellner diverges significantly from that between Hegel and Marx when it comes to the question of historical determinism. In their common, avid belief in the power of history and in the advancement of the human race by a dialectic path, Hegel as well as Marx are, of course, unmistakably products

---

[58]Jalalu'ddin Rumi was a twelfth century Persian Sufi poet. Whilst someone who believes that mankind will be raised from the dead is himself likely to have made up his mind about divine providence, the statement itself demonstrates that the problem of free will is an ancient and persistent one (Kane, R. 2001, p. xiii).

of one and the same Zeitgeist. Both believe in an ideal future and a quasi-deterministic 'higher' logic, which necessarily and reasonably unfolds. For both, history is a somewhat impersonal, extra-human or even supra-human entity. Despite the fact that Hegel builds his philosophical system in part on the 'will', and takes as his point of departure a perfectly abstract 'free will' (Hegel, 1956), there remains only a limited, and – ultimately – spurious role for human agency in the shaping of history. The ideal-type, individual will is, in Hegel's philosophy, trapped between Hegel's logic (which he holds to be universal and self-evident) and the quite clearly defined endpoint of the logic, the Weltgeist. Far from being free, the will is instrumental and thus indirect (Dyde, 1894; Taylor, 1975).

For Marx also, political action is – although possible, even necessary on one level – ultimately in vain if directed against the course of his understanding of history. Avineri skillfully argues in favour of a significant element of passion and agency in Hegel's and Marx' writings (Avineri, 1973). However, these are instrumental and the essential fact that both thinkers work with a pre-existing teleology remains. Ultimately, human beings are subjected to it. Other thinkers, such as St. Augustine (Augustine, 2003) – to take a very old example, or Ted Honderich (Honderich, 1990) – to take a modern one, have attempted to show that human agency and determinism are compatible, but they can do so only at the expense of blurring the concepts (as in Augustine's case) or by blurring the epistemological basis (as in Honderich's case). Meaningful individual agency, in the political sense relevant here, remains incompatible with any form of determinism.

As a theory, determinism cannot be refuted. Equally, it cannot be proven. This is why the problem remains one of the great contentious issues of philosophy. As Kant demonstrated, it remains essentially outside the realm of proof and reason, because it is – given our current state of knowledge – a matter of belief (Kant, 2004)[59]. Our experience can potentially be explained by a number of different narratives, including various deterministic ones. If one believes that history has an end, as Hegel and Marx did, one can interpret it accordingly.

However, as long as a deterministic argument cannot be proven, there is no reason why one should accept such an uncomfortable (and politically

[59]Those who profess to a deterministic worldview, of course, may well argue that it is not a matter of belief but a matter of science (e.g. Marx's pseudoscientific historical materialism) or a fact of life (e.g. God). However, there has so far been no irrefutable proof of any deterministic worldview. Thus it remains in the realm of speculation and belief.

devastating) proposition. Isaiah Berlin was profoundly puzzled as to why doctrines which, in the last analysis, deny individual responsibility and thereby ridicule an ordinary life filled with judgment and responsibility should nevertheless be so popular (Berlin, 1992). But what is the case for free will? How can we think about it and where can we delineate a sphere for individual agency? Roshwald argues that if one –

> '…contends that there are certain causal connections in social human issues, nobody would be so bold as to deny it. But our social activity consists of influencing those causal factors and thus modifying the course of society and history. This social activity itself may again be causally explained – one's action may be linked with upbringing, genetic factors, social environment, economic needs, and also with correct reasoning and an alert conscience. If all this is allowed for, indeterminism is saved. For, if indeterminism in respect of human issues has any meaning at all, it is the admittance of the significance of the determining factors of reason and conscience'.

To Roshwald, a central claim is the 'immensurability of the factor of human reflection', which as a variable shrinks or extends depending on the specific circumstances. It is 'bound to perplex those students of man and society whose ambition is to be called scientists in the sense of natural scientists' (Roshwald, 1956). Charles Taylor takes the issue of agency a step further. He not only believes that agents do have an idiosyncratic source of decision-making, but that they can even determine their idiosyncrasy. He developed a conception of man as a 'self-interpreting animal'. The self, he proposes, is not independent of the conception he has of himself (Taylor, 1989). Just as agency needs to be understood in its historical context, history equally needs to be understood as agent driven. It only makes sense by reference to the ways in which those undergoing historical transitions interpret their own experiences, give meaning to them and construct their worldview accordingly, in turn influencing history. If agency is to be considered seriously, it has to be a normative, purposive rather than a simply factual, instrumental endeavor (Abbey, 2004). The best argument for agency may well be originality. A 'self-interpreting animal' contributes, from within itself, a deeply idiosyncratic element to the process of continuing, evolutionary interpretation of and interaction with the outside world. It will add something new and original, something that cannot be explained by the logic of a larger mechanism. Can a nation equally be self-interpreting? Or is it merely the product of other historical forces?

Theories of Nationalism – Is Nationalism Inevitable?

The discussion about human agency and determinism is of particular relevance in the field of nationalism. Determinism in this context simply means that forces other than the nationalists themselves brought about nationalism. Nationalism, as an ideology, is itself oscillating between agency and historical determinism. On the one hand, it thinks of itself as seeking nothing but self-determination. On the other hand, however, nationalists tend to regard nationalism as something very natural, inevitable, a coming-into-ones-own and the result of an unstoppable historical process[60]. However, those who are subject to an ideology are rarely the best judges of it. Nationalism needs to be considered from the outside. The question is whether nationalism, as a historical phenomenon, is a product of agency (self-determination), or whether it is determined by history in one way or another? In short, is nationalism inevitable or is it contingent? Elie Kedourie and Ernest Gellner, from their respective idealist and materialist points of view again provide the best overview of the argument.

To Kedourie, the answer is clear – nationalism is contingent. It is artificial. Nationalists are agents, childish agents at that, who experience 'a spiritual restlessness' which makes them 'prodigiously eager for change'. Nationalist movements, he declares with more than a hint of contempt, 'are children's crusades', with the appeal of a secret movement – 'The enclosed, secret universe of plot and conspiracy would begin to exercise an obsessive compulsion of its own, from which escape was hopeless' (Kedourie). Nationalists are fakers of history, who instrumentalise the past in order to subvert the present (Kedourie). They are dreamers and dangerous hazardeurs, 'literary men who had never exercised power', unable to fully grasp the restraints, obligations and functioning of international relations. They operate in 'a hazy region, midway between fable and reality in which states, frontiers, compacts are at once both real and unreal' (Kedourie, 1993).

Nations have nothing natural or necessary about them. They are invented. Kedourie believes that the world is far too diverse to fit the specious classifications of nationalist anthropology. Furthermore, even if the existence of nations could be deduced from such classifications, 'it still

---

[60]The paradox of being a political entrepreneur (nationalist or revolutionary elites) making use of an ideology based on historical determinism has been extensively dealt with in communist thought. See, especially, Lenin's interpretation of Marx's historical dialectic (Lenin, V. I., 1950).

cannot be deduced what particular nations exist and what their precise limits are'. Nationalism, therefore, is far from being a historical, materialist, objective force 'ultimately based on will' (Kedourie). This view is part of Kedourie's overall theory of nationalism as a product of one specific school of thought which happened to gain a large following at a certain point in time. He gives two examples to support his view. Firstly, he shows how Napoleon used nationalist rhetoric for his own political purposes (Kedourie)[61]. Secondly, he explains that nationalism is not only artificial, but also a relatively weak historical force. Its role in the creation of nations has been only secondary. Great Power politics, not nationalism has created most European nations. Inversely, where nationalists could not find powers willing to take up their cause, 'their conspiracies and insurrections very often came to naught' (Kedourie, 1993). For Kedourie, therefore, nation states are as far from inevitable as possible. Not only are they not subjected to a materialist force, but even the idealist force, the key driver is hardly a potent ingredient in geopolitics.

Kedourie becomes slightly contradictory, here. He is an avowed critic of nationalism for all the harm it creates. But if it creates so much harm, how can it be a weak force? He vacillates between a contemptuous and a distressed perspective. The answer implicit in his writing is a chronological segmentation. He speaks of two types of nationalism – the original, rather ridiculous idea of it and the intimidating monster it created. He admits that even if nationalism is originally artificial, it nevertheless managed to create a modern need for the nation under the principle of an 'inter-national' order – 'Any state which is not a nation-state has its title and its existence perpetually challenged' (Kedourie, 1993). Like a self-fulfilling prophecy, nationalism, which starts as a 'spiritual restlessness', acquired a significant historical momentum. In principle, Kedourie's view of nationalism as a self-creating force comes very close to Charles Taylor's interpretation of man as a 'self-interpreting animal' in a constant productive battle with itself. It is an example of how we can through interpretation force our will upon reality – although, as was the case with Frankenstein's monster, we cannot control our creations.

Eric Hobsbawm, who agrees with Kedourie's interpretation of nations as historical inventions, offers an interesting explanation of the mechanisms

---

[61]He quotes him as saying – 'There will never be a fixed political stage of things until we have a body of teachers instructed on established principles. So long as the people are not taught from the earliest years whether they ought to be republicans or royalists, Christians or infidels, the state cannot properly be a nation.' (Kedourie, E., 1993, p. 77).

by which the idea is implemented. With reference to Karl Popper, he calls the process an exercise in 'social engineering' (Hobsbawm, and Ranger) – The key elements are education (to teach the new values and the revisionist national history), public ceremonies and festivities (relating to such key dates as the freedom struggle, the foundation or victories of the nation), public monuments (of national symbols or leaders), a cult of founding fathers, a national anthem and a flag, new national symbols (relating to the new values) and/or old national symbols (relating to a spurious historical continuity), historiography (adopting the past to the present), city, street or place names. These are just some examples of what is in the tool-kit of inventors of tradition. Nationalists in each country will pick and choose depending on what fits best in their particular circumstances (Hobsbawm, and Ranger, 1983).

Gellner, from his materialist vantage point, cannot accept Kedourie's and Hobsbawm's argumentation. Any theory proposing that nationalism is essentially, and primarily, an ideological whim, an invention and a human creation that appeared by a regrettable intellectual accident and that political life could do without it is, plainly speaking, a 'false theory' (Gellner). On the other hand, the opposite idea (usually expressed by nationalists themselves), namely that nationalism is a historical inevitability, is equally wrong[62]. Whilst he professes to take a middle point between necessity and contingency, however, Gellner, in reality, tilts heavily to the side of necessity by understanding nationalism as a logical and consistent outgrowth of modernity. As a phenomenon, rather than as a doctrine, nationalism 'is inherent in a certain set of social conditions; and those conditions, it so happens, are the conditions of our time' (Gellner, 1983). Whilst these conditions themselves may be accidental (if modernity itself is considered a historical contingency), and therefore nationalism, may, strictly speaking, not be inevitable, given the conditions of modernity, however, nationalism is the necessary outcome. This reading is corroborated by Gellner's aforementioned belief in the replaceablility of individual nationalist leaders. Nationalism, for all intents and purposes, is a historical force.

A similar approach to nationalism has been presented by Benedict Anderson. He also argues that it is the logical outcome of specific historical

[62]He writes that 'nationalism – the principle of homogenous cultural units as the foundations of political life, and the obligatory cultural unity of rulers and ruled – is indeed inscribed neither in the nature of things, nor in the hearts of men, nor in the pre-conditions of social life in general, and the contention that it is so inscribed is a falsehood which nationalist doctrine has succeeded in presenting as self-evident.' (Gellner, E., 1983, p. 125).

circumstances. Like Gellner, he emphasises the role of language and the reduction in linguistic variety witnessed in Europe before nationalism became powerful. The key driver for him, however, is not modernity, and the homogenising and atomising effects of the industrial revolution. Anderson pushes the historical focus back by about 250 years. To him, it was the effect of, what he calls 'print-capitalism', which first created a profoundly new sense of community among a growing number of people. The printing press enabled mass production of texts, for which capitalism in turn developed and cultivated a market. Large quantities of books were suddenly available in vernacular languages. These print-languages were, however, also new distillations from the many more spoken idiolects, thus creating new, larger, but anonymous 'imagined communities'. These new linguistic entities proved to be fertile breeding grounds for nationalist ideology and ultimately for the creation of modern nations (Anderson, 1991). Like in Gellner's theory, nationalism is the product of an impersonal historical force.

Whilst neither of the scholars discussed here takes nationalism and nations as perennial facts of human life, as some nationalists do, there is still a fundamental difference of opinion between those who, like Kedourie and Hobsbawm, regard it as an invention or idea which is the product of human choice (and may then acquire a force of its own) and those, like Gellner and Anderson, who argue that nationalism is the by-product of a larger socio-cultural momentum. Given the change – which itself may or may not be part of a larger historical determinism – Gellner and Anderson observe a development of natural language groups which made nationalism and the creation of nations more or less a formality. The role of material, impersonal force in their narrative is emphasised considerably at the expense of human agency.

Anderson does admit, however, that there is some role to play for elites. Print languages, once there 'could become formal models to be imitated, and, where expedient, consciously exploited in a Machiavellian spirit' (Anderson, 1991). Anthony Smith takes a similar middle-position, stressing the role of elites primarily in so-called 'subject vertical ethnies'. These are groups, in which modernity did not develop a community of equals and where there was subsequently far less systemic, external pressure for nation-building. Here, a 'secularising intelligentsia led by educator-intellectuals' plays a key role. It supplied the 'motor of transformation, as well as the cultural framework', furnishing the identity-definitions and goals for the new communal self (Smith, 1989).

The issue of agency vs. determinism is relevant to the overall argument in ways very similar to the issue of idealism vs. materialism. If nationalism has a deterministic momentum, there is very little room for individual agency. Individual agency, however, would mean two things. It obviously creates an outcome more arbitrary and therefore, again, frail, than if the outcome were determined by larger historical forces. Secondly, it gives nationalists room for manoeuvre. What the common identity is based on can be influenced by political entrepreneurs.

3.2.3 *The Past vs. Modernity*

How does change happen? Is it evolutionary or revolutionary? How much of the 'old' continues to exist in the 'new'? This question is crucial in the study of nationalism, where it is expressed in the following way – why did precisely those nations we know today develop and not others, and why is there a certain overlap between the new nations and certain pre-modern states or cultural units? Or, to reformulate – are nations products of modernity only, or does the past play a significant role in their creation?

The idea of evolutionary change has been made popular in the nineteenth century by Charles Darwin's detailed and comprehensive biological studies. Darwin proposed (like his intellectual predecessor Jean-Baptiste de Lamarck) that all forms of life share a common origin and have evolved from there[63]. Modern genetic research appears to corroborate this hypothesis, when it was discovered that there is a significant genetic overlap between even simple life-forms and human beings. The 'old' is thereby preserved in the 'new'. Change through random mutations is widely considered to happen in a piecemeal manner (Bowler, 2003; Ridley, 2004). The elegance and power of Darwin's biological theory has led thinkers to adapt it to the social sciences. In the 1960s, Karl Popper developed a theory of how ideas and knowledge changes which resembles Darwin's evolutionary theory[64]. Scientific progress, according to Popper, is an endless stream of 'corroboration' of existing theories and 'falsification'. Truth appears only in the negative and in the specific – a theory can never be proven as right,

---

[63]It was the second part of Darwin's theory, namely the method by which evolution happens, the 'survival of the fittest', which, together with Thomas Robert Malthus' earlier theory of population growth, exerted the greatest influence on nineteenth century strands of nationalist thinking (Russell, B., 1996, p. 657). Here, however, the idea of evolution is of primary interest.

[64]Popper's underlying rationale is not derived from Darwin's theories or any form of social Darwinism or sociobiology. To the contrary, it is a liberal preoccupation with fallibility and a strong warning against utopianism (Popper, K.,1994).

but only as wrong. Knowledge is built on what we know to be wrong. Once a theory is falsified, it is improved and adapted in the form of a new theory. Changes in our worldview are piecemeal (Popper, 2002).

Thomas Kuhn, by contrast, has provided a very interesting account of revolutionary change in his theory of scientific progress. He argues that facts are only scientific facts within the framework of a specific paradigm. These paradigms are invariably challenged by anomalies (problems or data) that cannot be accommodated within the existing framework. 'Revolutionary' scientists follow up on the anomalies. Over time, they become more and stronger. When they have gained a critical mass, they overthrow the old paradigm and establish a new one. Such change is not cumulative or evolutionary. It is a sudden and fundamental – a revolutionary – reconceptualisation of the world. As examples, he gives the transition from Aristotelian to Newtonian physics or that from Ptolemaic to Copernican cosmology (Kuhn, 1996). In such paradigm changes, Kuhn explains –

> '...one cannot get from the old to the new simply by adding to what was already known. Nor can one quite describe the new in the vocabulary of the old or vice versa.... Though scientific revolutions leave much piecemeal mopping up to do, the central change cannot be experienced piecemeal, one step at a time. Instead it involves some relatively sudden and unstructured transformation in which some part of the flux of experience sorts itself out differently and displays patterns that were not visible before (Kuhn, 2000).

According to Kuhn, therefore, there is some stickiness to human minds, which like to cling to what is known and familiar. However, once the tipping point has come, there is a radical break with the old. Whilst the object of inquiry remains the same, the subject's – the scientist's – point of view alters so dramatically that is seems to him almost as if he is dealing with an entirely new world. The planets exist unimpressed by our thinking, but Copernicus' 'planets' are fundamentally different from Ptolemy's 'planets'. It makes no sense to put them into any kind of relationship, to work with, say, a Copernican Venus revolving around the Sun, and a Ptolemaian Sun revolving around Earth. The new paradigm, whilst working with the same universe, is not using even fragments of the old paradigm. They are incompatible. A winning paradigm, according to Kuhn, is one which manages to gather a critical mass of the scientific community behind it.

There is important criticism of Kuhn's theory and, as the example of Popper showed, there are powerful alternative theories of scientific progress. Nevertheless, Kuhn gives a very interesting account of how change in people's minds may happen, and thereby offers a specific approach to theorising history. This can be so, because Kuhn's work is not merely epistemological, it is also describing the socio-political mechanism through which new knowledge is generated and adapted. Kuhn's theory of revolutions is describing matters of historical fact. A process like this may have gone on in the past, and may continue to go on in the future (Purtill, 1967)[65].

The debate over Kuhn's approach to change is continued in discussions of nationalism, which could itself be described as a paradigm. Incidentally, similarly to Kuhn's new scientific paradigm, nationalism, as a paradigm, has managed to gain wide acceptance among the 'community' (here, the entirety of the politicised population) and thereby secured a high degree of legitimacy as a political concept. To what extent, however, is the new paradigm dependent on previous social sentiments or institutions? Is the change modernity has brought about – ideally or materially – radical? Was it so radical that new political structures became possible or necessary; structures, which may have little or no relation to former political structures? In terms of this argument, the question may be posed thus – What is the role of the past in creating a nation? Can nationalism draw on primordial or quasi-perennial cultural elements in creating a nation? Are there traces of a cultural unity before nationalism? How strong is such a primordial or pre-modern element? How much substance does the claim of cultural continuity, so often put forward by nationalists themselves, have? As noted above, with theories of nationalism, the answer can only satisfactorily be given in the specific rather than in general. However, where the specific with regard to the general is located will have important political implications, namely on the stability of the nation.

The Philosophical Framework – Evolution vis-a-vis Revolution

Historians, philosophers of history and political scientists have proposed many different perspectives on how change happens. They range from those who, like Carlyle or Friedell, stress the power of great individuals such as

---

[65]Michael Mann, looking at power, rather than knowledge structures, has provided an argument for a mechanism similar to the one Kuhn describes. Historical change, according to Mann, is not evolutionary but 'neo-episodic'. What appears in retrospect to have been a continuous process was, in fact, the accidental consequence of episodic changes in human history, when the distribution of forms of power between social groups changed (Mann, M., 1986).

Martin Luther, Napoleon or Lenin, who shape history through their actions and thoughts (Friedell, 1927; Carlyle, 2002), to those, on the other side of the spectrum, who focus on gradual economic or social changes (Kennedy, 1989). In between, there are countless analyses of diplomatic and economic histories and the entire spectrum of international relations theory, some stressing agency (Hill, 2003) others systemic factors (Waltz, 1979)[66].

The issue can be taken up again in continuation of the comparison between Hegel and Marx. To Hegel, historical change is, in an implicit way, an evolutionary process. Calling his dialectic simply evolutionary change can be misleading, since the relationship of one stage to the next is complex in that the next step is usually the synthesis of the prior step and its antithesis. However, Hegel's theory is evolutionary in the broader sense, that there is a connection between the 'old' and the 'new'; the 'new' is arising from the 'old', not in a revolutionary, but in a controlled, linked manner. The process is comparable to pulling papers out of a tissue-box. The synthesis always retains elements of the prior stages. After all, to Hegel, history is nothing but the slow unfolding of the ever existing 'Weltgeist', its becoming explicit. As a thinker, Hegel was conservative, shying away from subversive or even revolutionary arguments (Hegel, 1991). Even blatant social or economic problems, he believed, could ultimately be incorporated by the integrative functions of the state. 'There is neither rebellion nor deviation' in his philosophy (Avineri, 1972).

In Marx's thought, there is much more space for radical change. He believes in radical change in history[67]. He also, in common with Hegel and as a result of their shared belief in historical determinism, understands history as moving through stages, where one historical stage produces from within it the next historical stage. Change, however, happens convulsively, in struggles and revolutions, until history will reach its final destination. In the Communist Manifesto, Marx emphatically states that Communists '...openly declare that their ends can be attained only by the forcible overthrow of all existing social conditions. Let the ruling classes tremble at the Communistic revolution' (Marx, and Engels, 1998). Whilst change itself happens radically, and the rupture in the 'superstructure' is also radical, the roots for change, the economic and social 'base' develop more slowly. The archetype of the proletarian himself, who developed under the

---

[66]See the earlier chapter – 'From Structural to Idiosyncratic Explanations in International Relations'

[67]In 'The German Ideology', Marx and Engels declare that 'revolution is the driving force of history' (Marx, K., and Engels, F., 1972, p.29).

capitalist system, provides a historical link between the 'old' and the 'new'. Essentially, however, the societies Marx portrays, the feudal, the capitalist and the communist, are very different. Like in Kuhn's scientific revolution, dissenters gain weight in the old system, until they are strong enough to overthrow it and establish their own, new system.

Nationalists (to Marx a capitalist, bourgeois group), reject the idea of such radical change and instead look upon history as a decipherable continuum in which some kind of identity thread is discernible. They build their theories on conceptions of history that stress a high degree of consistency or, at the very least, only evolutionary change. To them, there must be a clear link between the 'old' and the 'new'. Such a conception has been provided by Johann Gottfried Herder, the 'pioneer of the genetic theory of history' (Schmidt). He has, in a manner far less systematic than Hegel's or Marx's, advanced a philosophy of history which is essentially evolutionary, not revolutionary, stressing continuity (Schmidt, 1956)[68]. Such history is a basic force that 'awakens slumbering powers, develops germs, makes premature age youthful, and often changes apparent death to new life' (Schmidt, 1956)[69].

The task of the philosopher of history, Herder argues, is to discover the 'invisible medium' which relates the past with the present and future (Herder). This 'invisible medium' through which the 'old' and the 'new' are linked is the national character. It is running like a thread through the history of a community – a 'Volk'. The 'Volk' is the most natural socio-political unit (Barnard, 1963). This unity is recognised and preserved by way of education, through which the heritage of a 'Volk' is passed on (the 'genetic' element) and reappraised (the 'organic' element) (Herder, 1877). The key to this process is language which both awakens and perpetuates a community's sense of separate and specific existence.

---

[68]Stadelmann has argued that Herder has given the idea of organic growth far less weight in his later writings than in his early writings (which are valued more highly by him). Nevertheless, the idea persists (Stadelmann, R., 1928).

[69]Compare, the more recent exposition of the French historian Fernand Braudel. To him, a people retain a character throughout a succession of generations. Radical change is rare. There is constant adaptation, modification, adjustment. The fundamental impetus is provided by 'deep, underlying forces that invade our lives and indeed shape the world' (Braudel, F., 1995, p. xxxvi). Accidents of the historical and social circumstances of a period are far less significant than the collective mindset which derives from a nebulous, almost mythical and unconscious distant past, providing ancient beliefs, fears and anxieties – 'an immense contamination whose germs are lost to memory but transmitted from generation to generation' (Braudel, F., 1995, p.22).

This notion of the 'Volk', as a 'community sharing the consciousness of its own distinctive socio-cultural traditions' (Barnard, 1963), is perhaps Herder's most original and influential idea. It is also, despite the fact that Herder himself had the cosmopolitan outlook of the Enlightenment, directly linked to the development of nationalism in its more problematic forms (Kedourie, 1993).

Theories of Nationalism – Are there Primordial Roots?

Contrary to the fundamental nationalist assumption that the nation has a past that gives it identity, meaning and purpose (Kedourie, 1971), it is widely agreed that nationalism (and thus nationalist literature) itself is a modern phenomenon (Gellner, 1983; Anderson, 1991; Hutchinson, and Smith, 1994). Modernity in turn is intricately linked with historical revolutions, especially the political revolutions in the USA and France and the so-called Industrial Revolution[70]. European and American life in the nineteenth century was fundamentally different from life in the eighteenth century. Was this difference large enough to claim ownership of the phenomenon of nationalism, alone? Has there been a complete paradigm shift, as in Kuhn's scientific revolutions, within which nationalism only began to make any sense? Has history, in Marx' sense, produced new men? Has modernity eradicated all traces of 'genetic' history? Is the 'Volk', the distinctive socio-cultural tradition, passed-on and reinterpreted through the ages, a fiction retrospectively fitted to a radically new mindset and way of life?

Yes, Gellner would answer. The historical break modernity has produced, has been fundamental. Both the nation and nationalism are products of modernity and of the new way of life and production. The question, which comes first – the nation or nationalism? – is secondary to him. Hard pressed, he admits that there are many different nationalist experiences – some nations possess primordial roots (he calls them 'navels'), some can do without such roots, the large majority, however, have primordial roots invented for them by nationalist propaganda (Gellner, 1997). The issue is beside the point, however. What matters is the very

[70]A historical revolution is not necessarily the same as a revolution in the historicist sense. Revolutions may be historical events in their own right, drivers of history with a lasting impact as, for example, Michael Richards argues (Richards, M. D., 2004). Or, they may be primarily catalysts of changes that have taken place beforehand, making change official, rather than generating change themselves. This is what, for example, Jonathan Schell argues (Schell, J., 2005).

modern need for primordial roots (Gellner, 1997). Consequently, to Gellner, the role of the nationalist inventors of navels is limited to giving expression and a name to something which is already 'there' and converting it into a political movement. Kedourie, as shown earlier, concurs with Gellner that the nationalist past is an invention and the need for such a past is a modern one. The roots of this need are, in his opinion, found in ideational rather than material changes, of course, and the need is more a random romantic yearning (produced by the peculiar combination of enlightened with romantic thought) than an actual material necessity. Consequently, the inventor has a much more important role to play.

Anthony Smith has an argument with the so-called 'modernists'. He does allow for a significant impact of modernity which uprooted old orders, shuffled people around, created both power vacui as well as opportunities for what Kedourie called 'politics in a new style' (Kedourie, 1993). However, he believes that modernist theories only tell half the story – modernity can explain how a nation must operate in the modern industrial age, but it cannot explain why exactly those nations emerged that did emerge and not others (Gellner, and Smith, 1996). We have to include a primordial element in our understanding of nationalism in order to understand the link between 'old' (pre-modern) world and the 'new' (modern). The powerful sense of belonging, the emotional charge, the passion and the self-sacrifice inherent in nationalist sentiments only become intelligible with reference to primordial attributes of basic social and cultural links such as language, religion, territory and especially, kinship (Smith, 1998). Nations, according to Smith are both old and new, they are modern (i.e. products of the forces of capitalism, industrialism, urbanisation, the bureaucratic state and secularisation), but they also have a genetic history. The latter aspect limits the malleability of nationalist projects[71] by delineating what kinship and what territory can come into consideration as the focal point of nationalism. A nation is, therefore, not only a functional, but also a natural construct. Gellner with his functional approach, Smith argues, cannot explain the popular motivation and collective self-understanding which is essential to the success of any nationalism. There is some pre-modern substance to nationalism. Smith calls this substance 'ethnie'. It is a given imagined community which provides the groundwork for the later nation. Nationalists may have distorted and falsified the past, but they needed some past (Smith, 1989). In arguing thus, Smith takes sides

---

[71]A view implicit in, for example, the argument of Glazer and Moynihan that ethnic ties are the product only of elite interests (Glazer, N., and Moynihan, D. P., 1975).

with Clifford Geertz, who suggested that there are certain social 'attachments' derived from social practices that are 'natural' to a people. This provides the basis for an 'affinity'. These are pre-rational givens of social life (Geertz, 1967).

To show how the past played a role in nation-building, Smith developed two theories. One deals with what he calls 'lateral ethnies', the other with 'vertical' or 'demotic ethnies' (Smith). The first theory stresses 'bureaucratic incorporation', whereby a dominant ethnic core can spread out and gradually incorporate 'lower strata and outlying regions'. In this scenario, an upper-class ethnie is in control of a strong and stable administrative apparatus. It then uses this apparatus as a point of reference providing cultural regulation for all and thus defining and widening the cultural identity. (Smith). England and France are particularly successful examples of nation-building through this process of 'ethnic fusion'. Their success owed not so much to the mechanisms of the state as such, but rather to the 'sense of ancestry and identity' (rather than actual descent or race) of a 'relatively homogenous ethnic core' (Smith, 1989).

The second theory, concerning nation-building through a vertical, demotic ethnie, is particularly relevant to 'subject communities', such as India was before independence. In these communities, a basic fund of myths, symbols, memories, and values is transmitted from generation to generation throughout the territory and social strata. Organised religion provided the framework and mechanism to ensure persistence and diffusion (Smith, 1989). If religion is exchanged for education and language, Smith's subject vertical ethnie comes very close to Herder's concept of the 'Volk'. There is a key difference, however, which makes the 'ethnie' a less natural phenomenon than the 'Volk'.

As was described earlier, Smith believes that 'educator-intellectuals' play an important role in funneling the ethnie into a coherent national group. Whilst Herder works with a vaguely religious teleology (Barnard, 1963), Smith affirms the role of elite agency in driving events –

> 'At the centre of the self-appointed task of the intelligentsia stood the rediscovery and realisation of the community. This entailed a moral and political revolution… a new compact and politically active nation had to be created ("recreated" in nationalist terminology)…' People had to be '…purified of the dross of centuries – their divisions, alien elements, ignorance and so on – and emancipate themselves. That was the primary task of the educator-intellectuals.' (Smith, 1989).

The realisation of the community, however, is not so much the product of invention as Hobsbawm or Kedourie suggest. It is, rather, the product of manipulation, of patently selective, purposive rediscovery of the past (Smith). Elites work with the past, and they are restrained by the past – 'selection can take place only within strict limits, limits set by the pre-existing myths, symbols, customs and memories of vertical ethnies' (Smith, 1989). This is the link between the 'old' and the 'new'.

Paul Brass, broadly speaking, agrees with Smith. His position differs from Smith's only in so far as he sees no logical connection between primordial elements and the modern nationalist identity (Brass). He also thinks that the middle category Gellner proposes, the invention of navels by elites, is the most significant one. What matters is not, however, what exists, but rather the mere fact that people share a belief in a common descent (Brass). Many national projects give themselves a national identity only after they have created a state. At the same time, however, he, like Smith, rejects the purely instrumentalist viewpoint of Kedourie, which regards nationalism primarily as a pursuit of interests and advantage by elites in a context of almost unlimited cultural malleability (Brass, 1991). In order to be successful, elites must make skilful use of the available identity raw materials[72]. They emphasise certain aspects of a shared culture in order to build a political ideology –

> '...leaders of ethnic movements invariably select from traditional cultures only those aspects that they think will serve to unite the group and that will be useful in promoting the interests of the group as they define them. When they do so, moreover, they affect the self-definition of the group and its boundaries, often to such an extent that the ethnic community or nationality created out of a pre-existing ethnic group may be a very different social formation from its progenitor. [...] Consequently, whether or not the culture of a group is ancient or is newly-fashioned, the study of ethnicity and nationality is in large part the study of politically induced cultural change. More precisely, it is the study of the process by which elites and counter-elites within ethnic groups select aspects of the group's culture, attach new value and meaning to them, and use them as symbols to mobilise the group, to defend its interests, and to compete with other groups. In this process, those elites have an advantage whose leaders can operate most skillfully in relation both to the deeply-felt primordial attachments of group members and the shifting relationships of politics' (Brass, 1991).

[72]Compare, also – The 'psychological pre-adaptation theory' in anthropological research. Humans are therein seen as active agents with needs, desires and beliefs. Internalisation of social norms depends on the stimulation of these (e.g. Spiro, M. E., 1997).

Brass adds a new dimension to Smith's theory by suggesting that the varying thickness of cultural environments determines their usefulness for nationalist purposes.

> 'One possible route towards reconciling the perspectives of primordialists and instrumentalists may lie in simply recognising that cultural groups differ in the strength and richness of their cultural traditions and even more importantly in the strength of traditional institutions and social structure. The persistence over time, for example, of religiously based communal institutions among Jews and Muslims wherever they are found means that these cultural groups always form potential bases for ethnic movements. However, the mere persistence of the core religious traditions of such groups as these offers no prospect for predicting whether or not such movements will be effective in mobilising their members. Such cultural persistence suggests only that it is likely that the groups can be mobilised on the basis of specific appeals and not others and that, when ethnic appeals are made, the pre-existing communal and educational institutions of the groups will, if made available for the purpose, provide an effective means of political mobilisation. In short, the values and institutions of a persisting cultural group will suggest what appeals and symbols will be effective and what will not be and may also provide traditional avenues for the mobilisation and organisation of the group in new directions' (Brass, 1991).

Whilst it is very difficult, if not impossible to make precise judgments on the 'strength' or 'richness' of a culture, as Brass suggests, his argument is highly interesting where it overlaps with Smith's – whatever nationalist leaders are doing has to somehow resonate with something already there. An identity is presumably more solid ('rich', 'strong' – to use Brass' terminology), if there is a stronger connection between the old and the new. A nationalism based on at least some credible primordial elements would then be more stable than one which has little primordial ground under its feet.

3.2.4 *Identity, Stability and the Dangers of Ideological Politics*

National identity is here understood primarily in relation to political stability. It gives a nation an emotional backbone, and the people living in it a reason to want to be part of one specific state rather than another. Where the national identity is missing, it needs to be created.

Political stability is here understood as referring to the resilience of a state in the face of internal and external challenges. In the 2006 World Bank Report on Governance, political stability was measured by way of 'perceptions of the likelihood that the government will be destabilised or overthrown by unconstitutional or violent means, including domestic violence and terrorism' (Kaufmann, Kraay, et al. 2006). The most stable states are, consequently, those which both create little dissent and have found good ways to deal with dissent within their constitutions. They are peacefully resilient. A similar definition of stability was provided by Bremmer (Bremmer, 2006). What is measured by the World Bank is the 'perception' of how well a state can deal with political shocks, not the actual number and intensity of such shocks. Ake took the same approach – political acts such as political assassinations, coups d'etat, and frequent changes of the executive which are usually considered destabilising are, in fact, not necessarily destabilising. Stability has to be understood in context, since a 'form of behaviour that is stabilising relative to one political structure or pattern of political exchanges may be destabilising relative to another' (Ake). He warns against decontextualisation (i.e. statistics) and the risk of confusing political instability with political change, or political stability with a lack of change. Decontextualisation is, in his view, the main bias in scholarship, reflecting an undue preoccupation with elite interactions. The key to understanding stability is, therefore, to understand the political structure and pattern of political exchange (Ake, 1975). What, however, makes political structures – here, the nation state – stable? What determines whether a pattern of political exchange – here, a common identity – is stable? And how can stability be created if missing?

Ian Bremmer suggested that there is a significant positive correlation between the stability of a state and what he calls 'openness'. The correlation, however, only becomes effective at a certain point – 'For a country that is "stable because it is closed" to become "stable because it is open", it must go through a period of dangerous instability' (Bremmer); his book is accordingly called 'The J-Curve', where the bottom of the 'J' marks the point at which openness starts producing stability. Openness to him refers both to the extent to which a nation is 'in harmony with the crosscurrents of globalisation – the processes by which people, ideas, information, goods and services cross international borders at unprecedented speed', as well as the extent to which it is allowing 'the flow of information and ideas within [its]... borders' (Bremmer, 2006). Stability is best achieved in a liberal society with a democratic government and free-market capitalism. These are the conditions under which a state can be resilient in the face of change, like a healthy tree bending in a storm.

While focussing on the structural ramifications, he gives very little consideration to the emotional substance, however. The difference between a free trade zone and a nation is not clear. Political legitimacy, on which stability ultimately rests, is not only based on good governance, but also on identification. Centuries ago, it may have been enough to be a good ruler to be accepted by the people, but today, in an age of empowerment, democracy and nationalism, the government also needs to be accepted as being the specific government under whose authority the citizens feel they rightly belong. In the past, there have been cases in which free and open states have decided to break up and form smaller free and open states. If they do so peacefully, as the Czechs and Slovaks or a number of successor states to the Soviet Union have done, it would, by Bremmer's definition, not even be an instance of instability. However, if by stability is also meant the survival of the state within its existing boundaries, then, clearly, the state which has an internal cohesion is more stable than one which does not. Formulated differently, an ideology like nationalism which clarifies what constitutes the state and who is part of it, stabilises the state – in this case, the nation state – by giving it an identity, a shared emotional bond.

In his book, 'A Theory of Political Integration', Ake has argued that one of the crucial elements giving a political unit stability is a 'mutual identity between the political class and the governed' (Ake, 1967). This mutual identity can be provided by nationalism.

Nationalism, where it arises, can of course be both politically stabilising and destabilising[73]. Wherever the frontiers of a stipulated and mobilised nation do not overlap with the frontiers of the state, there is bound to be friction. If, however, the boundaries of a state and the concomitant nation significantly overlap, they can be mutually reinforcing, providing support for one another. In that respect, nationalism can fulfill a clear and practical political purpose – to serve as an identity-prop for the state. Myron Weiner describes political integration as a 'process of bringing together culturally and socially discrete groups into a single territorial unit and the establishment of a national identity within that unit' (Weiner, 1965b). Nationalism thereby persuades people that the specifics of the state – mainly its territorial extent – are the way they should be, i.e. that there is no more 'natural' or befitting organisation of the people in question.

This was Herder's idea of nationalism (Schmidt, 1956). It was also what Kedourie had in mind when he described how the French Revolution destabilised the European state-system by delegitimising the existing non-democratic, non-national order (Kedourie, 1993). The ideological fusion of nationalism and liberalism which survived throughout much of nineteenth

[73]For the different historical roles of nationalism, its causes and relations, see Hah and Martin 'Towards a Synthesis of Conflict and Integration Theories of Nationalism' (Hah, C.-D., and Martin, J., 1975).

century Europe is an expression of precisely this idea – a family ruling itself in liberté, fraternité and egalité. The 'who' and 'how' of political legitimacy is dealt with in conjunction. Smith also regards nationalism as arising out of a crisis of legitimacy brought about by the impact of rationalism and science. He argues that the new faith in mankind's own faculties of reasoning and understanding mechanisms of our world demanded 'complete freedom from any artificial constraints – social, religious or political' (Hutchinson, and Smith). To Smith, it was of 'signal importance' to the position of secular intellectuals in Europe and later also in Asia, Africa and the Americas, that 'rationalism and the scientific temper' emerged in societies which were still characterised by some form of authoritarianism. 'This meant that the quest for scientific truths necessarily took on the nature of a crusade on behalf of freedom of enquiry' (Hutchinson, and Smith). This development led to the break-up of the emotional mortar of pre-modern political life. However, since people need the emotional element in order to give them a sense of spatial and chronological belonging, historicists have developed nationalist responses to this crisis of legitimacy, giving people the feeling that political entities have origins and purposes, possess identities and boundaries in space (Hutchinson, and Smith, 1994).

In understanding the link between nationalism and legitimacy, Marxist thinkers are of help, because they critically evaluate what they view as persistent ideologies of 'false consciousness' through which ruling elites fabricate consent. Tom Nairn or Eric Hobsbawm suggested that nationalism is a political ideology, whereby the ruling class (the bourgeoisie) can mobilise the masses around their own developmental goals (Nairn, 1977; Hobsbawm, and Ranger, 1983). Without necessarily accepting the class-connotations, it suffices here to follow their categorisation of nationalism as an ideology, keeping in mind the relationship between ideology and power. Marx and Engels had a clear understanding of ideology as an instrument in the hands of rulers to exercise control through the state and to manufacture history according to their interests and goals. The myth thereby created, is that of a unified political community (Marx, and Engels, 1972). Torrance explains that in Marx's thinking, ideological doctrines have given certain concepts autonomous authority as ends in themselves. 'Thus they are thought to have a power over human actions that is independent, and indeed constitutive of the social relations in which they are used' (Torrance, 1995). To Marx and Engels, ideology as such (which itself remains vaguely defined) has negative connotations. It is some kind of a hypnosis which serves to defend the instable, unjust capitalist economic and political order. Nevertheless, ideology is clearly instrumental in creating a sense of legitimacy and thus political stability. It is endowed with vital political functions – structuring the social environment, giving it direction and meaning, and legitimising or delegitimising certain practices. At the very least, an ideology exercises power 'by creating a framework within which decisions can be taken and make sense' (Freeden, 2003). The paradigmatic framework itself in turn also fulfils an essential structural function of holding a community together through creating consensus[74].

Gramsci largely agrees with Marx' analysis of ideology, but by rejecting the separation Marx made between an ivory tower of philosophy (where ideologies are conjured up) and a 'real' world, he gives ideology a more permanent role in politics (Gramsci). He believes that it is impossible to separate 'scientific' from 'common' philosophy. The two are linked, because philosophies can become cultural movements, so-called 'faiths'. If one calls such a 'faith' ideology, then only on condition that 'the word is used in its highest sense of a conception of the world that is implicitly manifest in art, in law, in economic activity, and in all manifestations of individual and collective life'. This ideology serves to 'cement and to unify' the 'entire social block' (Gramsci, 2001). Gramsci, moreover, expands on Marx's understanding of ideology by adding a national-popular dimension to that of social classes (Simon, 2001).

A 'hegemonic class' plays a key role in generating ideologies by transcending its own class interests and combining them with those of other groups, classes or movements to create what he called a 'national-popular collective will' (Simon). Liberation struggles, for example, are particularly conducive to such a process (Simon). The key, for Gramsci, is that the ideology of the higher and the lower strata do not drift apart, that the elites remain in close contact with the masses. As particularly successful in this respect, he cites the Catholic Church and especially the Jesuit order, which ensured – even at the expense of the intelligentsia – that the 'scientific' and the 'common' aspects of the ideology remained connected (Gramsci, 2001). For Gramsci, there exists a continuous dialogue between popular thinking and the intelligentsia 'producing the kind of complex ideological positions that characterise the modern world' (Freeden, 2003). Remaining within the Marxian framework, one can say, that there is an interdependent and dynamic – but in Gramsci's case more evolutionary than revolutionary – relationship between the base and the superstructure.

---

[74]For Marx ultimately it is not ideas or ideologies which matter, but material conditions. Nevertheless, ideology has significant power (Torrance, J., 1995, pp.17–27).

For Gramsci, as well as for Marx, when speaking about ideology, social, political and economic concepts are integrated into a single system. This is congruent with historical experience – many nationalist movements have incorporated economic and political issues such as socialism or democracy (or, depending on the point of view, socialist movements have incorporated nationalist or democratic issues, etc.). Here, however, the focus is not on an all-encompassing ideology but only on the aspect of it which deals with the attempt to stabilise a specific political entity, the nation state. Nationalism, as Gramsci said of ideology as such, needs to transcend particular interests. Then, it can be 'social cement' serving the purpose of legitimising and thereby stabilising a political structure such as the nation state. Schöpflin called this the 'consent to be ruled'. He argues that –

> 'where a set of values and identity are broadly shared between different social strata, where they regard one another as sharing certain commonalities and respond to the same symbols, where they take the view that, whatever might divide them, they do share certain key moral aims and obligations, the basis for a redistribution of power becomes a less hazardous enterprise.' (Schöpflin, 2000).

How well can different types of nationalisms serve this central function of legitimising and stabilising a particular political unit (nation state)?

Firstly, Gramsci stresses that an ideology is more successful, if it is in tune with 'common' philosophy, with the sentiments of the masses. For theories of nationalism, this means that nationalism is stronger, where there is a higher receptivity for it. Thus, a nationalism which is based on a large scale material and social development (as Gellner argues) is able to provide a more stable prop for a nation state than one which is the result of an intellectual development (as Kedourie argues). For Gellner, the separation of people into homogenous groups often takes place smoothly, almost naturally, as a by-product of modernity. People voluntarily seek to become part of a 'high culture'. Nationalism is primarily an inclusive concept. If, on the other hand, nationalism comes first, as Kedourie suggests, and seeks to draw distinctions along linguistic or religious or somehow defined 'cultural' lines, it becomes an organising principle and an exclusive concept. People become emotionally charged (through ideological politics) with a national identity while still often living (Kedourie has Central and Eastern Europe in mind) in culturally very diverse conditions. That is (as the history of Central and Eastern Europe showed) a recipe for conflict[75]. Regardless

[75]The process can be violent in Gellner's scenario, too. The prior socio-economic change may bring significant turmoil and friction with it in its own right (for example, the

of the process by which historical change itself happens, after the change, once the nation state is created, it is either an on-the-ground-fact or the mere product of an elite ideal which may have little meaning for the people.

Secondly, if nationalism – of the materialist or idealist kind – were indeed the inevitable course of history, as many proponents of nationalism claim, nationalism would have a near absolute legitimacy. On the other hand, if nationalism is the product of elite agency, it would be just one way of dealing with modernity among many others (such as, for example, international communism). The legitimacy of such nationalisms and therefore their potential as props for nation states would be much lower. Thus, the issue is – how contingent is a specific nationalism, and how much does it blend into a larger historical context?

Thirdly, the long term strength of nationalism would be higher where it can evolve out of primordial roots. The stronger the link between the 'old' and the 'new', the more 'natural' a nationalism is. Where nationalism can connect to a people that have a strong understanding of a common history and culture, like for example the French or the British, the transition to the modern nation state is easier and the common identity holding it together is more grounded in the minds and hearts of its citizens.

Wherever nationalism is an arbitrary, artificial, imposed and elitist enterprise confronted with a complex historical, cultural and geographical situation, identity politics becomes crucial in order to stabilise the nation state. Kedourie describes how, in the new state which is no longer merely an administrative or simply a traditional feature of people's lives, but has become an internally pervasive, self-propelling unit with a purpose and value of its own, elites make conscious use of ideological politics (Kedourie). This 'new style of politics' links the idea of self-determination with that of nationalism and transforms the state from a mere organising principle into an emotional and moral entity – 'This then is the full extent of the claim – that the state should be the creator of man's freedom not in an external and material sense, but in an internal and spiritual sense' (Kedourie, 1993).

Figure 3.1 illustrates the point. Depending on the three dimensions idealism/materialism, agency/necessity and present/past, it can be deduced in how far a particular national project has sufficient natural stability. The

French Revolution). A war of independence or a revolution may be necessary to translate the new socio-economic conditions into a new political structure (for example, the US War of Independence). Furthermore, the nations created may not overlap territorially with the state and thus form oppressed minorities (for example, the Hungarians in Austria before 1867) or oppressing majorities (for example, the Hungarians in Austria-Hungary after 1867).

less natural stability there is, the higher the need to artificially generate stability through ideological politics.

Ideological politics, however, tends to come with a cost. It raises identity and ideals to the level of political values, standing next to, even surpassing the rational interest of the state.

> 'Interest, expediency, or the necessities of the case are not sufficient to justify political action. A metaphysical system must provide, from the outside, the norms of political behaviour, and a constant effort must take place in order to reconcile actions with first principles.' (Kedourie, 1993).

That is the problem of ideological politics – it conflates ideal (identity) and interest, it is 'necessarily and inevitably caught up in a perpetual disastrous and self-destructive tension between ends and means' (Kedourie, 1993). Thereby, nationalism (and Kedourie considers nationalism to be invented, arbitrary, ungrounded) –

> '...by its very nature... ran into extremes. It represented politics as a fight for principles, not the endless composition of claims in conflict. But since principles do not abolish interests, a pernicious confusion resulted. The ambitions of a state or faction took on the purity of principle, compromise was treason.' (Kedourie, 1993).

Kedourie cites Kant to make his point entirely clear. Kant argued that there are two natural differences by which nature prevents people from mixing – religion and language. These differences have a tendency to produce hatred and war (Kedourie, 1993). Ideological politics will, by necessity, exaggerate that effect. Gellner, who is not as pessimistic about nationalism as Kedourie is, primarily because he regards it as a historical by-product more than as the result of ideological politics, nevertheless shares some of Kedourie's apprehensions. He admits that nationalism does indeed see itself as a–

> '...universal, perennial and inherently – self evidently – valid principle.... This theory is dangerous not merely because it is false, but, more significantly, because the self-evident status which it ascribes to itself, and which indeed attaches to it, makes those who hold it fail to see that they are holding a theory at all.' (Gellner, 1997).

Maybe Kedourie is overly pessimistic. He can be criticised for generalising too much, failing to see the many and important nuances in nationalism. In some instances, where nationalism has turned violent as a result of ideological politics (for example, in the Balkans), his apprehensions are entirely justified. The devastating effect of ideological politics is, sadly, a historical fact. However, there are other cases in which nationalism has been peaceful. Other cases even, in which ideological politics has been largely constructive. There are three points to make in that respect – firstly, nationalism can serve as a source of political stability, secondly, elites can make conscious use of nationalism in this way, and thirdly, the more 'natural' nationalism can be made to appear, the more useful it will be for this purpose.

The two theoretical frameworks need to be understood in relation to each other. Here, their order is reversed, however. It is first necessary to understand the conditions, the challenges and choices of Indian nationalism. From these, the dynamic of the nation-building process can be deduced. Is India a natural nation, or is it a 'self-interpreting animal'. If it is the latter, how is ideological politics used? What is the content it is given? How is it applied? Once this crucial factor is understood, the application to foreign policy can be assessed through strategic culture.

4

Nationalism in India

'It intended to be itself. But what self? ...She could not understand what it all was. She only knew that it was not limited mechanical energy, nor mere purpose of self-preservation, and self-assertion.'

(T. H. Lawrence[76])

What is the need for ideological politics in the Indian context? Derived from the Indian experience of nationalism, this need can be understood to shape strategic culture in such ways as to create an inflection in Indian foreign policy (compare, Figure 1.2). The more precarious (i.e. the less natural) the Indian national identity is, the more acute is the need for a compensating ideological politics. The more the national identity relies on ideological politics, the more the process of national identity formation can be expected to have an impact on foreign policy. This will be discussed in Chapters 6 to 8. Since the challenges and choices of the Indian national project are taken as the origin of the dynamic that is responsible for the inflection, in impetus and direction, they need to be thoroughly understood.

In 1917, Rabindranath Tagore wrote that India is a 'no-nation' that never had a real sense of national unity. As a political entity, however, it was faced with the challenge of 'welding together into one body various races'. 'In my country', he continues, 'we have been seeking to find out something common to all races, which will prove their real unity'. This is necessary, because 'no nation looking for a mere political or commercial basis of unity will find such a solution sufficient'. Thus, 'men of thought and power will discover the spiritual unity, will realise it, and preach it' (Tagore, 1917). National unity in India, as Tagore well understood, had to be crafted. (Personally, Tagore deplored this because he believed that the idea of the nation is a deeply flawed one and alien to India.)

---

[76]From the novel *The Rainbow*, published by Penguin (1995), pp. 408–409

In 1947, when India celebrated its independence, it was still very much in the welding process. Far from being a 'nation' in the traditional European sense, it was 'a collection of states with a broad common culture, but many subcultures...' (Tanham, 1992). One had to go back over 2000 years to find an Indian, the Mauryan Emperor Ashoka, ruling an almost entirely unified Subcontinent. Traditionally, a highly regionalised country, India was not a compact political unit held together by a strong sense of belonging when it became independent in 1947. A number of factors, such as the inherent cultural multifariousness of India, but also the nature of its independence movement and the specifics of the transfer of authority from the British colluded to prevent this. Yet, India had important building blocks of a national identity, such as a democratic state, a clearly defined territory, a national flag, a national anthem, national heroes, a 'national movement' and other attributes of a nation. There was also too much emotional unity in the new state to call it a no-nation. India was somewhere in-between. Moreover, its path to unity was not simplistic, derived and reflexive, but rather innovative and at the same time authentic. What, then, happened in the thirty years between 1917 and 1947 in terms of a spirit of unity? What is the common denominator for India's astonishing mixture of ethnic groups, the plethora of mutually incomprehensible languages, multiple topographies and climates, religions and cultural practices, and extreme variations in economic development? What kind of national identity holds India together and what kind of nationalism does it spring from?

It is not easy to define what 'nationalism' actually means in the Indian context. It stands for a number of very different occurrences linked with modernity. In the nineteenth century, it became evident that India, like most of Asia and Africa, had fallen behind modern Europe in terms of technological know-how, organisation and military might. At the same time, India experienced the powerful mechanisms and ideas of a very modern nation, their British colonisers, at first hand. Modernity itself had a complex impact on India. It lead to an awakening of a national political consciousness, triggered by a new, modern experience of the foreign 'other'. This brought forth movements for political representation or even for independence, directed against a colonial system of suppression and exploitation. At the same time, it engendered an inward search in the desire to understand how India could have come under the sway of Britain, a relatively small island in a far away corner of the world. This led to social, cultural and religious reform movements, seeking to reinvigorate an ancient civilisation. By the twentieth century, political nationalism became associated with three distinct movements – the National Movement of the secular Indian Congress, the Muslim League, claiming to represent South Asia's Muslims, and the Hindu nationalists, identifying India with a specific version of Hindu culture. The Muslim League will not be of direct concern here, because it has realised its political goals outside the borders of today's Republic of India, in the states of Pakistan and what is today Bangladesh. Nevertheless, the Muslim League and Pakistan have been important for the national identity formation process of the Republic of India as a point of comparison and contrast. This will be explained here.

4.1 Historical Overview

Indian nationalism, according to Masselos, was the product of strong indigenous movements which arose and developed in the subcontinent. Their effectiveness, he asserts, comes from the 'application of lessons hammered out in the continuing debates over the techniques' by which 'senses of identity and opposition might best be expressed'. He continues to explain that such developments were necessarily protracted. And just as drawn-out was the evolution of the organisations whose purpose it was 'to express contemporary attitudes and to agitate, with varying enthusiasm, for the liberalisation of British rule and, ultimately, for freedom from its trammels' (Masselos, 2005). The history of the Indian independence struggle, was certainly 'protracted' – depending on the definition, it took as much as a century. Whether or not this was 'necessarily' so, is difficult to say. However, the fact that it did take long is in itself indicative of the specific nature of Indian nationalism. The historical overview will start with the mutiny of 1857. This starting point was chosen, not because it is the genesis of Indian nationalism (there have been expressions of cultural assertiveness and anti-colonialism before), nor because it is central to the attainment of independence. The uprising of 1857 can be regarded as a symbolic turning point, the conquest of India by a vast trading company had come to an end, and the Indian struggle for independence from an even vaster Empire was slowly picking up pace.

4.1.1 *Towards a National Movement*

In 1600, the British East India Company was founded in London in order to engage in spice trade between Europe and Asia. Twelve years later, it established its first toehold in the Indian port of Surat. Later, it set up trading points in Madras and Calcutta. In the eighteenth century, the Company evolved, in tune with its expanding commercial interests and the declining Mughal Empire, from a coastal trading partner into a significant landowner and military power. Under the 1773 Regulating Act, the – by now very large – Bengal, Bombay and Madras Presidencies were unified and subsequently administered from Calcutta. Company rule continued to expand by treaties and wars so that, by the 1850s, its influence was firmly established in almost all of India, either directly or indirectly, through the local princes it controlled. Whilst the Mughal Emperor was still sitting on his throne, the de facto ruler of India was the East India Company. Its hold on the country appeared solid, when, in 1857, Sepoys (Indian Company troops) mutinied and brought Company rule to the brink of collapse. For the first time, not a specific ruler or people, but a cross-section of Indians engaged the British.

The 1857 Uprising

The 1857 uprising – called a 'mutiny' or 'rebellion' by the British and the 'First War of Independence' by many Indians – was the most serious challenge to British rule in India in the nineteenth century. Following an incident which provoked religious resentments, many native soldiers in the Company's Bengal army mutinied against their British officers. Others joined, the mutiny spread across North India and such illustrious figures as Bahadur Shah, the last Mughal Emperor, or the *rani* of Jhansi (called the 'warrior queen') became involved. There were troop desertions, peasant uprisings and organised resistance. It took the Company half a year and a number of hard fought battles, especially in Delhi and Lucknow, to regain control of the situation.

In how far the events of 1857 had a nationalist motivation, or were merely outbursts of personal, social, or religious dissatisfactions coupled with personal interests and a random mass psychology, remains highly contested. S. B. Chaudhuri has argued the former case. He regards the uprising as a nationalist movement, because it was a concerted anti-foreign action, widespread geographically and deep-seated socially (Chaudhuri, 1965). Chaudhuri's work is a response to the thesis of R. C. Majumdar, who stated that the uprising cannot be classified as a national movement, because the motivation of the partaking fighters was not national independence, but rather personal gain (Majumdar, 1963). Jim Masselos also makes the issue of motivation the lynchpin of his analysis and comes to the same conclusion as Majumdar. He believes that whilst the anti-British nature did form a unifying bracket for an otherwise complex event, there was a decisive lack of anything positively unifying, such as a national idea. It was not a rising of Indians, but a rising of various oppressed peoples and did not inaugurate a movement for a new nation (Masselos, 2005). The conclusion that nationalism, at the time, was not a significant force, is underlined by the simple observations that the 'First War of Independence' was never followed by a 'Second War of Independence', and that independence came about only 90 years later and then not by war at all. However, 1857 gave later nationalists a powerful symbol of national resistance. This is where its importance lies. As was the case with the storming of the Bastille, it is not historical fact that matters, but historical impact – and that often depends on the posterior interpretation.

The Beginnings of the National Movement

Later in the nineteenth century, two distinct movements with nationalist connotations developed – one, secular and reform oriented, the other, religious and radical. The first, the liberal nationalist movement was initially represented by the Poona Sarvajanik Sabha (founded in 1870) and the Indian Association (founded in Calcutta in 1876). They worked to improve the colonial system in order to give Indians more of a say, and formed a quasi-political opposition with extensive political contacts with the Liberal Party in Britain. In 1885, under the reign of Lord Ripon, a Liberal Viceroy, the Poona Sarvajanik Sabha and the Indian Association organised and merged into the first Indian National Congress, held in Bombay. The Congress, designed as a yearly meeting to be held in a different Indian city each time, was established with the aim of putting the reform movement on a broader political footing. Its early leader, Pherozeshah Mehta, attempted to institute it as a parallel organisation to the British Liberal Party. The Congress, Gandhi later reminisced, 'brought together Indians from different parts of India, and enthused us with the idea of Nationality' (Gandhi, 1997).

Although the Congress was dominated by moderates, there was also a strong religious and revolutionary movement which did not seek mere reform through cooperation but full political independence. Independence was associated with religious self-realisation. Swami Vivekananda's interpretation of Hinduism was very influential. He provided a political approach to the religion, which had previously been neglected. Whilst the Vedanta philosophy teaches liberation from the world of material reality and is thus profoundly apolitical, Vivekananda stressed the idea of karma yoga, of self-realisation through courageous action. At the same time, Vivekananda, who had travelled extensively in the West, became an internationally recognised figurehead of Indian culture and religion and thereby a symbol of India's new self-esteem. Religious nationalists reached out to the masses by fusing their ideas with different regional religious cults, such as that of Kali in Bengal or of Ganpati in Maharashtra.

The partition of Bengal by Lord Curzon in 1905, widely resented in India, led to terrorism, further radicalisation and, with the revocation in 1911, to a loss of face for the British. Gandhi called it 'the real awakening' of the nation (Gandhi, 1997). It also put the unity of the Indian National Congress to the test. In 1905 and 1906, the moderate and widely respected leaders Gopal Krishna Gokhale and Dadabhai Naoroji managed to prevent an open break. The following year however, the radical fraction under Bal Gangadhar Tilak and Aurobindo Ghose broke away.

Tilak was jailed for a number of years and returned to Congress politics only by 1915, when, together with Annie Besant and C. R. Das, he manoeuvred the Congress into increasing opposition to the British. The passing of the Rowlatt Act after World War I, extending strict war-time measures into peace-time, caused significant outrage and further hardened the frontlines. The moderate Nationalists meanwhile founded a party modelled on the British Liberals, the National Liberal Federation. The most significant event to change the pace of the National Movement, however, was the massacre of approximately 1000 peacefully gathered Indians in Amritsar, in April 1919. The British were losing their nerve. It was under these circumstances that Mohandas K. Gandhi came to the fore and assumed leadership of the National Movement.

4.1.2 *Towards Independence*

The second part of the independence struggle, from approximately 1919 until independence in 1947, was characterised by a change of strategy from relying on cooperation to relying predominantly on non-cooperation, by the building of a strong political organisation and by linking the movement more with the masses. The British, to whom the need for change became increasingly clear, worked to protract their loss of control. The Congress attempted to speed it up, but not at all costs. Many different solutions were discussed until, finally, full independence was granted not to one, but to two successor states, India and Pakistan. The ultimate transfer of power itself was – as far as historical comparisons go – unusually cooperative.

Gandhi – From Mohandas to Mahatma

When Gandhi took the lead in the Indian National Movement after the First World War, he had already honed his skills as a leader and organiser of people in South Africa where he had led the Indian minority's struggle against racial discrimination. Despite his age (he was 46 at the time) and his considerable experience, he followed the advice of his mentor Gokhale to travel in India for one year, learn about the people and, in the meantime, abstain from making political statements. After he finished his journey, he began political action by orchestrating local resistance movements with a limited scope and clear goals in Bihar and Gujarat. This allowed him to learn more about conditions in India and improve his tactics along the way.

In 1920, Gandhi entered centre stage. At the September Congress meeting, he proposed non-cooperation by boycotting the upcoming elections and a declaration of self-rule (*Swaraj*) within a year as the cornerstones of his programme resolution. The resolution and with it Gandhi's leadership were accepted with a narrow majority. The boycott turned out to be key to Gandhi's consolidation of his position as leader. After the elections had passed without Congress candidates, no one had a stake left in the system of cooperation and most were prepared to walk Gandhi's path (Kulke, and Rothermund, 1998). When the peaceful boycott turned violent in a North Indian village in 1922, the British authorities used this as a pretext to arrest Gandhi and put him in jail until 1924.

In the late 1920's two new young leaders emerged – Jawaharlal Nehru (son of the respected congressman and lawyer Motilal Nehru) and Subhas Chandra Bose. Upset with the pace of events, they initially worked closely together in trying to radicalise the Congress and bring about independence more rapidly. Gandhi managed to co-opt Nehru into the Congress mainstream by paving the way for his presidency in 1929 and 1936. Nehru's main task as President was to make Congress politically functional. In order to do so, he had to leave the critical sideline in favour of a position of compromise in the mainstream. Although Nehru retained his own opinions and was frequently at odds with Gandhi, he became Gandhi's most loyal follower and key ally.

Subhas Chandra Bose, on the other hand, was fundamentally at odds with Gandhi when it came to means. Bose was willing to bring about independence by force – an unacceptable proposition for Gandhi. The two leaders were also at odds when it came to economic policy. Where Bose favoured rapid industrialisation, by authoritarian means if necessary, Gandhi was staunchly anti-industrial. Thus, when Bose became President of congress in 1938 and 1939, Gandhi opposed him and ultimately made his position untenable. Bose resigned and founded an independent party, the All India Forward Bloc. Later, during the Second World War, he staged a spectacular secret journey first via Afghanistan and Moscow to Nazi

Germany, then by submarine to Japan. He wanted to enlist the Axis powers' help for an invasion of India. Japan, whose forces were then rapidly advancing towards the Indian border in South East Asia, supported him. Bose took control of the Indian National Army (INA) and fought against the British to liberate India. However, the INA and the Japanese were forced to retreat and Bose himself died in a plane crash over Taiwan in 1945. He was no more than a 'meteor, which enters the earth's atmosphere'. He 'burned brightly for a brief moment only' (Kulke and Rothermund, 1998). The National Movement in India took Gandhi's path of peaceful resistance.

When in 1929, the British denied India dominion status, Gandhi put forward a resolution calling for complete independence. A year later, he started a new nationwide campaign, the 'Salt March'. In what turned out to be one of his most successful political manoeuvres, he ceremoniously and effectively broke the British salt monopoly which was a significant burden on the lives of ordinary Indians. The campaign was a resounding success – the media in India and abroad carried the brilliantly staged dramaturgy into millions of households while the British jails filled with *Satyagrahis* (non-violent fighters). Gandhi, meanwhile, drafted a carefully chosen eleven point programme demanding very specific political actions to support economic conditions of most social groups in India.

A good way out of the campaign for Gandhi, who feared that it may turn violent again, as well as for the British Viceroy, Lord Irwin, who did not know how to deal with the situation, presented itself with the Second Round Table Conference[77] on India. Gandhi agreed to take part and suspended the campaign. Irwin released most prisoners and legalised the production of small quantities of salt by households. Nehru was furious that Gandhi had given in to the British. The significance of the pact, however, was not in the details of it, but in the fact that the British Viceroy was willing to negotiate and make a pact with Gandhi in the first place, thereby giving him a quasi-official status as representative of Indians. The talks in London and Gandhi's meeting with Prime Minister Macdonald, on the other hand, were fruitless. Upon return, Gandhi reinstituted the campaign of civil disobedience, which was continued this time until 1933.

Gandhi's participation at the conference, as well as the Poona Pact on untouchability (the working basis of which was a communal award by the

[77]The First Round Table Conference was held in London several months earlier, but was invalidated by the absence of the Indian National Congress, the largest party to represent India.

British Prime Minister) brought Congress back into the British constitutional project. In 1934, Congress successfully contested at the elections to the British-Indian central parliament and, following the Government of India Act of 1935, contested and won in many provincial elections in 1936. As a consequence, Congress had to form a government in the provinces in which it had a majority and take political responsibility. Within Congress, there was vociferous opposition to this form of democracy by British grace. The old divide between those who wanted to achieve a change within the system using constitutional means and those who wanted to change the system using any means resurfaced again and again.

The Second World War ended the period of political cohabitation. When the British Viceroy Lord Linlithgow declared war in India's name without so much as consulting the Indian politicians, all Congress governments resigned in protest. Agitation, however, was limited to Gandhi's symbolic individual Satyagraha, in which one prominent congressman at a time would speak out against the war and be arrested. In 1942, Sir Stafford Cripps, tried to co-opt the Congress leadership into a more active role in India and in the war. He suggested they establish a national government in which the Viceroy would be confined to the role of representative head of state. The idea eventually foundered on Lord Linlithgow's resistance. Linlithgow was backed by Churchill. Nevertheless, Judith Brown argues that this was the point of no return – after the Cripps-mission, the British departure became inevitable (Brown, 1985).

Linlithgow's intransigence demanded an answer from Congress. The answer came in the form of the 'Quit India' campaign in which the British were asked to leave India immediately. The campaign was ill-conceived, before it could be given a programme, the entire Congress leadership was arrested and locked-up. The result was that Gandhi's moderating influence which for a long time had managed to subdue conflicts within Congress was no longer felt. The younger, more radical nationalists assumed control. In August 1942, there was a short outbreak of nationwide violence. Furthermore, the imprisonment of the Congress leadership left the political arena to Mohammed Ali Jinnah and the Muslim League, agitating for a separate homeland for the subcontinent's Muslims and thus a partition of post-independence India. The British, in the meantime, understood that the end of the war would bring a host of old and new problems and prepared to withdraw. Rothermund succinctly summarised what followed –

> 'Gandhi had asked the British to "Quit India" in 1942. "Divide and Rule" had been a safe watchword for a long time; now they found another one – "Divide and Quit."' (Kulke and Rothermund, 1998).

Jinnah and Partition

The partition of India and the foundation of the state of Pakistan was, more than any other comparable historical event, the work of just one man – Mohammed Ali Jinnah (Kulke and Rothermund, 1998). Jinnah was neither a religious radical nor a great leader of the masses. He was a tenacious and adamant political advocate of the Muslim minority. Initially, he was closer to Congress than to the Muslim League. However, after a long stay in Britain, he returned to Indian politics in 1936 in order to lead the Muslim League in the provincial elections. His manifesto, at that time, was still very close to that of the Congress. Partly for that reason, the Muslim League performed disappointingly in the elections. Jinnah now took on the role of an opposition politician. He began to see himself more and more as the caretaker of the Muslim minority only, moving continuously away from Congress with its pan-Indian outlook.

In 1940, the League passed the famous Lahore Resolution, calling for a separate homeland for South Asia's Muslim minority, to be called Pakistan. At that time, neither the idea nor the name 'Pakistan' was new. New was merely Jinnah's association with them (Kulke and Rothermund, 1998). He also professed the 'Two Nation Theory', echoing Alberuni's verdict of 900 years earlier, whereby –

> 'the Hindus and the Muslims belong to two different religious philosophies, social customs, and literatures. They neither inter-marry, nor dine together and, indeed, they belong to two different civilisations which are based mainly on conflicting ideas and perceptions.' (Cohen, 2004a).

During the war years, while the Congress leadership was in prison, Jinnah managed to solidify and improve his position within India as well as with regard to the British authorities. When, in 1944, he held talks with Gandhi, they could not find significant common ground. Gandhi wanted a treaty of federation before partition; Jinnah wanted complete partition first and possible treaties only between two sovereign states. Their failure to reach an agreement meant that the British would have to provide a solution. In July 1945, Viceroy Lord Wavell called the leading representatives of the Congress and the League to Shimla for a conference with the goal of establishing a provisional government. The conference, however, came to nothing. Jinnah demanded that the League nominate all Muslim ministers, thereby claiming the sole right to represent the subcontinent's Muslims. Congress, which did not accept the 'Two Nation Theory' and claimed to represent all Indians including Muslims, did not accept.

The situation for India changed significantly when, in 1945, the British Labour Party defeated the Conservatives and Clement Attlee succeeded Churchill as Prime Minister. The new government was unequivocally committed to Indian autonomy – in some unqualified form. Elections were called for in India, without, however, defining their scope and purpose. British policies were confused and improvised (Kulke and Rothermund, 1998). The elections produced two victors – Congress and the League, which drew most of the Muslim vote. The result fatefully resembled Jinnah's polarising 'Two Nation Theory'. The regional parties lost out. Thus strengthened, neither Congress nor the League was willing to compromise when the British sent a cabinet mission in March 1946 to resolve all problems. Even Attlee's personal attempt to mediate between Jinnah and Nehru in London was in vain. For some months, the League and Congress formed an uneasy and ineffective provisional government together. At the same time, first instances of large scale communal violence flared up in Calcutta and Bihar.

Viceroy Lord Wavell, who despite his best intentions was not the ideal man for the job, was eventually replaced. His successor, Lord Louis Mountbatten, a charismatic war hero and member of the royal family, was of a different calibre. When he arrived in India, he was equipped with a robust mandate to lead the colony into independence. He conceptualised a 'Plan Balkan', outlining the possible partition of India with all its consequences and provided a clear, very curt time schedule within which independence was to be accomplished[78]. The transfer of power would take place on 14 August (in Pakistan) and 15 August (in India), 1947. Except for Gandhi, all negotiating parties had by now accepted partition as inevitable. When Mountbatten finally indicated the borders of what was to become Pakistan, Jinnah was severely disappointed. Soon after the ceremonies, the 'Two Nation Theory' took a terrible toll on the ground. Violence broke out, first in the Punjab, then in Bengal, Bihar and other places as vast numbers of Muslims and Hindus relocated across the new borders.

---

[78]The British government suggested a modified version of Mountbatten's plan, attempting to avoid responsibility for partition by proposing to grant independence to the individual provinces of British India, which could then individually decide on their future. This proposition was angrily dismissed by Nehru, who preferred a British segmentation of India into large parts to such a 'balkanisation' with uncertain outcome. The episode shows just how insecure Nehru considered the common Indian national foundations to be at the time (Kulke and Rothermund, 2004, p.320).

Violence, however, was not the only problem the young countries faced. The status of the princely states was still unclear. They now had to decide whether to join India or Pakistan. Many of them dithered and procrastinated. This was the moment of glory for Sardar Vallabhbhai Patel. In an incredible tour de force, he travelled to almost all princely states and managed to have most of them sign an accession treaty with the Republic of India. Two key states, however, remained undecided – Kashmir and Hyderabad. In Hyderabad, the Muslim Nizam ruled over a predominantly Hindu people. He was hoping for independence, but since the country was entirely surrounded by the new Republic of India, that was unrealistic. In Kashmir, a Hindu Maharaja ruled over a predominantly Muslim people and the country was on the border of both new states. He had a realistic choice to go with either India or Pakistan. He decided to wait, Pakistan pressured him and India came to his aid – on the condition that he signed the accession treaty. Whilst the matter of Hyderabad was soon settled (when Indian soldiers made the decision for the Nizam), Kashmir remains the thorn in Indo-Pakistani relations.

4.1.3 *A Nation-in-the-Making*

Nationalism was manifold in India – there were traditionalists and modernists, community-based and universalist strands, radical and moderate approaches. There were different ideas of what the nation is and whom it encompasses once the British left. The Congress was very successful in integrating many of these diverse strands and some of the most brilliant leaders under its umbrella. Based on Mahatma Gandhi's ideas, the Congress occupied and shaped the mainstream of nationalism. Leaders with incompatible approaches to independence or nationalism, like Subhas Bose and Vinayak Damodar Savarkar (a cultural nationalist) were pushed to the fringes. The Muslim League was the only challenge to Congress nationalism that could acquire significant nationwide political influence before independence. Furthermore, the nationalisms were almost invariably intertwined with other ideas such as that of political self-determination, social liberation, progress or reform (Masselos, 2005). Nationalism – or the question of who should rule – was thus part of the much larger political package of how this rule should be exercised.

After independence and partition, the Congress managed to retain its status as a supra-party for a while, subsuming under it much of India's diversity. The National Movement, however, was an elitist enterprise. Although Gandhi was supremely skillful in inciting the Indian masses for certain specific economic goals, political independence or even social tolerance, by the time the British left India, the new state was not yet a nation based on a strong, popular identity. The main task for the national leaders was therefore to preserve the unity and territorial integrity of the new state and to give it a raison d'être – a national identity. India's heterogeneity precluded the 'easy' option of building a national identity based on some prior religious or linguistic identity. The Indian nation had to be a civic one in order to survive. In all this, Gandhi played a vital role as supra-political symbol of Indian unity and as builder of a value-consensus. He worked hard to preserve and strengthen the Indian national unity. After his death in 1948, Nehru took over as the leading architect of the greatest project of nation-building the world has ever witnessed. 'Nations are not formed in a day', Gandhi wrote, 'the formation requires years' (Gandhi, 1997). The process in India, however, is a particularly difficult and slow one. India is no nation like other nations. Its identity is a unique construct, defying ordinary definitions. The type of nationalism needs to be understood in depth, because it significantly shapes the basis for political unity as well as, ultimately, the nature of the nation's interaction with other nations. The three dimensions of particular relevance are – the idealism vs. materialism dimension, the necessity vs. agency dimension, and the past vs. modernity dimension. The three dimensions are not independent of each other but successively build one on the other. The first dimension determines in how far ideas or reality shaped nationalism, the second dimension determines what flexibility of action there was available for leaders to shape ideas, and the third dimension determines where leaders took their ideas from.

4.2 Idealism over Materialism

Modern India is both the product of the British as well as the product of its own traditions and nationalist movement. Whilst nationalists shaped a national identity, outside forces, such as great power politics played a key role in the actual establishment of the new nation state. The case of India, thus, partly supports Kedourie's point about the limited power of nationalism as a historical force, and its secondariness when it comes to actual state creation (Kedourie, 1993). Without wanting to diminish the role of the National Movement, it is nevertheless not coincidental that India's plea for independence was successful only once the British colonial power had been decisively weakened by the Second World War and felt it was in its own interest to release India into independence. There were, thus, significant exogenous pressures on British colonial rule. The general surging of nationalist sentiments in the colonised world, including India, as well as the actions of various nationalist leaders (especially Gandhi and Bose) added further endogenous pressure.

In the early twentieth century, the Raj still appeared to be more solidly entrenched than ever. The great capital architecture of Lutyens' New Delhi, planned from 1911 and finished in 1929, reflected this British confidence[79]. However, the effects of the First World War had already begun to erode the foundations of British rule, not immediately and directly (India loyally fought at Britain's side), but indirectly. India had become a partner rather than a colonial subject to Britain. This was evident to most political actors in Britain as well as in India. Constitutional reforms attempted to translate this power shift into political coin (Kulke and Rothermund). At the same time and as a result of reduced career prospects due to the reforms, the British government found it increasingly difficult to send its own citizens to serve in India and maintain the colonial administrative 'steel frame' (Kulke and Rothermund, 1998).

The Second World War completely reshuffled the global power relationships. Europe, including Britain, lost its dominant position in history to the new superpowers – the Soviet Union and the United States. The British were exhausted by the war effort. They found themselves incapable of maintaining a global empire in a new age which no longer supported a relatively effortless, imperialist European domination of largely non-politicised peoples. The world was now dominated by a strongly politicised global bipolarity which induced anti-imperialist ideologies such as communism and nationalism in Africa and Asia.

Elliot Roosevelt, President Franklin Delano Roosevelt's son and aide, describes a key scene between Roosevelt and Churchill preceding the signing of the Atlantic Charter, setting the tone for the Anglo-American alliance, in 1941. Roosevelt made clear to Churchill his desire to establish a post-war order free of despotism, including colonialism. Churchill, an arch-imperialist, rejected any proposition potentially undermining the foundations of British greatness. However, towards the end of the discussion,

---

[79]Khilnani writes that New Delhi was the 'summation of British efforts to hoist the imperial pennant on Indian territory... Delhi's attraction was both its rich historical associations as the seat of past imperial overlords, and its provision of a virgin space on which the marshaled layout of the canvas Durbar city could be engraved permanently into the rocky Indian landscape, the chosen site where a late imperial idea of power could be entombed' (Khilnani, S., 1998, p. 121; Volwahsen, A., 2002).

Churchill is forced to accept the ground realities. Without America, Britain won't stand. In the face of US opposition, 'British colonial policy would be a dead duck'. In this conversation, in which two fundamentally different worldviews came to clash, Elliot Roosevelt succinctly observes, how 'gradually, very gradually, and very quietly, the mantle of leadership was slipping from British shoulders to American' (Roosevelt, 1946; Dulles and Ridinger, 1955).

Whilst it can reasonably be argued that British weakness and global changes have played a significant role in bringing about Indian independence, the argument that India itself, as a coherent, modern nation state, is a product of the British is more difficult to sustain. Churchill, in a speech at the Albert Hall in 1931, famously declared –

> 'It makes me sick when I hear the Secretary of State saying of India "she will do this and she will do that". India is an abstraction… India is no more a political personality than Europe. India is a geographical term. It is no more a united nation than the Equator.' (Churchill, 1947).

James Fitzjames Stephen, a leading conservative Victorian intellectual, has argued that only a belligerent nation such as the British could suppress the internal differences and hostilities of India, and establish a unifying Pax Britannica (Stephen, 1883). Modern India, by this logic, was the creature of British imperial rule. And indeed, the British had a significant hand in the creation of the modern Indian administrative unit. In addition to the territorial unification under a single ruler, Rothermund lists the Indian colonial administration, the system of law, the educational system and the health system as key unifying accomplishments of British rule (Kulke and Rothermund, 1998).

However, as argued above, while British colonisation facilitated the modern state and transferred to India the idea as well as a model of a modern nation, they did not create an Indian nation. Despite having politically unified India to an extent rarely, if ever, witnessed in Indian history, the argument that India is an abstraction made concrete by British administrative organisation has two significant flaws. The first is that the British did not care to foster Indian unity. On the surface, their coherent sphere of power in South Asia was a result of their commercial and, later, geopolitical expansion and rivalries; it was not intended to become a unified realm. It thus included areas, such as Sri Lanka or Burma, which were traditionally not 'Indian'. Underneath the surface, they maintained divisions wherever it suited their interests (Kulke and Rothermund, 1998)[80]. Their system of indirect rule sustained a patchwork of princely states, they made a conscious attempt to co-opt the Muslims into their rule by giving them preferential treatment over the Hindus, they perpetuated and institutionalised religious and ethnic divisions in the army and they made no effort to improve ancient divisive practices such as the caste system (Dirks, 2001; Cohen, 2004a). In the end, they left the subcontinent divided (Panigrahi, 2004). The British did not create a unified nation. Their 'crown jewel' was the asymmetric product of a centuries-old historical process, the enormous outgrowth of a number of independent trading posts. India's administrative unity was accomplished, as Nehru said, 'incidentally as a side product of the empire's advance'. Later, when administrative unity began to work in favour of a developing national identity which challenged alien rule, 'we witnessed a deliberate promotion of disunity and sectarianism, formidable obstacles to progress' (Nehru, 2003).

The second problem is manifest in Churchill's comparison of India with both Europe and the Equator. The Equator has absolutely no shared culture, but Europe does; and so does India. As noted above, Europe and India have a comparable degree of cultural coherence. Europe happened to become a continent of nation states. Economic forces (as Gellner theorised) may well have set Europe on an inescapably divisive course. However, there is enough cultural unity to produce a viable European Union. British India, a continent of diverse peoples, happened to split into two (now three) parts. It did not remain unified in its entirety, but it equally did not become scattered into many fragments.

In India (as in Europe), there is an underlying cultural similarity which the Equator does not have. It enabled it to retain a vaguely felt common identity, despite repeated foreign conquests. Geography – the sea and the mountains – certainly plays a key role in this. India (again, unlike the Equator) has natural frontiers, within which Indian culture could develop. Rulers, foreign or not, could not retain territories outside them. The British expansion during the Great Game, for example, naturally stopped at the Khyber and Bolan Passes as well as in the Himalayas (Hopkirk, 1990). Furthermore, without going so far as to state that Indian nationalists have created 'convincing proof' that 'nationalist demands could not be left permanently unsatisfied and that withdrawal was a necessity that could not

[80]In 1858, Lord Elphinstone famously declared that he would safeguard British power in India by keeping the different peoples of India distinct, much like a steamer is secured by the division of the hull into water-tight compartments (Dirks, N. B., 2001, p.177).

be, nor should be, long denied' (Masselos, 2005), they nevertheless clearly played a significant role in bringing about the end of British rule[81]. In an age of faltering imperial power, India could thus be one of the first nations to gain independence. It was the path-breaker, not the follower of a historical trend.

On the whole, British rule in India had played a key role in creating a territorial and administrative unit which could subsequently become an independent state. Furthermore, a contribution of the Raj to India's development was that 'it occasioned the fundamental debate on the nature of her national identity, which in some ways continues to this day' (Parel, Hind Swaraj). It could do so, both phenomenologically, as the 'other' – at once challenger of the old and provider of modern ideas of democracy and meritocracy (Kulke and Rothermund, 1998), and materially – as provider of a modern state, which, according to Sharma, has woven together India's contradictions 'however clumsily' and to produce in India a modern state. However, Sharma continues, what needed to be done, was 'to identify the 'Self' that would determine the future course of India' (Sharma, 2003). The creation of the 'nation', of the modern unit that was to inhabit the independent state was the central task for Indian nationalism. It was inseparable from the struggle for independence.

There are a number of crucial questions pertaining to the nature of Indian nationalism. Was the nationalism found in India the driver for change, as Kedourie saw it, or was it merely a catalyst of change, as Gellner argued? Did the National Movement create Indian nationalism, or was Indian nationalism created by other historical forces? If nationalism in India was the natural by-product of social and economic changes, it would be likely to be both relatively stable and relatively unproblematic. If, on the other hand, nationalism was a product of the imagination of a small group infused into the large mass, it would be unstable, at least until reality has been adapted to the idea. This process, furthermore, has a high potential to create violence along the indistinct borders of a rough-and-ready demarcation.

4.2.1 *Limits of Materialist Explanations*

To determine in how far Gellner's materialist arguments can explain the emergence of nationalism in India in the nineteenth century, it has to be

[81]Gandhi's struggle had a significant effect both on the power structures in India and on British confidence in India and at home (Gregg, R. B., 1938). Bose's demonstration of organised violent struggle has also led to considerable concerns in London (Som, R., 2004).

understood, in how far the economic development in India under British colonial rule favoured the establishment of Gellner's 'high-cultures'. Did modernity, in the form of the Industrial Revolution significantly alter the Indian subcontinent before independence? Did economic change create anonymity, mobility, semantic work and atomisation within Indian society?

Karl Marx, writing in the mid-nineteenth century, observed a profoundly negative impact of British rule on the Indian economy. The traditional structures of manufacturing and village life were uprooted 'across the whole surface of Hindostan' by 'British steam and science' (Marx and Engels). What the British needed was raw materials and, later, a market. Colonial exploitation was more ruthless even than the despotic regimes which came beforehand. They, at least, at times reinvested some of the money they plundered and left the traditional economic structures more or less intact. The British did not do so. They exported India's wealth and uprooted its traditional economy. According to Marx, there 'cannot remain any doubt but that the misery inflicted by the British on Hindostan is of an essentially different and infinitely more intensive kind than all Hindostan had to suffer before' (Marx and Engels). Under British rule, the people of India (whose loss of wealth he symbolically equates with the loss of the gold jewellery even the simplest Indian family once held as a family treasure) found the colonial system uprooting their economic basis and throwing them 'into a sea of woes' (Marx and Engels, 1985).

Marx remained ultimately hopeful for India. Concerning the building of railways, he predicted that once such machinery is introduced 'into the locomotion of a country, which possesses iron and coals' there is no way to prevent it from industrialising itself. Therefore, the extensive network of railways will become 'the forerunner of modern industry' in India (Marx and Engels). He was proved wrong, however. Almost all machinery the British used in India and all of the rail tracks, carts and locomotives, were not produced in India, but imported from Britain (Kulke and Rothermund, 1998) and the main benefactors of the railways in India were, what Marx called the British 'millocracy', the mill-owning industrialists. His other hope also did not come to pass. Within his framework of a materialist dialectic, he expressed the expectation that the destruction of India's 'semi-barbarian, semi-civilised' communities will ultimately bring a revolution and liberation closer. Thus, 'whatever may have been the crimes of England', it could become 'the unconscious tool of history in bringing about that revolution' (Marx and Engels, 1985). We now know that such a revolution has not happened. To what extent British rule did actually manage to shake up the root structures of Indian society and in how far this may have had a long term decisive impact, is open for discussion. Marx, who was a much better economist than political philosopher, provided a sharp economic analysis, exposing the logic of a colonial system which was hardly conducive to Indian development.

Rothermund, reviewing the entirety of the British Raj, shares this assessment. On the eve of independence there were only few economically positive results to show for about two hundred years of colonial rule. Agriculture and industry were equally underdeveloped. This underdevelopment was, if not the direct intention of the British, indisputably a product of British economic policy and of the colonial system they had established – instead of encouraging and stimulating the industrial development, there were shortfalls, delays and structural deficits (Kulke and Rothermund, 1998). It is not surprising, therefore, that the subcontinent did not experience the economic and social turmoil that modernity brought to large parts of Europe in the nineteenth and early twentieth century. In 1600, when the East India Company was founded to exploit the riches of the East, India was producing about 22.5 per cent of the world's GDP (Britain, at the time, produced about 1.8 per cent). By 1870, Britain contributed about 9.1 per cent of the world's GDP. India, in the meantime, had been reduced to a 'poor third-world nation, a symbol across the globe for famine and deprivation' (Dalrymple, 2007). In subsequent decades, while many European countries experienced significant industrial growth, India stagnated. Between 1881 and 1931, the proportion of male workers in the industry actually declined from 10.6 to 8.4 per cent; between 1881 and 1901 the male industrial workforce declined even in absolute numbers (Roy, 1999). A de-industrialisation took place, with movements of labour from manufacturing into agriculture.

Broadly speaking, there are two main hypotheses as to why India did not experience industrial growth under colonial rule. They are briefly outlined. One explanation, exculpating the British, focusses on a large, cyclical downturn in the Indian economy. The long period of decline of the Mughal Empire caused supply-side problems. At the same time, there was a reduction in the Indian competitive advantage in the key cotton industry. The other explanation concentrates on the British impact. It stresses the effects of the incorporation of India into the British colonial economic system which caused a price shock in its key manufacturing tradable, cotton products. Clingingsmith and Williamson argue that both hypotheses are not only compatible but are reinforcing each other (Clingingsmith and Williamson).

Rothermund addresses an additional point. He argues that despite the fact that British rule brought some enablers of industrial development (such as the railways), industrialisation soon reached limits. Following Gerschenkron's theory of industrialisation in Europe, he identifies the scarcity of capital for investment into industry as a key limitation to economic development. There was a decisive lack of macro-financial structures to make funds available for investment, such as investment banks and state initiatives. This problem was compounded by a 'ruralisation' of money and a disadvantageous British currency policy (Rothermund, 1993; Kulke and Rothermund, 1998).

Thus, the economic conditions in India make the Gellnerian materialist approach to nationalism as a historical force irrelevant to the Indian pre-independence context. Kenneth Minogue was, therefore, well advised to use the Indian case as a starting point for a general critique of Gellner's theory –

> 'Again, consider India. Some elements of an industrial society developed under the British, especially during the First World War and others continued after independence. But the dominant strain of Indian nationalism was that of Gandhi, who was quite explicitly hostile to industrialism.' (Hall and Jarvie, 1996).

Given that there was no large-scale industrialisation in India under British rule, no 'high culture', in Gellner's sense of the word, could develop in India. There was no mobility, or atomisation, or anonymity on a mass scale. Traditional society, religions, castes, family and village life retained a firm grip on peoples' lives. The caste system is the most striking example. According to Gellner, nationalism occurred when the social stratifications of a static economy became disrupted and the new geographical demarcations of the high-culture developed (Gellner, 1983). The caste-system in India, however, representing the ultimate social stratification of a static economy, continues to exist and play an important role even unto this day.

It could be argued, of course, that there were other places from where a 'high culture' in Gellner's sense, could have originated. The Indian Civil Service had some amount of mobility and meritocratic equality as well as a common language, English. It has been proposed, furthermore, that the unity of views of the Indian Civil Service gave strength to India as a nation state (Roy). However, whilst the civil service certainly was an important structural cohesive under British rule, it was not the hotbed of a nationwide identity. The number of Indians in the upper echelons of the bureaucracy was, until the end of British rule, compared with the population as such, tiny. They were hardly enough to resemble a broad culture of nationalism compatible with Gellner's theory. Furthermore, with some notable exceptions, their position was conservative as their interests were naturally aligned with those of the colonial power. Indian soldiers in the Indian army may have become another focal point for the creation of a nationalist 'high culture', but after the 1857 mutiny, the British purposely emphasised the divisions among their Indian troops by drawing mainly on what they called the 'martial races', such as the Sikhs or Gurkhas, and by importing cultural Indian subdivisions into the army (Kulke and Rothermund).

The only occupations where Indian citizen were able to reach a relatively high status in terms of pay and influence and form significant networks were law and education. Thus, it was not surprising that these were also the first to articulate political aspirations (Kulke and Rothermund). However, this small group was not in the least representative of a bottom-up, popular 'high culture' on the scale Gellner envisaged. Thus, the British effect on Indian nationalism was to produce nationalist Indian elite communities. Or, more specifically still, individual nationalist leaders.

4.2.2 *First Intermediate Conclusion – Instability through Idealism*

What then, drove Indian nationalism? Nationalism in India was not the result of a social dynamic induced by economic changes. Instead, it is an idea, the product of the desires, beliefs and aspirations of individuals.

By way of speculation, it is likely that – applying Gellner's theory – economic growth would have created not one subcontinental high culture, but would have resulted in a number of idiom-based high cultures, for example a Tamil, Bengali, Kannada, Hindi and Urdu one. Bottom-up nationalisation in India would thereby have led to the creation of several nation states in the subcontinent. It could have also led to enormous bloodshed in the process.

A look at Europe can illustrate the issue. Like India, Europe has always been an area with a number of different languages and religions. Each region cherished its own idiosyncrasies and was governed independently by an aristocrat who often had only a limited bond with his subjects. On the other hand, Europe also shared an old, multi-layered common heritage and cultural affinities, as well as Pan-European social networks. The heritage was mainly the classical and the Judeo-Christian traditions of European life and thought, but also included pan-European myths based on, for example, the crusades, the reformation and counter-reformation, and the wars against Muslim invaders. The European common culture manifested itself in music, art or architecture, in an overlapping intellectual history and in an elite 'lingua franca', Latin throughout much of the Middle Ages and French until well into the twentieth century. Pan-European social networks were the Catholic Church or the intermarrying aristocracy. When nationalism became a potent force in the nineteenth century as a result of rapid industrialisation (following Gellner's theory), it led to a vivisection of the European cultural organism. Regional linguistic differences became stronger and were instrumentalised. National chauvinism and rivalries, especially between the rapidly industrialising states of Great Britain, France and, later, Germany took on a dreadful dynamic. In the wake of nationalisation and democratisation, history was reinterpreted, away from an elitist, European narrative and towards a popular, national narrative. Nationalism in Europe, possibly brought about by the materialist dynamics Gellner (or Andersen) describes, has severely damaged the fine web of Pan-European cultural links (Friedell).

The economic, social and intellectual dynamics of the industrial age have ultimately driven a Europe of nation states into disastrous wars (Hobsbawm). It was only after the Second World War that the idea of European unity, based on both an economic commonwealth and a shared culture, became a viable political project. Europe developed a supra-national umbrella organisation to organise the individual European nations according to a shared set of principles and values. Today, the EU is still more of a UN than a USA – sovereignty still rests more (but not exclusively) with the member states than with the European organisation. It is not a state.

India has taken a different route from a comparable starting point. Like Europe, it has always had both a significant shared culture as well as strong and diverse regional cultures. However, unlike Europe, where nationalism developed bottom-up (Smith) and not top-down, like Kedourie asserts (Kedourie), Indian nationalism follows Kedourie's theory more closely; the idea came before the fact. This probably made the creation of an Indian nation possible in the first place. On the other hand, however, the new Indian nation only had a limited identity-stability. It was based on an idea, and the idea itself, as will be argued below, is relatively abstract. If social and economic changes had produced regional nation states, as had happened in Europe, these would have been more stable both for being based on a prior ground-reality (homogenisation) as well as for being based on a 'thick' cultural affinity[82]. An Indian nationalism imposed on facts can be assumed

---

[82]Mishler and Pollack in their essay 'On Culture, Thick and Thin – Towards a Neo-Culturalist Synthesis' define 'thick' as opposed to a thin culture as (1) being important

to be less well embedded than one derived from facts. Ideological politics has to make up for a lack of natural stability.

4.3 Agency within Limits

Indian nationalism was a phenomenological process. But, was it also a Hegelian, teleological process, subject to an omnipotent 'higher logic' which necessarily unfolds? Or do we need to understand history through its key agents, and India as a 'self-interpreting animal' in Taylor's sense? An answer to this question has two main consequences – an inevitable nationalism would be both unoriginal and – supposedly – as a political force, more stable. India would be, for better or worse, merely part of a larger historical dynamic. If however, it is the product of conscious and original choices, an idiosyncratic response to the modern world, the nationalism would both be more flexible in content and effect as well as less stable. The nation would be in the hands of people rather than history.

Nehru wrote that the colonial situation created a 'unity of a common nationalism' and that the 'idea of a united and free India gripped the people'. Nationalism to him was not simply an artificial idea or sentiment imposed on the masses by an elite. It was, instead, 'the natural outcome of that fundamental unity which had been the background of Indian life for thousands of years... nationalism... is the dominant urge of the time and must triumph.' (Nehru, 2003). Indian nationalism, by this logic was the modern manifestation of a prior unity. The colonial experience merely brought it out. Such a statement, of course, is the typical battle cry of a nationalist leader, who is ever in need of giving his action both a historical and a popular legitimation. On the theoretical level, any proposition that colonial nationalism springs either directly from or in direct reaction to the West and that it took on a non-reflected, quasi-deterministic form, suggests that history has 'decreed' that Indians 'shall only be perpetual consumers of modernity'. In such a theory, according to the Indian scholar Partha Chatterjee, Europe and the Americas would be the only real subjects of history. They would have thought out on India's behalf 'not only the script of colonial enlightenment and exploitation, but also that of our anti-colonial resistance and postcolonial misery. Even our imagination must remain forever colonised.' Chatterjee continues to explain that he rejects such a

politically, (2) having a quasi primordial foundation, (3) being an 'a priori', (4) being externally differentiated, internally homogenous, durable and (5) providing political orientation (Pollack, D., 2003, pp. 237–257).

view not for sentimental reasons, but because he believes it to be a mistaken interpretation of anti-colonial nationalism –

> 'The most powerful as well as the most creative results of the nationalist imagination in Asia and Africa are posited not in identity but rather on a difference with the 'modular' forms of the national society propagated by the modern West.' (Chatterjee, Balakrishnan, G., 1996).

Was Indian nationalism a fabrication based on Western blocs of thought? Or, could Indian nationalism claim agency? And if so, then in what way? Where does originality and authenticity arise? The question has been a core issue for much postcolonial analysis.

4.3.1 *Idealism – The Dynamic of the Postcolonial Self*

Kedourie claims that nationalism – being based on an idea – arrived in the colonies, ('it is now generally agreed'), as a 'reaction against European domination' (Kedourie). In India's case, the nationalists have fallen victim to a European orientalism. Gandhi and other educated Indians, he points out, have 'adopted from European authors a romantic notion of the Indian past', and with 'this fiction' confront present reality. They conjured up an image of a people with specific characteristics and great moral strength. Such thinking was, for Kedourie, very much the usual symptom of the nationalist virus – 'There is, then, nothing particularly original in Gandhi's contrast between Europe's corruption and India's innocence'. He thinks it remarkable that Gandhi, 'this apostle of Indian tradition', has a picture of the Indian tradition 'entirely derived from European sources' (i.e. pre-packed and infected with nationalist thought and language) and that he himself even claims these sources as a 'warrant of his assertions' (Kedourie, 1971).

According to Kedourie's argument, the impact of colonialism was such that the elites in the colonies somehow got lost in between their traditional world and the new, European world – and subsequently decided to turn the idea of nationalism, 'Europe's latest gift to the world', against their oppressors (Kedourie, 1971). Being an avowed critic of nationalism, Kedourie regards it as a malignant idea, a disease almost, which spread from the coloniser to the colonised. To him, post-colonial nationalism was primarily built on a rebellious emancipation and (Western) utopian idealism –

> 'It developed rather among young officers and bureaucrats, whose families were sometimes obscure, sometimes eminent, who were educated in the

> Western methods and ideas, often at the expense of the State, and who as a result came to despise their elders, and to hanker for the shining purity of a new order to sweep away the hypocrisy, the corruption, and the decadence which they felt inexorably choking them and their society.' (Kedourie, 1993).

Of course, in this interpretation, where the independence movements focussed quite narrowly on a stereotypical, almost reflexive nationalism, there is little room for originality of thought or independent political agency. Kedourie also views the nationalist struggle between Congress and the Muslim League about partition in this light. There was little choice. Given the unfolding of the idea of nationalism in modern India, the subcontinent was simply –

> '...impaled on the horns of a dilemma which no man could surmount, a dilemma consisting of two propositions, one that India was two nations and the other that India was one nation. This dilemma dominated Indian politics because Indian politicians came to speak a Western political idiom'.

He elaborates on this point, explaining that Indians at the time were very impressed with all things European, and hence they imitated the fashionable idiom of nationalism. Nationalism in India, to Kedourie, was a reflexive, almost mechanical product of the European way of thinking. In picking up the language of nationalism –

> '...they were like many other Asians and Africans who also picked up the idiom. But in picking it up, did they know what the idiom assumed or implied? Did they have a clear view of the syntax or some idea of the etymology? It is safe to say that most who spoke this language rather took it for granted, accepted it unquestioningly, in the belief that it was the only possible language in the world, coeval with humanity itself, and unprofitable therefore much to examine and scrutinise.' (Kedourie, 1971).

If the European nationalists were already on what he called a children's crusade, the nationalists in the colonies, it seems, were on a crusade even more naïve, because it seemed childishly derived from a children's crusade. This assessment of Indian nationalism is incorrect. It assumes that the idea of nationalism, like a contagious virus, simply spreads without significant adaptation or modification and without a noteworthy intellectual contention with the conditions of colonialism. Nationalism, however, does not develop in such a linear way. The colonial experience did not simply encompass the concept of nationalism; rather, the colonial challenge demanded a reaction and created the Indian nationalism (Kulke and Rothermund, 1998). It was the burning glass, by which a 'hitherto vague and diffused self-consciousness coalesced for the first time into the articulation of a position vis-à-vis imperialist rule' (Som, 2004).

Possibly the most famous example of Hegel's phenomenological dialectic at work is that of the master and the slave – two fictitious individuals (non-socialised wills), not having met anyone else before, come into contact believing the whole world to be an outgrowth of themselves and subject to their will. They inevitably clash and one subdues the other. Whilst the victor, the master, has his view of the world confirmed and continues as before, the slave is confronted with an experience irreconcilable with his previous worldview. He consequently undergoes the painful but highly rewarding process of readjusting his worldview as well as his view of himself. Progress thus moves through the slave, whilst the master is being phased out of the argument (Hegel, 2004). As in Hegel's dialectic, the colonial experience posited the 'other' and triggered in Indian minds a new way to reflect and understand the 'self'. The colonial critique thus provided 'a ready reference point against which Indians could conceptualise and analyse their arguments regarding their traditional heritage and define and redefine their weakness and strength' (Som, 2004). But what precisely did colonialism trigger? Was it a mechanical, phenomenological process or was colonialism merely the initiator of something that turned out to be much more, namely, a new thought-product innovatively addressing the challenges of modernity?

One way to understand the relationship between the colonised and the coloniser is 'mimicry'. According to Homi Bhabha, this is 'one of the most elusive and effective strategies of colonial power and knowledge' (Bhabha, 1994). In Bhabha's version of the Master-Slave-Dialectic the colonial subject does not arrive at a synthesis, but is instead trapped within a futile but continuous process of gesturing towards the source of identity, the grounds of cultural origins and the image of home. The outcome can neither be 'original', because the act is a repetition, nor can it be 'identical', because it is defined by difference. Baucom called this the 'entrapment of the colonial subject' (Baucom, 1992). The colonisers encouraged mimicry in order to legitimise their own rule and normalise or de-originate the native, thereby making them the same, but not quite the same (Bhabha, 1990). This 'epic intention of the civilising mission' produces a discourse 'rich in the traditions of trompe-l'oeil, irony, mimicry and repetition'. The 'mimic man... becomes transformed into an uncertainty which fixes the colonial subject as a "partial" presence' (Bhabha, 1994). Indian national identity – in this narrative – is lost in translation. Bhabha has been criticised for offering an explanation of nationalism too cerebral and ethereal, and for a lack of interest in the socio-economic institutions and other forms of political practices (Parry, 2004). In Bhabha's narrative there is, moreover, a strongly fatalist element, leaving India with an unoriginal, derivative and fragmented identity, and no way to escape. This view does not do justice to the enormous achievement of the modern Indian state, whose identity surpasses the condition of mere mimicry.

Partha Chatterjee, by contrast, has argued that there is something deeply original about Indian nationalism. To him, any history of nationalism on the materialist (political) stratum must necessarily converge with the notion that Indian nationalism was unimaginative (Chatterjee, 1996). Chatterjee, therefore, instead focusses his analysis of Indian nationalism not on the openly political struggle for independence, but on the underlying development of a national idea. Quite like in Hegel's dialectic, the colonial master's power forced the politically aware Indians into a phenomenological inner sphere. In this inner domain, cultural difference could be used to prevent a complete loss of autonomy. Cultural traits became portrayed as markers of an essential and superior cultural difference from the coloniser – 'the domain of the "national" was defined as one that was different from the "Western"' (Chatterjee, 1993). In the 'inner domain' – he gives Bengal as an example – developed a literary, artistic, educational imagined community of a highly creative nature. This innovative Indian response to modernity is the escape route from the trap of colonial and postcolonial conditioning (Chatterjee, 1986). In this 'inner domain', nationalism 'launches its most powerful, creative, and historically significant project – to fashion a "modern" national culture that is nevertheless not Western' (Chatterjee, 1996). In Chatterjee's argument, Indian nationalism is a withdrawn or 'shy' reaction to the colonial power, which does not spill over into the outer, material domain.

Gyan Prakash, like Chatterjee and Bhabha, also views Indian nationalism as a 'search for a postcolonial modernity (an original identity) that has been tied, from its very birth, with its struggle against modernity (a derived identity)' (Chatterjee, 1993). Prakash, however, does not believe in the relevance of a distinction between an inner, spiritual domain and an outer, material domain (Prakash). Rather, he argues that hegemonic nationalism should be understood as a political project based on critiquing Western modernity while establishing India as a modern nation (Prakash). In this argument, as in Chatterjee's argument, the Hegelian dialectic is successful. The difference is (to use Hegelian language) that the synthesis – an Indian modernity – is also made explicit. India was, he argues, actualised as a 'culturally rooted moral community with a rational will to industrialise and achieve technological mastery'. Thus, India had to express itself in the language of modernity but its modern articulation had to be irreducibly different from its colonial expression (Prakash, 1999).

The crucial thought processes of Indian nationalism were not merely an emulation of or reaction to the West, but a creative synthesis, a particularly Indian approach to modernity. Bhabha's or Chatterjee's narratives may apply to some members of the second row of nationalists. It would be severely mistaken, however, to deny figures of world-historical significance such as Gandhi or Nehru the recognition that they have provided Indian nationalism with an approach both highly original and intensely political along the lines of Prakash's interpretation.

Bhabha, Chatterjee and Prakash, as well as Hegel, focus their attention on a larger phenomenological dynamic, encompassing something like a mass consciousness or a non-rational and implicit *volonté générale*. This perspective pushes political elites into the background. Their actions and ideas are essentially subsumed under this larger dynamic. Such a view runs counter to popular accounts of Indian nationalist historiography. How important was the role of elites?

The 'Subaltern' group of historians has provided a very influential critical assessment of the role of the elites in the National Movement. Guha, in particular, challenges the conventional narrative that Indian nationalism is perceived as 'primarily an idealist venture in which the indigenous elite led the people from subjugation to freedom', whereby 'the history of Indian nationalism is thus written up as a sort of biography of the elite' (Guha, and Spivak, 1988). Too little attention is paid, in his view, to the efforts and decisions made by the members of the rebellious subaltern classes. Nor is their conflictual relationship with the elites sufficiently explored. Guha's argument is highly relevant in understanding the manifold roots from which Indian nationalism developed and the complex dynamic which took a hold in India. However, the national identity towards which ideological politics are directed in the end depends to a significant degree on both a small leadership's ability to shape a consistent point of view from a multiplicity of interests and views and on the leadership's ability to present a unified view in nationalist historiography. As long as the subaltern voices do not become part of the mainstream and do not present a relatively coherent body of beliefs, they will not affect the 'official' national identity of the Indian state and the identity of those who matter for foreign policy. Spivak has elaborated on the troubles of making the subaltern voice heard (Spivak, in Ashcroft, Griffiths, et al. 2006).

Interpretations of Indian nationalism tend to emphasise a historical, sociological or anthropological narrative, be it simple and linear or complex and synthetic, prolific or barren, progressive or tragic. And they do so ultimately at the expense of individual (elite) agency. The argument proposed here, on the other hand, returns to the actors of popular historiography. They had the power to create a 'self-interpreting' nationalism. It was acting freely not only in Roshwald's sense of being free to pursue one's interests in the face of limiting circumstances, but free in the more elaborate, ethical and full sense used by Taylor – being capable of interpreting oneself and ones surroundings, and of developing strategies based on circumstances, judgment and values.

In how far such actors can effectively change the course of events and shape a country's identity, depends of course on the circumstances as well as on the character of the elites themselves. It is impossible to generalise. In the specific case of India, during the National Movement, there has been an abundance of unusually high calibre leaders. These individuals were capable of developing their own syntheses and innovative solutions to the problems faced by their country. Their views often diverged and sometimes conflicted. Nevertheless, Indian nationalism and Indian national identity bore their imprint. This is not to deny that impersonal forces or some kinds of group dialectics also played a significant role. It is to say, however, that within certain constraints, Indian nationalist leaders – especially Gandhi and Nehru – were able to make crucial choices concerning Indian national identity and the nature of the independent state. While non-agent-centered theories of a nationalist logic are very useful in explaining why nationalism arose in India in the first place, we have to look at the actors to understand how it manifested itself and why it took a specific direction. The British may have first exposed India to the concept of the modern nation. Their reverence to it, as well as the apparent strength of the British nation, may have made the idea very appealing to some Indian intellectuals (Brown, 1985). These then took up the challenge – and they did so in an imaginative manner.

4.3.2 *Second Intermediate Conclusion – Instability through Agency*

The primary concern of Indian elites has been the creation of a viable Indian nation state. Self-interest may have played a role in India, but was, in contrast to other postcolonial nationalist movements, not dominant. Although there remains an enormous gap between the ruler and the ruled, it would be misleading to view the elites as neo-colonial impostors. Their motives were fundamentally different from those of the British colonisers. This view challenges Chatterjee's argument that the elites merely sought to replace the colonial rulers and were not interested in truly emancipating the masses, and that their aim was not that of creating a new approach to modernity, but rather that of securing mass support for their own attempt at gaining power, thus creating an unequal, neo-colonial power relation. Instead, they provided a much needed modern self-interpretation of the Indian nation in the name of the silent masses from a patronising but largely disinterested position.

Gandhi is possibly the best example of Taylor's self-interpretation. He directed his powers of self-interpretation, as a private individual, at himself, and, as a political leader, at his interaction with others, at Indian society at large and at the state to come. The hallmarks of self-interpretation are authenticity and originality. Whilst the Indian National Movement always had idiosyncratic leaders and elements, it became truly unique and distinctive when Mohandas Gandhi took charge in 1920. He did not merely guide the political struggle, but 'imposed on it a unique moral code and a technique of action, that of non-violence' (Masselos, 2005). He did so by way of his own example, through his communication and through the concerted promotion and development of new leaders, infused with his ideas and spirit (the last of which, Morarji Desai, determined India's course until as late as 1979).

He certainly worked within a context. Western ideas made an impression on him. Yet, neither was his scope confined to the idea of nationalism, nor did he simply emulate what he found in the West. He was attracted mainly to radically humanist literature of writers such as Leo Tolstoy, Henry David Thoreau or John Ruskin, as well as to aspects of the New Testament, especially the Sermon on the Mount. None of these sources figure in Kedourie's account of the history of the idea of nationalism. Despite being an admirer of the British constitution and a British lawyer, Gandhi was firmly rooted in the Indian tradition. However, he also did not take Indian tradition for granted but significantly reinterpreted and updated it (Rudolph and Rudolph, 1983). Synthesising, selecting, emphasising, inventing, he 'evolved a pattern of thought and a programme of political action uniquely his own. The force of his individuality made him outstanding both in his Indian context and outside' (Masselos, 2005).

To argue that the content of Indian nationalism was the product of elite agency rather than of an inevitably unfolding historical dialectic, to argue, therefore, that nationalism was contingent is to argue that it is both original and relatively unstable. The idea of any person or group, however appealing to the masses and skillfully communicated, will always produce a more fickle popular sentiment than an idea driven forth by a determinist momentum. However, there are qualifiers which influence both stability as well as the identity-power of such a contingent nationalist idea. An elite can choose to link its idea to the past, thus usually trading-off originality for stability, innovation for primordial identity links. What use did the Indian nationalist elite make of the past?

4.4 The Selection of a Past – Neglect, Emphasis and Invention

Nationalist leaders in India as much as nationalists elsewhere claimed that the country which they seek to represent has an ancient lineage, a primordial 'national' identity. Nationalism, however, a political communal identity on a mass, anonymous scale, is a modern phenomenon in India (Khilnani, 1998; Talbot, 2000; Masselos, 2005). It links an imagined community to the question of who rules whom and sometimes, as in communist or democratic nationalist movements, even to the question of who rules how. It is therefore an oxymoron to call India an 'ancient nation'. It has an ancient culture, but is a modern nation like all other nations. The question is, how much of India's ancient culture is part of the identity of the modern Indian nation state? Is the modern Indian nation the result of a paradigm shift in Kuhn's sense? Is it a revolutionary reinterpretation of the political community? Or is the Indian nation the evolutionary outcome, the inevitable modern interpretation of a long term, possibly perennial, 'Indianness'? If elites shaped the mainstream Indian nationalism, what was the relationship of their ideas to India's past? How much was invented, how much selectively emphasised, and how much was simply rephrased in modern nationalist language?

4.4.1 *The Limits of Primordial Theories*

Rothermund distinguishes among three views of the Indian nation at the end of the nineteenth century. One view was that of the British bureaucrats. To most of them, India was not a nation. It was simply an amalgam of various cultures and peoples. Independence would be tantamount to chaos. Opposing this view, there were two broad stands of Indian nationalists. The moderates believed that India was not yet a nation. It needed to become one. This could best be achieved through a gradual political progress within the established framework. The radical extremists, such as Bal Gangadhar

Tilak or Aurobindo Ghose, on the other hand, believed that India was indeed a nation with a long tradition, which became paralysed by long periods of foreign rule and needs to be reawakened by conflict with the British authorities (Kulke and Rothermund, 1998).

One difficulty in talking about nationalism is that it is often impossible to discern between a nationalist's comments or writings qua politicised nationalist or qua objective analyst. If the radicals, for example, declare that India is an ancient nation, the question arises whether they believe what they say or whether their declaration is already politics? Do they still construct an identity, or do they already embody it themselves?

If we accept the previous argument that ancient nations do not exist, we can circumvent this problem. Regardless of whether or not a nationalist himself actually believes that India is an 'ancient nation', what counts is only the nature of the 'nation' he proclaims or builds. Let us assume, for the moment, that the nationalist is conscious in dealing with nationalism, that he is making use of the past in order to construct an identity. He would likely be using India's ancient, diverse and complex culture as the raw material for constructing 'his' Indian nation. What relationship is there between the materials and the construction? It could be possible that the material itself already is the construction (as in a cave) and the nationalist simply needs to recognise and communicate this. There would then be, a priori, an actual, underlying cultural unity or 'Leitkultur'[83], which naturally distinguishes India and designates a common denominator. It could also be the case, however, that the material has no particular meaning in itself, and for the construction anything can be used (as in a house). Elites would, then, simply fabricate an identity. The third option is, naturally, the middle ground. Is there local material which sets limitations and preferences for the type of construction that can be built with it (as in a house made with locally available materials)? In this case, elites would use the primordial

[83]The term 'Leitkultur' (lead culture) was used by Bassam Tibi to demarcate European cultural modernity. It incorporates secularism, reason, pluralism tolerance, and democracy (Tibi, B., 1998). Theo Sommer, publisher of the German weekly Die Zeit, used the term in an article referring to a 'German Leitkultur' to which immigrants should adapt (Sommer, T., 1998). The concept subsequently became heavily embattled in public. Leitkultur refers to the identity basis of a community, a canon of values and a cultural way of life, which regulates interaction and gives people a common sense of belonging. Norbert Lammert, President of the German Bundestag, said in an interview with the newspaper 'Die Welt' – 'If a Europe of diversity wants to conserve its national identities and yet develop a collective identity, it needs a political Leitidee (guiding idea), a common foundation of values and beliefs. Such a European Leitidee will inevitably refer to common roots, to a common history, and to common religious traditions' (Lammert, N., 2005).

raw materials at hand in such a way so as to serve their particular purpose – taking some, leaving others, combining them, and possibly importing some further materials to make the construction solid. They would be, however, limited by the local geography. The structure furthermore, would be useful only in relation to the surrounding environment. Building an igloo in the desert would be impossible and pointless. Only certain types of nationalism are functional under given conditions.

The belief that a country's past and social traditions present a single, visible thread available to the nationalist who just has to pick it up and transform it into a political movement, is a fiction. There is no cave to be discovered. Precisely this, however, is a common belief among nationalists. They like to present an uninterrupted, clear-cut (easily communicable) and usually romanticised and glorified 'national past'. It is also common to blend out parts of the past which contradict their specific political purpose and emphasise others leading to 'simplistic and stereotypical historical narratives of community consciousness' (Talbot, 2000). In that sense, nationalist historiography is a never ending battle for the interpretative high ground (Geary, 2002). Whilst simplistic nationalist historiography is a serious reduction of even relatively homogenous cultures, such as, say, Japan or France, it becomes a ludicrous proposal in India's case. Indian culture and history is extremely diverse and complex. It is one of changing cores and changing peripheries. There is no relatively easy linguistic, or historical, or ethnic, or even religious lever. India is fundamentally plural. It is, as Brass wrote –

> '...a multi-ethnic society in which there are a large number of ethnic groups which vary in size from highly localised caste and tribal groups to great language and religious groups, in which no single group is clearly dominant, and in which the boundaries between groups are not entirely fixed. These groups also vary enormously in the extent to which a self-conscious awareness of a common identity different from other groups exists among them.' (Brass, 1974).

This complexity creates enormous hurdles for all forms of nationalisms, even religious or linguistic ones, which are hampered by disunity along other dimensions such as labour or caste groups (Weiner, 1967). So what makes so many people into one people, if there is no archetypal Indian, as there is an archetypal Englishman or Frenchman, 'for the simple fact... that we are all minorities in India' (Tharoor, 2006)? It cannot be religion, or ethnicity, or language, or culture in the narrow sense. In 'The Great Indian

Novel', Tharoor's answer to this question is twofold – it is the geography which provides a natural framework and it is the foreigners, the Greeks, the Chinese, the Muslims, the Europeans who consistently perceived the people of Hindustan, living in the lands beyond the Indus and the Himalayas, as being one group (Tharoor, 1989). Geography and classification by foreigners are, however, merely external brackets. The question remains – what positively makes up the Indian identity for the Indian himself? What are the 'strong but invisible threads by which India is held together' (Nehru)? In an article in Catalyst, Tharoor expanded on this issue and called Indian nationalism the 'nationalism of an idea', an idea, as Tagore and Sen have explained, of 'one land embracing many' (Tharoor, 2006). Or, in Nehru's words, India is 'an elusive quality… a myth and an idea, a dream and a vision, and yet very real and present and pervasive.' (Nehru, 1946).

Yes, but which state embraces which lands – and why? What is the myth, the idea, the dream, the vision with which a majority of Indians can associate themselves? What is the unity, the structuring element in diversity? There is a Brahmanic, elitist, stratified cultural commonality and an implicit 'way of life' that may characterise India to a certain extent[84]. It may be sufficient social cohesive for the traditional, the rural and the poor masses; for all those, whose life is highly limited geographically and often deeply rooted in specific traditions. These people can be politically mobilised, and they do – much to the credit of the Indian democracy – take political initiatives in issues of direct concern to their everyday life. However, their need for an overarching identity is limited. The urban middle and upper classes, however, the potential political entrepreneurs and mobilisers, require more to associate themselves with India at large, they require a shared identity of some explicitness. This is where political nationalism comes in.

---

[84]In the essay 'Brahmanical Ideology and Regional Identities', Embree elaborates on the point that certain civilisational linkages provide a basis for modern political unity (Embree, A. T., 1989, pp. 9–27). Gandhi also occasionally espoused this view that India was one nation because there existed, from time immemorial, elites connected by pilgrimage – 'Our leading men travelled throughout India… They learned one another's languages, and there was no aloofness between them'. Those who first established the pilgrimage sites 'saw that India was one undivided land so made by nature. They, therefore, argued that it must be one nation. Arguing thus, they established holy places in various parts of India, and fired the people with the idea of nationality in a manner unknown in other parts of the world' (Gandhi, M., 1997, pp. 48–49). In Gandhi's case, the argument is probably more nationalist politics than personal belief.

As a result of the enormous complexity, however, not one but a number of nationalisms developed. Many of them were regional. On a supra-regional level, three main and competing nationalist approaches to interpreting India's past have been developed – the liberal-secular 'One Nation Theory' of the Gandhian/Nehruvian type and the Muslim and Hindu versions of the 'Two Nation Theory'. According to the former, India is a nation based on traditions transcending the divides of religion or language. According to the Hindu 'Two Nation Theory', India is based on a politically functional, concentrated tradition of Hinduism called Hindutva[85]. Of course, Kedourie is right when he says that both the 'One Nation Theory' and the 'Two Nation Theory' are fictions (Kedourie, 1971). This is beside the point, however. They are fictions related to a tradition and translated into an identity. They are thereby made real. How does this process happen?

Here, the focus is limited to the Gandhian/Nehruvian 'One Nation Theory' which prevailed and became the mainstay of Indian national identity. Gandhi's stance is true to the spirit of nationalism –

> 'The English have taught us that we were not one nation before, and that it will require centuries before we will become one nation. This is without foundation. We were one nation before they came to India. One thought inspired us. Our mode of life was the same. It was because we were one nation that they were able to establish one kingdom. Subsequently they divided us'.

Despite frequent excursions into Hindu tradition, Gandhi's interpretation of what constitutes India as a nation is not based on Hinduism, but rather on India's supra-religious 'faculty for assimilation', India's unique tradition of tolerance and pluralism. It 'has ever been such a country' (Gandhi, 1997). Parel explains this notion –

> 'When Gandhi says that the Indian nation has been created by a process of *samas* (a grammatical technique of forming a new word by integrating two or more pre-existing words) he means that though the nation is formed out of distinct ethnic, religious and linguistic groups, the new identity that emerges has an identity of its own. India in this sense is a nation. Gandhi is a cultural assimilationist in that all Indians, while retaining their sub-national identities, are supposed to share certain common values and symbols' (Parel, in Gandhi, 1997).

In particular, Gandhi refutes the idea that nationalism has a religious base. Religion is a private matter ('in reality, there are as many religions

---

[85]The 'Two Nation Theories' are discussed later. Of the two, the Muslim version is only of limited importance, because, being embodied in the state of Pakistan, it did not filter into Indian foreign policy directly.

as there are individuals'). Hindus and Mohammedans 'own the same ancestors, and the same blood runs through their veins' (Gandhi, 1997). Such a statement is – technically speaking – arbitrary. In a sense, the same blood runs through everyone's veins. However, it is politically highly potent. What Gandhi does is to emphasise certain traits in Indian culture, traits which, as seen here are not self-evident and positions them as flagship values of his Indian 'Leitkultur'. These are – secularism, pluralism and tolerance. While they are not omnipresent and dominant in Indian culture and history, they do nevertheless resonate with the people, because they have a foundation in India's past. There is an imaginary link between the Buddha, Ashoka, Akbar, and Gandhi. The link is, however, arbitrary to the extent that it is a highly selective reading of India's past, that an aspect of Indian culture is tacitly conflated with the *entirety* of Indian culture[86]. Does Europe have a deeply tolerant and peaceful tradition, because of the Stoa, Jesus Christ, Erasmus of Rotterdam and the EU? It is a fiction by virtue of its selectiveness.

However, the selection is based in an actual past (although this may be distorted). At the same time as focussing on certain traits, Gandhi entirely de-emphasises the Hindu-Muslim divide by depoliticising religion as such. His interpretation of Indian tradition thus runs directly counter to that of Jinnah's Muslim League or Savarkar's Hindutva movement. Given that rival nationalisms in India have made use of different interpretations of the past of one and the same culture, the question arises, what is the actual relationship between the past and modern nationalism? Were Indian nationalists able to simply instrumentalise tradition in any way for their own purposes? Or are there primordial links, cultural 'facts'? How malleable is India's past?

To answer this question, Paul Brass provides a very good starting point. Brass is concerned primarily with what can be called Indian sub-nationalisms, with ethnic movements within the Indian modern state representing only a fraction of the whole. These build their identities around their Hindu or Muslim religion or around a regional language. He emphasises the role of elites in creating ethnic nationalisms, the dynamics of elite competitions and their divisive nature (Brass, 1974; 1991; 2003). What is here considered to be the mainstream Indian nationalism, the pluralist nationalism of the Gandhian/Nehruvian type, is not in his focus. Nevertheless, his analysis of the role of elites in generating a community identity is highly instructive. As shown before, Brass thinks that nationalism

[86]To argue that India is a Hindu nation is at least as fictitious, if not more so – this argument rests on a distortion of both Indian history and Hindu religion.

is a product of elite machinations. They mobilise masses around symbols or ideas according to their own interests. They do so with varying degrees of success. However, they do not act in a cultural vacuum – firstly, they are 'constrained by the beliefs and values which exist within the group and which limit the kinds of appeals which can be made'. Secondly, he argues that in the process of mobilisation around ethnic identities, the elite 'simplifies those beliefs and values, distorts them, and selects those which are politically useful rather than central to the belief systems of the people in question.' (Brass, 1991). He asserts that the process of identity formation for an 'inter-ethnic, composite... national culture', such as the mainstream Gandhian/Nehruvian nationalism, is essentially the same as that for ethnic nationalisms.

In 'Ethnicity and Nationalism', Brass gives three examples for traditional symbols used by elites in South Asia for nationalist purposes – the cow, the Sharia and the Urdu language. Of the cow, for example, he says that it is 'always potentially a symbol that can be called up by Hindu religious or political elites to mobilise large numbers of Hindus either to build internal unity or to engage in action directed against Muslims' (Brass). These symbols do not have a political dynamic in themselves, but they resonate well, if used. Long persisting cultural communities, thereby, 'constrain the free manipulation of cultural symbols', without, however, entirely preventing their manipulation 'or even alteration of their meaning' (Brass). The symbols provided by a culture can be seen as building blocks for nationalists. Like Lego bricks, they have certain properties and are thus suitable for certain general types of structure. Each symbol relates to specific groups in specific ways. Brass describes, for example, that the Sharia is not a good symbol to mobilise the entire Muslim community. Some Muslims condone it, other reject it (Brass, 1991). However, the bricks can be put to use in very different structures. 'Hinduism', for example, has an entirely different symbolic meaning for Savarkar than for Gandhi. At the same time, however, it is clear that both Hindutva and Gandhi were products of India, representing facets of India. The men and their ideas had a heritage in India. Their nationalism was not as artificial as say, Ataturk's radically modernising nationalism in Turkey.

Looking at nationalism from an ethnic perspective, Brass has developed a pessimistic opinion of elites as acting only in their own interest – 'When primordial symbols are brought forth into the political arena, it is likely that a particular elite stands to gain from their use' (Brass). This opinion can be supported by countless examples of self-interested elites. The argument here is that Indian secular nationalism is an exception. To Brass, even to establish a nationalism based on an allegedly multiethnic consensus is simply tantamount to 'the freezing of a particular system of elite collaboration and elite advantage' (Brass, 1991). However, the leaders of India's mainstream nationalism, and especially Gandhi and Nehru, did not act primarily in their own interest. They developed a nationalism based on value symbols rather than more divisive and emotive symbols in order to ensure the survival of an Indian nation state. In doing so, they had to work with the relatively blunter identity-creating tool of abstract values instead of the sharper ones such as language, religion or ethnicity.

4.4.2 *Third Intermediate Conclusion – Instability by Choice*

We can take Brass' idea of the differing strength and richness of cultural traditions a step further to argue that a particular nationalism differs in strength and richness depending not only on the cultural basis but also on its affinity to the cultural framework within which it is developed, and on the way in which tradition is used symbolically. This is a matter of leadership choice. Symbols, as Lippmann famously wrote, are essential –

> '…for the real environment is altogether too big, too complex, and too fleeting for direct acquaintance. We are not equipped to deal with so much subtlety, so much variety, so many permutations and combinations. And although we have to act in that environment, we have to reconstruct it on a simpler model before we can manage with it' (Lippmann, 2004).

This simpler model – here, nationalism – can make use of different types of symbols. Elites give direction and thereby meaning to the reconstruction of the past.

There is an important distinction between symbols which are 'already there' and as concrete as the cow or the Sharia and more abstract political notions and symbols which need to be given a meaning first (such as, for example, a new constitution). The former are more easily communicated than the latter; and they are more readily available and easily wielded as political tools. Moreover, symbols which are simple and obvious, such as ethnicity, language, dress code or traditional living habits are more easily instrumentalised than abstract symbols such as political values. Ordinary people can more easily relate to them.

There is a further difference, namely that between 'emotional' political notions and 'rational' political notions – or values in the positive sense (Elder and Cobb, 1983). History has demonstrated time and again that it is easier to rally people around an idea, however absurd, that creates images of clarity, superiority, difference or enmity in the minds of a group, than it is to rally people around an idea requiring restraint, tolerance and differentiation. Masses unfortunately are more easily 'animalised' than 'civilised' by political leaders. For this reason, leaders are also more tempted to 'animalise' rather than 'civilise'. While the 'emotional' option is easily used in conjunction with symbols as emotional amplifiers, the 'rational' option is the result of a much more difficult political process for which symbols are less easily used. However, while symbols are powerful, wielding them by appealing to emotions tends to involve a loss of control. Symbols appealing to emotions are quicker unleashed and more difficult to channel than symbols appealing to reason. This is the reason why many liberal thinkers, such as Kedourie are afraid of the use of symbolism in ideological politics.

Clifford Geertz has identified five types of nation/state relations in multi-ethnic situations. They include – asymmetrical and symmetrical duality (one state, one nation, where the overlap is either perfect or imperfect), asymmetrical multiplicity (one nation in several states), multiple ethnic fragmentation (many nations in one state), and the most complex type of all, a non-hierarchical fuzziness, characterised by 'a relatively even gradation of groups in importance, from several large ones through several medium-sized ones, with no clearly dominant ones and no sharp cut-off points.' (Geertz, 1967). This, he argues, is where India belongs. The challenge of creating a common emotional bond for such a construct is immense.

Brass attempts to explain how this challenge was approached in India. He makes a distinction between nationalism and patriotism. His idea of nationalism is what could be called ethnic nationalism, an identity based on common language or religion as could be witnessed in Japan or Western Europe. Such a model, he rightly asserts 'is simply not relevant to the Indian subcontinent'. The model relevant to India is that of the multi-national state, as in the Soviet Union, Yugoslavia and Switzerland. 'These nations are bound together in a single political territorial unit by feelings of patriotism derived from ideology, memories of a common struggle against external or alien powers, and rational calculations of advantage... but not by a common nationality' (Brass, 1974). Brass' distinction between patriotism and nationalism is not followed here. What he calls patriotism is the pan-Indian emotive, identity-giving force of the Gandhian/Nehruvian mainstream nationalism. This force ensures the survival of India as a unified state.

With the benefit of hindsight, a look at Brass' examples is instructive. Of the three multi-ethnic states, two no longer exist. The Soviet Union as well as Yugoslavia were held together primarily by their totalitarian regimes using an anti-national ideology – communism – to legitimise themselves. After the regimes have gone, the states have broken up. Their common identity was clearly too weak to uphold the multi-ethnic state. Switzerland, of course, has survived; and it has survived precisely because of a strong national identity, or 'common nationality'. The identity is based on shared values and a shared history (including a freedom struggle) as well as on nationalist symbols (such as the flag) and historiography (such as the Rütli-Schwur). The mainstream Indian national identity, which has similarities to the Swiss national identity, is the product of nationalism, of a conscious nationalist identity-creation.

In terms of nation-building, the pluralist 'One India Theory' effectively trades-off a strong national identity for unity and equality. The second theory, Hindutva, strives to create a strong identity for a smaller community, working with exclusion and taking into account division. According to Thomas Pantham, 'the Hindutva ideology of militant, majoritarian nationalism rests on a power-political conception of religion' (Mehta and Pantham, 2006). Religion is used as a strong identity builder. India as a nation state and the mainstream nationalism took the other route. It opted for the 'soft' Gandhian/Nehruvian value-based liberal nationalism. A national idea based on more abstract notions than language, religion or 'thick' culture in order to hold together such a vastly diverse people, is a relatively weaker identity link.

Was there really a choice? Yes and no. Looking at India from a humane and responsible standpoint, an application of the 'Two Nation Theory' to the entire subcontinent would have created even more bloodshed than the India/Pakistan partition already did. After partition, there were approximately 40 million Muslims who became citizens of the Republic of India (today, there are approximately 150 million). Jinnah, when asked what they should now do, told them to become loyal citizens of India. To suggest that the Indian nation is based on a particularly defined Hindu heritage and that Muslims do not belong to it, is to invite self-destruction. Such a concrete, symbolic 'ethnic' nationalism would be, in Brass' words, a 'double-edged sword', a nationalism 'emotionally powerful' but 'dangerous to use', threatening civil disorder, because while unifying one group, it would be divisive in the society as a whole (Brass, 1991). Unfortunately, however, such dire consequences have not always deterred political entrepreneurs. In history, there are plenty of examples in which peoples and countries have shown a remarkable potential for radical self-destruction through civil war. And in India hardly a day goes by without religious clashes, fuelled by communalist ideologues. What can be said with some certainty is that the India we know today, in its present shape and make-up, would not be able to continue to exist under a less inclusive, more specific and 'ethnic' type of nationalism. In that sense, there is no real alternative to the Gandhian/Nehruvian mainstream nationalism and the 'invention' of India.

4.5 Creative Agency Nationalism

'Irreplaceable is only this – the vitality of the will and the power of realisation.'
(Werner Kaegi[87])

Nehru argued that the growth of a powerful nationalist movement in India has demonstrated the political unity of India, an India in which everyone, regardless of political views or religious persuasions, thinks in terms of national unity (Nehru, 2003)[88]. This implies that there was a unity first, then a bottom-up nationalism representing this unity, and finally, a nationalist leadership which simply needed to organise this sentiment into a political movement. While this is understandably the message of a nationalist arguing his case, nothing could, in fact, be further from the truth. Unity was and still is elusive. Nationalism and the process of nation-building in India were precarious and contingent. They were neither popular nor driven by a larger historical dynamic, material or phenomenological. They were not strongly based on symbols of the past. Nationalism was a product of thought rather than of actual conditions. It was, furthermore, a product of agency rather than of a phenomenological dynamic, and it was based on a mobilisation linked to a very selective view of the past in an abstract rather than concrete way. Had it been otherwise, the outcome (the state) would likely have been different. There was a serious lack of 'natural' emotional stability. In order to compensate for this lack and create a stable national identity (rather than simply an anti-British, pro-independence

[87]In multilingual nations, Kaegi writes, only a very strong state system can overcome the higher resistance of different language areas. Kaegi, a Swiss historian, has Switzerland in mind. Inversely, one may say that a state that seeks to build itself on multilingual (and multiethnic, – religious, and – cultural) foundations, needs to be made particularly strong (Kaegi, W., 1942, p. 33).

[88]In the same article, written in 1937 and entitled 'The Unity of India' (published in Foreign Affairs), Nehru argues that 'there is no religious or communal problem in India' and 'as a matter of fact India is a singularly unified area, so far as languages are concerned' (Nehru, J., 2003, Vol. 1, p. 38). In 1959, after partition and some years in government, Nehru had an entirely different view of the matter: 'In India we have had most distressing spectacles of conflict based on provincialism and linguism' (Nehru, J., 2003, Vol. 1, p. 63).

national identity) the ideological leadership of political entrepreneurs was required.

In the beginning of Hind Swaraj, Gandhi (speaking metaphorically of the 'editor') explained what is demanded of a political leader – his task is to 'understand the popular feeling and to give expression to it; another is to arouse among the people certain desirable sentiments; and the third is fearlessly to expose popular defects' (Gandhi, 1997). Gandhi is understating the role of leaders in India, including his own. He was certainly a great populist. He understood the Indian people like few others did. However, he used this quality, politically speaking, not so much as an instrument to manipulate the masses, but strictly as a way of gaining access to them. He was a great leader of people, and he had beliefs, ideals and visions he wanted to implement politically. Nehru, also a great leader, was, in contrast to Gandhi, prone to make deductive universal statements from his analyses of experiences. He speaks of the 'man of destiny'. 'Events', he wrote in his 'Discovery of India'–

> '…take place one after the other and the uninterrupted and unending stream of happenings goes on. We seek to understand a particular event by isolating it and looking at it by itself, as if it were the beginning and the end, and the resultant of some cause immediately preceding it. Yet it has no beginning and is but a link in an unending chain, caused by all that has preceded it, and resulting from the wills, urges, and desires of innumerable human beings coalescing and conflicting with each other, and producing something different from that which any single individual intended to happen. Those wills, urges, and desires are themselves largely conditioned by previous events and experiences, and the new event in its turn becomes another conditioning factor for the future. The man of destiny, the leader who influences the multitude, undoubtedly plays an important part in this process and yet he himself is the product of past events and forces and his influence is conditioned by them' (Nehru, J., 1946).

In this statement, Nehru also underplays the role of the 'man of destiny'. He is certainly embedded in the 'unending chain' of being. At the same time, however, he is not entirely a product of history (as Hegel maintained). There is significant room for individual agency, for 'self-interpretation' on the personal and political level. To write that a 'man of destiny, the leader who influences the multitude' is himself a product of 'past events' is to make the statement either contradictory or meaningless. However, without excessive hair-splitting, it can be assumed that Nehru's meaning was that a 'man of destiny' is part of a larger cultural framework, which provides, as he said, a 'psychological moment of action' (Nehru, 1946). The leader is furthermore, as Brass argued, constrained by the cultural instruments effectively available to him. Within these bounds, however, the actor, the leader, the political entrepreneur – and both Gandhi and Nehru were prime specimens of this historical type – can actively shape historical events.

His ability to do so is limited, of course, by the larger forces of history, by large scale intellectual and material changes and by the actions of other parties, countries or leaders. Nevertheless, there are times, when the room to manoeuvre is large, when individual leaders can make choices vast and significant, when they can shape events and effect something akin to Kuhn's scientific revolution[89]. Under such conditions, the question becomes not what is India, but rather how is India *interpreted*, what does it *become*? Nehru, very much interested in history, was, nevertheless not an historian, but a man of action. He acknowledged his debt to the past, but declares that 'we owe a duty to the future also, and perhaps that obligation is even greater than the one we owe to the past' (Nehru, 2003). The future demands political action and decisions. 'What new ideals or old ideals varied and adapted to the new world can we place before our people, and how can we galvanise the people into wakefulness and action?' The past is but a resource in this endeavor, important as a stabiliser, as a ready identity-glue to be used by leaders to establish a link with the people.

> 'It was the virtue of Gandhiji to keep his feet firmly planted in the rich traditions of our race and our soil and, at the same time, to function on the revolutionary plane. Above all, he laid stress on truth and peaceful means. Thus he built on old foundations, and at the same time, oriented the structure towards the future' (Nehru, 2003).

As has been shown before, nationalism is a highly complex phenomenon to which no single general theory can do justice. Whilst there are 'family resemblances' (for example, across concepts, expressions or effects), the dynamic of nationalism differs substantially from case to case. The key difference for the purpose of this argument is between nationalisms that developed 'bottom-up', as a materially or phenomenologically driven mass movement and those which developed 'top-down', as an elite project. In

---

[89]Nehru, for example, contrasts the 'old days' characterised by 'blind, unquestioning faith' with 'our age', an 'age of disillusionment, of doubt and uncertainty and questioning'. This, our age, begs leadership and the 'search for new ways, new aspects of the truth' (Nehru, J., 2003, Vol. 1, p. 78). At another instance, he calls his age 'an age of transition and change' (Nehru, J. 2003, Vol. 1, p.105).

the first case, a people's common identity was strengthened and, with the help of Kedourie's easily interchangeable or Gellner's opportunistic leaders, quite smoothly found a modern, political expression in the form of nationalism. The nationalism then demanded to be politically realised in a nation state. If the nation had some geographic cohesion and was not hindered by other states, the entire process could be relatively unproblematic and even related to democratisation. This was the case, for example, in Great Britain or in France.

In the second case, in which the historical identity-building force is weaker, elites play a much more important and active role. This was typically the situation in the colonised countries of America, Africa and Asia. Nationalism went hand-in-hand with a desire for independence, calling for the political emancipation of someone (a more or less fictitious nation) from someone (a colonial oppressor). The elites had the double task of mobilising a national identity in order to both legitimise and fuel a struggle for independence. In some countries they did so out of sheer self-interest, in others they did so out of idealism. In creating a nation 'top-down' these elite nationalists often worked symbolically with the existing identity-elements of a people's history and traditions. The struggle for independence itself was also a great unifier. However, once the struggle was won and a state had come into existence, this second unifier was lost. New states thus often suffered from a lack of national identity and thus a lack of unity and stability. There was an identity gap between what is externally defined as a state (through territory, government, administration, etc.) and what is internally felt as a nation (common identity). While there was a state, the nation to inhabit it was still in the making. The gap had to be patched up in the short term and filled in the long term. This was done by ideology, either in the form of nationalism (ethnic or civic) and/or in some other form, such as by creating a state unity based on a communist ideology. It was also done by leadership. This was the case in India.

The perspective on Indian foreign policy from the challenges and choices of nation building shows that ideological politics in India was necessary in order to provide an emotional backbone to political stability. It also shows that the Indian approach was original and creative. The following chapters will elucidate the type of ideological politics the two key Indian nationalist leaders, Gandhi and Nehru, pursued. An understanding of the need for ideological politics coupled with an understanding of the specific nature of ideological politics in India, will provide the explanatory thrust for an understanding of the idealist inflection in foreign policy.

5

Gandhi, Nehru and Ideological Politics

Things fall apart; the centre cannot hold;
Mere anarchy is loosed upon the world,
The blood-dimmed tide is loosed, and everywhere
The ceremony of innocence is drowned;
The best lack all conviction, while the worst
Are full of passionate intensity.

(W. B. Yeats[90])

Rationality itself... is ideology dependent.

(Harvey Siegel[91])

Ideological politics (especially nationalism), the conscious political manipulation of mass sentiments by elite agents, has strongly negative connotations. It tends to irrationally conflate ends and means and it usually does so in the service of an illiberal, chauvinistic creed. Violence is often the result – internally, in the Procrustean process of fitting reality to an abstract idea, and externally, in foreign policy, as one ideologically charged unit will contrast and clash with others. For these reasons, ideological politics is viewed with great skepticism by liberal thinkers.

Are there 'good' forms of ideological politics? Are there 'good' elite agents, both in the sense of 'morally good' and in the sense of 'capable'? Can Indian nationalism be different? Benedict Andersen argues that the historical experiences of nationalism in the West and in Russia have supplied all subsequent nationalisms, such as the Indian one, with a tool-

---

[90]'The worst are full of passionate intensity' – in his poem 'The Second Coming', Yeats warns of the 'Frankenstein effect' of arousing the masses through ideology (Yeats, W. B., 1920).

[91]Siegel discusses the positive role ideology can play in creating a culture of reason in his book 'Educating Reason' (Siegel, H., 1988, p. 66).

kit from which nationalist elites could chose the tools they like (Anderson, 1991). Kedourie similarly believes that nationalism in third world countries was a replication of a Western idea (Kedourie, 1971). If this is correct, if nationalism in Asia and Africa simply worked with a tool-kit made available for it by the West, then Indians indeed have nothing left to imagine (Balakrishnan, 1996). Ideological politics would have followed the same disastrous pattern as it did elsewhere.

In India, however, the national identity formation process, driven by key agents, has been original and authentic. The identity crafted is based on universal liberal values and ideological politics is applied with great caution. This national identity, however, has to be defended against communalist, derivative and dangerous rival ideological politics.

As shown in the previous chapter, India, for lack of a natural emotional stability heavily relies on ideological politics for its identity formation process. According to the model outlined in Figure 1.2, the identity formation process in India, however, did not cause an aggressive inflection of foreign policy, but an idealist one. The reason for this astonishing fact is found in the nature of Indian ideological politics as crafted by Gandhi and Nehru as well as in the character of these crucial political entrepreneurs.

In India, the scale of the political experiment (having one large, plural, democratic Indian state instead of many smaller, ethnically defined states) attempted by the National Movement was enormous. When the state came into being, the challenge of supplying it with a viable, functioning national identity was equally enormous. However, India had two key enablers – a long cultural history, providing essential traditions of social cohesion, and a strong, relatively selfless and highly original leadership. The leaders of the National Movement, mainly Gandhi and Nehru, were the burning glass through which a viable political identity was created out of an externally determined Indian state incorporating a multifarious Indian civilisation. They did so by instilling a specific value system (based on a highly selective interpretation of Indian history) into a sufficiently large part of the Indian public mind. In the absence of 'thick' cultural unity, specific universal values with an Indian hue were established as the hallmark of Indianness by way of ideological politics.

The focus of the analysis is on Mahatma Gandhi and Jawaharlal Nehru. There were, of course, a number of other, highly important leaders of nationalism, but Gandhi and Nehru, from the point of view of this argument, stood out. They are the crucial agents providing the link between ideological politics and international relations. There are three reasons for that. Firstly, in terms of individual importance, Gandhi and Nehru towered above their co-nationalists. Their impact on the history of modern India can hardly be overestimated. Gandhi, who was given the honorary title of 'Mahatma' (great soul), has been called 'the central driving force in the remaking of the Indian soul and the machinery of Indian politics' (Saunders, 1931). Gandhi was a character and a historical phenomenon of rare power. Whilst he led the struggle for independence and became the saintly, supra-political figurehead of the new state, Nehru had the most profound everyday impact on it. It is no exaggeration to say that, while the period of Indian history from 1919 to 1942 was 'the age of Gandhi' (Embree, 1989), 'in the years between independence in 1947 and his death in 1964, India in many ways was Nehru' (Som, 2004). To Tharoor, what India is today, both for good and ill, is owed in great measure to one man – to Nehru (Tharoor, 2003). His most important contribution is 'the very notion of Indianness'. Nehru, 'above all else... welded that India into a plausible nation', and through his writings, speeches, life and leadership – he can be credited with 'the invention of the India we know today'. To Nanda, 'no political leader with the exception of Gandhi, has ever stirred the minds and hearts of the people of India so long and so deeply as Nehru did' (Nanda, 2004). For almost half a century, therefore, from 1919, when Mahatma Gandhi started to fully engage the Indian freedom struggle, until 1964, when Jawaharlal Nehru died, during the decisive, formative years of the new nation, the fate of India was in the hands of two individuals.

The second reason why it makes sense to focus on Gandhi and Nehru is their mutually enforcing relationship. If they were of central importance individually, in conjunction, they more or less controlled the making of the modern Indian nation. Despite many and serious disagreements on specific issues, they remained very close allies in the struggle for independence. Although Nehru had a strong mind of his own, he was deeply influenced by Gandhi's thought and practice (Nanda, 2004, Nehru). The two formed, as Nanda put it, 'one of the longest, most intriguing, and fruitful partnerships in the history of nationalism'. Consequently, there is a high degree of coherence in their views and Nehru's great 'discovery' of India, 'was intertwined with his admiration for Gandhi' (Tharoor, 2003).

Thirdly, Nehru's extraordinary pre-eminence in the field of foreign policy together with his leadership in building a nation, suggest that in India, much more so than in most other countries at most other times, the link between the two fields was not only ideational, but institutionalised to the extreme – it was personalised. Furthermore, as Cohen argued, the 'Nehruvian core' of foreign policy thinking was influenced by Gandhi, directly through their personal relationship, as well as 'indirectly through the influence of the Mahatma on Indian thinking at large' (Cohen, 2001). For these reasons, the analysis of nationalism, as a dynamic influencing foreign policy, will concentrate on Gandhi and Nehru.

5.1 The Nature of Ideological Politics in India

As shown above, Elie Kedourie, to whom nationalism is both a fiction as well as a relatively weak factor in actually bringing about a nation state, nevertheless believes that nationalist politics is a significant and baleful historical invention. He contrasts what he terms 'ideological politics' with 'constitutional politics'. In constitutional politics –

> 'the object in view is to attend to the common concerns of a particular society, to safeguard it against foreign assaults, to mediate disagreements and conflicts between various groups through political institutions, through legislation and the administration of justice, and to uphold the law as being above and beyond sectional interests however important or powerful' (Kedourie, 1993).

In short, constitutional politics is good governance. Very little concern is given to the question of who governs whom. As per this definition, Indian independence would not have been necessary had the British adhered to the principles of good governance. Gandhi, knowing, of course, that this would make a farce of colonial rule, said the he had no objection to the British remaining in India 'as servants of the people', 'Your function will be, if you so wish, to police India; you must abandon the idea of deriving any commercial benefit from us' (Gandhi, 1997).

Ideological politics, Kedourie asserts, 'is very different' –

> 'Such a politics is concerned to establish a state of affairs in society and state such that everyone, as they say in old-fashioned novels, will live happily ever after. To do so, the ideologist will... look upon the state and society as a canvas which has to be wiped clean, so that his vision of justice, virtue and happiness can be painted on this tabula rasa'. The whole story is bound to go wrong, because 'the very attempt to wipe the canvas clean must entail arbitrariness, lawlessness and violence on a stupendous scale, such that the ideological vision of perpetual peace and joy must recede further and further into the horizon' (Kedourie, 1993).

Kedourie's critique of ideological politics as violent pipe dreams is influenced heavily by the thinking of Michael Oakeshott and Karl Popper[92],

[92]They taught together at the London School of Economics.

the latter using the term 'utopian social engineering' in place of 'ideological politics' (Oakeshott, 1978; Popper, 1994). This common liberal critique, was, with a view to India, also expressed by Homi Bhabha, who is wary about 'ideological manoeuvres through which 'imagined communities' are given essentialist identities' (Bhabha, 1990).

For Kedourie, of course, nationalism – along with communism or fascism – is just such an expression of ideological politics (Kedourie). The belief that, if each nation would be firmly established as a nation state, there would be no further need for war and perpetual peace would follow, is fallacious. Unfortunately, however, – so he argues – the fallacy has made quite a career – 'The greatest triumph of this ideological obsession is the enshrinement of national self-determination as the organising principle of international order' (Kedourie, 1993).

If the fictitious differentiating out of peoples into nations and the resulting violence is one side of ideological politics, then the internal homogenisation and the mobilisation of a national identity is the other. Kedourie explains how –

> '...by means of high philosophical words, rulers can better control the ruled, who are ensnarled by their literacy, and obtain their active support and their passive acquiescence. Thus, by a natural development, it is not philosophers who become kings, but kings who tame philosophy to their use. Such a political style calls forth a new class of literature – a Lenin discourses on empirio-criticism, and a Stalin expounds the principles of philology; a Hitler inaugurates his career with a *Mein Kampf*, while an Abd-al-Nasir crowns a successful coup d'état with a 'Philosophy of the Revolution' (Kedourie, 1993)..

He could have added Mao's famous *Little Red Book* or Muammar al-Gaddafi's *Green Book* to his list; but could he have added Gandhi's 'Hind Swaraj' or Nehru's 'Discovery of India'?

Kedourie's negative view of nationalism may be challenged at various levels. Philosophically one may, as Gellner has done, wonder if it makes any sense to condemn what to him is an impersonal historical force, at all (Gellner, 1983). At the system-level, one may ask, if nationalism may not be separable from the vile excesses which have given it a bad name. Such an argument emphasises the positive aspects of nationalism, such as liberal-democratic empowerment (Miscevic, 2000) or the success of nationalism as a political model. The real question is, however, put to the test – is good nationalism realistic? The risks involved in ideological politics, as pointed out by liberal thinkers such as Kedourie or Popper, as well as the empirical track record of identity politics, including nationalism, strongly point to a negative answer (Worcester, Bermanzohn, et al. 2002), if an answer can be given in such general terms. This is precisely the problem, however – general statements about nationalism may broadly indicate certain trends, propensities or 'family resemblances', but they cannot do justice to the large variety of specific nationalisms. Any claim about the nature of nationalism is likely to be contradicted by specific cases. In that sense, whilst Kedourie, from his generalist vantage point, may provide useful theoretical generalisations, his view is, by the same token, too detached and inflexible to account for all nationalisms. Nationalism is not always a shallow repetition and application of an idea born in Europe.

It is the third level of criticism which is the most important for this argument – the refutation of the universal nature Kedourie attributes to ideological politics in the specific case of India. In India, as shown above, ideological politics has not been a mere imitation. It had a profoundly original nature and a constructive effect. Furthermore, it contributed to the much larger enterprise of generating good governance or 'conventional politics'. To be sure, Indian 'ideological politics' could have followed Kedourie's simplistic and dangerous pattern. The fact that it did not, was mainly the merit of one man – Mohandas Gandhi. His politics was ideological in content. Yet, it was not violent, because it was flexible and practical in method. Gandhi, when he came to India from South Africa, realised, as much as Kedourie did, that simple copycat nationalism was harmful and that he was confronted with the 'difficulty' that 'the Indian nationalist is not national' (Gandhi, 1994). Henceforth, he developed his own, highly original approach to Indian nationalism and to politics as such, based on his conception of means and ends (Appadorai, 1986; Dalton 'Gandhi's Originality', Parel, 2000).

Kedourie failed to understand the deeply original nature of Indian nationalism. This becomes clear in his attempt to fit Gandhi into his framework. He recounts a correspondence on nationalism between Jinnah and Gandhi, in which Gandhi responds to Jinnah's 'Two Nation Theory' by saying – 'I am unable to accept the proposition that the Muslims of India are a nation distinct from the rest of India'. Kedourie condemns such an answer for its 'utter and absolute' nature, so characteristic of the ideological politics of nationalism. He continues – 'May we not see in these belligerent and frivolous logomachies a prelude to that bloody act consummated four years later on the lawn in New Delhi, a city desolated by wave upon wave of desperate and terrified refugees?' (Kedourie, 1971). Kedourie thus oddly condemns Gandhi for the consequences of a partition he was entirely opposed to. Apart from the fact that he gives Gandhi no credit for his ultimate acceptance of partition (which showed a mental flexibility not at all 'utter and absolute' in nature), nor for his extraordinary on-the-ground efforts to reduce the ensuing violence (fasting or walking from village to village quite unlike the usual ideological politician), he fundamentally misunderstands Gandhi as well as the theory of the Indian nation he stood for, for that of a chauvinist Hindu nationalism. To understand where Kedourie's misunderstanding stems from, it is useful to look further into a key aspect of ideological politics, namely the conflation of ends and means, of positive and of negative liberty.

5.1.1 *Positive and Negative Liberty*

The liberal thinker Isaiah Berlin was as skeptical about ideological politics as Kedourie was. He saw with great concern the tendency of idealists and romantics to equate the development of internal capacities for action with external opportunities for action, thereby plunging the concept of freedom into a muddle of arbitrariness. In the Essay 'Two Concepts of Liberty', he sets out to delineate and fence off an area of individual liberty from the machinations of ideological politicians. He distinguishes between an outer, negative freedom, that is determined by the personal space in which neither public authority nor other individuals can interfere, and the dubious concept of positive freedom related to ideas of autonomy and internal self-mastery. Only negative liberty is real liberty. 'The fundamental sense of freedom is freedom from chains'. Positive 'liberty' is a misnomer. It is really something else; for example, self-development or condition. Reducing liberty (negative liberty) is always an evil – however, sometimes this evil may be traded off against other, desirable goods, such as the negative liberty of others, law and order, or even self-development. Liberty is then not related to the form of government, it would be quite possible for someone to enjoy more liberty under a liberal-minded despot than under a democratic regime.

Berlin's argument is really concerned with definition and (in Spinoza's sense) with demarcation. He deeply resents the conflation of positive and negative liberty, because he regards this – very much as Kedourie does – as a route to disaster. In the introduction to 'Four Essays on Liberty', Berlin lays out his reasoning –

> 'The perversion of the notion of positive liberty into its opposite – the apotheosis of authority – did occur, and has for a long while been one of the most familiar and depressing phenomena of our time. For whatever reason or cause,

> the notion of "negative" liberty... however disastrous the consequences of its unbridled forms, has not historically been twisted by its theorists as often as or as effectively into anything as darkly metaphysical or socially sinister or remote from its origins as its "positive" counterpart'. While positive liberty 'can be turned into its opposite and still exploit the favourable associations of its innocent origins', negative liberty 'has, much more frequently, been seen, for better or worse, for what it was; there has been no lack of emphasis, in the last hundred years, upon its more disastrous implications. Hence, the greater need, it seems to me, to expose the aberrations of positive liberty than those of its negative brother' (Berlin, 1992).

A doctrine of positive freedom may lead to 'absurdities in theory' and (supposedly in conjunction with ideological politics) to 'barbarous consequences in practice' (Berlin, 1992).

Berlin gives two accounts of how the linguistic confusion of negative and positive liberty can lead to errors in thinking, errors in accountability and errors in politics – ultimately at the expense of human dignity. The first is the 'retreat into the inner citadel'. If freedom is related to capacities, to the ability to do what one wishes, then surely freedom could be increased not only by improving the ability, but also by contracting the wishes. One could become, in theory, a free slave. This idea is not alien to Indian tradition. It reflects the ascetic's attempt to achieve freedom from desires. He argues that actual negative liberty can only be increased by eliminating obstacles and not by withdrawing from them. Thus, while one may feel freer, one is not actually, objectively freer. There is nothing wrong with this per se. The problem arises only when the two are confused by the individual or by public authorities and the free market of value trade-offs is thus impeded by linguistic (and, hence, intellectual) fogginess (Berlin, 1992).

The second, even more devious confusion is the reverse approach – not to equate liberty with renunciation, but with self-realisation, with an increase in ability and knowledge. Such an approach stipulates that freedom lies in the realisation of truth, the overcoming of superstition and error, and in self-mastery. A political actor who proposes such an argument usually also has an opinion on what the 'truth' consists of. It is only a small step from here, via the assumption that the rational ends of all men coincide, to the absurd notion that someone can be coerced to be free, that x knows better what is in y's interest than y himself, that a *volonté générale* can override the expressed wish of an individual in order to realise his own 'real' self-interest, that platonic elites rule the masses by whatever means they see fit in order to achieve a collective ideal of self-realisation. This highly problematic claim to make people 'freer' all too easily leads to the re-education camps of the gulag archipelago; and it does so sanctimoniously under the cloak of liberty (Berlin, 1992).

Taylor has offered an interesting theoretical critique of Berlin's argument. He does not accept 'a view of freedom which doesn't involve at least some qualitative distinction as to motive...'. Freedom cannot be radically detached from either the specific individual subject exercising it or from the society within which it is exercised. One needs to want the right things in order to be free. This requires such abilities as moral discrimination or the prioritisation of motivations and desires into higher and lower ones. Charles Taylor's view of freedom is not just absence of external obstacles 'for there may be internal ones', even internal ones that the subject himself does not recognise. He therefore cannot be the final arbiter of his own freedom, 'for he may be profoundly mistaken about what he wants to repudiate'. If this is so, 'he is less capable of freedom in the meaningful sense of the word'. Freedom for Taylor is 'self-direction' – the absence not merely of external, but also of internal obstacles to freedom (Taylor, 1997). The idea of self-direction opens up a path towards original and authentic 'self-interpretation'.

At first, the argument may seem to be merely about the definition of the word 'freedom'. What Berlin describes as self-development, Taylor describes as (positive) freedom. However, there are two more fundamental disagreements. Firstly, Taylor thinks that a distinction between negative and positive liberty cannot reasonably be made. Both are part of the same, larger concept of freedom. Negative liberty without positive liberty does not make sense. Secondly, Taylor, as opposed to Berlin, does not regard the freedom to interpret oneself as a dangerous idea. When speaking about 'self-direction', Taylor steers clear of utopian and socio-political theories in a Hegelian or Marxian sense. To him it is foremost an individual exercise (Taylor, 1997). Gandhi's reasoning is not only in line with Taylor's, but goes significantly further.

5.1.2 *Gandhi and Benign Ideological Politics*

Gandhi very much and very consciously conflates positive and negative liberty[93]. His whole career was a protest against the 'double morality' that

[93]For a discussion of the relationship between Western thinkers, including Berlin, and Gandhi see 'Is there a Gandhian Conception of Liberty' by Anthony Copley. He concludes that Gandhi's lack of identification with the middle classes 'inevitably takes him away from a tradition of bourgeois liberalism' (Parel, A., 2000). While Gandhi certainly was not a

private and public ends and means are legitimately different (Nanda, 2004). He also, unlike Taylor, gave his theory and practice of freedom (Swaraj) a social and political dimension. In a panegyric on Gandhi, Nelson Mandela emphasises the 'interdependence of the social and the personal' in his thought, the desire for a 'simultaneous and interactive development of the moral person and the moral society', which is at the 'heart of his philosophy' (Mandela, 2000). Parel offers a four pronged typology of Gandhi's idea of freedom. On a spectrum stretching from negative to positive liberty (for, in truth, it is a spectrum), it reaches from national independence to political freedom of individuals, economic freedom of individuals, and self-rule (Parel, 2000). Parel writes that in Gandhi's view, 'self-realisation (*atmadarshan*) and politics (*rajyaprakaran*)... may not be radically separated... Individual regeneration and national regeneration constitute one continuum' (Gandhi, 1997). The two cannot be separated, because at the root of his philosophy lay his abiding belief in 'the law of authentic moral living' (Som, 2004). To Gandhi, politics started with the individual's control over his mind, and moral actions, it then continued to moral, fearless, upright society. Such a society cannot be fettered from the outside. Mere negative liberty (independence from the British) without positive liberty (self-development) would mean the same type of rule with a different mask – 'the tiger's nature, but not the tiger; that is to say... make India English, and when it becomes English, it will not be called Hindustan but Englistan. This is not the Swaraj I want'. By the same logic, colonisation is not primarily an expression of the physical, external constraint of negative liberty by a superior force, but rather an expression of Indian degeneration (lack of positive liberty). 'The English have not taken India; we have given it to them. They are not in India because of their strength, but because we keep them'. He compares the Indians to a *Bhang* addict and the British to the *Bhang* seller. The addict should not blame the seller but himself for his addiction; and the solution to his addiction will not lie in getting rid of the seller ('will not another take his place?'), but in overcoming the addiction (Gandhi, 1997). Like liberty, strength, to Gandhi, is not a physical condition, but a mental one. It is the 'absence of fear' (Gandhi, 1997).

The course of action Gandhi proposes in Hind Swaraj is nothing less than radical. India must reject modern civilisation and concentrate on its

---

bourgeois liberal, he had, however, many similarities in pattern of thought with liberals. Gandhi's search for truth through experimentation, for example, is not too different from Popper's theory of scientific progress through falsification. Both are interested in the achievement of goals under conditions of fallibility.

own venerable, humane and religious civilisation. Indian civilisation is great, but it must reawaken, and renew, purify and reinvigorate itself. He compares national unity to a clay-pot that will, under duress, break sooner or later. 'The way to save the pot is... to bake it so that no stone would break it. We have then to make our hearts of perfectly baked clay'. 'Defects' in the civilisation need to be 'purged'. This can be done through the 'new spirit that is born in us', brought about as a reaction to the condition of colonisation. 'In order to restore India to its pristine conditions, we have to return to it' (Gandhi, 1997).

This is typical nationalist talk. It is this language of ideological politics, prone to lead to violent chauvinism and inhumane utopianism, which sends shivers down the spines of Kedourie, Popper, Berlin or anyone who has witnessed excesses of ideological politics. The question of the dangerous nature of nationalism was also raised in India at the time, most prominently by Rabindranath Tagore ('The Illegitimacy of Nationalism', Nandy, 2003). Tagore saw nationalism as something wicked per se, as a 'cruel epidemic of evil that is sweeping over the human world of the present age, eating into its moral vitality' (Tagore, 1917). Nationalism would create violence and greed and enhance state power, possibly leading to even more tyranny (Dalton, 1993). Gandhi countered this by saying that he wanted to create a nationalism of an entirely different sort from that found in the West (Gandhi, 1994). And indeed, he did. The question is, then – why did Gandhi's positive doctrine of freedom not turn into 'a doctrine of authority and, at times, of oppression' to become a 'weapon of despotism' (Berlin, 1992)? How could it remain so 'remarkably free from utopianism, romanticism, fanaticism, and despair that have often shadowed moralism' (Parekh, 1997)? As it turned out, Gandhi's nationalism and ideological politics were highly original and moralistic adaptations of an otherwise problematic phenomenon. Gandhi brought 'idealism into the realm of practical politics' and demonstrated its 'viability' by not betraying his ideals with zealotry (Masselos, 2005). The explanation for this astonishing feat is found essentially in Gandhi's humble and philanthropic character.

The first reason is that Gandhi was firmly opposed to any form of monism, the belief that there is one knowable highest value or truth towards which all actions could and should conform. Here, his views converge with Isaiah Berlin's, to whom monism was a 'coherent fantasy'. However, their reasons for rejecting monism were not the same. Berlin argued, from an ontological standpoint, that there exists a plurality of values which are essentially incommensurable. They need to be traded-off against each other depending on the social or individual preferences. There is no perfectly good outcome; there is always compromise (Berlin, 1992). Gandhi, on the other hand, like Popper, looked at the problem from an epistemic perspective. Being intensely religious, he did consider God, truth, purity and Ahimsa as ultimately being one. He thus believed that there exists one supreme value. However, he did not profess to know it. He has only seen 'little fleeting glimpses' of the truth (Gandhi). Parel, in his introduction to 'Hind Swaraj', reminds of the Jain Rajchandra's early influence on Gandhi and the Jain concept of '*anekantavada*', the many-sidedness and fleetingness of truth. Parel, furthermore, suggests that Gandhi wrote Hind Swaraj in dialogue-style, because a dialogue is open-ended, thereby leaving 'little room for dogmatism' (Parel, 1997). Gandhi's autobiography is tellingly entitled 'The Story of my Experiments with Truth' (Gandhi, 1993a). An experiment in this sense is 'induced by the objective world, but it is essentially an operation within and upon oneself. To the end of his days, Gandhi attempted to master and remake himself' (Fischer, 2001). 'It is a bad habit', Gandhi writes, 'to say that another man's thoughts are bad and ours only are good' (Gandhi, 1997).

Whilst Gandhi was pretty sure of what he was against – colonial exploitation, discrimination of all kinds, religious intolerance, partition, the use of violence, modern civilisation and the use of machinery, urban life – his ultimate goal remained vague – to improve the quality of life for India's masses, to serve the ordinary Indian people (Gandhi, 1997). From his respect for the complexity of truth, as well as from a humble belief in his own fallibility[94], Gandhi drew the lesson of being flexible and pragmatic in his political approach. Hind Swaraj, according to Parel, is a theory 'of, and about, practice'. This 'requires that the theoretician be simultaneously the practitioner' (Parel, 1997). He had elaborate theories of what should be done and how, and of what would be counterproductive. These he was continuously putting to the test and adjusting them where necessary. He was adamant and highly disciplined with himself, or, as Schell expressed it – 'he belonged to a small class of people, many of them religious or political zealots, who are able to act according to their beliefs almost without condition or reservation' (Schell, 2005). Yet, he was not a zealot. He did not demand of others to unconditionally accept his views. Furthermore, while Gandhi could be extremely stubborn if he believed himself to be correct (often to the intense frustration of his fellow freedom fighters), he

[94]In his autobiography, he gives an account of his occasional blunders and even of a 'Himalayan miscalculation' (Gandhi, M., 1993a, p. 374).

also remained flexible and open to being persuaded by circumstances or arguments. Even where he was not persuaded, he was ready to play the political game and compromise in the name of unity. 'If we want unity, then the adjustment and readjustment, a series of compromises honorable to both parties and to a variety of opinions is to be effected' (Gandhi, 1994).

Despite his strong grounding in Indian traditions, 'experimenting with the truth', to Gandhi, also meant being open to outside influences. This also is not the typical trait of nationalist ideological politics, with its frequent xenophobic undertones. In a famous comment, Gandhi explained that 'I do not want my house to be walled in on all sides and my windows to be stuffed. I want the culture of all the lands to be blown about my house as freely as possible. But I refuse to be blown off my feet by any' (Gandhi, 1993b). Equally, his ideas were not really traditionalist, but rather universally oriented (Rothermund, 1965).

The fundamental reason, however, why Gandhi did not tend towards violent forms of ideological politics, was that non-violence formed part of his 'general theory of ends and means in politics'. 'Means have to be morally as defensible as ends themselves' (Parel, 1997). Unlike Lenin, Mao or a host of nationalist leaders who also experimented politically, he did not fall for the logic Kedourie, Berlin and Popper were most concerned about, namely that of trading-off present suffering against a vague future ideal. In Hind Swaraj, the ficticious questioner puts forward the ends-justify-the-means argument. Gandhi's answer to him is that the 'belief that there is no connection between the means and the end is a great mistake'. He elaborates on this point, making use of metaphors such as 'as is the God, so is the votary' or 'we reap exactly as we sow'. His point being that the nature of the outcome (the end) is influenced by the means. A stolen watch is not the same object as one given as a present. This is particularly true of violence. To use violence against violence only increases violence further, 'and so the battle grows' (Gandhi, 1997). Gandhi was thus a profoundly liberal thinker. His case demonstrates that true liberalism is not necessarily a Western and secular intellectual tradition (Engelmeier, 2003a).

Is Gandhi's non-violence merely a reasonable choice, a promising policy? Or is it based on principle? This is difficult to tell. Was Gandhi's flexible pragmatism greater than his belief in a principle? It could be that he was simply never confronted with a situation or an argument that could have led him to change his mind on non-violence. However, in how far he would have been willing to consider such an essential change in his philosophy is impossible to tell. Furthermore, on a logical plane, the elementary question is – whether the principle of non-violence is itself subject to trial and error? Liberal thinkers struggle with the same problem – are we free to abolish liberalism? Is liberalism a method or an a priori principle? At first sight, it seems as though Gandhi understands non-violence as a method. Parel notes that although non-violence –

> '...has its roots in Indian metaphysics, it is used in Hind Swaraj as a political, not metaphysical doctrine. Its exercise has to be guided by prudence not metaphysics. Circumstances modify the way in which the principle is applied. Casuistry, in the good sense of the term, is part and parcel of Gandhian moral reasoning on non-violence' (Parel, 1997).

Gandhi, for example, in comparing the Indian freedom struggle with the Italian one, makes a purely pragmatic argument for non-violence by stating that 'India can fight like Italy only when she has arms' (Gandhi, 1997). Brass argued that Gandhi's non-violence was a 'tactic which acknowledged the enormous potential for violence which existed in a highly fragmented and culturally heterogeneous society' (Brass, 2000). In his autobiography, he writes that 'I would risk violence a thousand times rather than emasculation of the race... but I believe that non-violence is infinitely superior to violence' (Saunders, 1931). The correspondence with Subhas Bose is instructive. He and Bose were, as Gandhi expressed it, 'sailing in different boats' with respect to the use of violence in the independence struggle. However, Gandhi 'made it clear that he would be the first to congratulate if his (Bose's) path proved to be the correct one' (Som, 2004).

However, the practical arguments become entangled in Gandhi's broader ideological outlook – 'To arm India on a large scale is to Europeanise it. Then her condition will be just as pitiable as that of Europe... The Indian nation will not adopt arms, and it is well that it does not'. The question whether non-violence is a principle or a pragmatic policy thus becomes hazy. Ends and means, interest and ideal are conflated – 'Only fair means can produce fair results, and... the force of love and pity is infinitely greater than the force of arms. There is harm in the exercise of brute force, never in that of pity'. Non-violence is, thus, a method, but the method is in turn embedded in Gandhi's larger idealistic worldview and the belief that good creates good and evil creates evil. To Gandhi, the non-violent 'soul-force' is the norm and what we call 'history' is merely a string of spectacular aberrations from the norm (Gandhi, 1997). Moreover, true and lasting victory lies not in vanquishing the opponent, but in winning him over and in reforming his soul (Parel, 1997). Doing good and doing the politically expedient is thus the same thing. Thus, Gandhi wrote that 'if every page of these chapters does not proclaim that the only means for the realisation of truth is Ahimsa, I shall deem all my pains in writing these chapters to have been in vain' (Gandhi, 1993a).

Since Gandhi is not dogmatic, he recognises that there are instances in which force may reasonably be used. He gives the example of preventing a child from running into the fire (Gandhi, 1997). Elsewhere, he explains that he would rather have India resort to arms than to remain cowardly in a state of dishonour (Gandhi, 1951). He also actively recruited for the Indian Army to fight in the First World War, and in 1938, he considered advocating the use of force against Nazi Germany (Gandhi, 1994). The use of force is attached to the condition, however, that it is employed either to help someone else (i.e. is not employed in self-interest), or is employed in self-defense (Gandhi, 1997). Gandhi's acceptance of the sending of Indian troops into Kashmir in 1947 can be understood under this second proviso (Woodcock, 1972). Given this central ambiguity about non-violence, Gandhi may be regarded not only as the originator of the idealist inflection of India's ambiguous foreign policy, but also as the originator of duality as such – of the conflation of ideals and interests, which is the conscious result of conflating positive and negative liberty, and ends and means.

By being open, flexible, pragmatic, non-violent, but above all by being deeply and humanely interested in the wellbeing of the ordinary Indian, Gandhi was able to avoid the baleful effects of ideological politics despite his conflation of positive and negative liberty. Gandhi ultimately found a very high level synthesis between belief and openness. Whereas belief is the common feature of ideological politics, the openness makes Gandhi a rare exception and deescalates the danger stemming from social engineering. It is Gandhi's evolutionary and experimental method of intellectual leadership coupled with a firm belief in the positive nature of mankind[95], which makes Gandhi a liberal despite being an idealist. According to Parekh, he was even 'transcending liberalism' (Parekh, 1997). He simply did not accept the idea of progress by violence. Popper, who shared Gandhi's epistemic apprehensions about the ends of political life, would not have been able to classify Gandhi. Gandhi was both 'utopian' in that he had larger moral and social, and not merely governance-related political goals. At the same time, however, he was consciously 'piecemeal' in his

[95]Gandhi's belief in the natural 'goodness' of mankind and the corrupting nature of modernity is strongly reminiscent of Rousseau's essay on the origins of inequality (Rousseau, J. J., 1992). However, whereas Rousseau believes to be in a position to solve mankind's illness from his desk – thus falling into the trap of ideological politics (Rousseau, J. J., 1993) – Gandhi's pragmatic approach and respect for the individual lead him to very different conclusions. (On Gandhi's idealism, see, Nanda, B. R., 2004, Gandhi, p. 267)

approach. He was then, in Popper's terminology, a 'piecemeal utopian engineer' (Popper, 1994; Gandhi, 1997). This specific approach results from Gandhi's character; he was, as Tagore put it, 'a lover of men not of ideas' (Nanda, 2004, Gandhi) – a harmless species, it seems.

5.2 Gandhi and the Challenge of Creating an Indian Nation

'But one dares to venture the opinion that no other leader in history in his own lifetime had done so much to make a people into a nation.'

(Ainslie T., Embree[96])

Gandhi did not envision India as a culturally homogenous, Western nation state based on exclusive nationalism. He looked upon India as a civilisation rather than a nation (Parekh, 1997). His nationalism, consequently, was highly inclusive. Furthermore, it retained a certain degree of 'anarchistic thinking' (Som, 2004). The result was, according to Rushdie, a national identity 'so spacious and pliable' that it would 'sustain and integrate a billion differences', 'far more original than the old idea of a "melting pot"' (Rushdie, 2006). Indira Gandhi has famously called India a 'salad bowl', a country in which particular identities do not necessarily blend into each other, but co-exist. In whichever way Indian identity is described, whether as a smelter or as a salad, it needed a container, a common, Pan-Indian 'pot' or 'bowl' with could contain all the different ethnic, regional, linguistic and religious identities.

Gandhi's 'particular genius', lay in his understanding of how the two, the salad and the bowl, the complex fabric of Indian social life and the essentially modern concept of a national movement could come together (Embree, 1989). His political struggle was twofold – It was directed at gaining independence from the British as much as it was directed towards making India fit for self-rule. That included making Indians understand that they were one people. Although Gandhi declared that India was an ancient nation, he was well aware that unity in a multi-stratified country was always precarious. In his endeavour to create an all-encompassing nationalism, he found himself in direct competition with groups who argued from the point of view of specific, demarcated and divisive Indian cultures. These were, most prominently, the Hindu nationalists and the Muslim League. Both propagated a 'Two Nation Theory'.

---

[96]This is the concluding statement of Embree's essay 'Gandhi's Role in Shaping an Indian Identity' (Embree, A. T., 1989, p. 172).

5.2.1 *Rival Nationalisms*

Vinayak Damodar Savarkar, a contemporary of Gandhi, offered the 'most mature and most extreme' interpretation of Hindu nationalism (Sharma). It was his belief that the source of national strength was national unity and that national unity, in turn, was based on a clearly and positively defined national identity and culture. Savarkar's aim was to establish a definition of what constituted such a Hindu identity (Sharma). His key work was, thus, entitled – *Hindutva – Who Is a Hindu* (Savarkar, 1969). The term 'Hindutva', coined by himself, is understood as the 'life of a great race', signifying the 'religious, cultural and racial identity of the Hindus'. For Savarkar, 'the story of independent India would be the story of the Hindu nation' (Sharma, 2003). In order to bestow historical weight and authority on this claim, he gave Hindu nationalism a primordialist grounding. The main argument in his book *Hindutva* is that the Aryans who settled in India in ancient times already formed an Indian proto-nation now embodied in the Hindus (Jaffrelot, 1996).

There are two key clashes between Gandhi's approach to nationalism and that of Hindutva, epitomised in Savarkar's demand to 'Hinduise all politics and militarise Hindudom' (Prasad, 1985)[97]. Hindutva was developed as a monochromatic, codified and exclusive concept of blood lineage (Sharma, 2003). 'The Hindus', writes Savarkar –

> '...are not merely the citizens of the Indian state because they are united not only by the bonds of the love they bear to a common motherland but also by the bonds of a common blood. They are not only a nation but a race – *jati*. The word *jati*... means a brotherhood, a race determined by a common origin, possessing a common blood. All Hindus claim to have in their veins the blood of the mighty race incorporated with and descended from the Vedic fathers' (Savarkar, 1969).

Such nationalism does not promote a plural society; to the contrary – there is a direct and long-term correlation between Hindu-Muslim tensions and the successes of Hindu nationalism (Brass, 2003). Against this stood Gandhi's supra-religious, inclusive nationalism. Secondly, behind Savarkar's demand to 'militarise Hindudom', was the idea that national reinvigoration could happen only on the basis of Kshatriya manliness and physical power. Gandhi, of course, believed that regeneration and national mobilisation would be a primarily spiritual exercise, based on non-violence and truth,

[97]On this, see the essay by Sudarshan Kapur, entitled 'Gandhi and Hindutva' (Parel, A., 2000).

rather than on violence. Thus, Savarkar's ideology, which was 'obsessively preoccupied with the themes of race, culture and militarism' (Bhatt, 2001), was fundamentally incompatible with Gandhi's, who regarded history as a social liability rather than an asset (Rothermund, 2003).

The second significant challenge to Gandhi's nationalism – and one he would ultimately not be able to fend off – was, of course, the Muslim League's 'Two Nation Theory'. This idea rested on the elite Indian Muslim sense of being culturally and historically distinct. A view that derives 'in part from the original Muslim invaders of the subcontinent, and in part from the willingness of some to abandon corrupt Hinduism for a peaceful and just Islam' (Cohen). On the other hand, as Islam had moved eastward and encountered other cultures, it adapted and transformed itself significantly. In India, the caste system crept into Muslim society and Hindu religious practices were incorporated into Islamic rituals. In turn, Islam had a profound impact on India, very notably, for example, in the Sikh sect. Furthermore, variants of Islam, like Sufism, found common ground with Hindus and Buddhists in their saint worship and mysticism (Cohen, 2004a).

To Gandhi, the 'Two Nation Theory' was not only an obvious impediment to Indian unity; it also represented a fundamentally different approach to nationalism and to modernity as such. It called into question his entire political project as based on self-development, non-violence and pluralism. Gandhi's religious-universalist and civilisational outlook, whereby he saw Muslims as Indians, was challenged by a national idea based on a Western-style cultural nationalism and attracted to modernity (Moore, 1983). Gandhi, for example, supported the Muslim religious Khilafat movement (1919–1924), which strongly resented the conditions imposed on the Ottoman caliph by the British. Iqbal and Jinnah, on the other hand, were much more impressed with Ataturk's modern Turkish state (Cohen, 2004a). The 'Two Nation Theory' undermined the Congress' claims to represent all Indians, including India's Muslims. It thereby made Congress not only potentially less Muslim and, by default, more Hindu, but also less universal and supra-religious. This new dichotomy between Muslims and Hindus was what most unsettled Gandhi[98]. Nehru, who eventually had to deal with this problem not only in theory but also in practice, expressed

[98]Merriam argues, that the monumental clash in ideology, ideas and personality between two leaders of rare prowess – Gandhi and Jinnah – ultimately made partition almost inevitable (Merriam, A. H., 1980).

the difficulty very well, when he wrote that –

> '...one of the biggest obstacles to the creation of the atmosphere we seek is the repeated declaration that Pakistan is an Islamic State... India claims to be something different while Pakistan goes on insisting on an Islamic State. If it is an Islamic State, then inevitably the conception of nationality, as it is understood today, has no meaning and the Muslims in India or most of them may well look to Pakistan as their homeland. That leads to disruptive tendencies working continuously and to a continuance of suspicion' (Nehru, 2003)[99].

During most of Gandhi's struggles – that is, before independence and partition – the ground reality in India was that Muslims lived interspersed throughout the entire subcontinent. Although there were Muslim majority areas, these were geographically disjointed and often incorporated large numbers of non-Muslims. How a 'Two Nation Theory' was ever to be effected without large scale human suffering remained a mystery to all parties involved right up until actual partition[100]. It is in this light, in which Gandhi's comment that 'Hindu Muslim unity... is the breath of our life' (Som, 2004) must be understood. These words proved to be tragically accurate when millions of Muslims as well as Hindus, including Gandhi himself, breathed their last as a result of partition.[101]

5.2.2 *'Integrative Nationalism'*

Gandhi's conception of nationalism was fundamentally different from Hindutva as well as from the Muslim 'Two Nation Theory'. He expanded on Bipin Chandra Pal's earlier notion of composite patriotism. Pal sought to unify all of India's religious groups in the struggle against the British (Kedourie, 1971). Gandhi went further. He sought to unify Indians across

---

[99]In calling Pakistan (which was founded as a secular state) an 'Islamic state', Nehru refers to a broadcast in the United States in February 1948, in which Jinnah said that the Pakistani constitution will embody 'the principles of Islam' (Nehru, J., 2003, Vol. 1, p. 174). In any case, the real problem was not whether Pakistan would choose to adopt Islamic principles (whatever that may mean), but rather the much more fundamental issue that Pakistan came into existence on the premise that South Asian Muslims needed their own homeland because their interests would not be secure in a Hindu-majority state.

[100]Lord Louis Mountbatten, last British Viceroy, initially thought the idea of Pakistan to be 'sheer madness' (Moore, R. J., 1983, p. 530).

[101]It is noted only in passing that Gandhi in promoting unity also and with great ferocity opposed the establishment of a separate electorate for the oppressed Dalits. He drew and continues to draw fierce criticism for this stance, especially from Bhimrao Ramji Ambedkar.

all communal groups, including caste (Hardiman, 2003). In order to do so, he had to find a value basis (which to him was civilisational) that could serve as the common identity for India's different linguistic, religious, caste and ethnic groups. The ideal Indian community Gandhi had in mind was to be based on truth, non-violence, pacifism, tradition, religious sentiments and equality (Som, 2004). To Gandhi, furthermore, these qualities or values resonated particularly well with India's traditions.

Hardiman called this his 'integrative nationalism'. It was 'broad and catholic' (Hardiman, 2003). For Gandhi it was imperative that Indian nationalism would secure, not threaten the fundamental right of each minority to follow its own way of life. He was trying to forge a polity bound together by 'a sense of "neighbourliness"' in which each group would respect the beliefs, and even prejudices, of its fellows for the good of the wider whole. It was on these terms that Gandhi achieved 'a strategic hegemony at this juncture in Indian history' (Hardiman, 2003).

Gandhi was above all a builder of consensus. He wanted to see a stable and thereby peaceful nation, capable of governing itself with honour, prudence and far-sightedness. Under his leadership, India developed a national identity, national pride even, based on a link between greatness and values; a link which was stipulated to be uniquely, or at least particularly, 'Indian'. The idea that India represented a unique, valuable and spiritually superior civilisation was 'a welcome salve to the injured pride' of a colonised people. Thus was nationalism 'which usually feeds on self-aggrandisement and militarism, wedded in India to a principle of self-restraint'. Gandhi had in effect 'nationalised the principle of non-violence. He brought it down from the ether of universal beliefs and gave it a terrestrial home – India'. He thereby, as Jawaharlal Nehru would later write, wrought in the consciousness of India a deep psychological change, 'almost as if some great expert in psychoanalytic methods had probed deep into the patient's past, found out the origins of his complexes, exposed them to his view, and thus rid him of that burden' (Schell, 2005).

Gandhi's nationalism based on morality, and directed against group, interest-based politics and tribal identities, was designed to solve two problems at the same time – to allow for external differentiation not against, but independent of the Western colonisers and to create a possibility for unifying a highly complex society, avoiding discrimination or marginalisation. He arguably achieved this extraordinary feat. It is doubtful whether it could have been accomplished by a lesser thinker and authority than Gandhi was. India, however, had the rare luck to have not only one, but two great helmsmen. For after independence, Nehru brought to bear his own vision of India, without, however, calling into question Gandhi's basic tenets of non-violent tolerance and pluralism.

5.3 Nehru and the Challenge of Creating an Indian Nation

> *'Sometimes I have had the feeling watching Nehru that he is a magician who conjures up a vision of a united, progressive India and that when he passes from the scene, the vision will disappear. It is a vision which he conjures up and he conjures up deliberately... He does it because he knows that India can advance only if it can see visions and dream dreams, if it draws on the best in its past, if it breaks with the worst.'*
>
> (Escott Reid[102])

Nehru would fit Kedourie's stereotype of a third world nationalist bred on Western ideas and intent on copying the admired colonisers much better than Gandhi did. In his *Discovery of India* Nehru freely states – 'I became obsessed with the idea of India... urging me to action so that we might realise some vague but deeply-felt desire of our hearts' (Nehru, 2003). Nehru also follows in the mould of 'positive liberty' thinking. He writes that –

> '...freedom is not a mere matter of political decision or new constitutions, nor even a matter of what is more important, that is, economic policy. It is of the mind and heart and if the mind narrows itself and is befogged and the heart is full of bitterness and hatred, then freedom is absent' (Nehru, 2003).

However, Nehru does not go as far as Gandhi to whom national independence was only one element in a larger religious-philosophical, ethical way of life. For Nehru, it was a sanguine political goal, a matter of pride and principle. He looked to the social sciences, especially history and economics, when phrasing his arguments. Gandhi, by contrast, sought the metaphor, the simple idea.

In terms of content, Gandhi and Nehru differed most sharply when it came to the issue of how poverty in India could be alleviated and how modernity should be approached. Nehru firmly believed in the possibility of progress though industrialisation and science. Where Gandhi advocated a return to the rural economy, Nehru wanted India to shed the old ways, which have ceased to have any purpose in the modern world. 'Old as we are', he said, with 'memories stretching back to the early dawns of human

[102]Escott Reid was Canadian ambassador in India during Nehru's time. He published critical reflections on Nehru under the title *'Envoy to Nehru'* (Reid, E., 1981, p. 233).

history and endeavour, we have to grow young again, in tune with our present time, with the irrepressible spirit and joy of youth in the present and its faith in the future' (Nehru). In that, India has much to learn from the West, which represents the 'spirit of the age' (Nehru, 1946). They had many other minor and major differences stemming from their essentially different characters and tempers, as well as their divergent approaches to life and to politics.

However, Gandhi's influence on and interest in Nehru, and Nehru's loyalty to Gandhi bridged these differences. As much as Nehru was an admirer of the West, he was primarily an admirer of Gandhi. The importance of Gandhi for Nehru can hardly be overestimated. Following the Madras Congress in 1927, a serious disagreement ensued between Gandhi and Nehru concerning the pace of change and the radicalism of the resolution passed. Nehru, provoked by Gandhi's chastisement, charged him with being hesitant and indecisive. However, when Gandhi suggested they make their differences public, Nehru recoiled. He pleaded with Gandhi that after all, he was an errant child in politics. He accepted Gandhi's leadership despite differences of opinion (Som, 2004). At the same time, however, Nehru was himself far too much of an original thinker and leader to simply follow Gandhi's leadership. He developed a view of India uniquely his own.

5.3.1 *A Very Personal Discovery of India – The Past and Nation-Building*

Unlike Gandhi and most nationalists anywhere and at any time, Nehru openly differentiates between a 'nation' as a modern phenomenon on the one hand, and a shared tradition on the other – 'India in the past was not, and is not even now wholly, a nation like France or England is today'. However, like Gandhi and other nationalists, he stipulates that there was an ancient, recognisable 'continuity of a cultural tradition through five thousand years', rivalled only by China (Nehru, 1946; 1949). 'India was Bharata', the holy land of the Hindus. It was held together by ancient pilgrimage sites, geography, Sanskrit, and a feeling of belonging. 'Every resident of the country felt a certain kinship with all others who lived in the great subcontinent'. Thus, he defines India as a 'group of closely allied peoples with a common culture and religion' – or, more poetically, likens India to 'the ocean' which 'received the tribute of a thousand rivers' but continued to be the ocean (Nehru, 2003). Nehru interprets Indian history as the history of a common people, whose cultural core – the village system, the arts, myths, a 'set of moral and mental qualities' – remained relatively stable despite foreign invasions, great diversity and internecine conflict (Nehru, 1946).

As Nanda writes, Nehru's interest in the past was not for its own sake, but primarily in relation to the present. To Nehru, the nationalist movement in India was the 'culmination of a historical process, which had been working itself out over the centuries' (Nanda, 2004, Nehru). Here, Nanda is arguably misunderstanding Nehru. As every nationalist, Nehru used the past for purposes of the present. It is unlikely (albeit not impossible) that Nehru has actually fallen victim to his own myth-making. He constructed 'his' India and gave it a heritage. Nehru himself was, however, the active and not the passive part. The process was not historically 'there', but was, rather, actively managed by nationalists. This becomes clear, when one looks at the actual make-up of Nehru's India, and the choices and selections he made.

Nehru's approach to India – the India he desired to exist, the India of his nationalist agitation – was the product of a selection process. Certain elements were left out, some were de-emphasised and others emphasised. Firstly, and demonstrating most clearly the moment of agency in his nationalism, there were aspects of India's tradition and mindset, which Nehru was very critical about and wished to discontinue. 'There was a great deal that had to be scrapped'. The caste system, for example, while it has some positive aspects (such as creating a strong social and cultural bond), is responsible for much suffering. It is an exclusive system, rigid and hampering progress. Another 'old failing' of India, Nehru identifies, is a tendency to be 'passive, static, quiescent' (Nehru, 1946). Nehru differs sharply from Gandhi when it comes to issues of tradition and modernity. Nehru admires the Western scientific mindset and vitality. India over the last centuries had 'undoubtedly deteriorated... the flexibility of her thought and structure gave place to rigidity' (Nehru, 2003), the 'dust and dirt of the ages... have covered her up... excrescences and abortions... have twisted and petrified her spirit' (Nehru, 1946). In order to face the future, India needs to renew itself, return to what made the country great, to the glorious, unifying past. What has made it great in the past? Nehru's answer is – openness, flexibility, the spirit of courageous scientific inquiry, heterodoxy.

From that standpoint, Nehru de-emphasises the Hindu and religious element in his India. Indian unity is 'essentially cultural... not religious in the narrow sense of the word' (Nehru, 2003). The difference between Nehru's discovery of India and the Hindutva conception of India can be exemplified in the case of emperor Akbar, a Muslim Mughal ruler of India. While he is conspicuously absent from Hindutva's list of national heroes, to Nehru, he was the 'great representative of the old Indian ideal of a synthesis of differing elements and their fusion into a common nationality' (Nehru, 1946). Although the Muslim conquest 'shook India', Islam eventually came into a highly productive cultural relationship with the older Indian traditions. New life forms emerged, which were 'truly a synthesis of the two and yet were essentially Indian' (Nehru). India, Nehru wrote, is a 'curious mixture of an amazing diversity and an abiding unity'. This unity is not based on some 'Hindudom' – and yet, it is fundamentally Indian. In Nehru's interpretation, while India is the product of a perennial Indian character, which has 'persisted through the ages' and has given the country 'a certain individuality', it has, at the same time, a 'composite culture' (Nehru). The various specific life-forms, including the Muslim and the Hindu ones, are – in their diversity – the manifestations of it. In Nehru's (and Gandhi's) interpretation of India, an excessive focus on religious (Hindu) aspects in nationalism doubly misses the point – it is a misrepresentation of Indian culture and it is a misrepresentation of Hinduism. Both are essentially tolerant, flexible and open. Hindu nationalism is not. From the 1930s onwards, the Congress leadership publicly disowned Hindu nationalism for being incompatible with their definition of Indian nationalism as based on tolerance and equality. The nation would not be constructed hierarchically, dominated by the Hindus (Pandey, 1990; Jaffrelot, 1996). In practical terms, Hindu nationalism, Nehru warned, could only end 'in a terrible catastrophe'. Such a prospect 'cannot be tolerated'. Nehru equally rejected the 'Two Nation Theory' as proposed by the Muslim League. In his autobiography of 1936, he scoffed at the idea of a Muslim nation within the nation. It is a vague, spread-out and indeterminate community. 'Politically, the idea is absurd, economically it is fantastic; it is hardly worth considering' (Nehru, 2003).

Whilst de-emphasising religious elements, Nehru attempted to base Indian unity on cultural values and a tolerant way of life. In his interpretation, 'some inner urge towards synthesis, derived essentially from the Indian philosophic outlook, was the dominant feature of Indian cultural and even racial development'. He repeatedly emphasises tolerance as his mantra. He knows that it is the cornerstone of Indian political unity and therefore makes every effort to communicate its historical, cultural legitimacy in India. In Nehru's *Discovery of India* it is a recurring theme. Nehru speaks of an 'atmosphere of tolerance and reasonableness, that acceptance of free-thought in matters of faith, that desire and capacity to live and let live, which are dominant features of Indian culture', of 'some basic ethical doctrines and a philosophic approach to life and a tolerance of other people's ways', of a 'tender humanity, a varied and tolerant culture, and a deep understanding of life in its mysterious ways'. He argues that 'it was the old tradition of India to be tolerant to all faiths and forms of worship' and that the 'philosophic ideal of Indian culture' is 'the integration of man and the stress of goodness, beauty and truth rather than acquisitiveness'. Ideas of 'religious and cultural toleration,' were 'inherent in Indian life' (Nehru). The essence of Indian thought is 'based on a fearless search for truth, on the solidarity of man, even on the divinity of everything living, and on the free and co-operative development of the individual and the species, ever to greater freedom and higher stages of human growth'. In Indian history, there is a 'freedom and flexibility of the mind and a tolerance of the spirit' (Nehru, 1946). India, over the centuries, has 'developed an aristocratic attitude which, secure in its own strength, could afford to be tolerant and broad-minded' (Nehru, 2003). In the final chapter of his *Discovery of India* he formulates the issue most forcefully –

> 'We can never forget the ideals that have moved our race, the dreams of the Indian people through the ages,… their love of truth and beauty and freedom, the basic values that they set up, their understanding of life's mysterious ways, their toleration of other ways than theirs, their capacity to absorb other peoples and their cultural accomplishments, to synthesise them and develop a varied and mixed culture… We will never forget them or cease to take pride in them. If India forgets them she will no longer remain India and much that has made her our joy and pride will cease to be' (Nehru, 1946).

Nehru understands that the matter is not so simple, however. Action is required. Choices have to be made. His interpretation of India – according to his writings, the correct interpretation of India – is in danger of being forgotten or lost. It needs to be recovered, reinvigorated, emphasised and filled with political determination and popular life. Nehru takes a lead in formulating Indian nationalism in such a way as to emphasise the tolerance and synthesis which lead to unity, peace and progress, and to combat the spirit of intolerance and segregation that holds India back and threatens to break her up[103]. Nehru was in the midst of an interpretative battle over the meaning and the shape of India. He was well aware of the potency and danger of the centrifugal forces, and he incessantly warned of them. The centrifugal forces are economic, social and political. In India, he wrote, history has produced instances of both 'the broadest tolerance and catholicity

[103]The view of the Hindu nationalists is, of course, the reverse. Stronger ethnic identity is the path to progress and unity, and the spirit of synthesis is detrimental to the country's development (Sharma, J., 2003).

of thought and opinion, as well as the narrowest social forms of behaviour. This split personality has pursued us and we struggle against it even today'. The split personality has force and historical depth –

> 'Throughout India's history we see the two rival and contradictory forces at work – those in favour of a synthesis and absorption and these fissiparous tendencies which separate. Today we face the same problem in a different context. There are powerful forces working for unity, not only political but cultural also. There are also forces that disrupt and lay stress on separateness'.

Nehru opposed all attempts to interpret and subdivide India into smaller national groups uncompromisingly and with a passion that is stirred in response to a credible threat. Thus he speaks of the 'utterly evil tendencies set in motion by Mr. Jinnah and the Muslim League'. Partition was 'inherently wrong and unnatural'. Nehru appealed 'to work continuously and deliberately for the promotion of national unity and emotional integration of all our people' (Nehru, 2003).

These statements and Nehru's actions as a statesman, as an educator, communicator and visionary, demonstrate the central element of agency in the formation of Indian nationalism. While the values Nehru again and again seeks to hammer into the Indian collective consciousness no doubt find numerous reflections in India's long and varied past, they are nevertheless a very personal and, with the political necessities and goals in mind, deeply practical discovery of India. Tharoor's suggestion that Nehru in a sense 'invented' India is thus not far off the mark (Tharoor, 2003). Nehru's invention was an act of ideological politics. Does Kedourie's theory about the derivative and potentially violent nature of ideological politics hold in Nehru's case? Was Nehru an idealist of the dangerous type?

5.3.2 *Pragmatism and Idealism*

Like Gandhi, Nehru combined values with pragmatism. Although he was more attracted by ideology than Gandhi was, he was also able to avoid the pitfalls of dogmatism, whilst nevertheless showing very strong leadership. This mixture of qualities, extremely rare as it is, was of fundamental importance to the development of the modern Indian identity.

About truth, Nehru wrote that while it may exist as an absolute, it 'cannot be apprehended in its fullness by the finite mind of man'. As man inquires into truth, new aspects of the truth come to mind. Hence, truth always has to be sought and renewed, in order to be 'a living truth of humanity... offering guidance in the present and for the future'. If any aspect of the truth has become petrified in a dogma, 'it ceases to grow and develop and adapt itself to the changing needs of humanity; other aspects of it remain hidden and it fails to answer the questions of a succeeding age' (Nehru). Nehru proposes a highly empirical, pragmatic 'scientific' approach to life, which refuses to accept anything 'without testing and trial', is ready to change previous conclusions 'in the face of new evidence', and relies only on 'observed fact' (Nehru, 1946). 'There is no room for bigots...,' he writes, 'we must cultivate the spirit of enquiry and welcome all knowledge whether the source of it is the East or the West' (Nehru, 2003). If European ideas have in any way contaminated Indian elites, as Kedourie suggested, it was, in Nehru's case, not the romantic, unrestrained, vindictive idea of nationalism, but rather the scientific, humane heritage of the enlightened liberals of the nineteenth century, such as John Stuart Mill[104].

Even if one can never be certain of having attained the truth, though, gaining knowledge, realising truth (and appreciating goodness and beauty) are 'the ultimate purposes of man'. This approach, if taken seriously, is fundamentally idealist. Not personal or national benefit, but achieving what is true and just, are the ends of life. However, given that 'truth' is abstract, only an 'ideal' goal, there is need for some more specific value guidance.

> 'Some faith seems necessary in things of the spirit which are beyond the scope of our physical world, some reliance on moral, spiritual, and idealistic conceptions, or else we have no anchorage, no objectives or purpose in life' (Nehru, 1946). 'There must be something permanent in the essential cultural and moral values which does not or should not change' (Nehru, 2003).

In this point, Nehru differs significantly from Gandhi who had not advocated that people take on any form of belief, but relied entirely on his values, reason and his own ability to communicate and persuade. Moreover, whereas Gandhi looked for improvement first within the individual, out of his own free will, Nehru is tending towards improvement top-down. Nehru believed in the idea of progress, into 'some vague conception of the perfect man and a better world'. Although Nehru admits that 'perfection may be impossible of attainment', '...some vital force urges us on' (Nehru, 1946). Such statements can be considered to be concretely and politically idealistic (as opposed to pragmatic and abstractly or personally idealistic). They are going in the direction of a utopian mindset – precisely what liberal thinkers such as Kedourie, Berlin or Popper feared most.

---

[104]In his *Glimpses of World History*, Nehru quotes a passage from Mill's work *On Liberty*, espousing the need for freedom of expression and the benefits of argument. Nehru calls Mill's attitude that of a 'philosopher, a seeker of the truth' (Nehru, J., 1949, p. 531).

Ironically, but not without some measure of historical congruency, Nehru ideologically petrifies Gandhi. The constant elements which should never be changed are those, he says, laid down by Gandhi – 'truth and non-violence'. He continues – 'we praise the Mahatma and we pay homage to his memory and yet we stray widely from the path he had pointed out to us. His basic lesson that only through right means can right ends be achieved is seldom remembered' (Nehru, 2003).

Despite these doctrinal ideological elements, Nehru, as a political character, remains elusive. Within each idealist Babushka doll, there is a pragmatic one[105]. The idealism is checked and balanced, in part at least, by Nehru's pragmatism, by his belief that no idea can retain its vigour and creativity without 'contact with life'. There is a constant need to adapt (Nehru, 1946). One of Nehru's key traits was the openness with which he presented his thought-processes and laid bare his own arguments. His style of interaction, writing and dialogue is not dogmatic; it is rather imbued with a deep sense of humanism. One of the prime examples is the inaugural speech entitled 'Culture and Wisdom', which he gave at the Indian Council of Cultural Relations in 1950. He attempts to explain what makes India culturally 'Indian', and how one is to deal with one's culture. Likening culture to a tree with stable roots as well as extravagant and fleeting flowers, he argues that culture must have both, depth and flexibility. While depth gives an identity and stability, flexibility is both expression of and condition for growth, progress and – life. The need for flexibility, coupled with the impossibility of grasping the truth entirely, implies that what is needed is openness and tolerance. Like Gandhi, he wanted to keep his intellectual windows open – 'the cultured mind, having roots in itself, should have its doors and windows open, imbibing other things'. He rejects the 'moral crusade', the positive assertion of an ideology based on a belief in being right (Nehru, 2003).

Nehru's idealism is not expressed in a specific 'positive' ideological exposition of the truth. It is, rather, expressed in a general belief in mankind. In line with the profound sense of optimism and can-do pervading his entire *Discovery of India*, in the address to the Institute of Cultural Relations, he declared that 'the right way is important' in dealing with one another – being open to others from the secure platform of one's cultural basis, 'a friendly approach brings a friendly response'. 'I have not the shadow of a doubt', he underlines, 'that it is a fundamental rule of human life that if

---

[105]Tharoor, more elegantly, formulated it thus – 'the paradox-ridden Jawaharlal Nehru… was India' (Tharoor, S., 2003, p. ix).

the approach is good the response is good. If the approach is bad the response is likely to be bad, too' (Nehru, 2003). This is idealism bordering on naiveté. The 'right way', for Nehru, is the way of tolerance and respect, the way of India since ancient times. That is his moral crusade. Like Gandhi, then, Nehru is fighting the same battle as liberal thinkers such as Kedourie, Berlin or Popper are, but also like Gandhi, he is doing so with the means they shun, the means of the politician – ideological politics.

5.4 Moral and Instable Nationalism

The national leadership had a number of levers at hand to craft a nation and come to terms with what Octavio Paz called the 'diabolically confused reality' and the 'enormous historical contradiction' (Paz, 1997) they were presiding over[106]. And they needed to make use of all of them – the state institutions, the political system and the Congress party organisation were important instruments of nation-building[107]. The Indian Constitution was a blueprint, based on a pious fiction and aimed at the nation-to-be. Economic policy took a central role. Development – industrialisation, autonomy and the reigning-in of poverty – was regarded as the most important task by Nehru (Nanda, 2004, Nehru). Economic planning and growth was at the same time considered a driver for unity, an act of unity

[106]Octavio Paz, a poet and diplomat, admits that his book about India is 'the child not of knowledge but of love' (Paz, O., 1997). Nevertheless – or perhaps for that reason? – his judgment is balanced and his insight is significant. Both are based on an intuitive grasp of India, which serves him well in trying to fathom the contradictions at work.

[107]There is an excellent and increasing body of literature on the political power structures in India, which can be analysed best by looking at the politics in individual states. Myron Weiner, in his path-breaking edited volume of state politics in India, has led the way (Weiner, M., 1968). A highly interesting regional study has been provided, for example, by V. M. Sirsikar. He argues that cohesion is provided by an internal multi-layered power-structure. Values and identities are conducive to success (Sirsikar, V. M., 1995). What on the local level is often factional, opportunistic identity politics, on the national level can become constructive nation-building politics. To an extent, the values and identity chosen, depend on the political use, the level of responsibility and representation of the actor (Brass, P. R., 1974; 1991). On a more general level, Kohli's 'Democracy and Discontent' is a key text. He identified a process of 'deinstitutionalisation' as the primary challenge to good governance in India (Kohli, A., 1990). More recently, a comprehensive study on governance in India was put forward by Subrata Mitra. He combines a neo-institutionalist and rational choice model to make sense of the puzzle of governance in India without taking recourse to cultural idiosyncrasies. He nevertheless gives ample consideration to the problems and uses of identity (Mitra, S. K., 2006). See, also, Sumit Sarkar's essay on the heritage of democracy in Kohli's edited volume on the success of India's democracy (Kohli, A., 2001).

and a symbol for unity. However, a nation is more than a community of common interests, such as a customs union or an area under common administration. A nation requires an emotional identity-glue – a sense of common identity. In how far did the National Movement manage to create what Gramsci called a 'national-popular will' and Schöpflin called the 'consent to be ruled'?

Gandhi's great intellectual contribution to Indian nationalism (as well as to social science at large) was his understanding that if Indians would withdraw their tacit consent, their cooperation, British rule would simply implode. Since the British were ultimately dependent on Indian opinion, they were vulnerable to Gandhi's key tactics – to confront the political opponents so forcefully and unequivocally with the 'truth' of their actions (i.e. the bigotry of their actions) that they were forced to either insist on a morally wrong course of action (which would be obvious and cause resentment) or to reconsider. He first developed this tactic in South Africa. It involved breaking discriminatory laws in a systematic and demonstrative manner, not by aggressive means, but by steadfast non-cooperation. In the resulting, dynamic confrontations with the authorities, his source of power was his ability to hold the moral high ground. He did so by keeping actions strictly non-violent, and by allowing room for dialogue and compromise. Thus, Gandhi forced the opponents into a confrontation on his terms and thereby – so the idea goes – into an acceptance of the nonconformity of their laws and deeds with their own principles.

Gandhi's strategy had two aims, one external, one internal. He wanted to gain independence from the British. And he wanted a unified, peaceful nation to take over after independence. His strategy was to combine the two goals into one – only a ripe society was able to wrest independence from the militarily superior British, and only such a society was worthy of it and could deal with freedom. He tried to educate Indians in order to make them more capable of fighting for independence and more capable of running their own state. He was building the nation at the same time as he was fighting for its independence. Gandhi linked morality with power – the better the nation, the stronger it is. He also linked power with morality – only the good deserve to be free.

This basic relationship between morality and unity became the mainstay of nationalism and later, under Nehru, of a national identity. 'Sometimes, though rarely', Nehru said, 'the group itself rises to a height of moral behaviour, forcing the individual to forget his narrow and selfish ways. More often the group falls below the individual standard' (Nehru, 1946). Gandhi and Nehru were working on this by – a historical rarity –

mobilising the masses responsibly and for responsible ends, transcending the petty pride of most nationalisms (Tharoor, 2003). The nature of the morality (an essentially liberal one) and the method of political agitation employed (one of trial-and-error) ensured that Gandhi's and Nehru's ideological politics did not take on a de-humanising dynamic of their own. At the same time, as the case of India challenges Gellner's materialist theory of nationalism, it calls his criticism of nationalist ideology and leaders as being simplistic and interchangeable into question. If nationalists cannot free-ride on a large scale socio-economic development, they must produce ideas and motivations. Kedourie believed that ideas are always mere reproductions of a basic morphology. The Indian example refutes this statement also. The nationalist leaders produced an original and creative ideology – not simply in terms of content, but in terms of an active, conscious and radical 'self-interpretation'.

From the perspective of national stability, there are two divergent results of the efforts of the National Movement. On the one hand, their choice for an all-encompassing Indian state, defined by values and not by linguistic, religious or ethnic community, made the task of nation-building a very difficult one indeed. Independence has given birth to a state marked by 'an immensely complex interplay between national consciousness and local collectivities based on religion and caste identity' (Talbot, 2000). George Jones wrote in the year of independence that 'complexity is the keynote of India. It remains an inconsistent mixture of races, languages, and religions' (Jones, 1947). There was no clearly defined 'nation' with a clearly demarcated territory which demanded its state in order to come into its own. There could not have been, unless there would have been what is nowadays euphemistically termed 'ethnic cleansing' on an enormous scale. The tragedies of partition appallingly demonstrated this. Instead, a state came into existence, which needed some kind of national identity to hold it together and justify its existence. On the other hand, the efforts of the National Movement to deal with this complexity by way of instilling a value-based nationalism were guided by some of the best leadership the age of anti-colonial nationalism has witnessed. Gandhi, Nehru and the other leaders of the National Movement were painfully aware of the underlying instability. Consequently, at the 'top of their goals, the sine qua non for everything else was an abiding faith in and determination to preserve the national unity and integrity of the country against all internal and external threats to it' (Brass, 2000). After independence, the Indian state and its government were faced with the terrible hatred, the violence and the mass migrations partition brought about. The borders were under dispute.

Kashmir and Hyderabad were only the largest of many unsolved issues of a successor state. The infrastructure threatened to break down. Soon, Gandhi, who single-handedly pacified vast tracts of the land, would be dead. The challenge of holding the country together was immense. Thus, for Nehru, the 'task of nation-building was a continuation of the freedom struggle'. Independence was the 'prelude to a massive reconstruction of the polity and economy' (Nanda, 2004, Nehru).

The result of the choices of the National Movement was a state that did not break up but continued to exist in a condition of precariousness for now almost 60 years, a vast political experiment which astonishes merely by survival and by its ability to absorb shocks and social tensions, which has developed a multilayered system of institutions and identities far more intricate than the designs of any one movement, let alone single leader could have been (Mitra, 2006). Gandhi's dictum that nations are not formed in a day but in years (Gandhi, 1997), encapsulates both – the aspect of agency ('are formed') and the aspect of instability. Given the difficulties, the specter of an exclusive, culturally defined 'strong' nationalism, the temptation to simply cut the Gordian knot (whatever the human cost) is ever present. So far, India has by-and-large managed not to fall into this trap. At the same time, it must not be forgotten that, while the Gandhian/Nehruvian nationalism became the basis of the modern Indian nation, the challenge posed to it by the Hindu and Muslim nationalisms did not die away but remained and shadowed the new state. A 'discourse of Hindu-Muslim difference was created that has struck deep roots in both communities and acquired a partly self-sustaining momentum that at the same time continues to be fed by political competition' (Brass, 2003). Partition on religious/cultural grounds has brought forth a constant challenge to the legitimacy of the value-based national project (Rothermund, 1998a).

The frailty of the Indian nation means that there is a constant uneasiness and intellectual struggle over what defines it. The Gandhian/Nehruvian nationalism is challenged by the diverse ground reality as well as by rival approaches to it. The key characteristic of this struggle is that it goes beyond the natural evolution of an identity which can never be fixed in time (Som, 2004). It is, more fundamentally, what Mitra recently called a 'game on the rules of the game' (Mitra, 2006), a debate about who could engage in the process and on what grounds. The basic identity crafted by Gandhi and Nehru remains challenged by culturalist, dangerous, ideological politics. It needs to be affirmed constantly. This instability and the value-basis of Indian nationalism have a profound effect on foreign policy. Nation-building and identity values both unconsciously spill over into foreign policy and consciously harness foreign policy for their ends.

The Hindutva movement proposed a different approach to nation-building – giving up pluralism in favour of relatively more cultural homogeneity. Had it been successful, it would almost certainly have led to enormous bloodshed. Unfortunately, however, such a prospect has not always prevented such political decision from being made. It is also thinkable that India could have undergone large scale social engineering, as Stalin has done in Russia or Mao in China, trading off democracy and individual rights for cohesion by destroying cultural identities and creating a nation of undifferentiated members. The option makes one shiver, but again it is unfortunately not without historical precedent. India could have also chosen a path of being split up into many ethnically, or linguistically homogenous groups. This also is an option promising enormous bloodshed. In any case, a culturally homogenous unit (established at the unthinkably high price) would ultimately provide more natural internal stability than a culturally complex unit.

Gandhi, Nehru and their key co-fighters and co-politicians chose a path that seems to be justified not only by actual events, but also by reason. However, the product of their approach, the Indian nation state they had to steer into the future, was an awkward one by the standards of modernity. It was an enormous, spectacular salad in a fragile identity bowl. Strengthening the bowl posed a significant challenge. The intensity of the required ideological politics was such that it could not stop at the gates of foreign policy. Identity became entangled in a realm usually preserved for strategy. At the same time, foreign policy, like all other levers, had to be used in order to prop-up the fragile identity bowl.

6

Foreign Policy and National Identity under Nehru

The strategic culture influencing Indian foreign policy under Nehru was – for all intents and purposes – the strategic culture of Nehru. The content of the strategic culture, the ideas of moral and political greatness, as well as the conflation of ideals and interests, are the product of the application of the national identity formation process onto the field of foreign affairs through the ideological politics described in the preceding chapter.

It would be wrong to think of the relationship between national identity and foreign policy as being a one way street – with an actor and an objective world upon which the actor impacts. An actor defines himself through his actions and through the reception of his actions by others. An identity built on and reflected by values takes on a dynamic of its own, it reflects back and forth, as in a gallery of mirrors, an image of the self in the world and an image of the world in the self. A second gallery of mirrors stands between the national identity and the identity of a political entrepreneur, each influencing the other. Nehru was both builder and – with his success – increasingly a consumer of a modern Indian identity. He believed what he wanted to believe and what he needed to believe in order to convince others of his version of Indianness. Like all great idealists, he was so convincing because he was himself taken in by his idea and vision, believing firmly in it, taking on the proposed identity himself[108].

Subsequently, foreign policy is not only consciously used to 'reflect' national identity. National identity also 'spills over' into foreign policy. The

[108]Ron Rosenbaum explores this idea in a highly interesting study entitled 'Explaining Hitler'. He asked himself in how far Hitler himself really believed his theories and argues he probably did, because he could not have been able to mobilise so many people for his outrageous ends if he had not believed in them wholeheartedly himself. He could otherwise not have been as convincing (Rosenbaum, R., 1998).

freedom struggle and the implementation of freedom (nationally and internationally) are 'different sides of the same coin'. One comes from the other –

> 'What the independent nation did with its opportunities and what it sought to achieve derived initially from the logic of the nationalist struggles and the ideas behind those struggles. The trajectory of the nation state thereafter continued to be influenced by the dynamics of those nationalist struggles' (Masselos, 2005).

The root cause of this inter-dynamic relationship is the essentially idealist (i.e. non-materialist), agent-driven nature of Indian nationalism. National identity and foreign policy are interlinked arenas of political entrepreneurship.

A related point, demonstrating the intimate relationship between Indian foreign policy and Indian nation-building from the opposite perspective, namely from foreign policy rather than from nation-building, was made by Appadorai (Appadorai, 1981; Jha, 2002). He argued that the effectiveness of foreign policy depends to a significant degree on national coherence and strength, which nationalism can produce. A weak national identity is thus a serious restraint on an effective foreign policy. Conse-quently, it can be inferred that a foreign policy which furthers national unity, improves its own power-base. Appadorai looks at pluralism, democracy and economics as limiting factors and concludes that –

> '...a united and strong nation is the sine qua non of an effective foreign policy. There is sound wisdom in Gladstone's observation that the first condition of a good foreign policy is a good domestic policy. A united people well above the poverty line and bereft of the baneful influence of casteism, communalism and regionalism is the only sure base for a sound foreign policy. To the extent that our top-leaders, supported by our people, realise the meaning of this statement and bend all their energies to secure unity and succeed in their efforts, to that extent they will not only improve India's image abroad, but will also enhance the ability of India to use foreign policy so as to achieve her national interests' (Appadorai, 1981, p. 232).

This is the other side of the coin analysed in this chapter. Here, the focus is not on what domestic unity can do for foreign policy, but rather on what foreign policy can do for domestic unity. Appadorai's statement, however, underlines the intimate interrelatedness of the two policy fields.

6.1 Idealism and Global Mission in Nehru's Foreign Policy

Nehru's greatness as a statesman, Nanda writes, stems from three primary sources – He was 'one of the principal architects of India's freedom', 'a nation-builder' and 'a champion of world peace' (Nanda, 2004, Nehru). These three policy projects did not exist parallely and independently of each other. They were interconnected – psychologically, of course, but also pragmatically and rationally. The freedom struggle, nation-building and foreign policy concepts reflected, conditioned and reinforced each other.

The link between a type of nationalism based on ethnic, religious or linguistic idiosyncrasy (providing a concretely defined and demarcated communal 'us') and a foreign policy based on a national interest is relatively straightforward, even natural. Both nationalism and foreign policy are concerned only with the welfare of a particular group. However, a type of nationalism based on values which are held to be universal, such as tolerance or non-violence or democracy or secularism (but are taken to have a particular cultural foothold in the specific nation espousing them), supports a foreign policy based on national interest only awkwardly. The belief that once the values are realised at home they should also be spread abroad, as well as the belief that international interaction should be based on principles comparable to those of intra-national interaction is usually not far off. Or, In Nehru's own words –

> 'Today we are freeing India. That is a great thing. But an even greater thing is the cause of humanity itself. And because we feel that our struggle is a part of the great human struggle to end suffering and misery, we can rejoice that we are doing our little bit to help the progress of the world' (Nehru, 2003).

India's freedom and independence must, therefore, be thought of 'in terms of the world and of world cooperation' (Nehru, 2003).

Since Nehru did not believe in laissez faire economics, he certainly did not have Adam Smith's famous maxim that it is not from the benevolence of the butcher that we expect him to provide our dinner, but from his regard for his own interest in mind, when speaking about the coincidence of the national and the global good. Global welfare is not simply a systemic side-product of national welfare. Nation and world are manifestly linked arenas of political entrepreneurship. What is true for India is true for all nations. 'It is quite impossible today to think of current events or of history in the making in terms of any one nation or country or patch of territory; you have inevitably to think of the world as a whole'. As much as values have to be defined, defended and enshrined in the domestic political struggle, 'a consideration of cultural and moral values and standards is essential if we have to solve the problems that afflict the world today'. (Nehru, 2003) Nehru, with his profoundly optimistic belief in the possibility of man-made progress, had global, system-level concerns. These were fundamentally linked to the project of Indian nationhood as based on common universal liberal values of peaceful coexistence. The very nature of these values demanded internationalisation.

At the same time, Indian value nationalism (like its US variant) facilitates and makes easier a more internationally oriented perspective. The government of a nation built on universal values can pursue policies which aim at 'a new era of international co-operation' (Nehru, 1946) with more internal and external credibility than states committed to a more narrow, concrete and non-moral national identity. Nehru explains that Indian nationalism was in this respect superior to the mainstream European type of nationalism, because it was –

> '...at no time opposed to internationalism... There was no necessary conflict between the two for, unlike the aggressive nationalism of Europe, it did not seek to interfere with others but rather to co-operate with them to their common advantage' (Nehru, 1946).

Nehru was a great educator, an old-fashioned 'father of the nation'. He produced a constant flow of messages, political-moral in content and more pedagogical than argumentative in purpose, elucidating his views, his visions and his reasoning – broadcasts and speeches to Indians, letters to his bureaucratic apparatus, talks and discussions with the political establishment. He also wrote, toured and spoke abroad, explaining India and the world to foreign statesmen and citizen alike (regardless of whether they expressed an interest or not). He understood the importance of communication for political unity. India, he argued, is a continent, not just a country, comparable to North America. 'Till the advent of modern communications and modern methods of transport, it was very difficult for such a vast area to hold together politically... A basic political unity was thus not possible in the past' (Nehru, 2003). In the modern age, however, a figure like Gandhi could reach the masses by way of newspapers, radio and modern transportation, producing effective nationwide symbols such as his salt march or the fasts.

This skill of stirring the hearts of millions of Indians through potent, clear simplicity, Nehru admired immensely about Gandhi. His own strengths were different. He was an intellectual, not a magician of the simple gesture. He consequently focussed his leadership on the elites, mainly on the political community, reaching into the bureaucracy, into the opinion-shaping circles and into the political processes in order to implant his understanding of India and of India's foreign policy guidelines into the Indian state machine.

From these efforts stems what Cohen called India's 'distinct civilisational identity', its idiosyncratic approach to foreign policy. It is a result of an agent-driven nationalism (ideological politics), capable of mobilising the people 'around a unique set of values, images, and ideas' (Cohen, 2001). The following sections will analyse the mechanism, by which the link between the Nehruvian national project (the 'civilisational identity') and foreign policy functions.

6.1.1 *Rationalism and Realism in Nehru's Foreign Policy*

Nehru had a highly sophisticated grasp of the geopolitical realities of his day. He understood the complex and ever moving balance of power, the role of rhetoric and propaganda, of fear and intimidation, the subtleties of power, psychologies of other nations and statesmen. He made mistakes in his assessments, of course, most notably in his evaluation of China and in his selective perspective on Stalin's Soviet Union. However, by-and-large, he was a more incisive, balanced and educated observer of the international scene than most other statesmen were or, indeed, are.

However, above and beyond the level of analysis dealing with distributions of power and with India's position in the tangles of international politics, Nehru was drawn to the larger problems of the age. Understandably, he believed that imperialism and the world wars had delegitimised Western claims to world leadership as well as Western theories of international relations based on the balance of power (and peace through deterrence) and a narrow focus on national interests without an active concern for substantial systemic improvements (Nehru, 1946). Furthermore, he quite rightly insisted that the invention of nuclear weapons had changed the rules of the game entirely. The Clausewitzian concept of war as a limited and fairly precise instrument in the repertoire of states, useful for the achievement of clearly defined political goals, is meaningless under conditions threatening nuclear annihilation. No possible political end could justify nuclear war. Nuclear destruction was, however, what the two power blocs threatened each other with. War and the threat of war became absurd propositions (Nehru, 2003; compare, Schell, 2005).

What was needed was a new world order in conjunction with a new approach to international politics, comparable to Gandhi's radically new approach to domestic political power struggle. Nehru was a fervent supporter of international law and organisations, a believer in the possibility of progress and the idea of a peaceful global civilisation. The end of European imperial domination and a renaissance of the newly independent nations, first in Asia and later in Africa, would bring about, he hoped, a radical change in climate. He repeatedly referred to, appealed to and sought to mobilise for his visions, the African and Asian states who shared a common history of oppression, the Asian states in particular who supposedly shared a vague notion of Asian values ('essentially peaceful'[109], quite the opposite of European power politics) and especially China, with which he believed India shared civilisational grandeur and the calm reason of antiquity.

Underlying this belief in the possibility of a new, better world order, was Nehru's confusion of realism (what states do) with a rationalism bordering on a utopian belief in man (what states would do if they were all interested in peacefully preserving the status-quo and took a long-term perspective, i.e. if they would behave moderately and respectfully rather than egoistically, like well-mannered members of a functioning society). Underlying this confusion was an exaggerated belief in the power of thought in shaping material reality (Nehru, 1960; Husain, 1961). Characteristically, Nehru wrote that now that India has gained independence, it has to engage with the world 'not only on the basis of principle...', but... – one would expect the sentence to finish with – also on the basis of interests, reality, or power. Instead, Nehru continues with the opposite – '...but also on the far more difficult plane of application of a principle in a complicated situation'. Nehru's world is one of our own making that can be consciously, purposely shaped by statesmen. For this reason, he stressed the need for a 'peaceful temper' and for 'ideological disarmament' (Nehru, 2003). With the right mindset and the will to act, one could then set to work on the structural causes underlying conflict – inequality, oppression and poverty.

Nehru's thinking originated in the experience of the Indian National movement, in which he was both leader and follower (of Gandhi). Naturally, as a nationalist leader, he believed – or at least stated – that it was the moral power of Gandhian resistance that brought about success and not the momentous geopolitical changes following the Second World War, including a serious weakening of the power of the British colonisers.

Nehru understood that his vision of the world was in part idealism. Idealism in the sense that he was pushing for change, for something that

---

[109]In a speech on BBC in 1951 entitled 'The Temper of Peace' (Nehru, J., 2003, Vol. 2, p. 433).

could become reality if the other nations of the world could be persuaded to join him. Idealism required a struggle with realism (Das, 1961). There was an opportunity for a better world, but in order to make this opportunity a reality, it was essential not to let the ideals be eroded by hypocrisy and instead 'to continually bridge the gulf between that idealism and that practice which is forced down upon us by circumstances' (Nehru, 2003). In how far he succeeded in doing so is another matter (Maxwell, 1974; Reid, 1981). In terms of his worldview, however, hope became intertwined with analysis, wish with fact. Reality is always in the making, but Nehru perhaps exaggerated the capacity of humans and nations to act for their common good. In 1950, for instance, following the North Korean attack on the South, he wrote to South Korea in utter disregard of the ground realities that 'our moral help is a big enough thing, which out-balances the petty military help of some other countries' (Gopal, 1993). Nehru's idealism has been affirmed by his experience of Gandhi's moral and rational power in the struggle with the British. Who could blame him for seeing in this unique struggle not a wonderful historical exception, but rather the prototype of a new order? And who could blame him, given the many close shaves of the Cold War such as the Cuban Missile Crisis, for believing that such change is absolutely vital for the survival of mankind? The effect of his idealism was, however, a very slow adjustment of Indian foreign policy to the realities of international politics.

6.1.2 *Foreign Policy Ideals as Unconscious 'Spill-Over' from Nation-Building*

The line between national politics and international politics, between the welfare of India and the welfare of the world at large became blurred, if not at times invisible, under Gandhi's leadership of the National Movement. The focus on values during the struggle for independence, together with the tendency of the great minds in the Indian intellectual tradition (of which Gandhi was a prime example) to emphasise the practical and universal implementation of values in everyday life and stress an essential ontological unity between ends and means (Zimmer, 1969), created an atmosphere profoundly unreceptive to considerations of national interest as based on an India-first ideology.

Gandhi believed that morality and reality are as inextricably linked as religion and politics are. Each would be meaningless without the other, they gave each other purpose. Morality needs to be tested and put to use in reality, it only makes sense in the realm of action. Action, on the other hand, needs to be guided by morality otherwise it is blind and meaningless. Reality is constructed by our actions. Idealism, therefore, 'could and did have a place in the tangles of Realpolitik' (Masselos, 2005). According to Parel, Gandhi even entirely rejected the modern principle of reason of state or national interest as a legitimate principle in international politics (Parel, 1997). Count Camillo Cavour, mastermind behind the Italian unification in the nineteenth century and as much an icon of Realpolitik as Otto von Bismarck, was, for instance, denounced by Gandhi for his 'machinations', which 'disgrace that portion of the history of Italy' (Gandhi, 1997). This judgment is all the more remarkable, because Cavour helped Italy (by way of his 'machinations') to become an independent and unified state in the face of great power opposition – a situation not unlike India's own. The principles upon which Cavour's actions were based, those of a national interest with no recognition for 'the higher law of dharma' are fundamentally 'inconsistent with non-violence' (Parel, 1997).

In a Young India Article in 1925, Gandhi laid out how his patriotism included 'not only the welfare of India but the whole world'. The Indian national idea 'wants to organise itself or to find full self-expression for the benefit and service of humanity at large' (Gandhi, 1994). Nehru quotes Gandhi's idea of nationalism in his *Discovery of India* –

> 'My (Gandhi's) idea of nationalism is that... if need be the whole of the country may die, so that the human race may live... I do want to think in terms of the whole world. My patriotism includes the good of mankind in general. Therefore my service to India includes my service to humanity...' (Nehru, 1946).

In light of other remarks by Gandhi, this seems like hyperbole, but it shows that his universalist sense of mission, in combination with a particularly Gandhian idea of self-sacrifice (which was not entirely shared by most other nationalists including Nehru), far exceeds the universalism of the French Revolutionaries or of the founding fathers of the United States. In a way, it was the price Gandhi (and after him, Nehru) paid for a highly original approach to nationalism, the price for avoiding the 'narrowness, selfishness, exclusiveness which is the bane of modern nations' (Gandhi, 1994).

Crucially, however, as explained above, the unity of ends and means was tied in Gandhi's mind not only by principle but also by expediency. There was no real conflict of interest between the good of the part and the good of the whole, between the good of India and that of the world. He believed in the inherent utility of moral action and felt that immoral policies would sooner or later backfire and destroy the actor, here – the precarious construct called the Indian nation (Narain, 1987).

The logical link that became ingrained in Nehru's mind was an unusual conflation of morality and necessity. It was a belief that the very general civilisational challenge to affirm moral principles (worthy ends in themselves) by moral action, on the one hand, and the much more specific political challenge to affirm the internal construction of the Indian nation, both spiritually and physically, using the specific political instrument of moral action (including rhetoric), on the other hand, were essentially one and the same. Under the roof of Gandhi's overarching and fundamentally philanthropic belief that the good and the useful, the ideal and the interest coincide, this path to nation-building was understood as involving no compromise with interests. It was seen, rather, as a synthesis of ideal and interest on a higher level. This link – translated by Nehru into a new grammar of foreign policy – became the basis of an Indian exceptionalism.

This exceptionalism drew further strength from Gandhi's highly critical perspective on Western modernity and his efforts at building an identity on the premise that it is the tendency of the Indian civilisation 'to elevate the moral being' while it is the tendency of material Western civilisation 'to propagate immorality' (Gandhi, 1997). Although Nehru did not share Gandhi's wholesale condemnation of Western modernity (to the contrary, he embraced the Western way of life and sought to emulate its socio-economic achievements), he believed that Indian civilisation had certain advantages over Western civilisation with regard to avoiding conflict. Western civilisation seemed to him 'to lack something to give it stability, some basic principles to give meaning to life' (Nehru, 1946)[110].

Nehru (among many others) was deeply impressed by the un-precedented coincidence of morality and power and thus political success, which Gandhi represented. It struck a deep chord in him. In his *Discovery of India* Nehru declared, full of admiration and with profound satisfaction – 'I don't know of any other nationalist movement which has been so free from hatred... His (Gandhi's) nationalism... was entirely free from any aggressive trend'. It was so, because Gandhi's nationalism and political ambition was not directed simply at evicting the British qua occupiers in a zero-sum world confined by lust for wealth, power or glory, but it was directed at a future which held more and better things in store for everyone, including Indians (and, presumably, the British). Gandhi changed the rules of the game. Nehru shared his essentially optimistic approach to politics.

---

[110]The quote also refers to the link between principles (values) and political stability.

Long before independence, he wrote that a free India would work for the 'establishment of a real world order based on freedom and democracy, utilising the world's knowledge and resources for the progress and advancement of humanity' (Nehru). The 1940 All India Congress resolution gave institutional expression to this claim. Non-violence was affirmed and a call was made for the establishment 'of a new and juster political and economic order'. Depending on practical realities, free India would lead the way and 'do its utmost to give effect to this policy of disarmament'. It will 'peacefully labour' to ultimately produce a 'comity of free nations for the peace and progress of the world' (Nehru, 1946). Nehru himself stressed the need for complete, global disarmament in the interest of world peace and proposed a new world order in which justice and equality made true and lasting cooperation among nations possible. He suggested the establishment of an international peace-keeping force to keep aggressors at bay (Nehru, 2003).

After independence, laying out the basic principles of Indian foreign policy to be presented before the UN in 1948, Nehru stated that –

> '...in world affairs generally we should stand for everything that promotes peace and avoids war and everything that puts an end to any imperialist domination of one country over another. At the same time, we should work for close cooperation between nations with a view ultimately to help in the establishment of some world order.' (Nehru, 2003).

He also referred to 'One World' (Nehru, 2003). The ideas were ultimately diplomatically enshrined as 'peaceful coexistence' under the tenets of 'Panchsheel'.

The continuing stress on the same values – peaceful engagement of others for mutual benefit, tolerance and non-interference, respect and equality, and especially the inseparability of ends and means – from the Gandhian-led struggle for independence during which Nehru played a major role, through to Nehru's long tenure as Prime Minister of an independent state, suggests that there is a considerable 'spill-over' effect. Nehru, the critical but enthused first disciple of Gandhi, and Nehru the statesman and politician were not two different individuals. They held similar ideas, adjusted by time and situations. In fact, Nehru managed to retain an unusually consistent personality throughout a life tested by challenges and temptations spawning the depths of prison cells and the heights of glory and power. Given Nehru's centrality to Indian foreign policy, the personal 'spill-over' and the political and national 'spill-over' are intimately connected.

6.1.3 *Foreign Policy Ideals as Conscious 'Reflections' for Nation-Building*

Nehru believed that Indian ideals of pluralism and tolerance could not be taken for granted. Although they were supposedly deeply rooted in Indian history and traditions, they had to be affirmed domestically, but also through international relations. Indians 'have to live up to them'. There are too many people in India, who 'talk of high philosophies and our ancient greatness, but act in narrow grooves and show intolerance to our neighbour' (Nehru, 2003). Nehru frequently and harshly castigated India for its shortcomings while holding before it a shining ideal – the 'super-India', that was within and could now be materialised. Because this relationship between Nehru and India almost took on the nature of a mystical ritual, Escott Reid called him 'the high priest of India' (Reid, 1981). Foreign policy was one of the main stages on which the ritual was performed.

The supposedly benign tradition on which Nehru built the Indian national identity is projected outwards in international relations to other peoples – and through this projection again reflected back to Indians themselves. Indian national identity is affirmed through interaction, not so much in Wendt's systemic intersubjective sense, but in a more purposive manner. By clarifying to others what India stands for, Nehru both clarified directly to his own people and expected that a befitting resonance would resound from abroad. In a radio broadcast in 1956, he drew a portrait of the Indian people for the citizen of the USA –

> 'Through the centuries, India has preached and practiced toleration and understanding... Her sons journeyed far and wide, braving the perils of land and sea, not with thoughts of domination, but as messengers of peace or engaged in the commerce of ideas as well as of beautiful products. During these millennia of history, India has experienced both good and ill, but throughout her chequered history, she has remembered the message of peace and tolerance'.

While India wants to become dynamic and modern (like the USA), it is not willing to do so at any price. On its path to modernity, it will continue to adhere 'to the moral and spiritual aspects of life' (Nehru, 2003).

In internal communication, too, foreign policy was used to reflect an image of the self and contrast it with others. In a 1950 broadcast to the Indian nation, Nehru declared that he would 'with all humility and prayerfulness' guide India's foreign policy so as to ensure peace and cooperation with other nations. 'We try not to be swept away by passion and anger but to maintain the temper of peaceful approach' (Nehru, 2003).

War, and the disruption and emotional reactions which war causes would have endangered the young nation's complex organism. Calm and stability were political necessities to be enshrined by national identity. War was not only a danger because of the imminent dangers of losing lives or territories, or because the costs of a war would divert crucial resources away from domestic development. War was also likely to be fought with Pakistan, threatening to emotionalise India along communal lines and breaking up a national identity built on supra-communal values.

War, however, could not always be avoided. And when it came, it had to be explained in the language of peace and national values. Following the 'Chinese aggression' in the Himalayas in 1962, Nehru, in a nationwide radio broadcast, explained to the Indian people –

> 'We are men and women of peace in this country, conditioned by the ways of peace. We are unused to the necessities of war. Because of this, we endeavoured to follow a policy of peace even when aggression took placc on our territory in Ladakh five years ago. We explored avenues for an honorable settlement by peaceful methods. That was our policy all over the world... But all our efforts have been vain...' (Nehru, 2003).

The Indian desire to manifest its value identity through reflection and recognition was most visible and focussed in its relationship with Pakistan. Pakistan, although then still a secular state, was a communalist (Muslim) national project. It stood in glaring opposition to the Indian value-based, non-communalist (non-Hindu) project. For Nehru, the conflict with Pakistan was not primarily about land and frontiers in Kashmir or elsewhere (although being of Kashmiri descent himself, he did have a strong personal, emotional attachment to the land). It is a question of competing identities – each denying the legitimacy and right to exist of the other in an existentialist antagonism[111]. While India, he argued, 'stands for a secular state and for freedom of its component parts to live their autonomous lives' (the ideals of pluralism, tolerance and peaceful co-existence), Pakistan represents the dangerous communalist project, which – in contrast to a peace-loving India – 'by the very nature of its objectives and ideology, is aggressive in outlook'. These 'disruptive and subversive' communalist policies in turn provoke mirror communalist sentiments of 'unwisdom and lack of vision' of Indian Hindu nationalists, threatening the very core of the young Indian nation ('weakening the basic conception of the Indian state').

---

[111]The existentialist antagonism is comparable to that between the USA and the Soviet Union during the early phases of the Cold War (Engelmeier, T. F., 2003b).

> 'It is not Kashmir, therefore, but rather a much deeper conflict that comes in the way of friendly relations between India and Pakistan... We cannot give up the basic ideals which we have held so long and on which the whole conception of our state is founded' (Nehru, 2003).

Other nations must become cognisant of this fundamental difference between the evil and the good offspring of the British Raj, between the Cain and the Abel, between the Kauravas and the Pandavas. 'The patent contrast of warlike Pakistan and peaceful India is too obvious not to be noticed by even the casual observer' (Nehru, 2003)[112].

The internal construction of the identity was matched externally by a desire for recognition of the identity that was created. 'Out of some postcolonial inferiority complex', Vikram Chandra explains, 'we Indians are longing for recognition in the international arena' (Trojanow, 2006). But recognition for what? Recognition is always sought for something that generates pride, for some kind of 'greatness'. In India's case, the case of a poor, backward country, it was moral and political-historical greatness. The 'spill-over' and the 'reflection' effects coincide in their mutual grounding of these perceptions of greatness. Nehru's strategic culture was infused with the ideas of the identity formation process. In foreign policy, they took on the form of a conception of India's moral and political greatness, as well as a conflation of ideal and interest.

6.2 The Idea of Greatness

To Nehru, whose mind was filled with a poetic grasp of historical, moral and cultural meta-structures, and who was a firm believer in mankind and in its progress, it seemed natural that a country considers itself to have a special historical mission. Somewhat contemptuously, he notes that every country has some notion of a 'special dispensation from Providence', of being chosen and unique in some way, and that 'others may be good or bad but secondary, somewhat inferior human beings'. He wondered how such a sentiment could persist in all nations without exception (Nehru, 2003). He is right, of course, in that many – if not most – nations tend to overestimate their own importance, judgment and integrity. In that sense, nations are merely agglomerations of individuals and share (and amass) their basic flaws of subjectivity and self-aggrandisement.

---

[112]US special envoy to India, Strobe Talbott, observed the 'the prevailing inclination of many Indians was, for many years, not to accept the logic or the legitimacy of the two-nation theory. They regarded the idea of Pakistan not just as a mistake but as an insult to the idea of India' (Talbott, S., 2004, p.7).

However, the 'special dispensation from Providence' nations feel they have, can differ significantly in quality as well as intensity. Only few countries believe in a mission that transcends their own nation and incorporates others, fewer still believe that their mission is to make the world as such and for all a better place. The French revolutionary armies sought to bring their ideals to Europe, Lenin and Trotsky believed in their duty to carry the communist revolution into the world, the USA since the Second World War believes that it is a beacon of freedom (democracy, free-market) and needs to encourage others to follow. Such a sense of mission is based on a certain sense of political importance (i.e. the capability to change the world) and on a strong belief in the universal value of a message together with a sense of historical novelty (i.e. the nation has made a civilisational advance, often by way of revolution, that others should now follow). In history, few of the nations with such a sense of mission were willing to sacrifice their own interests for their ethereal ideal when they came into conflict. More often, the mission became an instrument of national power and influence.

In terms of the intensity with which 'a special dispensation of Providence' is communicated, there is an important difference between stable and instable nations, between those that have something to prove to others and themselves, and those who feel comfortable and secure in their identities. In nations which are emotionally settled and politically stable, the sense of uniqueness may at times erupt in chauvinistic terms (an excess of self-certainty), but more often it is tacitly understood and deemed self-evident, requiring neither excessive expression nor demonstration before others in order to acquire validity in the eyes of the members of the nation themselves. In less stable nations, on the other hand, the belief in a special role may be part and parcel of public diplomacy and slip into foreign policy decisions. Furthermore, there is a significant difference between countries whose belief in their own greatness is a narcissist one, and those, who believe that their greatness should be of benefit to the world at large. Some countries have a sense of mission, and system-level goals which may come into conflict with the national interest, others don't. Some countries build identities on values they consider essentially universal, others build theirs on differentiation (Sen, 2006).

The Indian case is highly particular. The 'special dispensation from Providence' is at once universal in claim and idiosyncratic in nature[113], it

---

[113]An important early intellectual, shaping the idea of Indian cultural greatness and universal mission was Swami Vivekananda. In a famous passage from a speech held in

is as strongly articulated as it is built on frail foundations. Foreign policy, in the absence of a direct external threat, was used in the assertion of India's nationhood, to reaffirm its independence and identity, more so than as a means of securing direct national interests, such as economic or security benefits. Non-alignment in particular served this purpose by facilitating the quest for national unity as well as for national identity (Rothstein). It did so in two ways. Firstly, it reaffirmed the independence and the sovereign equality of the state. It 'seemed to symbolise freedom and independence' (Rothstein). Non-alignment ensured that India would not become subject to the USA or the Soviet Union in one of the two Cold War blocs just after it gained independence (Rana, 1976). It would remain an independent actor on the world scene and thereby confirm its national independence in the eyes of its own people. The country's size and regional position gave India, like Indonesia or Egypt, the opportunity to shun the great power protection rackets, at least for some time. For the same geostrategic reasons, Pakistan did not have such a choice. Nehru's charismatic and visionary leadership enabled India to seize the opportunity fully. By demonstrating that India was not only independent, but an entirely sovereign and idiosyncratic player in world politics, it assumed a position of political greatness and importance that is the hallmark of a key regional power in a multipolar international system.

Secondly, non-alignment enabled the state to establish 'a position separate from, and indeed implicitly morally superior to, the great power blocs'. This sense of moral greatness was as much the product of a national identity as it was meant to further strengthen this identity. It lay at the roots of the continuing misunderstandings between India and the West, lasting for most of the second half of the twentieth century – 'All the conferences of the non-aligned, the summit meetings, and the declarations of Third World brotherhood (and First World duplicity) may have seemed meaningless and hypocritical rhetoric, but it should be remembered that the goals the elites sought were primarily ceremonial and symbolic' (Rothstein, 1976). Being 'good' or 'moral' logically begs comparison with the unethical. It does so even more, when it is used in a national project as a common

Colombo, he gives an early example of the somewhat chauvinistic belief in the global relevance and preeminence of Indian culture – 'If there is any land on this earth that can lay claim to be the blessed *Punya Bhumi*, to be the land to which all souls on this earth must come to account for Karma, the land to which every soul that is wending its way Godward must come to attain its last home, the land where humanity has attained its highest towards gentleness, towards generosity, towards purity, towards calmness, above all the land of introspection and of spirituality – it is India' (Vivekananda, S., 1918, Vol. III, p. 105).

denominator to differentiate between an 'us' (Indians, Asians) and a 'them' (Europe/USA, 'the West', recent history, etc.) (Sayegh, 1964). Underlying the foreign policy strategy of non-alignment or foreign policy guidelines such as Panchsheel are values, a notion of the good. These values were not – as nationalists claim – fundamental, or even natural, to the Indian culture and people. They were rather indispensable elements of the Indian national project, the building-blocs of a common psyche.

India's 'special dispensation from Providence' as enshrined in the national identity thus engendered a particular sense of mission derived from a belief in a moral uniqueness of universal relevance and a historical-political understanding of importance. Both required external validation or recognition in order to become credible or 'real' in the eyes of Indian politicians, the strategic community and the wider politically aware Indian populace.

6.2.1 *Moral Greatness – The Sense of Uniqueness*

Both Gandhi and Nehru professed humility. Gandhi, with his simple white cloth, walking barefoot through India and sleeping in villages and ashrams was an icon of modesty and restraint. Nehru was slightly different. He did not shun luxury and enjoyed the lifestyle that came with being Prime Minister of India. Personally, as Reid wrote, he 'does not give the impression of being a humble man… in his pride and sensitiveness he reflects the pride and sensitiveness of India' (Reid, 1981). In international relations, like Gandhi, he had respect for other nations and cultures and he warned that 'we should avoid… adopting a self-righteous pose and making remarks and aspersion, which may wound the self-respect of individuals'. In reality, however, he, like Gandhi, was convinced that India had a capacity for moral greatness which sets her apart and that there are 'some lessons in India's peaceful revolution which might be applied to the larger problems before the world today' (Nehru, 2003).

Coexisting with, and even to some extent underlying, Gandhi's humbleness and Nehru's cosmopolitanism was a certain nationalist moral pride that Indian culture is particularly susceptible to plural, tolerant and respectful inter-group relations. The values which have become the mainstay of Indian nationalism gave India an exceptional position in the comity of nations. In Hind Swaraj, Gandhi, writing primarily to his own Indian countrymen, portrayed India as a superior civilisation –

> 'I believe that the civilisation India has evolved is not to be beaten anywhere in the world. Nothing can equal the seeds sown by our ancestors. Rome went,

> Greece shared the same fate, the might of the Pharaoh's was broken, Japan has become westernised, of China nothing can be said, but India is still, somehow or other, sound at the foundation' (Gandhi, 1997).

In writing this, Gandhi attempted to uplift his countrymen. He wanted to instill in them a sense of pride in their own nation. In the face of a militarily and economically superior coloniser, he went for history and moral superiority as sources of such pride.

> 'Civilisation is that mode of conduct which points out to the man the path of duty. Performance of duty and observance of morality are convertible terms… civilisation means "good conduct". If this definition be correct, then India, as so many writers have shown, has nothing to learn from anybody else. And this is as it should be'. Ancient Indians, he explains, 'saw that kings and their sword were inferior to the sword of ethics, and they, therefore, held the sovereigns of the earth to be inferior to the Rishis and the Fakirs. A nation with a constitution like this is fitter to teach others than to learn from others' (Gandhi, 1997).

Of course, such statements were meant primarily for a domestic audience and originated in a period marked by the profound dismay and low spirits of colonisation. However, the seed that would later become an important identity-constituent, a pride in the Gandhian/Nehruvian India, is already visible.

Nehru transported this nationalist sense of moral greatness into the field of foreign policy after independence. In India, he argued, the symbols of national greatness have not been great military commanders 'but men like the Buddha and, in our own times, Gandhi, both messengers of goodwill and peace' (Nehru, 2003). Such a statement obviously contrasts (Nehru does not even need to say it) with the European tradition of leadership from Alexander the Great to Napoleon in which not goodwill or peace are dominant, but a search for glory, power and conquest[114]. Indeed, Nehru elsewhere wrote that India has 'a great deal worthy of a great country and

[114]It is interesting to compare the Iliad and the Mahabharata on this point. Both epics have been composed at a similar time (700–400 BC), depicting similar warrior societies at the dawn of history. Both are describing a great war between two rival armies whose ranks are filled with heroes. Both wars are protracted wars of annihilation in which an entire generation of heroes dies. In both epics a central question has to be answered – what are the men fighting for? Of course, there are the simpler minds fighting for wealth, power or a woman. But what motivates the greatest heroes? What motivates an Achilles and an Arjuna? For Achilles, the answer is, glory. For Arjuna glory is not enough. He fights for a higher, divine right. As described in the Bhagavad Gita, he requires Krishna's revelation of the laws of dharma to entice him to slaughter his opponents.

compares very favourably with the squabbles and incessant conflicts of the little countries of Europe' (Nehru, 2003). This is not only because of the nature of Indian thought (the Buddha, Gandhi), but also because of the permeation of this philosophy into the everyday lives and traditions of Indians. In India, philosophy and religion, though in its higher manifestations confined to the elect, 'has been more pervasive than elsewhere and has had a strong influence in moulding the national outlook and in developing a certain distinctive attitude of mind' (Nehru, 1946)[115]. In contrast to most other countries, where 'manly' qualities of strength and prowess are emphasised, Nehru wrote that India appears to have more feminine than masculine qualities. Essentially, India ('she') is 'gentle and peaceful even though on occasions she may indulge in brutal and callous behaviour'. No country in the world, he argues, abhors the idea of war as much as India (Nehru, 2003). India takes the moral high-ground in the international arena and is willing to go 'further than many nations in her acceptance of real internationalism and the co-ordination of, even to some extent the sub-ordination of the independent nation state to a world organisation' (Nehru, 1946).

India's supposed moral greatness is, of course, part of the Gandhian/Nehruvian nationalist interpretation of India's past, according to which India has 'deep reserves of wisdom and inner strength' and a characteristic intellectual preference for 'the goodness and self-sacrificing nature of the man' (Nehru, 1946). The concept of coexistence is the basis of Indian thinking. India consequently is naturally a peaceful, open-minded and tolerant neighbour.

> 'We have not been, broadly speaking, a proselytising people. We accept other religions and faiths tolerantly. We do not think that our view must necessarily prevail over others. There are many aspects of truth, and how can we presume to limit it to one particular aspect which appeals to us?' (Nehru, 2003).

For these moral qualities of the Indian nation, Nehru firmly believed that the world will benefit if India can make its influence felt, for India would always be working for peace and co-operation and against aggression (Nehru, 1946). India should seek to take a lead in bringing about a new world order. It should take a global responsibility, even if other countries in their narrow-mindedness (i.e. adherence to the concept of reason of state) hesitate (Nehru, 2003). It can and should do so, because of its superior insight and because of its particularly benign constitution.

---

[115]Why this is not the case with other religious ethics, such as, say, Islam (Lewis, B., 2003) or Calvinism (Weber, M., 2001) is difficult to say.

This superior insight and benign constitution cannot be taken for granted, however. Nehru's communication strategy has two cutting edges – India is morally great is his message to the world; India must live up to its own moral greatness is his message to Indians. It is a high risk strategy. The world must believe what (Nehru says) Indians are in order for Indians to believe what (Nehru says) they are – and vice versa. Thus, the real reason why Nehru loves India is not found in India's past, but in the promise it holds of what it can be. It is Nehru's 'faith in her today' and his belief 'that she will stand for truth and freedom, and the higher things in life'. If Indians want India to stand for the 'great aims and ideals which Gandhi placed before us all', they need to think and act accordingly, resisting the temptation to be 'carried away by the passion of the moment or by thoughts of petty advantage'. Externally, Nehru proclaims that India is not aggressive (i.e. mission accomplished) – internally, he proclaims that it must not be aggressive (i.e. mission not yet accomplished)[116].

> 'If we indulged in aggression, we should be false to all that we have stood for and all that Gandhiji taught us… Whatever may happen in other countries, let us remain calm, and let us try to remain true to Gandhiji's teachings' (Nehru, 2003).

At its ('her') best, India can be a beacon of tolerance and peace, and a symbol of hope for a new, better world order for other nations –

> 'The story of India's long struggle for freedom under Gandhiji has powerfully impressed the world and, more especially, the Asian countries as well as the people of Africa. The tradition and Gandhiji's name are tremendous assets. In the eyes of large numbers of people we have stood for certain principles and we have adopted a certain technique and policy which brought us success. Because of that, they still look to our country for a certain kind of lead and for advice based on experience.' (Nehru, 2003).

6.2.2 *Political and Civilisational Greatness – The Sense of Importance*

Nehru wanted to bring India into the modern world and with India shape the modern world – both to improve the world and to return to India a sense

[116]A recent study on problems of intercultural management between Germany and India has noted that the 'language of accomplishment' in India is fundamentally different from that in Germany, leading to misunderstandings and disappointments in business relationships. A project will often be declared 'finished', while still being in process (Wildemann, R., 2007).

of authenticity and pride. India was, in his mind, a nation to be 'looked up to, in consonance with India's glorious past' (Fisher, 1967). He wanted to interact on equal terms with the world's most powerful nations. In 1949, he informed the US ambassador that the United States and India had much to give to each other, for they were both nations of actual (presumably the USA) or potential (presumably India) significance. Nehru was certain that India could be very important to the USA as an Asian partner in leadership (Gopal, 1993). India, in his mind, was one of the few key power centres in a multipolar world, the natural organiser and final arbiter in South Asia, with an influence extending into the farther parts of Asia (Nehru, 2003)[117]. Even in the world as such, Nehru was convinced that India 'cannot play a secondary part'. India's importance was a constant theme in Nehru's speeches and correspondence. He spoke of 'an important part' (Nehru, 1946), a 'growing part', a 'vital role' (Nehru, 2003) for India in world affairs.

Where did this belief in India's political importance come from? Its traditional measures of power were meager. The economy was small and backward and its armed forces incomparably weaker than those of the advanced industrial societies. The sources of India's importance, as Nehru saw it, were three – its potential and resources, its history and civilisation, and its moral greatness and the vital positive contribution India could make to the future course of history.

The resource argument is based primarily on the fact that India is home to the world's second largest population. Its human resources are immense. Its territory is also vast. Nehru saw India as 'one of the very few countries' which have the resources and capacity to act independently and thus play a key role in international relations. Such real independence was at the time the privilege of only two countries – the United States of America and to the Soviet Union. China and India are the only other nations, 'potentially capable of joining that group' (Nehru, 1946; 2003). This puts India conceptually into the same league as the USA, the Soviet Union and China.

In terms of cultural, historical importance, Nehru took pride in tracing India's role in world history back to the earliest days of human civilisation. Since then, Indian scientists, merchants, poets, thinkers and prophets have, in the course of an illustrious and ancient history, contributed significantly

---

[117]Nehru seemed to be oblivious to the fact that as long as India was not strong enough in real terms (economically and militarily) to actually dominate the Subcontinent, its ambitions were bound to create antagonism (e.g. Pakistan) and draw in outsiders (e.g. China, the USA).

to the development of the world. Under Gandhi and Nehru, India became a beacon of hope for the oppressed nations of Africa and Asia. At the end of Hind Swaraj, Gandhi quotes a number of Western writers who profess to the civilisational greatness of India. He wanted to uplift Indians and make them realise that they belong to a great and ancient country. The ideas transported by the quotes have subsequently filtered into the Indian national consciousness. These are some examples – 'We are constrained to bend the knee before [the genius] of the East and to see in this cradle of the human race the native land of the highest philosophy' (Victor Cousin[118]). 'It cannot be too well understood that our [the British] position in India has never been in any degree that of bringing civilisation to savage races. When we landed in India we found there a hoary civilisation, which during the progress of thousands of years had fitted itself into the character and adjusted itself to the wants of highly intellectual races' (J. Seymour Keay[119]). 'If I were to ask myself from what literature we here in Europe... may draw that corrective which is most wanted in order to make our inner life more perfect... I should point to India' (Max Müller[120]). 'Among nations possessing indigenous philosophy and metaphysics... Hindustan holds the first rank in point of time' (Friedrich von Schlegel[121]).

Furthermore, India's sense of political greatness is fundamentally linked to its sense of moral greatness. First of all, a sense of moral greatness is the product of an inflated image of the self. The same inflated image can easily produce a sense of political and civilisational greatness. Secondly, if a nation has a value-based sense of mission, it naturally wants to be heard and taken seriously – this is in the nature of universal values. It assumes a certain capability of implementing and enforcing them.

The self-image of being a great nation has found a reflection in India's policy of non-alignment. Apart from the debate about its success as a policy, it was fundamentally important in terms of the identity-building process of an old culture in a newly independent state. Non-alignment communicated that India could and would act independently of other powers, judge matters according to its beliefs, and analyse and make choices entirely based on its own principles, interests and identity. 'If I join any of these big groups [NATO or the Warsaw Pact]', Nehru said, 'I lose my identity; I have no identity left, I have no views left' (Nehru). India,

[118]French philosopher (1792–1867)

[119]British MP and Banker living in India in the nineteenth century

[120]German indologist (1823–1900)

[121]German philosopher (1772–1829)

however, because of her greatness and importance, could afford to have an independent foreign policy identity. Nehru firmly believed that it could stand on its own feet. India does not need protection from others. It would shape its own niche in world affairs, which fits in 'with the genius of her people' (Nehru, 2003). West Germany, after the Second World War, by contrast, did the exact opposite, foregoing a (dubious) offer by Stalin for unification on the basis of neutrality and some kind of non-alignment. Adenauer – equally a great statesman and leader – decided to steer the country into the Western alliance. By doing so, he politically subsumed it under the power of the USA and France, foregoing all claims for national greatness and firmly anchoring the new state's identity in the West (Mann, 1966).

6.2.3 *Recognition*

Identities are social constructs and as such need outside affirmation; identities still half-way between the minds of ideologues and the hearts of the people, and thus at flux and insecure, are in even greater need of recognition by others. Nehru's frequent references to the ideals of 'Indianness' in front of Indian audiences show that Indian national identity was far from secured and fixated. Internal affirmation would need to be supported by external affirmation – through recognition by other states of the projected political identity of India.

Nehru was initially successful in finding such recognition. In the mid-1950s, following the Korean War (and India's involvement as an arbiter in the repatriation of prisoners), Nehru was at his zenith as global statesman, powerfully projecting his image of India into the world. He had become 'a world figure whose stature had little relation to his country's strength and whose constituency extended far beyond India'. He put the new Indian state firmly on the international map, giving foreign statesmen and peoples a frame of reference. His India thus became the 'chief symbol in the world's eyes of national freedom and progress, and international goodwill' (Gopal, 1993).

Nehru has frequently been criticised for pursuing policies that created nothing but hot air, while disregarding, even harming the national interest, for talking where others acted, for concerning himself with the thankless and unappreciated task of moralising while others followed his lead only insofar as it suited their interests and parted company as soon as it became a burden. He has furthermore been criticised for insincerity and bigotry, for espousing ideals he himself did not live up to (e.g., Maxwell, 1974; Reid,

1981; Kapur, 2004). Regardless of these considerations, Nehru did for a time achieve a status for India and projected an image of India in line with the ideals on which the Indian nation was to be built. He received a significant degree of recognition for it. It is difficult to assess exactly how important this recognition was in the nation-building process, particularly with respect to the other important building blocs, such as domestic communication of political values, economic policy or the process of institutionalising democratic structures. There can be no doubt, however, that international recognition was a source of pride and affirmed the Indian national-project. It can be assumed then, that it crucially helped support a fragile national frame.

The recognition for India's approach to international relations declined, however, after the mid-1950s. Other nations, especially the NATO members and China, began to resent the 'sense of moral superiority' and India's 'open role of the preacher', which was so out of tune with India's actual importance in terms of power. Non-alignment thus became regarded as an undue projection into international politics of a 'specifically Indian morality' (Maxwell, 1974). In the West, Nehru's moralising was considered to be based on a double standard with a partial blindness to the Soviets[122]. In the Soviet Union it was not taken seriously, while the Chinese resented India's leadership of the Third World (Reid, 1981). Indian morality was no longer perceived by others as quite as universal as Nehru made it out to be, it became increasingly viewed as vainglorious, proud and self-serving moralising.

Where recognition was denied, a strong sentiment of defiance and self-assertion in the face of what was considered unjust aggression became the most powerful link between foreign policy and national identity. Kashmir and the struggle with Pakistan, while providing ample opportunity for demarcating the different and rival national-projects, was of limited usefulness when it came to actual conflict. The danger of stirring communalist reactions from Hindu nationalists in India was significant. Interestingly, the disastrous 1962 war against China led to a 'massive reinforcement of Indian unity' (Gopal, 1993). Tharoor describes how –

> '...for the first time since that midnight moment of independence, the country rallied together as one – housewives knit sweaters for the soldiers on the Himalayan front and donated their gold jewellery to the servicemen's fund,

---

[122]Nehru's significantly delayed stance on the Soviet oppression of Hungary in 1956 as opposed to his strong and immediate support of Nasser's Egypt during the Suez crisis of the same year is often cited as evidence.

movie-goers stood respectfully to attention as the national anthem, played in theatres after the film, school children discovered a sense of patriotism... In the moment of his greatest failure, the preeminent voice of Indian freedom gave a new boost to a nationalist resurgence. War and defeat, destroyed illusions but nurtured resolve, tightening the bonds Nehru had helped put in place' (Tharoor, 2003).

Skillfully communicated by Nehru, the Chinese invasion gave rise to a common feeling of betrayal and of being morally right. However, such a feeling depended on the prior formulation of the ideals and identity that characterise the Indian nation, on the shared feeling of commonality. War put stress on the system – and it made it stronger rather than breaking it. Indian national identity successfully survived a serious test.

6.3 The Idealist Inflection as a Conflation of Ideal and Interest

Nehru should not be mistaken for a lofty and otherworldly idealist, out of touch with the realities and necessities of an anarchical world. He was quite ready to use hard power when necessary. 'India', he wrote, 'will of course take all necessary steps to strengthen her defenses and she has the industrial and other resources to do so... There is no doubt that India can build up an efficient defense apparatus'. He analyses the international power balance, possible threats to India and the likelihood of their occurrence (Nehru). With respect to Afghanistan, for instance, he writes (in the true spirit of Kautilya's Mandala strategy, whereby an enemy's enemy is a friend) – 'Afghanistan, being anti-Pakistan, automatically is a little more friendly to India. We should take full advantage of this fact' (Nehru, 2003). Nehru's actual realpolitik in Hyderabad, Kashmir or Goa, has already been noted in the introduction. His farsighted border-treaties with Sikkim, Bhutan and Nepal are also more reminiscent of sphere-of-interest-thinking than of idealism.

Whatever policy India pursues, Nehru declared that 'the art of conducting foreign affairs lies in finding out what is advantageous to the country'. One may earnestly talk about international goodwill, peace and freedom, 'but in the ultimate analysis, a government functions for the good of the country it governs...' (Maxwell, 1974). So 'realism of course there must be'. No nation can afford to base its foreign policy 'on mere goodwill and flights of the imagination' (Nehru). What is realism, however? And what is the national interest? Nehru rejects the narrow self-interest of the so-called realist as 'far too limited by past myths and dogmas', regarding 'ideas and social forms, suited to one age, as immutable parts and as unchanging parts of human nature and society, forgetting that nothing is so changeable as human nature' (Nehru, 1946).

Nehru, however, believed in human progress. In his mind, the good of the country and the good of the world converged. His long-term objective was 'to seek out points of convergence between the interests of India and the interests of world peace' (Nanda, 2004, Nehru). Range wrote extensively on the concept of 'enlightened self-interest' in Nehru's policies (Range, 1961). Underlying Nehru's worldview was the belief that inter-national cooperation and goodwill was as much in the interest of the individual nations as intra-national cooperation and goodwill was in the interest of the different Indian communities. International peace was seen as a prerequisite to national peace and development as much as India's national independence and development was seen as a significant boost for world peace. Even before independence, in the 'Quit India' Resolution of the 1942 Bombay Congress, an appeal was made to Britain and the USA for Indian independence 'in the interest of world freedom'. The continuation of British rule, so the argument went, would make India 'progressively less capable of defending herself and of contributing to world peace'. It prevents India from 'functioning in its own interest and in the interest of humanity'. 'The freedom of India [interest] must be a symbol of and prelude to the freedom of all other Asiatic nations [ideal]' (Nehru, 1946). This appeal and the (ineffective) 'Quit India' campaign did not push for Indian independence at all costs. Already then, the Indian National Congress showed a deep concern for world affairs. India's struggle for independence must not undermine Britain's struggle against Nazi Germany, from a global perspective, by far the greater evil. Bose chose a different path. He tried to free India by any means possible, including armed struggle. He was ready to enlist the help of anyone who had an interest in helping, including fascist Germany and militaristic, imperial Japan. This is where he parted ways with both Gandhi and Nehru (Som, 2004).

After independence, the global perspective and national interest remained strongly connected. In Nehru's eyes, national interest as viewed in opposition to or competition with that of other nations is a flawed concept. The fate of the world is a shared one – 'I cannot forget the world and isolate myself in India. The fate of every country is linked up together now and success or failure will be the common lot'. Thus, a policy of peaceful cooperation designed to bring about a just world order should be pursued 'not only on the ground of principle, but also from the point of view of practical necessity'. The interests of India as well as that of the world dictate the same principled stance. What helps India, helps the world and vice-versa. Ideals and interests converge. 'Whether we look at this question [nonalignment] from the point of view of narrow self-interest or the larger one of world peace, the only policy we can pursue is one of nonalignment' (Nehru, 2003). In the chapter on 'Realism and Geopolitics' in the 'Discovery of India' (Nehru, 1946), Nehru explains his worldview, based on the conviction that a purposive development of mankind is possible and can be achieved through good rather than bad (fallacious) policies and his confidence in the ultimate sanity ('real' realism) of a humane and peaceful approach.

Where did such a belief come from? Nehru was a firm believer in the Gandhian principle, that moral ends can ultimately best be achieved by moral means, that immoral means may bring short-term Pyrrhic victories, but in the long-run will damage the ends and even (in a spiritual sense) the actor himself (Nehru, 2003). 'I have become more and more convinced', Nehru wrote in 1948 –

> '...that so long as we do not recognise the supremacy of the moral law, in our national and international relations, we shall have no enduring peace. So long as we do not adhere to the right means, the end will not be right and fresh evil will flow from it' (Nehru, 2003).

On this account, he became less rigorous with time. Before independence, in 1927, he declared that India did not need arms – 'We have no interests... which require the protection of armed forces and even if we had such interests it is better for them to suffer than to be protected at the point of the bayonet'. Later, during his long time in office, he was forced to adjust his position. In a letter to Thakin Nu of Burma, and with a view to events in Kashmir, he wrote that 'it is obvious that your Government must meet rebels with force'. He later repeatedly declared that he was no pacifist (Nehru, 2003).

Nevertheless, the basic conflation of ideals and interests, the conviction that India's best policy was to make the world a better place, remained. In a world where other nations do not respect the need to place the common good on an equal footing with the national good or fail to see an ultimate connection between the two, but seek only to serve their own interests from a point of view which must have seemed cynical to someone like Nehru, in a world, moreover, where India cannot single-handedly determine and enforce rules of conduct, this policy has an element of idealist stubbornness that can only be explained by reference to the internal nation-building process – to an unconscious 'spill-over' of universalist national ideals, and to a conscious 'reflection' of national ideals through the international arena.

The strategic culture, as driven by the identity formation process, causes a preoccupation with the ideas of moral and political greatness, as well as a conscious (reflective) and unconscious (spill-over) conflation of ideal and interest in foreign policy. While the idealist inflection presents itself to the external observer of Indian foreign policy as a duality or an ambiguity, from the inside, from within the phenomenological perspective of the nation-building process, it presents itself as a conflation of realism and idealism.

7

Foreign Policy and National Identity Today[123]

This book attempts to understand the phenomenological basis of a specific, observed fact in Indian foreign policy – the idealist inflection. As previously outlined, working with strategic culture (the locus of the phenomenology in foreign policy) requires that the persistence of its key traits is investigated over time. The traits, as identified in the preceding chapter, are – the notion of moral greatness, the notion of political greatness and the conflation of ideals and interests. The persistence of these traits in the thoughts of the current strategic elite are analysed using the results of interviews.

Whilst under Nehru, Indian foreign policy could easily be pinned down to him personally and to his own views and writings, the India of today presents a much more complex picture. Congress has since lost its dominant position. No leader as incontestable and powerful, experienced, cosmopolitan and visionary in terms of foreign policy has emerged since Nehru's death. (No such leader, it may be argued, is needed in a functioning democracy.) Despite various efforts, India has not yet developed an institutional and intellectual architecture for a solid long-term national foreign policy strategy to guide and underpin the decisions of successive governments. The picture is, thus, much more scattered. There is an awe-inspiring multiplicity of often very well reasoned and argued views, voiced by the current strategic community.

---

[123] 'Today' refers not only to the time when the interviews were conducted (2005 and 2006), but – as explained in the chapter on method – to the current thinking of the current strategic elite, which was interviewed in 2005 and 2006, but whose experiences, analyses and views are the product of a longer period during which they were involved in the foreign policy process.

Moreover, the India of today is a fundamentally different place than the India of the 1950s and 1960s. It is a country with much more power. It possesses nuclear weapons and its economy has shown significant growth over the last 15 years. By the middle of the century, its population is expected to be the largest in the world and its economy the third largest[124]. The security environment, too, has changed radically. The end of the Cold War and the colossal rise of Chinese power are the most marked features. Non-alignment in the specific meaning of the Cold War no longer makes sense. The momentum of decolonisation and the ideologies of socialism and communism have ebbed away.

Very much has changed – and yet there appear to be significant constants in Indian foreign policy thinking. Has Nehru really bequeathed to India a timeless identity reflected in its foreign policy, as Chaulia suggests (Chaulia, 2002)? Is there a 'strong if evolving common core' (Cohen, 2001), that is, a widely shared vision of national greatness, uniqueness and pride? If so, what does it consist of?

According to Stephen Cohen, there were, in 2001, three main foreign policy lobbies in India (Cohen, 2001). On the one hand, there were the advocates of a 'firm India' who believe that India should act as a powerful, confident state. They view the idealist element in Indian foreign policy as a severe limitation and, trusting in an inherent responsibility, advocate that India use force freely. The USA, Israel or China are, to them, the shining examples of how to position oneself in the international arena. Indira Gandhi's legacy and the shadow of the 'Indira Doctrine' are clearly discernible. The nuclear bomb is strongly promoted as a symbol of national power. All idealist, civilisational shibboleths are to be shed (Subrahmanyam, 2005). India needs to be willing to act unconditionally according to its national interests (Kumaraswamy, 2004). The most prominent voice at the extreme end of the spectrum is the 'nuclear maximalist' Bharat Karnad who proposes a significant arms build-up, a low tolerance doctrine and security through what Melvyn P. Leffler has called 'a preponderance of power' (Karnad, 2002; Leffler, 1992).

The second group identified by Cohen is positioned on the other side of India's foreign policy spectrum – the peace-mongering proponents of a

---

[124]Population projection from population reference bureau (http://www.prb.org). India is expected to have the world's largest population (1.6 billion), surpassing China (1.4 billion), in 2050. Economic projection from Goldman Sachs (http://www2.goldmansachs.com/insight/research/reports/99.pdf). India is expected to have the highest long-term growth potential of the BRIC states (around 6% p.a.) and become the third largest economy after China and the USA in 2050 with a GDP of around US$ 25 billion (accessed on 3 March, 2007).

'conciliatory India'. They want to deal with Pakistan and China by way of territorial compromise, questioning the logic of defense-led economic development, a bigheaded approach and interventions in neighbouring countries. On the nuclear issue, they suggest moderation and limitation. Furthermore, whilst the 'firm India' lobby rejects any outside role in the region (especially of the USA or the UN in Kashmir), the conciliatory voices are – marginally – more inclined to accept it. With regard to Kashmir, they hope for an eventual settlement of the conflict by way of establishing democratic institutions and generously accommodating Kashmiri nationalism within the Indian state (Ganguly, 2001).

The third group advocates a 'didactic India'. India, they argue, is unlike any other country. It is a civilisational state which should deploy its cultural and moral greatness as a valuable diplomatic asset. Other countries must be made aware of the moral quality of Indian foreign policy. According to this view, it should be possible to –

> '...persuade foreign officials of the wisdom and moral correctness of the Indian position, say, by stating the Indian case and supplementing political arguments with information about India's great civilisation, its cultural and economic accomplishments, and its democratic orientation.' (Cohen, 2001).

Indian culture and her unique experiences as a plural, democratic mega-state should be promoted abroad as sources of national power as well as for the benefit of the international community. At times the 'moral' aspect of 'moral greatness' prevails, and at times the 'greatness' part of 'moral greatness' prevails.

The three lobbies cannot easily be sorted into the political spectrum. There are representatives of each in all the major parties, and the parties change their views over time. Nehru's own daughter presented a hard-line ('firm India') 'Indira Doctrine', while the Hindu nationalist BJP initiated an assuaging ('conciliatory India') 'bus diplomacy'. The first two schools are essentially concerned with solving problems. The last ('didactic India') is concerned also with reflecting, communicating and propelling a national identity. Both the 'firm India' lobby and the 'conciliatory India' lobby at times take recourse to Indian history in order to authenticate their views (e.g. to Kautilya/Curzon/Indira Gandhi or Ashoka/Akbar/Mahatma Gandhi, respectively). The 'didactic India' group is providing the underlying worldview.

How much of the ideas of moral and political greatness, as linked to the Indian national project, remain in the thinking of the foreign policy community across the spectrum? And in how far is the conflation of ideal and interest, the idea that an 'essentially just and moral' India 'would do well by doing good' still manifest in the minds of Indian policy makers (Cohen, 2001)? Has Nehru's identity project filtered down into the lower echelons of society, into the bureaucracy and into political discourses? Has it succeeded in becoming 'sticky'?

Mitra and Singh have discovered, in a questionnaire on Indian values and political opinions in 1996 (published in 1999), that a majority of Indians have a conciliatory attitude towards Pakistan and 'a tendency to accommodate differences'. 44.6 per cent agreed with the statement 'India should make more efforts to develop friendly relations with Pakistan'; only 17.6 per cent disagreed. To Mitra, 'the high level of support for policies resembling those advocated by the Gujral doctrine among highly educated Indians is most significant'. Mitra concludes that there is no natural antagonism between the Indian and the Pakistani people. The nuclear bomb, however, is also supported by more people (36.1 per cent) than rejected (25.9 per cent), with particular force among college graduates (63.9 per cent supporting the bomb) (Mitra, 2001). A possible explanation for this seeming paradox is that both – dialogue (values) and the bomb (greatness) are essentially identity-goods. The nuclear bomb is widely considered a proud symbol of India's leading role in the world. To many Indians it is not paradoxical to hold, at the same time, that India is a force for peace in the world. In fact, as seen above, some Indians argue that the acquisition of the bomb is a step closer to global nuclear disarmament. It is possible to formulate four hypotheses from Cohen's classifications and from the information of the Mitra/Singh research –

(1) A belief in moral greatness still exists among the strategic community, although in the absence of a towering figure it is probably less loudly voiced and more implicit today.
(2) A belief in political greatness still exists among the strategic community. It can be expected to have increased as a result of the economic boom and India's nuclear weaponisation. The link between political and moral greatness may have become less strong.
(3) Recognition and external affirmation is sought more for political greatness and less for moral greatness.
(4) The conflation of ideals and interests, between ends and means has become less strong. While the ideal of a peaceful world is still upheld, it no longer stands in the way of pragmatic politics which

points in the opposite direction. The justification for the nuclear bomb is a prime example.

7.1 The Idea of Greatness Today

The changes in political mentality observed here are the products of a process spanning the last 60 years. Within this process, there has been significant fluctuation. Some of them occurred naturally with different administrations. Nehru and his successors, from Shastri to Indira Gandhi, Desai, Rajiv Gandhi, Rao, Vajpayee, Gowda, Gujral and Manmohan Singh all held their own views, had their own concerns and goals, were working with different advisors and experts in different international circumstances, responding to different challenges. Opinions also sometimes react to immediate, emotional foreign policy issues. The nuclear tests or the Kargil war, to name just two, recent examples, were moments in India's foreign policy with considerable emotional potential. They could sway the arguments and emphases of the strategic community, even the opinions about both India and the world. On the other hand, however, the interviewees are highly intellectual and very well informed. They are much more capable of giving a stable opinion than a less well informed, or a less well educated casual observer. Moreover, the interview years, 2005 and 2006, saw no major foreign policy emotionalisers.

The results link two points in time – today's worldview to that of the earlier Nehruvian era. In between, there have been significant shifts – both rhetoric and actual – in the conduct of Indian foreign policy. All of Nehru's successors to this day have made their own contributions. Nehru, himself, had to go through reassessments of his worldview. Indira Gandhi is particularly noteworthy, because she has given Indian policy a new and entirely unsentimental perspective. She remained, however, broadly within the Nehruvian strategic and ideological paradigms (Malhotra, 2006). Nehru's framework has evolved over time and so has the strategic community. Is it sufficient, then, to take two points to draw a line? The answer is positive, because the points are in reality lines, themselves. Nehru's time in office lasted for all but 17 of the 60 years of Indian foreign policy. And the vast majority of the interviewed experts, while giving their current assessment, have accompanied, analysed and shaped Indian foreign policy for many years, often reaching well back into the administration of Indira Gandhi. Their view can be expected to be tempered and balanced by a big picture spanning the last 20–30 years.

The elite interviews, conducted with both, decision-makers and observers with significant opinion-shaping powers, demonstrated that the view of India's role in the world – connected with the view of what constitutes India – has evolved significantly since Nehru. Most markedly, the language has been significantly toned down and messianic elements are almost universally rejected. Indian national objectives are being assessed realistically, on the basis of Indian material needs and capabilities. The conflation of ideals and interests has, accordingly, become less significant.

What has remained, however – and this is the Nehruvian core – is a belief in the special Indian political and cultural experience of tolerant pluralism and in the universal relevance of this experience. There still is, consequently, a claim to work on system-level goals. There is also seriousness to this claim. These goals are to be approached, however, from the point of view of a 'good international citizen', working through established processes of international cooperation rather than by way of leadership, and by way of example rather than lecture.

Sixty years of a largely successful shared national experience have left a strong mark on the Indian polity. The mere fact of survival, to many observers a miracle, has given Indians (politicians and people alike) reason for pride and confidence. During most of these sixty years, Nehruvian national ideals have been pre-eminent. Despite a continuing challenge from Hindu nationalism (the outcome of which is by no means certain), the need, the possibility and, indeed, the beauty, of living peacefully in a modern pluralist society have become entrenched in the minds of large swathes of society. The need as well as the temptation for hyperbolic rhetoric and symbolic actions in affirmation of these ideals has considerably lessened with the success of 'ideological politics'.

The strategic community retains a belief in the greatness of Indian society. It is, as under Nehru, twofold – on the one hand, India is considered to be of significant importance to the world by virtue of its population, culture, history and – increasingly – economy. This is fairly common national chauvinism or, more positively expressed, a patriotic self-appreciation. And, indeed, this sense of belonging to a culture and state that can be proud of its achievements is not unfounded. The belief in moral greatness is, nowadays, less simplistic and more confident. However, underneath a surface of diplomatic, educated politeness still lurks a widely held self-perception of a vague civilisational superiority – especially with respect to Pakistan, China and the West – based on a stipulated peacefulness and tolerance. However, 'the message, as well as the messenger has ripened' (Haidar)[125].

7.1.1 *Moral Greatness – The Sense of Uniqueness*

Except for some notable exceptions, none of the interviewees were much inclined to attribute to India the alleged cultural moral superiority of Nehruvian rhetoric. The sense of mission, the 'spill over' has declined significantly, and so has the willingness to instrumentalise foreign policy to project and 'reflect' an image. The perception of India as an intrinsically moral nation that has made a great civilisational leap (during the National Movement) and now has the capacity, or even the duty to become a guru for the unenlightened is today widely rejected. Moral grandstanding is considered anachronistic and counter-productive. There are too many unpleasant memories associated with it. However, the idea of moral greatness has not entirely disappeared from the thinking of the strategic community. What used to be 'the moral language of a poor country with a high opinion of itself' has now become a more humble but nonetheless 'broad consensus on restraint as a value and as a necessity' (Joshi) of a country increasingly more at ease as a great power.

Nevertheless, The strategic community in India still seems to be instinctively 'more comfortable with moral language' than in most other nations (Rajagopalan) and – based on India's civic achievements – there is a limited, less loudly voiced 'feeling of moral exceptionalism' (Subrahmanyam). This creates, as has been the intention of the nation's founding fathers, a 'political sense of belonging' (Mansingh).

A number of interviewees remain close to the Nehruvian image of India. Without excessively emphasising it, they share an underlying belief in an inherent Indian moral quality as defined by its culture[126]. The vast majority of interviewees in this group did not drive towards culturalist explanations directly. They did, however, when asked, state culturalist assumptions underlying their perception of foreign policy. There are significant differences in the assessments of how far cultural patterns of behaviour do or, indeed, should filter into the foreign policy process. (Although, there is a widespread agreement that messianic impulses should be avoided.) However, there is little doubt for most, that the understanding of the self, as fixated by an understanding of one's culture, is somehow

[125]This and the following quotes and references are from the conducted interviews.

[126]For a critical examination of culturalist arguments, see chapter 2, section 2.2.2 on 'The Myth of a Benign Tradition'.

reflected in a worldview, in foreign policy assessments and ultimately in actions. Moreover, there is widespread agreement, in this group, that Indian culture has a distinct aversion to aggression, that 'aggression is intrinsically alien to the Indian psyche' (Khare), that India is 'essentially peaceful' (Varma), or that 'Indians loathe violence' (Nandy)[127]. To Parthasarthy, too, 'in terms of history and character, India is fundamentally peaceful'. The people are 'fundamentally opposed to war'. Benignity is, to him, 'instinctive'. Chattanath argues that 'the larger trait of peacefulness is more pronounced in Indian culture than the impulses of violence'. He asks the interesting question, in how far Gandhi was a product of India, and whether he could have succeeded with his tactics of peaceful mass mobilisation in any other place than South Asia. While much more skeptical about the idea of an essential peacefulness, Rajagopalan, nevertheless makes out a 'high cultural conduciveness' for Gandhian and Nehruvian ideals in India – as opposed to, say, Bose's more violent approach.

A recurring theme in culture-based arguments proposing a peaceful Indian mentality, is the historical assertion that India has never sought imperialist expansion outside its borders, was peacefully spreading its religion without proselytising, and has tolerated many forms of worship on its soil (Chattanath, Varadarajan, Varma, Singh, Sinha). Parthasarthy argues that India is historically not used to realpolitik and that the National Movement taught it an enormous appreciation for the limits of violence. Kanti Bajpai, who is skeptical about the applicability of culturalist arguments, nevertheless suggests that Indian restraint in the use of force may simply be the human norm, but that many other nations have experienced the 'barbarising' effects of total wars, which India has not[128]. For Ashis Nandy, much of the moral Indian self-image is simply a reflection of Western romantic illusions and expectations which India has appropriated.

The central theme, however, for most members of this group (as it had been for Nehru) is not peacefulness but a syncretic tolerance as the 'defining characteristic of Indianness' (Kaul). Peacefulness is seen as a product of Indian tolerance. Hindus, according to Khare, understand themselves to be a tolerant people. The chauvinistic, simplistic Hindu-nationalism is still a minority view. Jaswant Singh argues that India is

---

[127]As an example, Nandy compares the rate of homicides in the USA with that in India. The ratio is approximately 10:1 (personal interview with the author, 2005).

[128]The argument opens-up questions – (1) Why has 'barbarisation' happened elsewhere in the first place? And why has it never happened in India? (2) Was partition violence not precisely this kind of 'barbarisation'? (3) Do other countries, which have also not been 'barbarised' by war on their soil, show the same restraint in the use of force?

pulled together by an 'innate understanding of the notion of "Dharma"'. Sinha believes that in India certain 'civilisational values' have been 'nurtured over centuries' and that Indian foreign policy is 'deeply rooted' in these civilisational values and 'in the Indian benign and tolerant psyche'. In terms of foreign policy, tolerance is generally understood as an acceptance of international diversity and the legitimate needs, views and interests of others. India uses war, but prefers not to. It believes in a diplomatic, cooperative approach to solving conflicts. India has an 'accommodative spirit'. There is 'no excessive triumphalism' after wars, no irredentism and no long term enmity (Subrahmanyam).

Tolerance is often traced to an inherent dislike of clear definitions, to a 'Hindu fuzziness' (Varma) and a culture that traditionally works with 'shades of grey' rather than with 'black and white' (Kapoor) and is 'moving, flexible, and porous' (Kaul, Jha). Tolerance, thereby, is not so much the result of an explicit, value-based choice for non-aggressive interaction, but rather the implication of what Varma called an 'amorphous, pliable and essentially pragmatic worldview'. There is, he argues, a 'harmonious schizophrenia' in the Indian mind, which loves to moralise but does not enforce the morals or even take them entirely seriously. Such a quality stands in direct contrast to, for example, the ruthless German execution of Nazi ideology. In India, 'there is no fulcrum to ideologically mould the masses', it is an 'essentially non-monolithic and non-radical culture' flanked by a 'healthy sense of self-preservation', which is highly suspicious of demagoguery. In this, Varma does not follow Nehru directly. Nehru sees a stronger link between values and actions. He also believes that Indian tolerance is a positive cultural quality rather than merely a side-product of 'fuzziness' (or, that 'fuzziness' is itself a purposive cultural quality). His conclusions regarding the effects of Indian culture are the same, however[129]. Bajpai transfers the concept of 'fuzziness' from the religious-cultural to the political-historical. He proposes that India as a concept has always been in flux, with 'changing centres and changing peripheries'.

A second, widely accepted explanation for a cultural tolerance is a particularly Indian argumentative tradition as recently expounded in a book by Amartya Sen (Sen, 2005). It is understood as a general readiness (in terms of open-mindedness) and ability (in terms of flexibility and patience)

[129]Varma stresses that there is no naïve otherworldliness about Indian culture. He refers to the entrepreneurial and materialist instincts of the rising Indian middle classes which show an acute interest in the spoils of this world.

to enter into significant dialogue (Nath, Chattanath). Parthasarthy and Sinha also stress patience as an Indian quality. A less frequent explanation is the Gandhian idea of the 'popular wisdom' of Indian village culture (Chattanath), whereby a practical, everyday tolerance is the result of introvert, self-sufficient and base-democratic village structures. The basic goodness of common village life is contrasted with a violent communalism which is the product of elite manipulation, mental colonisation and, when turning into riots, of mob psychology (Chattanath, Kaul, Varadarajan).

Jyotirmaya Sharma, on the other hand, is very critical of Indian moral exceptionalism. He believes that the 'holier than thou' mentality, based on a sense of 'moral pride' and a 'teacher's pet psychology', is wholly unfounded. The idea of a tradition of tolerance is a 'great but common self-deception'. Cultural and civic explanations for it are bogus. India has no history of a higher morality than other countries (if, indeed, such a comparison can be made in the first place). There may be some degree of restraint. It is, however, a by-product of other aspects of Indian culture. His opinion thus resembles that of the proponents of 'fuzziness'. Only, his view of Indian culture is far less positive than the harmless 'fuzziness'. On the interpersonal level, restraint springs from a certain disinterest and ignorance, becoming a merely 'repressive' tolerance (the opposite of the Christian ideal of 'compassion'). Poverty and caste are 'structural violence' and forms of 'slow exterminism'. On the international level, restraint comes from the inability to deal with threats head-on – an 'inability to look reality in the eye', a lack of strategic culture and structural weaknesses such as corruption, poverty, instability. He comes to the conclusion that 'Indian foreign policy is like a virgin – willing but scared'. In this particular view, cultural benignity is nothing but a delusion or fig leave. However, the mere belief in it has some impact.

The majority of the interviewed strategic community was much more comfortable with the idea of a 'structural restraint' than with a 'cultural benignity' in characterising Indian foreign policy. (Albeit a number of interviewees used both approaches.[130]) The restraint, in this line of thinking,

[130]See also, for example, the works of Sunil Khilnani and Pratap Bhanu Mehta who argue that India's key quality is the idea of syncretic pluralism, developed from cultural roots within the current civic framework (Khilnani, S., 1998; Mehta, P. B., 2003). Prime Minister Manmohan Singh shares this opinion. At a recent conference in New Delhi, he explained that 'India's unique contribution to the world has been the notion of the many-sidedness and the constant and continuing discovery of truth… Our democracy, like our civilisation, has been built on the notions of "unity in diversity" and inclusive pluralism'. He adds that he believes 'our experience can be of some help to the world community' (Singh, 2005a,

is the product of political-structural factors. Modern India, so the argument goes, has developed a plural, tolerant, functioning society which naturally seeks good relations with others and avoids war. There is significant pride in the moral quality of India's civic achievements. All the more so, since this achievement appears to stand in a marked contrast to the significant friction between the individualistic, legalistic, materialistic and strictly secular West and the world of Islam, reaching from troublesome and often unsuccessful immigration to terrorism and war. India succeeds, where the West (the main rival for the moral high-ground) fails.

India's version of pluralism is seen as a role model for the globalising world, for 'equality', 'unity' and even 'modernity'[131] in 'diversity', where 'diversity' is a meaningful cultural concept, filled with communal, traditional and religious life. This, in combination with other factors (civic, cultural or both), institutionalised India's restraint in the use of force in international relations. The 'nuclear moralism' (Joshi), embodied in a commitment to no first use, minimal deterrence as well as (in the long run) denuclearisation, must be understood under the heading of restraint, rather than cultural benignity.

The quality of restraint is usually portrayed as a permanent, but cultivated as opposed to encultured feature of the modern Indian state, which will not change as India will become more powerful. Apart from the structural pluralism, India's 'political culture' does not feed on resentment or chauvinism. There is no need for conflict – India is 'territorially satisfied' (Haidar) and 'at peace with itself' (Varadarajan). There is no ambition comparable to China's with regard to Taiwan, to include into India the partitioned Muslim states of Pakistan and Bangladesh or territories which were formerly part of the British Raj (Haidar). India has 'forgiven the West for partition' and has accepted it (Gandhi).

These types of argument for a structural restraint are based on the logic of a plural and democratic civil society (Ansari, Chattanath, Varadarajan). On one hand, as the Indian nation-builders around Gandhi and Nehru were acutely aware of, in order to make a multicultural society work, it is necessary to establish tolerant, plural values (Subrahmanyam). On the other

---

p. 21 and 24). At the same conference, Sonia Gandhi said that India's 'many diversities are cemented by secularism and a long tradition of tolerance. This makes us an example for a world where nations are torn apart by sectarian violence...' (Gandhi, S., 2005, p. 32).

[131]Bernhard Lewis considers the inability of Islamic culture to come to terms with modernity and to develop a meaningful modern Islam as a central failure, creating disorientation, fear and ultimately violence (Lewis, B., 2002). India, so is the broadly held consensus, has managed to develop a culture at once traditional and open.

hand, as in a self-fulfilling prophecy, 'internal social engineering and stratification' has created a stable and non-aggressive society, a 'self contained civilisation' (Sahni). Tolerance was thereby 'institutionalised' (Karnad). What differentiates India from other nations with plural and tolerant societies is that India, through its particular approach to pluralism has managed to 'defuse the idea of the "other"' (Malhotra), thereby keeping xenophobia at bay. This achievement is widely believed to be India's main contribution to international relations (Basham, Jha, Malhotra, Varma). In dealing with cultural complexity, India is a 'laboratory for the world' (Bhattacharya).

For Indian foreign policy, successful pluralism induced a preference for a 'conciliatory middle path', readily attempting to reconcile seemingly incompatible differences (Mansingh). It is the success in building a viable, even inspirational, Indian modernity, rather than some mystical primordial quality that makes India a stable, content and cooperative nation. Jha even goes so far as to call modern Indian society 'profoundly pacific'. India, he argues, is the prime representative of the 'post-national type', transcending the 'Westphalian System' by defusing the insider/outsider distinction and thus avoiding the fears and aggressions associated with homogenous, closed understandings of the self. In India, there is 'true' or 'natural' multiculturalism as everyone is in a minority in some sense (religious, linguistic or ethnic) and no single group is dominant (Jha, Khare). Yet, every group can unfold freely – long, local histories, vernacular systems of law, schooling and community traditions 'cover about 80 per cent of the need for self-expression'. And because the system works fairly well for everyone, everyone has a stake in the system (Jha). The functioning pluralism of the civil society is understood to make India a content, status-quoist and peace-oriented member of the international society.

Harish Khare adds to the Indian pluralism a number of other elements which are instrumental in bringing about a structural restraint. Indians are fond of international organisations and treaties because they are good at working them. They are, moreover, bound to them by a strongly legalist mindset. This, in turn, comes from the experiences of British law during colonisation and of the National Movement. These experiences are consonant, however, with a prior cultural Indian legalism (Brahmanism). Moreover, the role of the military in Indian politics has always been limited and the 'state system is weak', giving the Prime Minister far less power to start a war, than for example the US President has (Basham, Khare).

Another line of argument, pursued by a few interviewees, is that of political and social 'complexity'. It is akin to the argument of Hindu cultural 'fuzziness' in that it sees foreign policy restraint largely as a by-product of a lack of readily deployable power. Managing the Indian Leviathan – colossal, democratic, plural, unequal, and miraculous in its inner mechanisms – is so complex a task in itself that it leaves no room for adventurism. One would have to be a 'megalomaniac' (Khare). For Inder Malhotra, domestic complexity is 'the key' to understanding restraint in Indian foreign policy (also, Mansingh, Subrahmanyam).

A significant minority of the interviewees rejected the idea that Indian foreign policy is in any way determined by cultural or structural restraint. Some do not like the idea of national policy styles as such. To Hamid Ansari, there is no tangible difference between India and other countries in terms of restraint and morality. To C. Raja Mohan, cultural or structural factors provide no more than a limited 'stickiness' in the decision-making process. Similarly, Varun Sahni does not attribute much significance to cultural or structural factors. He allows for only a very limited non-aggressive character. Voll considers Indian restraint – cultural or structural – as mere 'value talk' of political elites steeped in a self-righteous 'Brahmanic mindset'. There is no connection with actual foreign policy decisions. Vanaik describes Indian moral aspirations as hypocritical and bigot, and disproved by actions.

Only Bharat Karnad systematically questioned the proposition that if culture or civic society do play a role in the foreign policy process, it will be towards restraint and benignity. He challenges the idea of a moral India by stressing the 'war-like traditions' as exemplified in the Arthashastras, the Mahabharata ('a story of war'[132]) and the Vedas ('entirely amoral texts'), which outbalance non-aggressive and otherworldly 'fringe concepts'. However, even he is willing to attribute to India some special capabilities in dealing with conflict arising from modernity and diversity. India is 'the ultimate melting pot'. It is culturally less prone to think in terms of a strict insider/outsider distinction than, for example, the Chinese (Middle Kingdom/barbarians). For that reason, Pakistan has significant difficulties in defining itself against India.

On the whole, Nehru's message has, it seems, arrived and taken root. The ideals of tolerance, pluralism and restraint are embedded in the strategic community. A significant change can be observed in that civic and structural factors of a modern society are emphasised over cultural factors. The latter, however, still retain some clout. The self-righteous style of

---

[132]Chattanath gives an opposite interpretation. For him, the war is purely symbolic of an inner struggle for enlightenment.

communication and sense of mission has subsided. In overall terms, the concept of moral greatness is now less pronounced.

7.1.2 *Political Greatness – The Sense of Importance*

While the strategic community's sense of India's moral greatness is somewhat receding, its sense of India's political greatness remains strong. Compared with Nehru's time, it has changed insofar as it is no longer primarily based on history, culture and individuals. Two other very powerful symbols of India's political greatness have come to the fore – the economic success story, especially in high-tech sectors, and India's nuclear weapons (which, according to Haidar come 'with a dose of chauvinism'). These symbols stand for India's global technological and social-political competitiveness and for a widespread 'sense of destiny', an understanding of being on the right side of history, that the future is Asia's to take and that 'time works in India's favour' (Sinha). India's enormous population is, on balance, no longer regarded as a drag on development, but as a source of power – as a vast pool of human resources, from highly trained professionals to unskilled labourers, and an even larger pool of consumers. India is considered a great power, one of six[133] power centres shaping the world of tomorrow. There is a strong sense that 'India counts for a lot, that it is one of the key forces in global history' (Bajpai). This sense reflects and springs from a 'stunning sense of self-esteem' (Joshi).

Given that the interviewees were invariably highly educated, and often cosmopolitan and experienced intellectuals, the sense of importance was naturally not communicated directly and crudely. It was tacitly understood, to be read between the lines, or at most reflected upon as a general phenomenon. However, it was almost always there – mostly in the form of a certain ease and confidence. It seems as though India's perceived actual importance has significantly reduced the need for communicating it (Mallavarapu). India is no longer belittled as a colossal, poverty-stricken and otherworldly anarch. It has arrived at the centre of global attention[134]. Of course, Indian power is still largely implicit and potential rather than factual and there are many serious challenges on the way to realising it. However, the 'sense of destiny' has fundamentally changed the perspective on the facts. To most interviewees it is plain to see where this great sub-continent is heading. In the case of a number of them, patriotic enthusiasm

[133]The United States, Russia, China, India, the European Union, Japan.

[134]See, for example, the recent studies by Stephen Cohen, Sandy Gordon and Naunihal Singh (Gordon, S., 1995; Cohen, S. P., 2001; Singh, N., 2006).

further blurred the line between potential and actual importance. It was also manifested in the references made by interviewees. The focus of attention was firmly set on the USA (the hegemon) and China (the paragon). 'Lesser' powers, such as Japan, Britain, France, Germany and Russia, are – although still significantly more powerful than India in economic and military terms – neglected. It appears as though they are already 'left behind' in the imagination of the future. A sense of political greatness could, thus be easily traced. However, there is no consensus on what political greatness actually means. Economic power is, of course, key. But some see it as a source of greatness in its own right, while others see it as a vehicle for technology leadership, political influence, military power or cultural attractiveness.

Nehru's perception of national greatness as the greatness of a civilisation, although a minority view among the interviewees, still carries some weight. Some regard it as 'crucial for a Pan-Indian identity' (Joshi). It came up in three variations. Firstly, India, as one of the great actors in world history, is seen as having a natural duty and right to play 'a leading role in world affairs' (Malhotra). Of course, today, there is widespread consensus that Tanham was right when he criticised India for confusing being a great nation with being a great power and that lasting influence needs to be backed by a strong power base (Rajagopalan, Malhotra). However, being an actual-potential great power with a rapidly growing economy and internationally leading centres of technological excellence, India is now at once a great nation and great power. In the opinion of a number of interviewees (as, indeed, had been Nehru's opinion) this is not news, however. India had been important throughout most of known history. What is happening today is therefore not a rise but a renaissance of Indian power. Economically, India (like China) used to be one of the wealthiest parts of the world. Now it is resurging. Culturally, too, after 1000 years of stagnation, India is reawakening (Chattanath).

Secondly, the Nehruvian ideals of national autonomy, sovereignty and non-alignment still play some role (Rajagopalan, Joshi). In economic terms, Indians take pride in the fact that economic growth is a largely domestic effort – with little foreign direct investment, it is predominantly financed and driven by Indian entrepreneurs (Bhattacharya, Mallavarapu). Politically, Sinha follows the Nehruvian logic when he says that India has a 'natural leadership of the third world'. India, the former centrepiece of the British Empire, set in motion the great wave of decolonisation after the Second World War. Other African and Asian countries looked up to it. It was able to offer them a democratic example and an autonomous, 'third way' during the Cold War. Today, India can show the other former colonies how to be successful economically and politically. India's profile is now sharper and must be recognised because it is backed by strength (Sinha).

Thirdly, a significant minority of interviewees still thought of Indian political greatness in Nehruvian culturalist terms, whereby 'civilisational and cultural weight is more significant than wealth and military power' (Varma). Such a culturalist view often comes in conjunction with a sense of culturally-based moral greatness. Jaswant Singh argued that greatness derives from the fact that 'the spirit of the ancient Indian nation has never been conquered', that indeed, India is – culturally – 'unconquerable'. It is a great source of ideas and religion in its own right and not so much a consumer of foreign ideas.

A majority of the interviewees, however, thought about greatness primarily in terms of power. Culture, civilisation or values were of secondary concern. Power is usually understood as economic and military power. India's dramatic rise in power is exemplified by its no longer associating itself with the G-77 (of developing states) but with the G-4 (of states seeking a permanent seat on the Security Council[135]) (Kapoor). Interviewees, who thought along these lines, tended to identify a strong sense of strategic rivalry with other great powers, especially China, and much less so with the USA. India must not allow either to be hegemon in Asia or to interfere with a broadly defined sphere of interest. This sphere matches Indian greatness and is increasingly thought of in terms of far-reaching energy needs and economic opportunities. Conceptualisations of India's national security sphere are approaching those of the Viceroys Curzon and Minto[136], with a broad definition, which was valid during the peak of British imperial influence (Karnad, Mohan, Unnikrishnan). However, most interviewees who stressed the economic and military aspects of greatness nevertheless appreciated the cultural aspects as great reservoirs of 'civilisational soft power'. As sources of this power, Unnikrishnan lists – (1) a wealthy and widely dispersed diaspora (especially in the USA), (2) India's cultural influence in South Asia and, to a lesser extent, in South East Asia, (3) India's importance and authority in religious matters, (4) The

[135]The other three are – Japan, Germany and Brazil.

[136]Lord Curzon and the Earl of Minto were Viceroys of India from 1899–1905 and from 1905 to 1910, respectively. They defined a sphere of interest for India, encompassing the Indian Ocean and reaching from Iran to South East Asia. This was at the height of the so called 'Great Game', the geopolitical rivalry between the Russian and British Empires in the Middle East and Central Asia (Prasad, B., 1979; Mohan, C. R., 2003, pp. 204–236).

entertainment industry (especially Bollywood), (5) India's global trade and business links, (6) its IT and service industry links, (7) democracy (India is the main non-Western role model, the largest democracy and the most successful former colony), and (8) a – rapidly diminishing – moral authority deriving from the spiritual aura of Gandhi and Nehru.

7.1.3 *Recognition and the Conflation of Ends and Means*

International recognition and respect has been very important for successive Indian governments since Nehru[137]. In part, this may be for reasons of post-colonial insecurity (Mallavarapu). In part, it may spring from a very status-oriented 'Brahmanic mindset', which stresses etiquette, hierarchy and rules, and places significant emphasis on each member's position within a given system (whereby the international system is an ideational approximation to the caste system) (Luce, Malhotra)[138]. By the logic of the argument proposed here, however, recognition is primarily needed (and, thus, more or less consciously sought) for a representative national 'greatness' as a differentiating and stabilising factor in the process of nation-building, helping the formation of a national identity through external validation. It is at once a 'reality check' and a call for identity affirmation. In fact, most interviewees linked recognition to a sense of greatness. Depending on the perception of greatness, recognition is sought for moral or cultural qualities, for civic achievements, for a civilisational history or for power – economic, technological and military.

In conjunction with India's economic rise, the emphasis in terms of a global leadership role has tilted towards economic and technological success; cultural pride is still important, but less strongly communicated. Under Nehru, culture, in terms of morality and civilisation, was the primary source of desired respect. This change is significant in its effect on the conflation of identity and strategy. In terms of strength, the relationship between a desire for recognition and actual (economic) success is inconclusive. Whilst for some interviewees, India's economic success and growing influence engenders a heightened desire for recognition and offers

---

[137]Tanham, in his 1992 study of Indian strategic thought, wrote that – 'Indians strongly believe that India's size, population, history, culture, and recent achievements make India a world nation. They resent the fact that their country is not yet considered a world power, even a regional power... They feel a real need for a world position and for the world's recognition of that position' (Tanham, G.,1992, p.49).

[138]The same point has been made by several outside observers of India. Compare, for example, Tanham – 'the caste system has given Indians a hierarchical view not only of India but of the world; they rank nations by size, culture, and power' (Tanham, G.,1992, p.16).

opportunities to actually receive the due respect, for others the actual success is generating sufficient self-assurance in itself. In the latter case, everyday business and political relations replace the need for political statements, thus further facilitating a pragmatic foreign policy[139].

Mansingh argued that the West has, in the past, judged India only by the standards of its own particular interests. It failed to engage India in terms of India's specific civilisational and moral identity. The rapid economic growth has now, however, triggered a new appreciation for India and facilitated engagement on a more equitable level. 'The glory of India', Singh said, 'is finally being recognised'. According to Varma, there is a strong desire in India to regain the standing and recognition of an ancient civilisation. He calls this India's 'rightful place' on the world stage. Subsequently, it is India's 'grand strategy' to reassert itself 'as one of the world's great nations' (Varma, Kursheed)[140]. Other interviewees regarded recognition as naturally following in the wake of economic success, and thus nothing to be particularly pushed (Haidar, Scindia). It is difficult to assess, however, how important recognition is for each interviewee. Few addressed the issue directly. It manifested itself mostly in conceptions of greatness.

The changing focus of recognition, from recognition for moral greatness to recognition for political greatness and from cultural issues to civic and economic issues is reflected in a changing appreciation of Nehru and the foreign policy associated with him. For many, he is still the central personality in the history of the modern Indian state. They see his status and influence as a national symbol reaching far into the contemporary political processes. To others, he represents a vainglorious, old-fashioned India that has failed to take its rightful place. And finally, his legacy of idealist folly is being overcome. Among the interviewees there were slightly more negative than positive verdicts. Gandhi, on the other hand, while no longer a point of reference in terms of policy decisions, is almost universally revered as a national icon. He is, however, interpreted almost at will – as anything from a shrewd master tactician in the service of the national interest to a saintly spirit in the service of all mankind.

---

[139]In a speech at the Institute for Defense Studies and Analyses (IDSA), C. Raja Mohan described Manmohan Singh's foreign policy as being characterised by a 'a rare tranquility… This tranquility is built around the new self-assurance based on India's high economic growth rates of the last decade-and-a-half. It also reflects a new national confidence that, as its economic weight increases, India will begin to matter much more in world affairs in the years to come' (Mohan, C. R., 2005, p.37).

[140]At times, there is a flicker of the 'place in the sun' rhetoric that characterised a jingoist, rapidly growing, newly powerful German empire under William II.

As noted in the introduction (with respect to written sources), assessments of Nehru depend to a large extent on the foreign policy perspective of the analyst, here the interviewee. Those who greet India's 'pragmatic turn' (Mansingh[141], Varadarajan) and 'new realism' (Joshi)[142], either to a greater or lesser extent disassociate themselves from Nehru (Haidar, Kapoor, Nath, Joshi) or stress his realism and give little credence to his idealism (Karnad, Mohan). Those who continue to value his system-level goals tend to regard Nehru as the still fundamentally relevant architect of India's grand strategy (Basham, Kaul, Rajagopalan, Bajpai, Subrahmanyam). They tend to stress the rationality and pragmatism of an idealism which was nevertheless based on genuine values (Ansari, Jha, Kursheed, Mansingh, Malhotra).

Almost all interviewees observe a 'pragmatic turn' away from idealism (or moralising) in Indian foreign policy since the economic and nuclear revolutions of the 1990s. Ashis Nandy, Vidhya Subrahmanyam and Siddharth Varadarajan were the only interviewees concerned about a new emotionalisation of foreign policy issues, this time not elitist and idealist but popular-democratic and communalist. Nandy observes a serious threat to a restrained foreign policy emerging from an increasingly jingoist middle class. The protests against US President Bush's visit to Delhi and political concerns about the reactions of Indian Shia constituencies to policies concerning Iran were given as examples of a foreign policy influenced by communal pressures (Varadarajan, Subramanyam).

All other interviewees, however, concentrated on the shift towards pragmatic realpolitik, or, as Mansingh put it, on 'India's emancipation from Gandhi and Nehru' (Mansingh). This change is seen as the product of a learning process. India 'has learned many lessons and adjusted its policy accordingly' (Sinha, Parthasarthy). For Mohan, contemporary India has a strongly interest-oriented foreign policy. It is essentially a continuation of the Curzon/Minto tradition (Mohan). Haidar regards contemporary Indian foreign policy as essentially pragmatic. Since independence, he argues, India has 'moved across a spectrum from moralpolitik to realpolitik' as it stumbled into the 'deeper waters' of international politics. Kursheed also sees Indian foreign policy as having become significantly more pragmatic

[141]In a speech at the Institute of Defense Studies and Analyses (IDSA), Mansingh said that in the 1990s, 'Indian foreign policy, freed from the shackles of an ideological past, entered a new pragmatic phase' (Mansingh, L., 2005, p. 44).

[142]This perception is widely shared. See, for example, Mitra – 'Beyond the constants of Indian politics... Indian diplomacy has acquired a new pragmatism and a tone of confidence that distinguishes it from its earlier avatars' (Mitra, S. K., 2005, p. 32).

as a result of the experience that 'morality does not pay'. Throughout the history of independent India, there has been a 'slow, but steady evolution – rather than revolution – away from Gandhian principles' (Kursheed, Parthasarthy). Kapoor, on the other hand, observes a 'sharp turn' towards pragmatic foreign policies, based primarily on economic considerations. Ansari traces a pragmatically pursued and interest-driven new foreign policy primarily to India's energy policy. India's willingness to be pragmatic may, furthermore, as Unnikrishnan argues, exceed its actual pragmatism in the absence of a clearly defined national strategy. For instance, Indian restraint towards Pakistan may not be the result of choice, but rather of an inability to decide whether India wants a stable or an instable neighbour (Subrahmanyam, K.).

Again, depending on the assessment of Nehru's policies, the 'pragmatic turn' is either regarded as a resurgence of pragmatism (in this view, Nehru was already essentially pragmatic in his moralpolitik, but his successors subsequently mistook means for ends) or as a more or less radical turn away from Nehruvian idealism. Interestingly, almost all interviewees, even those very critical of Nehru, have accepted some basic idealist elements of Nehruvian foreign policy. To Mohan, for instance, India still has a moral overall frame of reference in its foreign policy. Haidar argues that while the 'idealist spirit' and 'desire to single-handedly reshape the world' is gone, India nevertheless still 'rejects pure realpolitik'. Others see Nehruvian idealist reflexes ingrained in policy making. Kapoor believes that they occasionally flare up, most recently in the Indian stance on US policy towards Iraq and Iran. Unnikrishnan suggests that the difficulty to develop a national strategy comes in part from an idealist element in the Indian worldview.

With respect to the duality between ideals and interests, a majority of interviewees is skeptical. Some, like Bharat Karnad, Achin Vanaik or Inder Malhotra, do not see much idealism in the first place. Hence there is no duality. Others, who regard the idealism as more substantial, see no conflict between it and pragmatic policies. They reject the strict Gandhian unity between ends and means. There is 'no Cartesian divide between mind and matter, ends and means', Nath argues, 'moralism and pragmatism can coexist'. Idealist ends, Mohan believes, do not stand in contradiction to a strictly power political approach to achieving them in foreign policy. Others look at the matter historically, asserting that while there may be a clash between idealist ends and pragmatic policies, in the past, the two mostly dovetailed (Varadarajan, Singh). Nandy believes the duality exists, but that India has been 'quite successful at mediating the clash'.

A number of interviewees (albeit a minority) follow the Nehruvian logic that there is no clash between interest and ideal, because the ideal is simply 'the larger, global aspect of the same solution' (Chattanath). In this line of argument, Nehru's legacy and Panchsheel are 'still part and parcel of India's foreign policy'. The legacy is one of practical idealism. In that sense, there is no contradiction between realism and idealism (Basham). To Kursheed, there is also no contradiction – 'India wants to be powerful in order to be peaceful'. He regards this as credible, despite nuclear weaponisation, because there is 'very little jingoism' among the foreign policy community and a 'stable national psyche'.

A significant minority of the interviewees see the duality between interests and ideals as both real and problematic. Mansingh explains that the strength of the moral momentum generated by the National Movement is such that 'India continues to struggle with ideals and reality'. The situation has improved significantly, however. For Chattanath, the Indian approach to international relations is marked by an uneasy balance between contract, cooperation and power. Rajagopalan argues that India refuses to unconditionally play the power game. A morally motivated restraint comes into the equation both at the tactical level (where India does not use force as freely as others do) and on the strategic level (where India does not systematically balance Chinese power). Kaul describes Indian foreign policy as 'pragmatic' as well as 'benign', to Jha it is 'pragmatic' as well as 'peaceful'. Sahni believes that there is clearly a moral quality in Indian foreign policy. It is, however, balanced by increasingly interest-based policies. Sinha argues that India still has an idealistic framework, and that 'idealism needs to be combined with realism – and vice versa'. The role of idealism in Indian foreign policy is, as Mansingh explains, an existential one –

> 'If India had associated itself with the USA and Great Britain, India would have been a world power, with a seat in the Security Council. But India chose the opposite path – to side with the weak. The choice was correct, because of India's identity. Siding with the USA and playing the Great Power game would have created a great sense of betrayal of the National Movement.'

The same sense of identity and mission still exists somewhere in the Indian strategic community. Although it is becoming weaker, it is by no means gone (Mansingh)[143].

---

[143]The duality is evident in widely accepted statements such as this by Uday Bhaskar – 'Great nations must remain committed to lofty moral principles and humane values, but it

Pragmatism is, therefore, albeit much more prominent today, still coupled with substantial idealist concerns. The inflection still exists, although at a much more restrained level. What does that mean in terms of the hypotheses?

(1) A belief in moral greatness still exists among the strategic community, although in the absence of a towering figure it is probably less loudly voiced and more implicit today – This is true. With the addition that moral greatness is today seen more as a civic achievement of the Indian plural, secular democracy rather than as a basic, cultural feature. The sense of mission is almost entirely gone. It is replaced by a more careful sense of exemplariness.

(2) A belief in political greatness still exists among the strategic community. It can be expected to have increased as a result of the economic boom and India's nuclear weaponisation. The link between political and moral greatness may have become less strong – This is not true. The belief in India's political greatness seems to be, if anything, at par with the Nehruvian era. Today, the sense of political greatness is based in roughly equal share on a newfound pride in economic success and the more traditional pride in India's culture and history. Since India has become less concerned with cultural aspects of greatness and has instead increased its power, moreover, there is a more solid connection today between the self-esteem and the perception by others. What Cohen has called 'one of the central puzzles of contemporary India', namely the 'large disparity between India's own view of its "greatness" – past, present, and future – and the skepticism in this regard voiced by many others' (Cohen, 2001), has become less puzzling as the gap between actual power and the sense of importance has narrowed.

(3) Recognition and external affirmation is sought more for political greatness and less for moral greatness – This is true in part. A desire

---

merits repetition that the power of principle can be most effectively pursued when it is accompanied by the principle of the relevant power of the times' (Sisoda, N. S., and Bhaskar, C. U., 2005, p. xx). Inversely, the duality means that realism will be guided by idealism. As Cohen writes – 'Whether India veers towards the greater use of force, towards a more conciliatory approach, or towards a mixed policy, its decision will be justified in terms of the broad principles that help hold this pluralist, secular, former colonial state together. There is a widespread agreement that its policies should promote anticolonialism; the vision of a just, equitable, and nonnuclear world; antiracism, democracy, and economic justice; and national dignity' (Cohen, S. P., 2001, p. 65).

to be recognised for moral greatness has become less pronounced, although it still exists. In terms of political greatness, the desire for recognition has shifted in focus from civilisational, historic, demographic greatness to political and economic greatness. It is still important. Overall, it seems as though the need for recognition, moral and political, is reduced.

(4) The conflation of ideals and interests, between ends and means has become less strong. While the ideal of a peaceful world is still upheld, it no longer stands in the way of pragmatic politics which point in the opposite direction. The justification for the nuclear bomb is a prime example of this. There has been a significant shift towards pragmatic foreign policy unimpeded by ideological or idealist considerations. The conflation of ideals and interests, and the duality in foreign policy still exists – although at a reduced level.

These inside-out findings on Indian strategic culture correlate with the outside-in perspective given in the introductory chapter of this book, that Indian foreign policy is becoming increasingly more pragmatic, driven by strategic considerations based on realism, while an idealist inflection (the conflation of ideal and interest) still exists at a reduced level. How can the change towards a more pragmatic strategic culture be explained?

7.2 Changes in India's Strategic Culture since Nehru

Per se, change does not require an explanation. It is the norm, rather than the exception. Not everything changes all the time, but everything changes sometime and something changes all the time. Malleability is the natural morphological condition of all constitutive elements of history. States, polities, peoples, cultures, actors, environments, interests, pressures, opportunities, threats, explanations, beliefs, approaches – and with all these, national identities – are subject to change in an unending maelstrom of intersubjectivity, generating new experiences, lessons, emotions, structures, technologies, knowledge and obliterating, superseding, synthesising the old. The supposed individuality of a nation is masking a changeable core. India, with its manifold, uncontrolled and quite possibly uncontrollable vitality, constructed around overlapping shades of grey which facilitate its everyday life, has a particularly fluid identity (Kakar and Reif, 2006). At the same time, identities are 'sticky' – elements of it enter the unconscious and survive generations and significant external changes. The important question is therefore not if the Indian national identity changes, but exactly why it changes in the particular period under investigation, and what has remained stable.

As the interviews demonstrated, a significant part of the Nehruvian national project has taken root in the identity of the Indian foreign policy community. Irrespective of many necessary adaptations in terms of actual foreign policy, especially the 'pragmatic turn' and the significantly toned down rhetoric, there remains a core understanding of India as a nation with a particular moral capacity – and consequently, duty. The duality continues to exist. However, the gap between interests and ideology has become smaller. Idealism plays a far less powerful role in determining foreign policies than it did under Nehru. Why is that? According to the argument proposed here, idealism has its roots in the Indian nation-building process. It was a risky, precarious project, driven by ideologically motivated politicians (spill-over). In order to succeed, they made use of ideological politics and sought to affix an identity, using all levers at the disposal of a political entrepreneur, including value-based, idealistic foreign policy (reflection). There are two hypotheses, therefore – either the national project has been successful and is no longer in need of ideological stabilisation, or foreign policy is, for one reason or another, no longer a preferred instrument of identity building.

7.2.1 *National Stability Today – Continuing Need for Nation-Building*

The great Gandhian/Nehruvian project of nationalism is, in spite of an ongoing and serious challenge from a rival Hindu nationalism, taking root. Salman Rushdie, one of the most thoughtful observers of Indian life, is optimistic that 'India is more mature than many can imagine... in my opinion, the power of the idea of India is being underestimated' (Rushdie, 2006). Ideology has, over time, produced 'something new in the subcontinent – a state stronger than society' (Embree, 1989). The very success of ideological politics may ultimately make it irrelevant. To some extent this is the case. The Republic of India has lived through 60 years, some of them highly turbulent, most of them accompanied by internal insurrections, terrorism, separatism and war, but by-and-large, the vast experiment has been a success. India has survived, and even blossomed in parts, based on plural and secular political ideals. Over the last 60 years, Indians have proved that they are willing and ready to live by these ideals, and in turn they have had ample time (an overwhelming majority of Indians were born and grew up after 1947) to ingest them. This is the result of the aforementioned extensive research project of the Indian electorate by Mitra and

Singh. A questionnaire was sent to 9,000 randomly selected voters of the 1996 election to assess political values, partisan and issue preferences and political participation, taking note of their age and communal identities. It transpired that young voters were more willing to disapprove of the 1992 demolition of the Babri mosque in Ayodhya, more willing to negotiate on Kashmir, and less willing to accept separate communal family law codes (Mitra, and Singh, 1999). As stated before, however, it would be premature to call the nation-building mission accomplished. There are still significant sources of instability.

The main threat to the national project in the long term is poverty. The stability of any state depends to a significant extent on the ability of the economy to satisfy the needs of the population and to open up opportunities and prospects for economic and technological progress. Economic interdependence engenders a sense of community among the stake-holders. Consequently, a successful economy, closing the link between abstract rights, values and identity on one hand, and a people's concrete needs for education, work, food, water, shelter and a dignified life on the other, is a key building-bloc (if not, today, the key building bloc) of political legitimacy (Rothermund, 1998b; Jayal, 1999). A country failing to develop an economic base, will eventually fail as a state (although India has lived with abject and widespread poverty for a surprisingly long time).

Nehru was very much aware of the centrality of economic development and made it his top priority. As Paz explained, 'in the struggle against separatism, especially that of the Hindu nationalists, the national economic interests are the allies of the secularism of the state' (Paz, 1997). For a long time, however, India achieved little more than the infamous 'Hindu rate of growth' of around 3 per cent per year. Most of this growth was swallowed up by population growth. The net effect on the average Indian was small. In the last 15 years, however, following economic reforms set in motion by the Rao government (with the current Prime Minister Manmohan Singh as Minster of Finance), growth has picked up significantly to rates between 6 per cent–8 per cent. India is set to make considerable progress in terms of average incomes and education in the next decades.

This positive economic picture has led Pavan Varma to argue that a new Pan-Indianness is emerging, bringing people together and shaping them into a community. Tourism is one example –

> 'Whether travelling by road, by train or by air, Indians are no longer strangers in any part of their country. This is a new feeling and is changing the way they

define and identify themselves. Even in the farthest outposts there is something representative of India as a whole. And however marginalised an Indian, a part of him or her is influenced by a larger, transcendent India. Perhaps the most ubiquitous element of this subcontinental continuity is the Government of India (GOI)' (Varma, 2004).

A growing network of shared commercial interests and exchanges is further complementing the political framework. This reinforces national cohesion. 'As a result of economic growth, Indians are preoccupied by issues other than religious issues' and if the current dynamic continues, socio-structural barriers such as the caste system will become less important (Kakar and Reif, 2006)

The problem with economic growth as it is today, however, is that it is not creating one India, but two Indias – one that profits from growth, the burgeoning new middle class, and one where nothing changes, the rural, poor and illiterate India. The divide is growing almost as rapidly as the economy as a whole.

> 'There is no doubt that coexisting along with the "shining face" of a burgeoning India is the dark face of continuing poverty, deprivation and unequal opportunities. It is a supreme irony that India today can be viewed in effect as two Indias, the smaller India, yet running into more than 300 million people as a fraction of her billion plus population, that is strident, aspiring and competitive, and the larger India, that is deprived and still awaiting the opportunity to share in the full fruits of democratic equity and development' (Som, 2004).

The problem of unequal growth becomes all the more drastic and dangerous in terms of national cohesion, if the two separate economic spheres overlap partially with other, older religious differences. Muslims in India participate far less in economic growth than Hindus do. The figures are alarming ('The Economist', 2006).

The relationship between economic development and national stabilisation along Gandhian/Nehruvian lines is thus far from clear. Communal tension and violence in India sometimes comes in the wake of poverty and chaos, as is the case of Bihar. Gujarat, on the other hand, being one of India's richest states, is also highly divisive. Furthermore, wealthy non-resident Indians (NRI) and person's of Indian origin (PIO) provide most of the funding for the Hindu extremist organisation RSS.

The India of today is still far from stable. It is a giant with feet of clay. Although the Tamil or Punjabi separatist movements have subsided and other movements such as that of the Naga and Mizo have been co-opted into the Indian nation, the central authority of the state is still challenged in vast tracts of the country – Kashmir, Bihar, the North East Provinces and the vast tracts of land effectively under Naxalite control (or rather under the control of local warlords) are just the most prominent examples. Furthermore, relations between the two main religious groups, Hindus and Muslims, are far from peaceful. The 2002 burning of a train in Gujarat (in which Muslims killed Hindus) preceded communalist riots (in which Hindus killed Muslims), and the continuing tensions over Ayodhya have been the most prominent recent cases of communalist violence. But –

> '...hardly a month passes in India in which a riot does not occur that is large enough to be noted in the press.... Indeed, it is likely that not a day passes without many instances of quarrels, fights and fracases between Hindus and Muslims in different places in India, many of which carry the potential for conversion into large-scale riots' (Brass, 2003)[144].

Each riot and each case of friction plays into the hands of those who want to remodel Indian national identity along communal lines and are willing to accept considerable instability in the process.

India, therefore, is still in the nation-building process. What Tanham wrote in 1992 is still relevant – 'India's most pressing strategic concern is its own internal unity' (Tanham, 1992). Today, as the memories of Gandhi and Nehru are fading and no individuals of comparable charisma take their place, there is a real danger of disenchantment. People need an identity as well as money. The latter can only go so far in substituting the former. The struggle for a plural, tolerant and secular nationalism is not over. Despite the success of 60 years of statehood, therefore, there is still a need for ideological politics. The reason why the duality in foreign policy has

[144]A list of recent large terrorist activities in India with a communalist background further illustrates how serious and persistent the problem is – 13 December, 2001, a terrorist attack on the Indian parliament leads to the death of eight people and the five attackers. 27 February, 2002, the mentioned Gujarat incident and the ensuing riots led to up to 3,000 deaths. 25 September, 2002, soldiers storm a Hindu temple occupied by Hindu extremists and kill 30. 26 August, 2003, at least 52 are killed by terrorists in train bombings in Mumbai. 29 October, 2005, a series of bombings in Delhi kill 60. 7 March, 2006, three explosions in Varanasi kill 20. 11 July, 2006, explosions in trains and train stations in Mumbai kill at least 180. 8 September, 2006, at least 37 die in two bomb attacks during a Muslim festival in Maharashtra. 19 February, 2007, in an attack on a train connecting India and Pakistan, 69 are killed. 26 August, 2007, bombings in public spaces in Hyderabad kill at least 42 (Deutsche Welle 2006). The year 2008 saw new heights of terorism with attacks all across the country, culminating in the 60 hour battle between extremist terrorists and Indian security forces in Mumbai, in November.

become less pronounced is, thus, probably found in a changing perception of the utility of foreign policy as an instrument of nation-building or in a reduced spill-over.

7.2.2 *Ideology in Foreign Policy Today – Costs Exceed Benefits*

The spill-over effect from national identity to foreign policy has – as the interviews have shown – become less strong. This is not a necessary development. In the case of the USA, for instance, the spill-over effect fluctuates significantly over time and from administration to administration around a relatively high long-term trend[145]. Depending on the mood in a country and depending on the intellectual currents and the preferences of individual leaders, it may become more or less pronounced. That is not to say, however, that in the Indian case one cannot find good reasons to explain the reduction in spill-over.

One reason is, quite simply, that Nehru had his own very strong character, visions and experiences, and once he was gone, India's foreign policy was naturally less defined by his paradigms. Nehru spent most of his life in British India. The larger part of his political life was dedicated to the service of the National Movement rather than, as Prime Minister, to an independent country. He was very close to Gandhi and strongly influenced by him in many ways. The ideology of the national project was their creation. The spill-over effect thus took part not only within one political society (with a 'sticky' identity and, perhaps, a degree of path dependency), but within one mind.

A second reason, related to the first, is that Nehru was a particularly charismatic and visionary leader. It was his personal style to mix ideological with pragmatic concerns and to define ideal-type goals. Others – especially his daughter Indira Gandhi – were far less concerned with the promises of a far away future and far more concerned with a task at hand[146].

A third reason, also related to Nehru as an individual, is that the Indian political environment is today less determined by a 'great man' (or, of

[145]It was, for example, arguably stronger in the Carter administration (Democrat) than in the Reagan administration (Republican) and is stronger now, after the end of the Cold War, under the Bush Administration (Republican) than under the previous Clinton administration (Democrat). In all administrations since F. D. Roosevelt, however, a clearly discernible identity spill-over can be detected.

[146]However, even Indira Gandhi had ingested the duality. Indian foreign policy, she argued, is 'a projection of the values which we have cherished through the centuries as well as our current concerns' (Gandhi, I., 1977, p. 164).

course, 'great woman'), a father/mother of the nation, a political entrepreneur. As in a fast growing family business, after the initial founder generation, the later leadership is more preoccupied with managerial than entrepreneurial tasks. As such, it is less guided by the intuition and personality of a leader and more guided by the exchange and evaluation of arguments among a group of decision-makers within a stable institutional framework. The spill-over in the latter case is naturally less.

A fourth, more general reason is that the spirit of the age has changed. After the Second World War and to a lasser and lesser extent throughout the Cold War, ideological arguments were considered extremely relevant and were frequently used. The current mood, it appears, is one of pragmatism and the focus is no longer so much on fundamental debates about the ideal society, but on economic competitiveness and the generation of wealth. The mood today is, in Popper's terminology, a piecemeal one and not a utopian one. Much of Nehru's language would today appear anachronistic. The spill-over is, furthermore, no longer as straightforward in terms of content. Nehru's apocalyptic fears, as well as his high hopes for international affairs have (for now) not become reality. The world as such took a pragmatic middle-path between armed conflict and peaceful coexistence.

It seems as though the value identity has become deeply ingrained in the minds of India's decision-makers and with that, it seems as though the desire to proclaim the values has given way to a more subdued and confident disposition. India has undergone a learning process. The most significant insights were, perhaps, that firstly India has far too little power to decisively change the international system, and secondly, that moralising is seldom appreciated. A country or statesman may start off with many ideals, but then, as Nehru himself explained, comes some 'knocking about process', bringing 'a sense of realism' (Nehru, 2003). Nehru was distressed by the fact that as Prime Minister the choice is 'seldom between good and evil' – it is usually 'between a greater evil and a lesser evil' (Reid, 1981). This experience contradicts the belief in the Gandhian paradigm that only good means produce good ends and vice versa. A number of shocks (the British and US role at the UN over Kashmir, the China war, etc.) have sped up this realisation and set in motion a process that continues to this day. Today, it is hard to imagine any Indian decision-maker making a statement with the same idealist fervour, bordering on the naïve, as this, India will –

> '...help the realisation of that one world towards which we are inevitably being driven, even though our passions delude us and our minds from understanding

> it. The Indian people… will grow in stature and lose their narrow nationalism and exclusiveness. Proud of their Indian heritage, they will open their minds and hearts to other peoples and other nations, and become citizens of this wide and fascinating world…' (Nehru 1946).

While a learning process and a changed configuration of Indian politics have limited the spill-over effect, there are also good reasons for no longer using foreign policy to reflect an identity. Rothstein argued that eventually, the ceremonial and symbolic pay-offs of an ideological foreign policy could no longer cover the cost as other ever more pressing concerns, which foreign policy could help solve, such as population and food pressures, economic growth, unemployment, trade or aid became increasingly significant (Rothstein, 1976). This is true for India. The balance was decisively turned in favour of a pragmatic foreign policy in the 1990's due to radically new global and domestic circumstances.

The world system of bipolarity collapsed in the early 1990's. The results were that on the one hand India's key international ally, the Soviet Union, suffered an enormous loss of power while on the other, the USA became the single, unrivalled superpower. More broadly, the international system suddenly acquired an immense new dynamic and complexity. In Asia, the strategic environment subsequently came under significant pressure with the fast economic growth of first the 'Asian Tigers'[147], South East Asia and then – of world historical significance – of China. This created new opportunities and new threats, new friendships and new rivalries. The steel frame of the Cold War had given way to a unipolarity rapidly transforming itself into multipolarity – the balance of power is vibrantly shifting around. India needs to react decisively and pragmatically to these new circumstances.

The domestic Indian power calculus has also changed radically. Indian economic growth has generated new needs and interests which cannot be hampered by ideological concerns. Foreign policy is increasingly important as a key facilitator of economic growth rather than as a platform for identity representation. It needs to support trade links, ensure a stable energy supply and deal with global pollution, copyright or technology regimes. Today, as Bertsch argued with a view to India's nuclear policy –

> '…practical issues are vying with larger issues of morality for autonomous space on the national agenda…The new generation of Indians is more concerned about completing the second stage of nation-building, what Samir Amin referred to as the process of "national consolidation". This second stage

[147]Hong Kong, Singapur, Taiwan and South Korea.

> requires allocation of national resources and values towards an optimal utilisation of national capabilities and potential. While moral considerations would continue to under-gird the conduct of its nuclear policy, practical considerations are also not to be lost sight of' (Bertsch, Gahlaut, et al. 1999).

A second key driver for a pragmatic foreign policy is India's increased power, especially its nuclear status. This invites heightened attention and concern from other powers which spend more time calibrating Indian moves and expect it to act reasonably and predictably.

Malik believed that, as a result of the rapid expansion of Indian power and interests, India can no longer be called a status-quoist power in the full sense of the term. India may be less expansionistic and more subtle than China, but like China, its natural projectory will lead it to undo the current balance of power. Today, both India and China, 'are non-status-quoist powers – China in terms of territory, power and influence; India in terms of status, power and influence' (Malik). In a very interesting comparison, he shows how India's relationship with China matches China's with the USA. Both relationships are between a challenger and an established power. In both cases, the challenger is asking for its due in terms of respect and accommodation of security interests (Malik, 2004).

In any case, India needs to pursue a very active foreign policy as it becomes increasingly more entangled in international politics.

> 'From starving nation to economic superpower; from nuclear pariah to responsible nuclear power; from membership of G-77 to special invitee of the G-8; from trade union leader to a seat with the global management team, it has taken India close to six decades to advance from the base of the mountain to the summit. And the view from the mountaintop looks quite different from the landscape India surveyed six decades ago' (Mansingh, 2005).

Using foreign policy for nation-building purposes is, today, much more costly than it was under Nehru. At the same time, the necessity and inclination to do so has become less.

8

Conclusion – The Identity–Strategy Conflict

The vast area encompassed by the new state of India shared only a vague notion of community and internal cohesion when the National Movement began its struggle for an independent state. At independence, in 1947, the modern, political, explicit national 'self' was still under construction and heavily embattled. It was a political project of un-precedented proportions which could probably only be made to work under a combination of factors which rarely come together neatly, but, despite serious hiccups, did so in the Indian case – inspired and incorrupt leadership which can slowly be replaced by accepted and functioning democratic institutions, relatively stable and peaceful circumstances internally and externally, and (for a long time only a limited) economic growth. The emotional and intellectual stabilising frame, within which these factors are applied to a specific geographical area and community, is the sense of national identity. The ideas and ideals on which the national identity is based lay down the terms of interaction.

The success of the national project relied heavily on the ability of political entrepreneurs to create a sense of national unity based on a common identity. This required a specific interpretation of the past and the propagation of this interpretation through nationalism or what Kedourie has called 'ideological politics' – the emotional mobilisation of many Indians along certain pseudo-ontological characteristics. The choice made by Gandhi, Nehru and most successive Indian political leaders was for a national identity based on values both universal in nature and national in their specific expression – tolerance, non-aggression, and a pluralist, supra-religious, interactive and peaceful coexistence.

Given that Indian nationalism was an elitist undertaking, given that there were serious contending nationalisms, especially the Muslim and Hindu versions of the 'Two Nation Theory', and given that the task of pulling together such a vast number of people with such widely different traditional, economic, geographic, linguistic, ethnic, and religious circumstances, the task of creating a common national identity was enormously challenging. Was there an alternative? There was probably not a peaceful one. Any ethnic or religious or linguistic, simple, straightforward nationalism would have arguably risked a Thirty-Years-War-type scenario in unprecedented dimensions.

The value-based nationalism, on the other hand, was both all-encompassing and weaker, because more abstract and less easily discernible by people. It is always more simple to base a community on visible differentiators such as colour of skin or language or any other outward symbols, such as religious signs, than it is to base a community on shared values; values moreover, that are universally applicable. Outwardly visible symbols facilitate a negative definition of the self (an Indian is someone who is not Muslim, not white, not Urdu speaking, etc.). Values are more difficult to use negatively, especially if they are universal. It is Gandhi's greatest achievement that he managed to emotionally mobilise masses in a positive, complex way, around values. He is the shining counter-example to the fascist or communist ideologists who plagued the twentieth century by arousing the masses with appeals to base instincts and desires for superiority, simplistic community and clear differentiation. His ideological politics was thus not harmful – it did not debase the masses but elevated them. The great balancing act between the need to create a national identity on the one hand and the need to avoid divisive and simplistic identities was continued by Nehru and successive governments.

The price to pay for the abstract, value-based approach to national identity was – especially after the enigmatic and symbolic figure of Gandhi was gone and the straightforward struggle for independence (allowing for a degree of negative definition of the self) was exchanged for the much more complex realities of independent statehood – a less stable national identity than could have been achieved by, say, a religious Hindu-nationalism[148]. This strategic choice, made in the face of an already

[148]Again, such a national identity would first cause the violence concomitant with a large scale reorganisation of people along cultural/ethnic/religious dimensions into relatively homogenous territorial unity. Only then could such a 'thick' cultural nationalism produce stability.

enormously difficult national project, required that all levers including foreign policy were used for the purpose of stabilising national identity. At the same time, a national identity based on universal values quite naturally spilled-over into the field of foreign policy. The two effects were related insofar as a foreign policy contradicting the values held internally, would have made the identity and the political entrepreneur far less credible vis-à-vis the target group of ideological politics.

Foreign policy being an elitist undertaking in general and in India in particular, was of course a lever which only applied to a select, politically aware segment of the society. This segment, however, was a particularly important multiplier for the overall national project. The result of both spill-over and reflection of a value-based identity was a strategic culture that supported an idealistic inflection of foreign policy. At times, this dovetailed neatly with foreign policy interests; at other times, it came in conflict with them. The result was a real idealism–realism duality in Indian foreign policy. National identity – both as a work-in-progress consciously advanced and as a fact unconsciously applied – thus came into conflict with the application of foreign policy strategy, based solely on a consideration of the national interest.

Today, this conflict between identity and strategy, and the duality between an idealist and a realist element in Indian foreign policy is significantly reduced. The interviews showed that it still exists, however. The unconscious 'spill-over' effect is probably stronger than the conscious 'reflection' effect. There is a continuing need for national stabilisation through ideological politics. The costs, however, of using foreign policy for this purpose (the 'reflection' effect) have significantly increased. Foreign policy as a whole has taken on a much more complex and vitally important role today, the opportunity costs of hampering strategy with identity-concerns has risen significantly. At the same time, the 'spill-over' effect has also become more subtle as – to use Salman Haidar's fitting expression – the message and the messenger has ripened. However, given that the national identity based on universal values as promulgated by Gandhi and Nehru has taken root in some segments of society and is still heavily embattled in others, the identity element will continue to play a role in foreign policy.

Per se, it seems as though any infringement on the range of options open to a foreign policy maker and any infringement on his or her rational, strategic analysis, negatively affects the quality of the outcome. Kumaraswamy, for instance, has argued that the realist and the idealist motivations clearly obstruct and compromise each other. India's constant vacillation leads to its idealism being rendered incredible by realist policies and its efforts at realpolitik being constantly hampered by ideals. The result is that, since 1947, the country has followed a minimum or lowest-common-denominator strategy of security. It survived. Yet, it could not free itself of its ideological fetters and perform professionally in the international arena. It could not gain a more wide-ranging and substantial 'security beyond survival' (Kumaraswamy, 2004). Is this really true? What are – ultimately – the costs and the benefits of an idealist inflection, the resulting foreign policy duality and the recurrent conflict between identity and strategy?

8.1 Drawbacks of a Duality

As Kumaraswamy pointed out, the most important drawback of a duality is that the foreign policy cannot unconditionally serve the security interests and the advancement of national power and influence. Key concerns may be crowded out by ideological considerations, stopping Indian foreign policy makers from taking necessary actions decisively and timely. The current economic growth will further India's long term power potential. At the same time, it will multiply the associated national interests and thus the demands on foreign policy makers (Kennedy, 1989). China, moreover, has emerged as an extremely dynamic factor in regional and global relations with aspirations of deep concern for India's security – for instance in the Indian Ocean and in Central Asia. Pakistan remains a rival, the Kashmir issue unresolved. Nuclear weapons have given their antagonism an extremely dangerous new dimension.

There are many issues India needs to deal with urgently, pragmatically and decisively – its bilateral relationships, especially with the USA, Pakistan, China and Russia, its energy supply lines, new trade links, regional security, and policies on terrorism and nuclear non-proliferation are just some of them (Kumaraswamy, 2004; Sisoda and Bhaskar, 2005). The centerpiece of the Indian foreign relations puzzle continues to be Kashmir.

Energy is one case-in-point. Crude oil prices serve as price leader in the energy sector. In 2003, they were around $30 per barrel. In 2005, the price peaked at around $70 and the long term outlook is for an oil price around $60[149]. Part of the reason for the rapid rise in oil prices is supply insecurity, generated by international crises such as the Iraq war. The underlying reason for the long term trend is, however, the rapidly rising energy demand from newly industrialising economies, foremost, China and

---

[149]Bloomberg (6 May, 2007)

India. Their fast rising demand for energy is thus matched by an equally fast rise in energy prices. If India cannot satisfy its energy requirements, its economic growth will stall. Being a latecomer to the global energy game, it needs to catch up fast with geopolitical realities and practices in order to carve out a sustainable position for itself (Chellaney, 2005; Khosla, 2005). Unnikrishnan consequently regards the problem of energy supply as the most vital long term national security issue for India[150]. The Singh government's establishment of an inter-ministerial Energy Coordination Committee in 2005 highlights the importance of the issue.

In order to secure vital energy needs, India will, in the foreseeable future, depend on importing large quantities of fossil fuels. In covering these needs, India is competing with the USA, the EU, China, Japan and other economies. In order to succeed, it has to be willing to deal with countries that are considered 'pariah' states by some of its competitors. And India has shown such willingness. It has invested in Sudan, Burma and signed a long-term energy contract valued at $22 billion with Iran (Dadwal, 2005). India is particularly dependent on the Gulf Region. It is the largest supplier of fossil fuels. Furthermore, a huge Indian expatriate community of up to 3.5 million is employed there. Their remittances exceed $7 billion per year. It is a major trading partner with a trade volume of $18–20 billion per year. Iran's geopolitical relevance with respect to its location 'behind' Pakistan cannot be underestimated either (Ansari, 2005). These very sensitive issues of national security require a tightrope balancing act with India's important strategic partnership with Israel and the recently improved relationship with the USA. There is very little space for idealism and ideological concerns in the great energy game.

Idealist concerns may impede not only pragmatic action, they may also – much more harmfully – impede realist, bold and interest-oriented strategic thinking. Indian foreign policy making has frequently been criticised as ad hoc and lacking strategic depth and clarity (Tanham, 1992; Subrahmanyam, 2005). There has been a lack of clarity in what interests to pursue and about the possible trade-offs. As a result, India has often behaved erratically and, especially from an outside perspective, unpredictably. Except for the obvious danger of taking wrong decisions, there is a broader danger of sub-optimal foreign policy outcomes. There is a 'transaction cost' in terms of power – a greater cohesion in the country's strategy 'will enhance the transformation of India's potential strength into an effective role in South

[150]Interview with the author (2005)

Asian security' – and vice-versa (Mitra). There are further significant costs involved in the process of 'tough learning' through recurring conflicts with reality. The duality can also create mistrust and apprehensions in other countries who may find the Indian approach irritating. It is conducive to misunderstandings and can thereby escalate security situations. Many other countries, from a perspective distorted by their own interests and beliefs, are unwilling to regard the idealist element as substantial. Mitra has analysed the glaring gap between the inside-out and the outside-in views of India, which are, he argues, further compounded by the contradiction between an exaggerated Indian perception of its own importance as a great power, not matched by the resource commitment to substantiate such claims (Mitra, 2003).

The most prominent example of the negative effect of the duality in terms of outside perceptions is the relationship between India and the USA, in many ways a clash of rival exceptionalisms. Each state could not understand the actions and intentions of the other because each state refused to understand the ideological and moral underpinnings of the other state's foreign policy. In India, policy-makers could not understand why the USA – a secular and democratic state with shared values and institutions – does not favour India over Pakistan (Mitra, 2005). Equally, the USA for a long time had problems understanding India's unequal non-alignment. The relationship has now improved substantially. The end of the Cold War has given both players a chance to rethink relations. Strong economic links make an improvement attractive and important. The China factor and the struggle against global terrorism have brought them still further together. The nuclear deal signed in 2006 has eliminated the last major obstacle to good relations. The improvement in this extremely important relationship has become possible because the USA and India have both reduced the ideological content in their relationship and have become significantly more pragmatic in their mutual dealings.

8.2 Benefits of a Duality

Sunil Khilnani has argued that the salient idealist/realist duality in Indian foreign policy must not necessarily produce a number of bad compromises (as Kumaraswamy believes). If handled well, the duality may be brought into a synthesis on a higher strategic plane and India may benefit from its irregularity. Since India, in his view, is still militarily and economically weak for the foreseeable future, it should adopt a diplomacy based on wit, moral discipline, persuasion, the intelligent pursuit of self-interest and the use of 'soft power'. In order to do so, it needs to be more flexible and engagingly active than it was in the past.

The vision Khilnani has, follows Nehru's example. Nehru, he argues, crafted a 'relatively effective policy of state... based not on hard power, but rather on a dexterous combination of moral legitimacy and realpolitik'. Today, the two elements need to (and can) be reorganised to suit the contemporary geopolitical condition. India can be a 'bridging power' (Khilnani), bridging across 'the varieties of hard and soft power in today's world'[151]. This would be truly innovative. There is no precedent for such a 'bridging power'. India would reinvent its own role and influence the nature of global interaction. This is not too much to ask because, 'after all, part of what it takes to be a great power is the capacity not just to conform to existing definitions but to re-define – as Gandhi did for another age – what power and greatness are' (Khilnani, 2005).

India should operate 'with a more nuanced conception of power'. 'More nuanced' supposedly refers to the traditional realist conception of power. The idealist element, so the argument goes, creates goodwill and political capital. 'Legitimacy is certainly a good in itself; but it also has instrumental value, and is part of the armory needed to conduct realpolitik'. India 'must be willing to play a role in the global "battle of ideas"'. Focussing on its democratic and pluralist value – legitimacy, Khilnani believes, will give India considerable power and assures its independence as well as its indispensability. This is not only good for India – it is also good for the world. 'Encompassing elements of both hard and soft power, India could become a power that provides the essential connective tissue, the connectivity that a fragmenting world requires' (Khilnani, 2005). Mitra agrees with Khilnani, that India can fulfill a new and significant bridging role as a result of its history and of its limited involvement in the disastrous wars of ideology that have shaped the twentieth century. India, he suggests, has an innate 'heuristic capacity to understand ideology' and the 'intellectual resources to negotiate across cultures'. Panchsheel, 'in its second coming', not as an ideology, but as a practical doctrine of foreign policy, 'should be able to build heuristically on the innate, universal desire for peace, understanding of difference and respect for the dignity of man' (Mitra, 2005).

---

[151]The distinction between hard and soft power was first made by Joseph Nye in his book 'Bound to Lead – The Changing Nature of America's Power' (Nye, J. S., 1990; 2004). Whereas hard power is the ability to influence other states through coercive means, soft power is the ability to indirectly influence the behaviour or interests of other states through cultural or ideological means.

Let us assume that India does indeed have such qualities – as a result either of history and tradition or (as argued here) of the national identity formation process – does the argument hold? Given that currently there are still significant deficits in the strategic process, it is doubtful if India can really perform such a complex strategy with a pay-off expected only in the distant future. More importantly, however, the assumption underlying such an argument is precisely the Nehruvian conflation of ideal and interest outlined in this book. The special Indian 'heuristic' and 'bridging' qualities may dovetail (like expedient tools) with the national interest in certain circumstances which require soft-spoken diplomacy. However, the same quality may also be a disadvantage, when forceful, even ruthless action is called for. To take the case of energy strategy again – it is possible that India, based on its intercultural qualities, will have an advantage in establishing good relations with the oil producing countries. Will that be enough, however, to outbid a concerted effort by China or the USA, who present a mixed package of monetary, technological, political, even cultural inducements as well as threats backed-up by credible force? Would India not make the same mistake again, as it had done under Nehru, when the non-aligned states turned out to be firmly non-aligned against India during the war with China? What happens with the heuristic qualities, if they are out of tune with the national interest? If they are scrapped, they can hardly be considered constitutive qualities of an Indian identity, or sincerely held values. If the duality is real – and this book supports such a view – they cannot simply be scrapped. They are therefore, not part of a ('bridging' or other) strategy but part of an identity. What does that mean in terms of the national interest?

A capacity for cross-cultural mediation is highly relevant in the world today. India does have invaluable experiences in democratic inter-cultural life which it could and should share with others. It would thereby contribute to global stability. This is a worthy goal. However, achievements at the system-level should not be mistaken for achievements at the national level. The relationship between 'good behaviour', in the sense proposed by Khilnani and Mitra, and national interests can only be a long-term one. Acting according to values over a long period of time and demonstrating the seriousness of the values, upholding them in certain situations against considerations of national interest, can establish a credibility that may indeed serve the long term national interest. Thus, a real duality – where ideals are not merely expedient tools for a middle power, but form a guideline for foreign policy behaviour alongside and level with the national interest – can be beneficial. Values thereby help successive administrations, even generations, to keep track of a reputation that may ultimately serve the national interest. What can be expected of a credible reputation for restrained, predictable, even non-aggressive behaviour?

It would generate trust. India would be seen by other states as constituting a lower risk (Deudney, and Ikenberry, 1991). This would potentially reduce the number of states who regard India with antagonism and suspicion and increase the number of states willing to cooperate. The negative effects of the 'security dilemma'[152] would be reduced. This could come with a tangible pay-off in terms of reduced security spending for India. According to a 1997 study by Mahbub ul Haq, the potential dividend for a sustainable peace with Pakistan, for India could have been – Rs 2,111 billion (US$ 40 billion), had security expenses been frozen at the 1996 level and Rs 3,198 billion (US$ 60 billion) with a 5 per cent reduction (Haq, M. u., 1997). These are significant sums – especially so for a country with such pressing non-military needs as India has. Arguably, a concrete result of the credibility and trust has been the willingness of the USA to accept India as a 'responsible' (capable, careful and non-prolife-rating) nuclear weapons state. This severely reduced the economic and security costs of nuclearisation.

The inverse of this argument is, of course, that India may be regarded as weak, as unwilling or incapable of defending its interests, even its borders, and thus invite adventurism and conflict from more assertive states. This negative effect of a credible reputation for restraint is not to be underestimated and needs to be addressed clearly. The Kargil Review Committee Report, for instance, stated that in the Pakistani military, there is a persistent view of India as a vacillating and unprofessional military opponent, encouraging it to test India's defenses (Kargil Review Committee, 2001).

The most important long-term advantage of a continuing duality in Indian foreign policy and of a credible adherence to values, is the idea of the 'peaceful rise' and of a 'gentle giant'. Here, a comparison with China is instructive. China is rising fast to become a global economic giant and superpower. In an international system characterised by balance of power considerations, such vast tectonic shifts need to be managed very carefully if major disruptions in global order are to be avoided and antagonistic, reactive power-shifts are to be minimised (Shambaugh, 2005). The USA, for instance, managed its rise much better in the twentieth century than

---

[152]A 'security dilemma' is a situation in which two or more states are unintentionally drawn into conflict by mutually aggravating security concerns (Herz, J. H., 1950; Jervis, R., 1976; Roe, P., 2005).

Germany did in the late nineteenth century. China's leadership is acutely aware of the importance of soothing its path to power. Deng Xiaoping's firmly held maxim was that China should disguise its ambition and hide its claws. Today the notion of 'peaceful rise' is the mantra of the Chinese leadership, which has, in December 2005, published a White Paper entitled 'China's Peaceful Development Road'. Evidently produced for external consumption, it is available in English on the website of 'People's Daily', the official newspaper of the Communist Party of China[153]. The paper stresses five points – (1) China has a peaceful approach to modernisation; (2) China's growth will promote world peace and development; (3) it will be endogenous; (4) China seeks to engage in mutually beneficial relations with other nations, in order to (5) build a 'harmonious world of sustained peace and common prosperity'.

The effect of Chinese 'smile diplomacy' has been a remarkable improvement of the difficult relations around its rim during the last couple of years. Japan, South Korea, the ASEAN states, the former member states of the Soviet Union and India have been engaged in negotiations and confidence-building diplomacy. China became the first non-member to sign up to ASEAN's Treaty of Amity and Co-operation in 2003, committing itself never to use force against its members for any reason. It organised the 'Shanghai Five' talks in the mid-1990s (since 2001, institutionalised as the Shanghai Co-operation Organisation) to resolve border issues with the former member states of the Soviet Union. Relations with India have warmed significantly since Vajpayee's visit to Beijing in 2003. They are increasingly stabilised by growing trade flows. In the territorial disputes, in which China is the status-quo power, it can live comfortably with interminable low-level discussions. Despite a very difficult historical heritage and severe diplomatic hiccups, relations with Japan are equally marked by a common desire to cooperate (The Economist, 2007d). China's growing economic reach, not only as a low-cost production powerhouse, but increasingly and more importantly as an investor and importer, makes it an attractive international partner. Other countries want to partake in China's growth and profit from it – but they are also weary of it.

The reason is that the attraction of an authoritarian state like China is limited by the 'concern that it could become a threat in the future' (Nye, 2004). Thus, while China 'appears to have signed up wholeheartedly to an

---

[153]See: *http://english.people.com.cn/200512/22/eng20051222_230059.html* (accessed on 5 December, 2006)

international order of globalised trade and rules-based relations among states' (from which it has gained significantly), 'Chinese intentions about what to do with its power in the long run remain deeply ambiguous' (The Economist). Why, The Economist asks, are there 'so few takers outside China for its self-proclaimed doctrine of 'peaceful rise''?[154] Its answer is that – apart from the frightening scale of 1.5 billion people rising in itself, or a rapidly rising military budget with periodical displays of assertive prowess such as firing missiles into the seas next to Taiwan in 1997 (when the USA dispatched two aircraft carriers to the region as a response) and shooting down an old weather satellite in 2007 – it is mainly the political and social setup that makes China a particularly threatening giant – 'With no attractive ideas or values to appeal to neighbours, it falls back on a resurgent nationalism that scares them instead' (The Economist, 2007a). 'Smile Diplomacy' will remain incredible with room for serious suspicion and misperceptions, as long as China does not develop a stable and moral (i.e. transparent, democratic) domestic social and political structure. China is still run by a non-democratic, closed-state apparatus. Communist values have been dropped or reduced to a farce by practically unfettered capitalism. There is a 'moral vacuum at the heart of Chinese life', which gives room to 'raw and volatile forms of nationalism' lurking 'just beneath a usually placid surface' (The Economist). These erupted, for instance, in response to the NATO bombing of a Chinese embassy in Belgrade in 1999 or during the anti-Japanese riots in 2005. According to Singapore's elder statesman Lee Kuan Yew, passing on the lessons of history to a more jingoist generation that never experienced the horrors of war is China's 'big problem' (The Economist, 2007b).

This has consequences in terms of power and interests. The charm offensive has a purpose – to build trust in order to smoothen the path for Chinese growth and make China's new power palatable to others, thus avoiding the costs and risks of friction and conflict. If it fails, China will have to deal with more difficulties and in doing so, it will be forced to use more costly and clumsy 'hard', coercive power. Inversely, 'when the society and the culture of the hegemon are attractive, the sense of threat and the need to balance it are reduced' (Nye, 2002)[155]. This is in line with Sun

[154]This rise is, historically speaking, of course more accurately described as a renaissance. China used to have a share of between 20 per cent and 30 per cent of the world economy. It currently has around 15 per cent (Maddison, A., 2003).

[155]Josef Joffe, in a description of how the USA manages to make their enormous power palatable to others, comes to the conclusion that 'great powers remain great if they promote

Tzu's advice that it is much better to achieve one's ends without making a battle necessary that it is to win a battle (Sun Tzu, 1988). The Chinese concept of a peaceful rise is regarded as a strategy – and not as a structural factor. According to Tellis, it will probably 'satisfy Chinese interests until it becomes a true rival of the United States'. At that point, he predicts, China will face a 'strategic crossroads' between 'strident assertiveness' and 'deepened accommodation'. Tellis leaves open the path China will choose. He advises a cautious approach, however. Washington should manage its relationships in Asia carefully in order to counteract Beijing's grand strategy which seeks to drive a wedge between the USA as the regional hegemon and its partners (Tellis, 2005). This statement, of course, is at least as indicative of US strategic culture and grand strategy (to preserve its hegemonic status for as long as possible) as it is of Chinese culture and strategy. Furthermore, Tellis may or may not be correct in his analysis and predictions. In the context of the argument presented here, Tellis' statement is useful, however, to demonstrate something else. It shows that the Chinese idea of 'peaceful rise' does not have sufficient credibility. The USA – presumably the ultimate target of the smile diplomacy – remain skeptical (Government of the United States, 2006; The Economist, 2007c). As long as 'peaceful rise' is considered the product of interests rather than values, and thus is understood to be a strategy, the question will always arise, what happens when this strategy is no longer expedient? If China cannot convince others that it is structurally benign, its strategy will not succeed.

A second, positive example, demonstrating the pay-off of embedded values and the resulting credibility which exceeds the strategic realm is the German unification. Like China's or India's rise, the prospect of German unification seemed to upset a balance of power. Furthermore, it was viewed with serious suspicions and apprehensions by many European nations, especially, Poland, the Soviet Union, France and Britain, which had strong historically grounded fears of German aggression. In the years between 1989 and 1990, the crucial question for the four control powers (The USA, the Soviet Union, France and Britain) was whether they could trust a unified Germany to remain unthreatening once all restrictions on sovereignty had been released. The USA answered the question unconditionally positively and eventually managed to convince the other powers. The underlying reason why the USA trusted Germany, and the reason why the European powers could eventually be persuaded to do so, too, was not diplomatic

---

their own interest by serving those of others' (Joffe, J., 1997, p. 27). This would be the next step following a 'peaceful rise'.

skill or clever strategy (although that played a role as well). It was the late, unexpected pay-off of a value-based West German foreign policy – Adenauer's unconditional integration into the Western political and defense structures, the success of the European project, to which Germany tied itself, West Germany's firmly established democratic institutions and civil society, a clear long-term commitment to systemic improvements in Europe and a very restrained foreign and defense policy (with a limited army and no weapons of mass destruction) have created the political goodwill and trust, within which the 'German problem' could be satisfactorily solved once and for all (Zelikow, and Rice, 1997).

India can profit, much like Germany has done, from a credible value base. It can sell its 'peaceful rise' to its neighbours and to the current global power brokers more credibly than China can. In part, this is simply due to the fact that India is years behind China in terms of economic development. Its economy is still far smaller (roughly one third of China's) with slightly lower predicted growth rates (around 7.7 per cent, compared to China's 8.0 per cent)[156]. However, in as far as domestic political and social structures determine if two counties 'feel good towards each other or… regard each other with irritation and disappointment' (Talbott, 2004), if they see each other as friends or enemies, partners or rivals, emphasise the opportunities or the threats brought about by change (Wendt, 1996), democratic, plural India has a structural advantage. Whatever its growth and power, it will most likely provoke less hedging and counter-balancing, less suspicion and fear by other states. Its companies may be able to invest more easily in other markets. Interpersonal cultural, academic or tourist exchanges are more facile. India's structural duality can make a gentle rise credible. It can do so, moreover, precisely because it is structural and not merely a foreign policy strategy because India at times acts against its national interest for reasons of value, identity and political structure. These values, the identity and political structure are relatively transparent. India's 'gentleness' has more credibility than China's. From a Western perspective, the 'comfort level' is higher with India than with an undemocratic, opaque China rising systematically and ambitiously[157]. The idealist inflection may be a good

---

[156]Indian GDP in 2005 was $785.5bn. China's in the same year was $2228.9bn. Average annual growth between 2005 and 2009 is predicted to be 7.7 per cent in India and 8.0 per cent in China. The World Bank classifies India in the 'Low Income Group' and China in the 'Lower-Middle-Income Group'. 'India at a Glance' (http://devdata.worldbank.org/AAG/ind_aag.pdf) and 'China at a Glance' (http://devdata.worldbank.org/AAG/chn_aag.pdf), accessed on 11 April, 2007.

[157]Lalit Mansingh, in a personal interview with the author (2005)

strategy in that sense. However, it is credible, precisely because it is not a strategy, but rooted in identity. The identity anchor, moreover, creates a possibility for generating a long term climate favourable to a 'peaceful rise' because it transcends individual decision-makers, governments, even generations. Thus, values may support strategy, but they are themselves outside of the realm of strategic thinking.

Being firmly entrenched, India's idealist element may also be a crucial corrective for chauvinistic interferences in the pursuit of an interest-based foreign policy. The idea of moral greatness, as it is thought of today, can thus be understood as capping the potentially harmful effects of the idea of political greatness. The German empire at the end of the nineteenth century did not have such a corrective. As its powers grew, chauvinism began to interfere with realpolitik. The results were disastrous – most of all for Germany. India may be spared such a fate because of a stable idealist element. As India will become increasingly more powerful, other countries will be analysing it in this manner, and decide on their policies towards it accordingly.

8.3 Comparability of the Indian Case

National identity is (one could almost say 'by definition') idiosyncratic in content. Being Indian is supposedly a unique attribute of some people and not others. The precise effects of this national identity depend to some extent on the specific nature of the Indian national identity. Comparability, however, is given. The theoretical link between nationalism and foreign policy can be transferred to different scenarios, from the concrete to the abstract. Comparability, it should be kept in mind, however, is always imperfect and limited to certain aspects of a case study.

The most concrete comparisons are given by states whose national identity formation is similar to India's. The USA, for example, has chosen – as India has – to focus on transcendental values rather than cultural assimilation in seeking to bring together ethnic, religious and linguistic diversity. The values are abstract and liberal, as are India's. US national identity is built on concepts such as 'individualism' (on the social level), 'the American dream' (on the economic level) and 'freedom' and 'democracy' (on the political level). Together, these values become the foundation for an 'American way of life'. These ideas are linked in some way to real or fictitious shared experiences (the 'Boston Tea Party', 'Manifest Destiny' and the 'Conquest of the West' or the 'Battle of

Alamo'). The constitutive value concepts crop-up in foreign policy decision-making. They do so, as in India's case, as a combination of moral greatness and sense of mission, a sense of importance, and – a product of the last two – a conflation of ideal and interest, creating a duality in foreign policy comparable to India's. It was expressed in foreign policy-decisions and justifications from Woodrow Wilson's Fourteen Points, to the Truman Doctrine ('the free peoples of the earth look to us'[158]) and George W. Bush's Iraq war. Bob Woodward quotes Bush in his meticulously researched book on the decision-making before the Iraq war –

> 'Let me make sure you understand what I just said about the role of the United States. I believe that the United States is the beacon of freedom in the world. And I believe we have a responsibility to promote freedom that is as solemn as the responsibility to protect the American people, because the two go hand-in-hand. No, it's very important for you to understand that about my presidency' (Woodward, 2004).

The Democrat and Former Secretary of State, Madeleine Albright, hardly suspect of carrying neoconservative intellectual baggage and a firm opponent of the Iraq war, nevertheless shared some fundamental assumptions. She thinks of the United States 'as an inspiration to people everywhere', with a 'duty to free people' (Albright). Locating the convergence between 'doing what works best' and 'doing what is right', is her 'ultimate goal' – 'as it should be for the policy-makers of a nation that has, from the earliest days, sought to be judged both by its prowess and by its ideals' (Albright, 2006).

Except for the challenge of forming a nation out of a highly diverse people, India and the USA share important founding myths, both have been colonies (both have been colonised by Britain), both were able to create a national idea around a struggle for independence, towering leadership (Washington, Franklin, Hamilton, Gandhi, Nehru), and a set of values that set them apart from both their coloniser as well as from the evil, violent ways of a European world in general. Both countries formulated their national values as international human rights. Both countries, however, compromised their values from the beginning. At home, they did so by sustaining radically segregated, unequal societies. Abroad, they engaged, from the outset, in wars and European-style realpolitik within regions

[158]US President Harry Truman, on 12 March, 1947. His speech to Congress became known as the Truman Doctrine (see: *http://www.yale.edu/lawweb/avalon/trudoc.htm,* accessed on 9 April, 2007).

demarcated as their spheres of interests (the Monroe Doctrine, India's occupation of Hyderabad or Goa). Both countries have mixed ideals and interests in many ways, on many levels.

There are, of course, enormous differences between India and the USA, too. In terms of nationalism, the main difference is that the people who made up the United States were immigrants of various sorts, voluntary or involuntary, economically or politically motivated, from Europe, Asia, Latin America and Africa. These people were often ready to start a new life and take on a new identity, merging into a new nation. The USA became a melting pot. India, on the other hand, is made up of a diversity of communities with ancient roots and structures, geographically and socially far less mobile. Thus, it became a salad bowl. In terms of values, this is expressed in the different emphases within the liberal spectrum – individualism and freedom in the USA, tolerance and pluralism in India.

The most important difference in terms of foreign policy is that the USA is far more powerful than India. It has the ability to back its worldview and can go much further in implementing it. It has power at the system-level where India only has ideas and ideals. This may significantly diminish the problematic effects of an idealism–realism duality. It may also lead to larger mistakes as the Vietnam and Iraq wars demonstrate. Furthermore, because the USA is a much more stable national entity than India is[159], it is likely that the effect of nationalism on foreign policy is more of the 'spill-over' than of the 'recognition' kind.

There are also some comparable contexts which, although overlapping less strongly with the Indian case than that of the USA, nevertheless share some fundamental mechanisms. The Soviet Union and Yugoslavia, both multiethnic states, turned to communist ideology (rather than nationalism) in order to bridge internal gaps. Communism (at least in the Leninist/Trotskyist version), as much as the liberal, capitalist values of the USA (and India's values), is a universalist ideology. Its meaning for one state is intimately related to its applicability in the world at large. This helps explain the Manichaean, zero-sum reaction of the US governments to the Soviet Union at the outset of the Cold War. The two blocs were based on ideologies competing for the same universal space. If one side is right, the other must be wrong. If one side is wrong, it has a fundamental identity problem (Engelmeier, 2003b). The ideological and identity aspect during the Cold War is comparable to the ideological and identity aspect in the

[159]This could be because of the economic success of the USA which validates the myths of national identity on an everyday level.

India–Pakistan rivalry – if the 'Two Nation Theory' Pakistan is founded upon is correct, then the 'One Nation Theory' India is founded upon is incorrect. In both cases, what one side says about itself negates (or at least seriously disturbs) the identity of the other side.

A further way in which comparisons with the Indian case may be fruitful is to look not at the content of the national project (universal values), but at the context of the national project. The Indian experiment has been and still is precarious. Foreign policy provided a further lever for national integration. Many other countries, at times of domestic instability, have been tempted to bolster their internal cohesion by way of positioning themselves against an 'other', or by projecting their own identity onto the international arena. Kedourie's ideological politics is not confined to the domestic arena. Instances of ideological foreign policy abound in the history of the twentieth century.

8.4 Back to the International Relations Debate

This study uses an element of comparative politics (a unit-internal dynamic) to complement realist international relations theory. It proposes that an understanding of identity, more specifically, of the identity formation process, can be – as in the Indian case – a crucial aspect of understanding a country's foreign policy behaviour.

The approach differs from that of Alexander Wendt's constructivism in two ways. Firstly, the identity formation process analysed here is not an intersubjective one taking place in the realm of international relations as Wendt proposes (Wendt, 1992; 1994; 1996). It is one that originates within the state itself, and has a purpose and mechanism independent of considerations pertaining to foreign policy. The identity formation process is an elite-driven attempt at creating national unity. Secondly, the realist paradigms are not rejected or supplanted by an identity process. Waltz' structural realism is taken as a theoretical, abstract fix-point in international relations (Waltz, 1979; 1995). It provides a point of orientation, as the equilibrium does in economic theory. Reality will never precisely match the theoretical abstraction. In fact, Waltz never suggested as much, but rather admitted that his theory is better at saying what will happen (the balancing of power) than at saying when it will happen (the concrete behaviour of individual states at certain historical junctions).

The argument here goes much further, however. It shows how in the Indian case (and quite possibly, in the case of other states, too) there is a substantial and persistent inflection away from the realist norm, as triggered by a political issue with an independent origin and purpose, but with a partially overlapping dynamic – the national identity formation process. To continue the comparison with economic theory – there is a structural 'problem' (as seen from a strategic foreign policy perspective) in Indian foreign policy which prevents a free movement around the equilibrium. The idealist inflection of Indian foreign policy is determined with respect to a hypothetical realist foreign policy (Figure 1.1).

The results of the Indian case analysed here, show that the realist claim that countries wishing to survive in an anarchic environment will, within a reasonable time span, sooner or later converge towards a balance of power behaviour, is incorrect (Waltz, 1979). The international system is not the only significant determinant of foreign policy in India. While structural realism may still be the leanest, most elegant overall theory of international relations, trusting entirely in it will lead to 'errors in judgment and theory'. India, this great and difficult political experiment, requires a much closer look.

Bibliography

Abbey, R. *Charles Taylor*. Cambridge, Cambridge University Press. (2004).

Aberbach, J. D., J. D. Chesney, et al. 'Exploring Elite Political Attitudes: Some Methodological Lessons.' *Political Methodology*. (1975). 2: pp. 1–27.

Aberbach, J. D. and B. A. Rockman 'Conducting and Coding Elite Interviews.' *Political Science and Politics* 35(4). (2002). pp. 673–676.

Adorno, T. W. 'Aspects of Hegel's Philosophy.' *Hegel: Three Studies*. T. W. Adorno. Cambridge, MIT Press. (1993). pp. 1–52.

Ake, C. *A Theory of Political Integration*. London, Dorsey. (1967).

Ake, C. 'A Definition of Political Stability.' *Comparative Politics* 7(2). (1975). pp. 271–283.

Alberuni. *Alberuni's India*. New Delhi, S. Chand. (1964).

Albright, M. K. *The Mighty and the Almighty: Reflections on America, God, and World Affairs*. New York, Harper Collins. (2006).

Anderson, B. *Imagined Communities: Reflections on the Origin and Spread of Nationalism*. London, Verso. (1991).

Angell, N. *After All*. London, H. Hamilton. (1951).

Ansari, H. 'Imperatives of Indian Policy in West Asia.' *Emerging India: Security and Foreign Policy Perspectives*. N. S. Sisodia and C. U. Bhaskar. Delhi, Institute for Defence Studies and Analyses. (2005). pp. 247–254.

Appadorai, A. *Essays in Indian Politics and Foreign Policy*. New Delhi, Vikas. (1971).

Appadorai, A. *The Domestic Roots of India's Foreign Policy: 1947–1972*. New Delhi, Oxford University Press. (1981).

Appadorai, A. *Indian Political Thinking in the Twentieth Century: An Introductory Survey*. New Delhi, South Asian Publishers. (1986).

Aron, R. *Peace and War: A Theory of International Relations*. New York, Praeger. (1968).

Ashcroft, B., G. Griffiths, et al., Eds. *The Post-Colonial Studies Reader*. London, Routledge. (2006).

Augustine, S. B. o. H. *Concerning the City of God Against the Pagans*. London, Penguin. (2003).

Avineri, S. *Hegel's Theory of the Modern State*. London, Cambridge University Press. (1972).

Avineri, S. 'The Instrumentality of Passion in the World of Reason: Hegel and Marx.' *Political Theory* 1(4). (1973). pp. 388–398.

Axelrod, R. M. *Structure of Decision: The Cognitive Maps of Political Elites*. Princeton, Princeton University Press. (1976).

Bajpai, G. S. 'Ethical Standards on World Issues: Cornerstone of India's Foreign Policy.' *Foreign Policy of India: A Book of Readings*. K. P. Misra. New Delhi, Thomson. (1977). pp. 91–96.

Bajpai, K. 'War, Peace and International Order: India's View of the World.' *Project on Conflict or Convergence: Global Perspectives on War, Peace and International Order*. Harvard Academy of International and Area Studies. Cambridge, Weatherhead Center. (1998).

Baker, G. P. and P. M. S. Hacker. *Wittgenstein: Understanding and Meaning*. Oxford, Blackwell. (2005)

Bakshi, G. D. *The Indian Art of War: the Mahabharata Paradigm (Quest for an Indian Strategic Culture)*. New Delhi, Sharada. (2002).

Balakrishnan, G. *Mapping the Nation*. London, Verso. (1996).

Ball, D. 'Strategic Culture in the Asia-Pacific Region.' *Security Studies* 3(1). (1993). pp. 119–149.

Barnard, F. M. 'Herder's Treatment of Causation and Continuity in History.' *Journal of the History of Ideas* 24(2). (1963). pp. 197–212.

Basrur, R. M. 'Nuclear Myths and Counter-Myths.' *New Quest* 129. (1998). pp. 161–167.

Basrur, R. M. 'Nuclear Weapons and Indian Strategic Culture.' *Journal of Peace Research* 38(2). (2001). pp. 181–198.

Basrur, R. M. *Minimum Deterrence and India's Nuclear Security*. Stanford, Stanford University Press. (2005).

Basu, P. K., B. Chellaney, et al. 'India as a New Global Leader.' Retrieved 6 May, 2007, from *http://fpc.org.uk/fsblob/377.pdf*. (2005).

Baucom, I. 'Narrating the Nation.' *Transition* 55. (1992). pp. 144–153.

Bayly, C. A. 'The Pre-History of "Communalism"? Religious Conflict in India, 1700–1860.' *Modern Asian Studies* 19(2). (1985). pp. 177–203.

Berger, T. U. 'Norms, Identity and National Security in Germany and Japan.' *The Culture of National Security: Norms and Identity in World Politics*. P. J. Katzenstein. New York, Columbia University Press. (1996). pp. 317–356.

Berger, T. U. *Cultures of Antimilitarism: National Security in Germany and Japan*. Baltimore, The Johns Hopkins University Press. (1998).

Berlin, I. S. *Four Essays on Liberty*. London, Overseas Publications Interchange. (1992).

Berry, J. M. 'Validity and Reliability Issues in Elite Interviewing.' *Political Science and Politics* 35(4). (2002). pp. 679–682.

Bertsch, G. K., S. Gahlaut, et al. *Engaging India: U.S. Strategic Relations with the World's Largest Democracy*. New York, Routledge. (1999).

Bhabha, H. K. *Nation and Narration*. London, Routledge. (1990).

Bhabha, H. K. *The Location of Culture*. London, Routledge. (1994).

Bhargava, R. 'Indian Secularism: An Alternative, Trans-Cultural Ideal.' *Political Ideas in Modern India: Thematic Explorations*. V. R. Mehta and T. Pantham. Thousands Oaks, Sage. (2005). pp. 285–306.

Bhatt, C. *Hindu Nationalism: Origins, Ideologies and Modern Myths*. Oxford, Berg. (2001).

Bilgrami, A. 'Secular Liberalism and Relativism.' *Political Ideas in Modern India: Thematic Explorations*. V. R. Mehta and T. Pantham. Thousands Oaks, Sage. (2005). pp. 307–325.

Booth, K. *Strategy and Ethnocentrism*. New York, Holmes & Meier. (1979).

Booth, K. 'The Concept of Strategic Culture Affirmed.' *Strategic Power: USA/USSR*. C. G. Jacobsen. London, Macmillan. (1990). pp. 121–130.

Bowler, P. J. *Evolution: the History of an Idea*. Berkeley, University of California Press. (2003).

Bozeman, A. B. *Politics and Culture in International History: From the Ancient Near East to the Opening of the Modern Age*. New Brunswick, Transaction Publishers. (1994).

Brass, P. R. *Language, Religion and Politics in North India*. London, Cambridge University Press. (1974).

Brass, P. R. *Ethnicity and Nationalism: Theory and Comparison*. New Delhi, Sage. (1991).

Brass, P. R. *The Politics of India Since Independence*. Cambridge, Cambridge University Press. (2000).

Brass, P. R. *The Production of Hindu-Muslim Violence in Contemporary India*. Seattle, University of Washington Press. (2003).

Braudel, F. *A History of Civilizations*. London, Penguin Books. (1995).

Bremmer, I. *The J Curve: A New Way to Understand Why Nations Rise and Fall*. New York, Simon & Schuster. (2006).

Brown, D. M. *The White Umbrella: Indian Political Thought from Manu to Gandhi*. Berkeley, University of California Press. (1953).

Brown, J. M. *Modern India: The Origins of an Asian Democracy*. New Delhi, Oxford University Press. (1985).

Bull, H. *The Anarchical Society: A Study of Order in World Politics*. London, Macmillan. (1995).

Carlyle, T. *Heroes and Hero Worship*. Washington, Ross and Perry. (2002).

Carr, E. H. *The Twenty Years' Crisis, 1919–1939: An Introduction to the Study of International Relations*. London, Macmillan. (1946).

Chatterjee, P. *Nationalist Thought and the Colonial World: A Derivative Discourse*? London, Zed Books. (1986).

Chatterjee, P. *The Nation and its Fragments: Colonial and Postcolonial Histories*. Princeton, Princeton University Press. (1993).

Chaudhuri, S. B. *Theories of the Indian Mutiny, 1857–59: A Study of the Views of an Eminent Historian on the Subject*. Calcutta, World Press Private. (1965).

Chaulia, S. S. 'BJP, India's Foreign Policy and the "Realist Alternative" to the Nehruvian Tradition.' *International Politics* 39(2). (2002). pp. 215–234.

Chellaney, B. 'India's Future Security Challenge: Energy Security.' *India as a New Global Power* Retrieved 6 May, 2007, from *http://fpc.org.uk/fsblob/377.pdf*. (2005).

Churchill, W. S. *Maxims and Reflections*. London, Eyre and Spottiswoode. (1947).

Clausewitz, C. v. *Principles of War*. Mineola, Dover Publications. (2003).

Clingingsmith, D. and J. G. Williamson. 'India's De-Industrialization under British Rule: New Ideas, New Evidence, Working Paper.' *International Trade and Economic History Initiative*. Centre for Economic Policy Research. (2005)

Cohen, S. P. *India: Emerging Power*. Washington, Brookings Institution Press. (2001).

Cohen, S. P. *The Idea of Pakistan*. Washington, Brookings Institution. (2004a).

Cohen, S. P. 'Indo-Pak Track II Diplomacy: Building Peace or Wasting Time?' *Security Beyond Survival: Essays for K. Subrahmanyam*. P. R. Kumaraswamy. New Delhi, Sage. (2004b). pp. 192–217.

Croce, B. *History as the Story of Liberty*. London, G. Allen and Unwin. (1941).

Dadwal, S. R. 'An Energy Crisis in the Making?: India's Policy Options.' *Emerging India: Security and Foreign Policy Perspectives*. N. S. Sisodia and C. U. Bhaskar. Delhi, Institute for Defence Studies and Analyses with Promilla. (2005). pp. 307–326.

Dalrymple, W. 'Plain Tales from British India.' *The New York Review of Books* LIV(7). (2007). pp. 47–50.

Dalton, D. *Mahatma Gandhi: Nonviolent Power in Action*. New York, Columbia University Press. (1993).

Das, G. *India Unbound*. London, Profile. (2002).

Das, M. N. *The Political Philosophy of Jawaharlal Nehru*. London, Allen & Unwin. (1961).

Desch, M. C. 'Culture Clash: Assessing the Importance of Ideas in Security Studies.' *International Security* 23(1). (1998). pp. 141–170.

Deudney, D. and G. J. Ikenberry. 'The International Sources of Soviet Change.' *International Security* 16(3). (1991). pp. 74–118.

Deutsch, K. W. *Nationalism and Social Communication: An Inquiry into the Foundations of Nationality*. Cambridge, MIT Press. (1966).

Deutsche Welle. 'Terrorismus in Indien – Eine Chronologie.' Retrieved 26 August, 2006, from *http://www.dw-world.de/dw/article/0,2144,2752406,00.html*. (2006).

Dexter, L. A. *Elite and Specialized Interviewing*. Evanston, Northwestern University Press. (1970).

Dirks, N. B. *Castes of Mind: Colonialism and the Making of Modern India*. Princeton, Princeton University Press. (2001).

Dixit, J. N. *India's Foreign Policy: 1947–2003*. New Delhi, Picus. (2003).

Dixit, J. N. *Makers of India's Foreign Policy: Raja Ram Mohun Roy to Yashwant Sinha*. New Delhi, HarperCollins. (2004).

Donnelly, J. *Realism and International Relations*. Cambridge, Cambridge University Press. (2000).

Duffield, J. S. 'Political Culture and State Behavior: Why Germany Confounds Neorealism.' *International Organization* 53(4). (1999). pp. 765–803.

Dulles, F. R. and G. E. Ridinger. 'The Anti-Colonial Policies of Franklin D. Roosevelt.' *Political Science Quarterly* 70(1). (1955). pp. 1–18.

Dunne, T. and B. C. Schmidt. Realism. *The Globalization of World Politics: An Introduction to International Relations*. J. Baylis and S. Smith. Oxford, Oxford University Press. (2001). pp. 141–161.

Durant, W. *The Case for India*. New York, Simon and Schuster. (1930).

Durant, W. *Kulturgeschichte der Menschheit: Das Vermächtnis des Ostens*. Lausanne, Editions Rencontre. (1965).

Dyde, S. W. 'Hegel's Conception of Freedom.' *The Philosophical Review* 3(6). (1894). pp. 655–671.

Easterby-Smith, M., R. Thorpe, et al. *Management Research*. London, Sage. (2002).

Elder, C. D. and R. W. Cobb. *The Political Uses of Symbols*. New York, Longman. (1983).

Embree, A. T. *Imagining India: Essays in Indian History*. New Delhi, Oxford University Press. (1989).

Engelmeier, T. F. 'Is a Global Order Based on a Liberal Conception of Human Rights Desirable and Possible?' *Two Essays on Global Order*. T. Engelmeier. Frankfurt, M.E.C.H. Academy. (2003a). pp. 8–79.

Engelmeier, T. F. 'NSC 68 and the Early Dynamic of the Cold War.' *Two Essays on Global Order*. T. Engelmeier. Frankfurt, M.E.C.H. Academy. (2003b). pp. 80–110.

Erikson, E. H. *Young Man Luther: A Study in Psychoanalysis and History*. New York, Norton. (1958).

Erikson, E. H. *Gandhi's Truth: On the Origins of Militant Nonviolence*. New York, Norton. (1969).

Fearon, J. D. 'Domestic Politics, Foreign Policy, and Theories of International Relations.' *Annual Review of Political Science* 1(1). (1998). pp. 289–313.

Finnemore, M. 'Constructing Norms of Humanitarian Intervention.' *The Culture of National Security: Norms and Identity in World Politics*. P. J. Katzenstein. New York, Columbia University Press. (1996). pp. 153–185.

Fischer, L. *The Life of Mahatma Gandhi*. New Delhi, HarperCollins India. (2001).

Fisher, M. W. 'India's Jawaharlal Nehru.' *Asian Survey* 7(6). (1967). pp. 363–373.

Freeden, M. *Ideology*. Oxford, Oxford University Press. (2003).

Friedell, E. *Kulturgeschichte der Neuzeit*. München, Beck. (1927).

Fromm, E. *Die Kunst des Liebens*. Zürich, Manesse. (2002).

Fukuyama, F. *The End of History and the Last Man*. New York, Maxwell Macmillan International. (1992).

Fukuyama, F. *Trust: The Social Virtues and the Creation of Prosperity*. New York, Free Press. (1995).

Fuller, J. V. *Bismarck's Diplomacy at its Zenith*. New York, H. Fertig. (1967).

Gaborieau, M. 'From Al-Beruni to Jinnah: Idiom, Ritual and Ideology of the Hindu–Muslim Confrontation in South Asia.' *Anthropology Today* 1(3). (1985). pp. 7–14.

Gandhi, I. 'India and The World.' *Foreign Policy of India: A Book of Readings*. K. P. Misra. New Delhi, Thomson. (1977). pp. 161–171.

Gandhi, M. 'The Gita and Satyagraha.' *Selected Writings of Mahatma Gandhi*. R. Duncan. Boston, Beacon. (1951). pp. 45–70.

Gandhi, M. *An Autobiography: The Story of My Experiments With Truth*. London, Beacon. (1993a).

Gandhi, M. *The Penguin Gandhi Reader*. New Delhi, Penguin. (1993b).

Gandhi, M. *The Collected Works of Mahatma Gandhi*. New Delhi, Ministry of Information and Broadcasting. (1994).

Gandhi, M. *Hind Swaraj and Other Writings*. Cambridge, Cambridge University Press. (1997).

Gandhi, S. Democracy and Progress. *India and the World: A Blueprint for Partnership and Growth*. N. Bhandare. New Delhi, Roli. (2005). pp. 30–35.

Ganguly, S. *Conflict Unending: India-Pakistan Tensions since 1947*. New York, Columbia University Press. (2001).

Geary, P. J. *The Myth of Nations: the Medieval Origins of Europe*. Princeton, Princeton University Press. (2002).

Geertz, C. *Old Societies and New States: The Quest for Modernity in Asia and Africa*. New York, Free Press. (1967).

Gellner, E. *Thought and Change*. London, Weidenfeld & Nicolson. (1964).

Gellner, E. *Nations and Nationalism*. Oxford, Blackwell. (1983).

Gellner, E. 'Reply to Critics.' *Poznan Studies* 48. (1996). pp. 623–686.

Gellner, E. *Nationalism*. London, Weidenfeld & Nicolson. (1997).

Gellner, E. and A. D. Smith. 'The Nation: Real or Imagined?' *Nations and Nationalism* 2(3). (1996) pp. 357–388.

Giddens, A. *The Constitution of Society: Outline of the Theory of Structuration*. Cambridge, Polity Press. (1984).

Gilbert, A. 'Marx on Internationalism and War.' *Philosophy and Public Affairs* 7(4). (1978). pp. 346–369.

Gilpin, R. *War and Change in World Politics*. Cambridge, Cambridge University Press. (1981).

Glazer, N. and D. P. Moynihan. *Ethnicity: Theory and Experience*. Cambridge, Harvard University Press. (1975).

Glenn, J., D. A. Howlett, et al. Introduction. *Neorealism versus Strategic Culture*. J. Glenn, D. A. Howlett and S. Poore. Burlington, Ashgate. (2004). pp. 3–20.

Goffman, E. *The Presentation of Self in Everyday Life*. Garden City, Doubleday. (1959).

Goldstein, K. 'Getting in the Door: Sampling and Completing Elite Interviews.' *Political Science and Politics* 35(4). (2002). pp. 669–672.

Gopal, S. *Jawaharlal Nehru: A Biography*. New Delhi, Oxford University Press. (1993).

Gordon, S. *India's Rise to Power in the Twentieth Century and Beyond.* London, Macmillan. (1995).

Government of India. 'Lok Sabha Debate on Resolution Condemning the USA-led Invasion of Iraq.' Retrieved 27 May, 2007, from *http://164.100.24.208/debate/debtext.asp?slno=5585&ser=iraq&smode=t.* (2003).

Government of the United States. 'Annual Report to Congress: Military Power of the People's Republic of China.' Retrieved 4 May, 2007, from *http://www.globalsecurity.org/military/library/report/2006/2006-prc-military-power.htm.* (2006).

Gramsci, A. *Sections From the Prison Notebooks.* London, The Electric Book Company. (2001).

Gray, C. S. 'National Style in Strategy: The American Example.' *International Security* 6(2). (1981). pp. 21–47.

Gray, C. S. *Nuclear Strategy and National Style.* London, Hamilton Press. (1986).

Gray, C. S. 'Strategic Culture as Context: The First Generation Fights Back.' *Review of International Studies* 25(1). (1999). pp. 49–69.

Gregg, R. B. *The Power of Nonviolence.* London, Routledge. (1938).

Guha, R. and G. C. Spivak, Eds. *Selected Subaltern Studies.* Oxford, Oxford University Press. (1988).

Gujral, I. K. 'Aspects of India's Foreign Policy.' Retrieved 8 March, 2005, from *www.stimson.org/southasia/?sn=sa20020116302.* (1997).

Gujral, I. K. *Viewpoint: Civilization, Democracy and Foreign Policy.* New Delhi, Allied Publishers. (2004).

Guzzini, S. and A. Leander. *Constructivism and International Relations: Alexander Wendt and his Critics.* New York, Routledge. (2006).

Hah, C. D. and J. Martin. 'Toward a Synthesis of Conflict and Integration Theories of Nationalism.' *World Politics* 27(3). (1975) pp. 361–386.

Hall, J. A. and I. C. Jarvie. *The Social Philosophy of Ernest Gellner.* Amsterdam, Rodopi. (1996)

Hanrieder, W. F. 'Dissolving International Politics: Reflections on the Nation-State.' *The American Political Science Review* 72(4). (1978). pp. 1276–1287.

Haq, M. u. *Human Development in South Asia.* Karachi, Pakistan Human Development Centre and Oxford University Press. (1997).

Hardiman, D. *Gandhi in His Time and Ours: The Global Legacy of His Ideas.* London, Hurst. (2003).

Hay, S. 'Anthologies Compiled from the Writings, Speeches, Letters, and Recorded Conversations of M. K. Gandhi.' *Journal of the American Oriental Society* 110(4). (1990). pp. 667–676.

Hegel, G. W. F. *The Philosophy of History*. New York, Dover. (1956).

Hegel, G. W. F. *Elements of the Philosophy of Right*. Cambridge, Cambridge University Press. (1991).

Hegel, G. W. F. *The Phenomenology of Mind*. Mineola, Dover. (2004).

Held, D. Sovereignty, National Politics and the Global System. *Political Theory and the Modern State: Essays on State, Power, and Democracy*. D. Held. Stanford, Stanford University Press. (1989). pp. 214–242.

Herder, J. G. v. *Herders Sämtliche Werke, 33 Bände*. Berlin, B. Suphan. (1877).

Herz, J. H. 'Idealist Internationalism and the Security Dilemma.' *World Politics* 2(2). (1950). pp. 157–180.

Herz, J. H. *Political Realism and Political Idealism: A Study in Theories and Realities*. Chicago, University of Chicago Press. (1951).

Hill, C. *The Changing Politics of Foreign Policy*. New York, Palgrave MacMillan. (2003).

Hobbes, T. *Leviathan*. Cambridge, Cambridge University Press. (1991).

Hobsbawm, E. J. *The Age of Empire, 1875–1914*. London, Weidenfeld and Nicolson. (1987).

Hobsbawm, E. J. *Age of Extremes: The Short Twentieth Century, 1914–1991*. London, Michael Joseph. (1994).

Hobsbawm, E. J. and T. O. Ranger. *The Invention of Tradition*. Cambridge, Cambridge University Press. (1983)

Hoffman, A. and K. Longhurst. 'German Strategic Culture in Action.' *Contemporary Security Policy* 20(2). (1999) pp. 31–49.

Hoffmann, S. *Gulliver's Troubles; Or, The Setting of American Foreign Policy*. New York, McGraw-Hill. (1968).

Honderich, T. *A Theory of Determinism, Vol. 2: The Consequences of Determinism*. Oxford, Clarendon. (1990).

Hopkirk, P. *The Great Game: On Secret Service in High Asia*. London, Murray. (1990).

Huberman, A. M. and M. B. Miles *The Qualitative Researcher's Companion*. Thousand Oaks, Sage. (2002).

Hume, D. *Selected Essays*. Oxford, Oxford University Press. (1998).

Husain, S. A. *The Way of Gandhi and Nehru*. London, Asia Publishing House. (1961).

Hutchinson, J. and A. D. Smith. *Nationalism*. Oxford, Oxford University Press. (1994)

Inden, R. B. *Imagining India*. Oxford, Basil Blackwell. (1990).

Isaacs, H. R. *Scratches on Our Minds: American Images of China and India.* New York, John Day. (1958).

Jaffrelot, C. *The Hindu Nationalist Movement in India.* New York, Columbia University Press. (1996).

Jayal, N. G. *Democracy and the State: Welfare, Secularism, and Development in Contemporary India.* New Delhi, Oxford University Press. (1999).

Jepperson, R. L., A. Wendt, et al. 'Norms, Identity, and Culture in National Security'. *The Culture of National Security : Norms and Identity in World Politics.* P. J. Katzenstein. New York, Columbia University Press. (1996). pp. 33–78.

Jervis, R. *Perception and Misperception in International Politics.* Princeton, Princeton University Press. (1976).

Jervis, R. 'Realism, Game Theory, and Cooperation.' *World Politics* 40(3). (1988). pp. 317–349.

Jha, N. K. *Domestic Imperatives in India's Foreign Policy.* New Delhi, South Asian Publishers. (2002).

Joffe, J. 'How America Does It.' *Foreign Affairs* 76(5). (1997). pp. 13–27

Johnston, A. I. *Cultural Realism: Strategic Culture and Grand Strategy in Chinese History.* Princeton, Princeton University Press. (1995a).

Johnston, A. I. 'Thinking About Strategic Culture.' *International Security* 19(4). (1995b). pp. 32–64.

Johnston, A. I. 'Strategic Culture Revisited: Reply to Colin Gray.' *Review of International Studies* 25(3). (1999). pp. 519–523.

Jones, D. Soviet Strategic Culture. *Strategic Power: USA/USSR.* C. G. Jacobsen. London, Macmillan. (1990). pp. 35–49.

Jones, G. E. 'India Today.' *Far Eastern Survey* 16(20). (1947). pp. 229–232.

Judd, C. M., E. R. Smith, et al. *Research Methods in Social Relations.* Philadelphia, Harcourt Bracee Jovanovich College Publishers. (1991).

Kaegi, W. Die Entstehung der Nationen. *Historische Meditationen.* W. Kaegi. Zürich, Fretz & Wasmuth. (1942). pp. 9–37.

Kahn, H. *The Nature and Feasibility of War and Deterrence.* Santa Monica, Rand. (1960).

Kakar, K. and S. Kakar. *Die Inder: Portrait einer Gesellschaft.* München, Beck. (2006).

Kakar, S. and A. Reif. 'India is the Subconscious of the West (Interview).' *Universitas* 61(723). (2006) pp. 961–970.

Kalton, G. *Introduction to Survey Sampling.* Beverly Hills, Sage. (1983).

Kane, R. *Free Will.* Malden, Blackwell. (2001).

Kant, I. *Critique of Pure Reason*. Mineola, Dover. (2004).

Kanwal, G. 'India's Strategic Culture Must Change to one that is Pro-active.' *ORF Strategic Trends* III(48). (2005).

Kapila, S. *India's Defence Policies and Strategic Thought: A Comparative Analysis*. Noida, Simsid Books. (2003).

Kapur, A. Eclipsed Moon and Rising Sun. *Security Beyond Survival: Essays for K. Subrahmanyam*. P. R. Kumaraswamy. New Delhi, Sage. (2004). pp. 52–82.

Kapuscinski, R. *Meine Reisen mit Herodot*. Frankfurt am Main, Eichborn. (2005).

Kargil Review Committee. 'Recommendations.' Retrieved 16 March, 2007, from *http://mod.nic.in/newadditions/annexb.pdf*. (2001).

Karnad, B. *Nuclear Weapons and Indian Security: The Realist Foundations of Strategy*. New Delhi, Macmillan. (2002).

Katzenstein, P. J., Ed. *Cultural Norms and National Security: Police and Military in Postwar Japan*. Cornell Studies in Political Economy. Ithaca, Cornell University Press. (1996a).

Katzenstein, P. J. Introduction: 'Alternative Perspectives on National Security.' *The Culture of National Security: Norms and Identity in World Politics*. P. J. Katzenstein. New York, Columbia University Press. (1996b). pp. 1–32.

Kaufmann, D., A. Kraay, et al. 'Governance Matters V: Governance Indicators for 2002–2005.' Retrieved 12 March, 2007, from *http://wwwr.worldbank.org/wbi/governance/govmatters5/*. (2006).

Kautilya. *Arthashastra*. Delhi, Penguin Books India. (1992)

Kedourie, E. *Nationalism in Asia and Africa*, London: Weidenfeld and Nicolson. (1971).

Kedourie, E. *Nationalism*. Oxford, Blackwell. (1993).

Kennan, G. F. 'The Sources of Soviet Conduct.' *Foreign Affairs* XXV (July 1947). (1947). pp. 566–582.

Kennan, G. F. *Around the Cragged Hill: A Personal and Political Philosophy*. New York, W.W. Norton. (1993).

Kennedy, P. M. *The Rise and Fall of the Great Powers: Economic Change and Military Conflict from 1500 to 2000*. New York, Vintage Books. (1989).

Keohane, R. O. *After Hegemony: Cooperation and Discord in the World Political Economy*. Princeton, Princeton University Press. (1984).

Keohane, R. O. *Neorealism and Its Critics*. New York, Columbia University Press. (1986).

Keohane, R. O. and J. S. Nye. *Power and Interdependence: World Politics in Transition*. Boston, Little. (1977)

Khilnani, S. *The Idea of India*. New York, Farrar Straus Giroux. (1998).

Khilnani, S. 'India as a Bridging Power.' *India as a New Global Leader* Retrieved 6 May, 2007, from *http://fpc.org.uk/fsblob/377.pdf.* (2005).

Khosla, I. P., Ed. *Energy and Diplomacy*. New Delhi, Konark. (2005).

Kier, E. 'Culture and Military Doctrine: France between the Wars.' *International Security* 19(4). (1995). pp. 65–93.

Kier, E. 'Culture and French Military Doctrine.' *The Culture of National Security: Norms and Identity in World Politics*. P. J. Katzenstein. New York, Columbia University Press. (1996). pp. 186–215.

Kim, M. *India: Neorealism versus Strategic Culture*. J. Glenn, D. A. Howlett and S. Poore. Burlington, Ashgate. (2004). pp. 75–104.

Kissinger, H. *Diplomacy*. New York, Simon & Schuster. (1994).

Klein, B. The Textual Strategies of the Military: Or, Have you Read Any Good Defence Manuals Lately? *International/Intertextual Relations: Postmodern Readings of World Politics*. J. Der Derian and M. J. Shapiro. Lexington, Lexington Books. (1989). pp. 97–112.

Klein, Y. 'A Theory of Strategic Culture.' *Journal of Comparative Strategy* 5(3). (1989). pp. 3–23.

Kohli, A. *Democracy and Discontent: India's Growing Crisis of Governability*. Cambridge, Cambridge University Press. (1990).

Kohli, A. *The Success of India's Democracy*. Cambridge, Cambridge University Press. (2001).

Kondapi, C. 'Indian Opinion of the United Nations.' *International Organization* 5(4). (1951). pp. 709–721.

Krasner, S. D. 'Realism, Imperialism, and Democracy: A Response to Gilbert.' *Political Theory* 20(1). (1992). pp. 38–52.

Krause, K. Conclusion. *Cross-Cultural Dimensions of Multilateral Non-Proliferation and Arms Control Dialogues*. K. Krause. Ottawa, Department of Foreign Affairs and International Trade. (1997). pp. 188–221.

Krause, K. and A. Latham. 'Culture and Construction of Western Non-Proliferation, Arms Control and Disarmament Practice.' *Cross-Cultural Dimensions of Multilateral Non-Proliferation and Arms Control Dialogues*. K. Krause. Ottawa, Department of Foreign Affairs and International Trade. (1997). pp. 19–48.

Kripalani, J. B. 'Gandhian Revaluation of Values.' *Gandhi and the Contemporary World: Studies in Peace and War*. K. Misra and S. C. Gangal. New Delhi, Chanakya. (1981). pp. 21–29.

Kromrey, H. *Empirische Sozialforschung Modelle und Methoden der Datenerhebung und Datenauswertung*. Opladen, Leske und Budrich. (1998).

Kuhn, T. S. *The Structure of Scientific Revolutions*. Chicago, University of Chicago Press. (1996).

Kuhn, T. S. *The Road Since Structure: Philosophical Essays, 1970–1993*. Chicago, University of Chicago Press. (2000).

Kulke, H. and D. Rothermund. *Geschichte Indiens von der Induskultur bis Heute*. München, Beck. (1998).

Kulke, H. and D. Rothermund. *A History of India*. New York, Routledge. (2004)

Kumaraswamy, P. R. 'National Security: A Critique.' *Security Beyond Survival: Essays for K. Subrahmanyam*. P. R. Kumaraswamy. New Delhi, Sage. (2004). pp. 11–32.

Kupchan, C. *The Vulnerability of Empire*. Ithaca, Cornell University Press. (1994).

Kux, D. *Estranged Democracies: India and the United States, 1941–1991*. New Delhi, Sage. (1994).

Lammert, N. 'Auch die EU braucht ein Ideelles Fundament.' *Die Welt*. Hamburg. (2005).

Lantis, J. 'Strategic Culture and National Security Policy.' *International Studies Review* 4(3). (2002). pp. 87–101.

Larus, J. *Culture and Political–Military Behavior: The Hindus in Premodern India*. London, Minerva. (1979).

Latham, A. 'The Role of Culture and Identity in Indian Arms Control and Disarmament Policy.' *Cross-Cultural Dimensions of Multilateral Non-Proliferation and Arms.Control Dialogues: Research Report*. K. Krause. Ottawa, Nonproliferation, Arms Control and Disarmament Division, Department of Foreign Affairs and International Trade. (1997). pp. 103–125.

Lebow, R. N. and T. Risse-Kappen. *International Relations Theory and the End of the Cold War*. New York, Columbia University Press. (1995).

Leffler, M. P. *A Preponderance of Power: National Security, the Truman Administration, and the Cold War*. Stanford, Stanford University Press. (1992).

Legro, J. W. 'Military Culture and Inadvertent Escalation in World War II.' *International Security* 18(4). (1994). pp. 108–142.

Legro, J. W. 'Culture and Preferences in the International Cooperation Two-Step.' *The American Political Science Review* 90(1). (1996). pp. 118–137.

Lenin, V. I. *What is to be Done? Burning Questions of our Movement*. Moscow, Foreign Languages Publishing House. (1950).

Lewis, B. *What Went Wrong? Western Impact and Middle Eastern Response*. Oxford, Oxford University Press. (2002).

Lewis, B. *The Crisis of Islam: Holy War and Unholy Terror*. New York, Modern Library. (2003).

Liddell Hart, B. H. *Strategy*. New York, Meridian. (1991).

Lippmann, W. Public Opinion. New York, Dover. (2004).

Luckham, R. 'Armaments Culture.' *Alternatives* 10(1). (1994). pp. 1–44.

Lynn-Jones, S. M. and S. E. Miller. *Global Dangers: Changing Dimensions of International Security*. Cambridge, MIT Press. (1995).

Mabbett, I. W. 'The Date of the Arthashastra.' *Journal of the American Oriental Society* 84(2). (1964). pp. 162–169.

Machiavelli, N. *The Discourses*. London, Penguin. (1970).

Macmillan, A., K. Booth, et al. 'Strategic Culture.' *Strategic Cultures in the Asia-Pacific Region*. K. Booth and R. B. Trood. New York, St. Martin's Press. (1999). pp. 3–26.

Maddison, A. *The World Economy: Historical Statistics*. Paris, Development Centre of the OECD. (2003).

Majumdar, R. C. *The Sepoy Mutiny and the Revolt of 1857*. Calcutta, K. L. Mukhopadhyay. (1963).

Malhotra, I. *Indira Gandhi*. New Delhi, National Book Trust. (2006).

Malik, J. M. 'India and China: Bound to Collide.' *Security Beyond Survival: Essays for K. Subrahmanyam*. P. R. Kumaraswamy. New Delhi, Sage. (2004). pp. 127–165.

Malik, V. P. 'India's Strategic Culture.' *The Tribune*. Chandigarh. (2002).

Mandela, N. 'The Sacred Warrior.' TIME. (2000).

Mann, G. *Deutsche Geschichte des 19. und 20. Jahrhunderts*. Frankfurt, S. Fischer. (1966).

Mann, M. *The Sources of Social Power*. Cambridge, Cambridge University Press. (1986).

Mansingh, L. 'Foreign Policy Imperatives for a Post-Nuclear India.' *Emerging India: Security and Foreign Policy Perspectives*. N. S. Sisoda and C. U. Bhaskar. Delhi, Institute of Defense Studies and Analyses with Promilla. (2005). pp. 43–58.

Marx, K. *Capital: A Critique of Political Economy*. London, Penguin. (1976).

Marx, K. *Marx : Later Political Writings*. Cambridge, Cambridge University Press. (1996).

Marx, K. and F. Engels. *The German Ideology*. New York, International Publishers. (1972).

Marx, K. and F. Engels. *Collected Works*. New York, International Publishers. (1985).

Marx, K. and F. Engels. *The Communist Manifesto: A Modern Edition*. London, Verso. (1998)

Masselos, J. C. *Indian Nationalism: A History*. New Delhi, New Dawn Press. (2005).

Maxwell, N. *India's China War*. London, Cape. (1970).

Maxwell, N. 'Jawaharlal Nehru: Of Pride and Principle.' *Foreign Affairs* 52(3). (1974). pp. 633–643.

Mearsheimer, J. J. 'Back to the Future: Instability in Europe after the Cold War.' *International Security* 15(1). (1990). pp. 5–56.

Mehta, P. B. *The Burden of Democracy*. Delhi, Penguin. (2003).

Mehta, V. R. and T. Pantham, Eds. 'History of science, philosophy and culture in Indian civilization.' *Political Ideas in Modern India: Thematic Explorations*. New Delhi, Sage. (2006).

Menon, R. *The Mahabharata: A Modern Rendering*. Delhi, Rupa. (2004).

Merriam, A. H. *Gandhi vs. Jinnah: The Debate over the Partition of India*. Calcutta, Minerva Associates. (1980).

Miscevic, N. *Nationalism and Ethnic Conflict: Philosophical Perspectives*. Chicago, Open Court. (2000).

Miscevic, N. *Nationalism and Beyond*. Budapest, Central European University Press. (2001).

Misra, K. P. *Foreign Policy of India: A Book of Readings*. New Delhi, Thomson. (1977).

Misra, K. P. *Non-Alignment and Neutrality: Proceedings of the Indo-Austrian Seminar*. New Delhi, Indian Council for Cultural Relations. (1982).

Mitra, S. K. 'War and Peace in South Asia: a Revisionist View of India-Pakistan Relations.' *Contemporary South Asia* 10(3). (2001). pp. 361–379.

Mitra, S. K. 'The Reluctant Hegemon: India's Self-Perception and the South Asian Strategic Environment.' *Contemporary South Asia* 12(3). (2003). pp. 399–417.

Mitra, S. K. *Engaging the World: The Ambiguity of India's Power*. India in World Politics, Berlin. (2005).

Mitra, S. K. *The Puzzle of India's Governance: Culture, Context and Comparative Theory*. London, Routledge. (2006).

Mitra, S. K. and V. B. Singh. *Democracy and Social Change in India: A Cross-Sectional Analysis of the National Electorate*. New Delhi, Sage Publications. (1999).

Mohan, C. R. *Crossing the Rubicon: The Shaping of India's New Foreign Policy*. New Delhi, Viking. (2003).

Mohan, C. R. 'Rethinking India's Grand Strategy.' *Emerging India: Security and Foreign Policy Perspectives*. N. S. Sisoda and C. U. Bhaskar. Delhi, Institute for Defence Studies and Analyses with Promilla. (2005). pp. 33–42.

Moore, R. J. 'Jinnah and the Pakistan Demand.' *Modern Asian Studies* 17(4). (1983). pp. 529–561.

Morgenthau, H. J. *Scientific Man vs. Power Politics*. Chicago, The University of Chicago Press. (1946).

Morgenthau, H. J. *Politics Among Nations: The Struggle for Power and Peace*. New York, Alfred A. Knopf. (1963).

Moyser, G. and M. Wagstaffe. *Research Methods for Elite Studies*. London, Allen & Unwin. (1987).

Mukherjee, B. *Kautilya's Concept of Diplomacy: A New Interpretation*. Calcutta, Minerva Associates. (1976).

N-TV. 'Terroranschlag in Indien - Dutzende Tote in Hyderabad.' Retrieved 26 August, 2006, from *http://www.n-tv.de/843725.html*. (2006).

Naga, K. *Theories of Diplomacy in Kautilya's Arthashastra*. Calcutta, Writers Workshop. (1997).

Nairn, T. *The Break-up of Britain: Crisis and Neo-Nationalism*. London, NLB. (1977).

Nanda, B. R. *Indian Foreign Policy: The Nehru Years*. New Delhi, Vikas. (1976).

Nanda, B. R. *Three Statesmen: Gokhale, Gandhi, and Nehru*. Oxford, Oxford University Press. (2004).

Nandy, A. *Bonfire of Creeds: The Essential Ashis Nandy*. New Delhi, Oxford University Press. (2003).

Narain, J. *Gandhi's View of Political Power*. New Delhi, Deep & Deep. (1987).

Nehru, J. *The Discovery of India*. London, Meridian Books. (1946).

Nehru, J. *Glimpses of World History*. London, Lindsay Drummond. (1949).

Nehru, J. *An Autobiography*. London, Bodley Head. (1955).

Nehru, J. *Nehru on World History*. London, Bodley Head. (1960).

Nehru, J. *India's Foreign Policy: Selected Speeches, September 1946 – April 1961*. New Delhi, Publications Division, Ministry of Information and Broadcasting, Government of India. (1961).

Nehru, J. *The Essential Writings of Jawaharlal Nehru*. New Delhi, Oxford University Press. (2003).

Nietzsche, F. W. *The Gay Science*. Cambridge, Cambridge University Press. (2001).

Nizamani, H. K. *The Roots of Rhetoric: Politics of Nuclear Weapons in India and Pakistan*. Westport, Praeger. (2000).

Noelle-Neumann, E. and T. Petersen. *Alle, Nicht Jeder: Einführung in die Methoden der Demoskopie*. Berlin, Springer. (2000).

Nye, J. S. *Bound to Lead: The Changing Nature of American Power*. New York, Basic Books. (1990).

Nye, J. S. 'Limits of American Power.' *Political Science Quarterly* 117(4). (2002). pp. 545–559.

Nye, J. S. *Soft Power: The Means to Success in World Politics*. New York, Public Affairs. (2004).

Nye, J. S., Jr. 'Nuclear Learning and U.S.–Soviet Security Regimes.' *International Organization* 41(3). (1987). pp. 371–402.

Oakeshott, M. J. *Experience and Its Modes*. Cambridge, Cambridge University Press. (1978).

Onuf, N. G. *World of Our Making: Rules and Rule in Social Theory and International Relations*. Columbia, University of South Carolina Press. (1989).

Palit, D. K. *War in High Himalaya: The Indian Army in Crisis, 1962*. London, St. Martin's Press. (1991).

Pandey, G. *The Construction of Communalism in Colonial North India*. Delhi, Oxford University Press. (1990).

Panigrahi, D. N. *India's Partition: The Story of Imperialism in Retreat*. London, Routledge. (2004).

Parekh, B. *Gandhi: A Very Short Introduction*. Oxford, Oxford University Press. (1997).

Parel, A., Ed. *Gandhi, Freedom, and Self-Rule*. Lanham, Lexington Books. (2000).

Parry, B. *Postcolonial Studies: A Materialist Critique*. London, Routledge. (2004).

Paz, O. *In Light of India*. New York, Harcourt Brace. (1997).

Perkovich, G. *India's Nuclear Bomb: The Impact on Global Proliferation*. Berkeley, University of California Press. (2001).

Pipes, R. 'Why the Soviet Union Thinks it Could Fight and Win a Nuclear War.' *Commentary* 64(1). (1977). pp. 21–34.

Pollack, D., Ed. *Political Culture in Post-Communist Europe: Attitudes in New Democracies*. Aldershot, Ashgate. (2003).

Poore, S. 'What is the Context? A Reply to the Gray-Johnston Debate on Strategic Culture.' *Review of International Studies* 29(279-284). (2003).

Poore, S. 'Strategic Culture.' *Neorealism versus Strategic Culture*. J. Glenn, D. A. Howlett and S. Poore. Burlington, Ashgate. (2004).

Popper, K. *The Open Society and Its Enemies*. London, Routledge, 2002. (1994).

Popper, K. *Conjectures and Refutations: The Growth of Scientific Knowledge*. London, Routledge. (2002).

Prakash, A. Introduction. *Emerging India: Security and Foreign Policy Perspectives*. N. S. Sisodia and C. U. Bhaskar. New Delhi, Institute for Defence Studies and Analyses with Promilla. (2005). pp. 1–14.

Prakash, G. *Another Reason: Science and the Imagination of Modern India*. Princeton, Princeton University Press. (1999).

Prasad, B. *Foundations of India's Foreign Policy: Imperial Era, 1882–1914*. Calcutta, Nayad Prokash. (1979).

Prasad, N., Ed. *Hind Swaraj: A Fresh Look*. New Delhi, Gandhi Peace Foundation. (1985).

Price, R. and N. 'Tannenwald. Norms and Deterrence: The Nuclear and Chemical Weapons Taboo.' *The Culture of National Security: Norms and Identity in World Politics*. P. J. Katzenstein. New York, Columbia University Press. (1996) pp. 114–152.

Purtill, R. L. 'Kuhn on Scientific Revolutions.' *Philosophy of Science* 34(1). (1967). pp. 53–58.

Pye, L. W. 'Introduction: Political Culture and Political Development.' *Political Culture and Political Development*. L. W. Pye and S. Verba. Princeton, Princeton University Press. (1965). pp. 8–11.

Radhakrishnan, S. 'The Supreme Spiritual Ideal: The Hindu View.' *Eastern Religions and Western Thought*. S. Radhakrishnan. New Delhi, Oxford University Press. (1974). pp. 35–55.

Raghavan, V. R. 'Strategic Culture: A Military Perspective.' *Emerging India: Security and Foreign Policy Perspectives*. N. S. Sisoda and C. U. Bhaskar. New Delhi, Institute of Defence Studies and Analyses with Promilla. (2005). pp. 17–31.

Rajagopalan, R. 'Restoring Normalcy: The Evolution of the Indian Army's Counterinsurgency Doctrine.' *Small Wars and Insurgencies* 11(1). (2000). pp. 44–69.

Rana, A. P. *The Imperatives of Nonalignment: A Conceptual Study of India's Foreign Policy Strategy in the Nehru Period*. New Delhi, Macmillan. (1976).

Rana, A. P. 'The Nehruvian Tradition in World Affairs: Its Evolution and Relevance to Post Cold War International Relations.' *Nehru's Foreign Policy: Fifty Years On*. S. Mansingh. Dclhi, Mosaic Books. (1998).

Rana, A. P. 'Nehru's Foreign Policy Design and its Relevance to a Globalizing World.' *Nehru Revisited*. Mumbai, Nehru Center. (2005).

Range, W. *Jawaharlal Nehru's World View*. Athens, University of Georgia Press. (1961).

Ray, A. K. *Western Realism and International Relations: A Non-Western View*. New Delhi, Foundation Books. (2004).

Reid, E. *Envoy to Nehru*. New Delhi, Oxford University Press. (1981).

Rengger, N. 'Culture, Society, and Order in World Politics.' *Dilemmas of World Politics: International Issues in a Changing World.* J. Baylis and N. J. Rengger. Oxford, Oxford University Press. (1992). pp. 85–106.

Richards, G. *The Philosophy of Gandhi: A Study of his Basic Ideas.* London, Curzon. (1991).

Richards, M. D. *Revolutions in World History.* New York, Routledge. (2004).

Ridley, M. *Evolution.* Oxford, Blackwell. (2004).

Ringmar, E. 'Alexander Wendt: A Social Scientist Struggling with History.' *The Future of International Relations: Masters in the Making*? I. B. Neumann and O. Wæver. London, Routledge. (1997). pp. 269–289.

Risse-Kappen, T. *Cooperation Among Democracies: The European Influence on U.S. Foreign Policy.* Princeton, Princeton University Press. (1995).

Rivera, S. W., P. M. Kozyreva, et al. 'Interviewing Political Elites: Lessons from Russia.' *Political Science and Politics* 35(4). (2002). pp. 683–688.

Roe, P. *Ethnic Violence and the Societal Security Dilemma.* London, Routledge. (2005).

Roosevelt, E. *As He Saw It.* New York, Sloan & Pearce. (1946).

Rosecrance, R. N. *Action and Reaction in World Politics.* Boston, Little. (1963).

Rosecrance, R. N. *International Relations: Peace or War*? New York, McGraw-Hill. (1973).

Rosecrance, R. N. *The Rise of the Trading State: Commerce and Conquest in the Modern World.* New York, Basic Books. (1986).

Rosen, S. P. 'Military Effectiveness: Why Societies Matter.' *International Security* 19(4). (1995). pp. 5–31.

Rosen, S. P. *Societies and Military Power: India and its Armies.* Ithaca, Cornell University Press. (1996).

Rosenbaum, R. *Explaining Hitler: The Search for the Origins of his Evil.* New York, Random House. (1998).

Roshwald, M. 'The Case for Indeterminism.' *The British Journal for the Philosophy of Science* 7(27). (1956). pp. 240–242.

Rotberg, R. I. 'The Failure and Collapse of Nation-States.' *When States Fail: Causes and Consequences.* R. I. Rotberg. Princeton, Princeton University Press. (2004). pp. 1–50.

Rothermund, D. *Die Politische Willensbildung in Indien: 1900-1960.* Wiesbaden, Harrassowitz. (1965).

Rothermund, D. *An Economic History of India: From Pre-Colonial Times to 1991.* London, Routledge. (1993).

Rothermund, D. 'Conflict as a Challenge to Legitimacy: A Historical Perspective.' *Legitimacy and Conflict in South Asia.* D. Rothermund and S. K. Mitra. New Delhi, Manohar. (1998a).

Rothermund, D. Epilogue. *Legitimacy and Conflict in South Asia.* D. Rothermund and S. K. Mitra. New Delhi, Manohar. (1998b).

Rothermund, D. *Mahatma Gandhi.* München, Beck. (2003).

Rothstein, R. L. *Alliances and Small Powers.* New York, Columbia University Press. (1968).

Rothstein, R. L. 'Foreign Policy and Development Policy: From Nonalignment to International Class War.' *International Affairs* 52(4). (1976). pp. 598–616.

Rousseau, J. J. *The Social Contract and the Discourses.* London, D. Campbell. (1993).

Rousseau, J. J. *Discourse on the Origins of Inequality.* London, University Press of New England. (1992).

Roy, N. C. *The Civil Service in India.* K. L. Mukhopadhyay: Calcutta. (1958). pp. xx. 328.

Roy, T. *Traditional Industry in the Economy of Colonial India.* Cambridge, Cambridge University Press. (1999).

Rudolph, S. H. and L. I. Rudolph. *Gandhi: The Traditional Roots of Charisma.* Chicago, University of Chicago Press. (1983)

Rushdie, S. Interview. *Spiegel Special: Literaturland Indien.* (2006). pp. 19–21.

Russell, B. *History of Western Philosophy.* London, Routledge, 2000. (1996).

Sagan, S. D. 'The Perils of Proliferation in South Asia.' *Asian Survey* 41(6). (2001). pp. 1064–1086.

Saunders, K. 'Mahatma Gandhi Seen Through His Autobiography.' *Pacific Affairs* 4(3). (1931). pp. 201–209.

Savarkar, V. D. *Hindutva: Who is a Hindu*? Mumbai, Veer Savarkar Prakashan. (1969).

Sayegh, F. A. *The Dynamics of Neutralism in the Arab World: A Symposium.* San Francisco, Chandler. (1964).

Scheffler, I. 'Vision and Revolution: A Postscript on Kuhn.' *Philosophy of Science* 39(3). (1972). pp. 366–374.

Schell, J. *The Unconquerable World: Power, Nonviolence, and the Will of the People.* London, Penguin. (2005).

Schelling, T. C. *The Strategy of Conflict.* Cambridge, Harvard University Press. (1960).

Schmidt, R. J. 'Cultural Nationalism in Herder.' *Journal of the History of Ideas* 17(3). (1956). pp. 407–417.

Schnell, R., P. B. Hill, et al. *Methoden der Empirischen Sozialforschung*. München, R. Oldenbourg. (1989).

Schöpflin, G. *Nations, Identity, Power*. New York, New York University Press. (2000).

Schuman, H. and S. Presser. *Questions and Answers in Attitude Surveys: Experiments on Question form, Wording, and Context*. New York, Academic Press. (1981).

Scobell, A. *China and Strategic Culture*, Carlisle, Strategic Studies Institute. (2002).

Sen, A. K. *The Argumentative Indian: Writings on Indian History, Culture, and Identity*. London, Allen Lane. (2005).

Sen, A. K. *Identity and Violence: The Illusion of Destiny*. New York, W. W. Norton. (2006).

Shambaugh, D. L. *Power Shift: China and Asia's New Dynamics*. Berkeley, University of California Press. (2005).

Sharma, J. *Hindutva: Exploring the Idea of Hindu Nationalism*. New Delhi, Viking. (2003).

Siegel, H. *Educating Reason*. London, Routledge. (1988).

Simon, R. *Gramsci's Political Thought*. London, The Electric Book Company. (2001).

Singer, J. D. 'The Level-of-Analysis Problem in International Relations.' *World Politics* 14(1). (1961). pp. 77–92.

Singh, B. 'The Sources of Contemporary Political Thought in India: A Reappraisal.' *Ethics* 75(1). (1964). pp. 57–62.

Singh, J. *Asian Security in the 21st Century*. New Delhi, Institute for Defence Studies and Analyses. (1999a).

Singh, J. *Defending India*. New York, St. Martin's Press. (1999b).

Singh, M. Inaugural Address at the Hindustan Times Leadership Initiative 2005. *India and the World: A Blueprint for Partnership and Growth*. N. Bhandare. New Delhi, Roli. (2005a). pp. 16–24.

Singh, M. 'Speech at the India Today Enclave, New Delhi, 25 February, 2005.' Retrieved 2 May, 2007, from *http://meaindia.nic.in/speech/2005/02/25ss01.htm*. (2005b).

Singh, M. 'Indian Foreign Policy has had a Basic Consensus.' Retrieved 28 November, 2006, from *http://www.rediff.com/news/2006/feb/15guest1.htm*. (2006).

Singh, N. *India: A Rising Power*. New Delhi, Authors Press. (2006).

Sirsikar, V. M. *Politics of Modern Maharashtra.* Mumbai, Orient Longman. (1995).

Sisoda, N. S. and C. U. Bhaskar, Eds. *Emerging India: Security and Foreign Policy Perspectives.* New Delhi, Institute for Defence Studies and Analyses with Promilla. (2005).

Skocpol, T. *Social Revolutions in the Modern World.* Cambridge, Cambridge University Press. (1994).

Smith, A. D. 'The Origins of Nations.' *Ethnic and Racial Studies* 12(3). (1989). pp. 349–356.

Smith, A. D. *Nationalism and Modernism: A Critical Survey of Recent Theories of Nations and Nationalism.* London, Routledge. (1998).

Snyder, J. L. *The Soviet Strategic Culture: Implications for Limited Nuclear Operations.* Santa Monica, Rand. (1977).

Snyder, J. L. *The Ideology of the Offensive: Military Decision Making and the Disasters of 1914.* Ithaca, Cornell University Press. (1984).

Snyder, J. L. 'The Concept of Strategic Culture: Caveat Emptor.' *Strategic power: USA/USSR.* C. G. Jacobsen. London, Macmillan. (1990). pp. 3–9.

Snyder, J. L. *Myths of Empire: Domestic Politics and International Ambition.* Ithaca, Cornell University Press. (1991).

Som, R. *Gandhi, Bose, Nehru, and the Making of the Modern Indian Mind.* Delhi, Viking. (2004).

Sommer, T. 'Der Kopf zählt, nicht das Tuch - Ausländer in Deutschland: Integration kann keine Einbahnstraße sein.' *Die Zeit.* Hamburg. 30. (1998).

Spencer, H. *First Principles of a New System of Philosophy.* New York, D. Appleton. (1865).

Spengler, O. *Der Untergang des Abendlandes: Umrisse einer Morphologie der Weltgeschichte.* München, Beck. (1919).

Spiro, M. E. *Gender Ideology and Psychological Reality: An Essay on Cultural Reproduction.* New Haven, Yale University Press. (1997).

Spirtas, M. 'A House Divided: Tragedy and Evil in Realist Theory.' *Security Studies* 5(3). (1996). pp. 385–423.

Stadelmann, R. *Der Historische Sinn bei Herder.* Halle/S., Niemeyer. (1928).

Stephen, J. F. 'Foundation of the Government of India.' *Nineteenth Century* 80. (1883). pp. 541–563.

Subrahmanyam, K. 'Evolution of Indian Defence Policy.' *A Centenary History of the Indian National Congress: Vol. IV (1947–1964).* B. N. Pande. New Delhi, Vikas Publishing House. IV (1947–1964). (1985). pp. 505–580.

Subrahmanyam, K. *Shedding Shibboleths: India's Evolving Strategic Outlook.* New Delhi, Wordsmiths. (2005).

Subrahmanyam, K. 'Sonia's Choice.' *Indian Express*. New Delhi. (2008).

Sun Tzu. *The Art of War*. Boston, Shambhala. (1988).

Swaine, M. D. and A. J. Tellis. *Interpreting China's Grand Strategy: Past, Present, and Future*. Santa Monica, Rand. (2000).

Tagore, R. *Nationalism*. London, Macmillan. (1917).

Talbot, I. *India and Pakistan*. London, Arnold. (2000).

Talbott, S. *Engaging India: Diplomacy, Democracy, and the Bomb*. Washington, Brookings Institution Press. (2004).

Tanham, G. 'Indian Strategic Thought: An Interpretive Essay.' Santa Monica, Rand: p. 105. (1992).

Taylor, C. *Hegel*. Cambridge, Cambridge University Press. (1975).

Taylor, C. *Sources of the Self: The Making of the Modern Identity*. Cambridge, Cambridge University Press. (1989).

Taylor, C. 'What's Wrong With Negative Liberty.' *Contemporary Political Philosophy: An Anthology*. R. E. Goodin and P. Pettit. Oxford, Blackwell Publishers. (1997). pp. 418–429.

Tellis, A. J. *India's Emerging Nuclear Posture: Between Recessed Deterrent and Ready Arsenal*. Santa Monica, Rand. (2001).

Tellis, A. J. 'A Grand Chessboard.' *Foreign Policy* Jan/Feb 2005(146). pp. 53–55.

Tharoor, S. *The Great Indian Novel*. New Delhi, Penguin Books. (1989).

Tharoor, S. *Nehru: The Invention of India*. New York, Arcade. (2003).

Tharoor, S. Interview. 'You Can't Feel the Country's Pulse.' *Afternoon Dispatch and Courier*. (2005).

Tharoor, S. 'The Idea of India.' *Catalyst*. Salt Lake City. (2006).

The Economist. 'Don't Blame it on the Scriptures.' (30 November, 2006). (2006). p. 34.

The Economist. 'The Great Game in Asia.' (31 March–6 April, 2007). (2007a). p. 12.

The Economist. 'Heavenly Dynasty.' (31 March–6 April, 2007). (2007b). pp. 15–16.

The Economist. 'Reaching for a Renaissance.' (31 March–6 April 2007). (2007c). pp. 3–5.

The Economist. 'Smile Diplomacy.' (31 March–6 April, 2007). (2007d). pp. 7–8.

Thomas, R. 'India's Place in a West-Dominated World.' *Security Beyond Survival: Essays for K. Subrahmanyam*. P. R. Kumaraswamy. New Delhi, Sage. (2004). pp. 33–51.

Tibi, B. *Europa ohne Identität? Die Krise der Multikulturellen Gesellschaft*. München, Bertelsmann. (1998).

Torrance, J. *Karl Marx's Theory of Ideas*. Cambridge, Cambridge University Press. (1995).

Trojanow, I. 'Unermessliches Indien.' *Universitas* 61(723). (2006). pp. 907–923.

UPA. National Common Minimum Programme of the Government of India. New Delhi, Government of India. (2004).

Van Inwagen, P. *An Essay on Free Will*. Oxford, Clarendon. (1983).

Varma, P. K. *The Great Indian Middle Class*. New Delhi, Viking. (1998).

Varma, P. K. *Being Indian: The Truth About Why the Twenty-First Century Will Be India's*. New Delhi, Viking. (2004).

Vivekananda, S. *Complete Works*. Almora, Advaita Ashrama. (1918).

Voltaire. *Essai Sur les Mœurs et l'Esprit des Nations et Sur les Principaux Faits de l'Histoire Depuis Charlemagne Jusqu'à Louis XIII*. Paris, Garnier Frères. (1963).

Volwahsen, A. *Imperial Delhi: The British Capital of the Indian Empire*. München, Prestel. (2002).

Walker, R. *Applied Qualitative Research*. Aldershot, Gower. (2002).

Waltz, K. N. *Theory of International Politics*. Reading, Addison-Wesley. (1979).

Waltz, K. N. 'The Emerging Structure of International Politics.' *The Perils of Anarchy: Contemporary Realism and International Security*. M. E. Brown, S. M. Lynn-Jones and S. E. Miller. Cambridge, MIT Press. (1995). pp. 42–77.

Waltz, K. N. 'International Politics is Not Foreign Policy.' *Security Studies* 6(1). (1996). pp. 54–57.

Waltz, K. N. 'Interview with Kenneth Waltz.' *Review of International Studies* 24(3). (1998). pp. 371–386.

Waltz, K. N. 'Structural Realism after the Cold War.' *International Security* 25(1). (2000). pp. 5–41.

Watts, J. 'Chinese General Warns of Nuclear Risk to US' (16 July, 2006). *The Guardian*. London. (2006).

Weber, A. *Kulturgeschichte als Kultursoziologie*. Heidelberg, Leiden. (1935).

Weber, C. *International Relations Theory: A Critical Introduction*. London, Routledge. (2005).

Weber, M. *The Religion of India: The Sociology of Hinduism and Buddhism*. Glencoe, Free Press. (1958).

Weber, M. *The Protestant Ethic and the Spirit of Capitalism*. Los Angeles, Roxbury. (2001).

Weiner, M. 'India: Two Political Cultures.' *Political Culture and Political Development*. L. W. Pye and S. Verba. Princeton, Princeton University Press. (1965a). pp. 199–244.

Weiner, M. 'Political Integration and Political Development.' *Annals of the American Academy of Political and Social Science* 358(1). (1965b). pp. 52–64.

Weiner, M. *Party Building in a New Nation: The Indian National Congress*. Chicago, University of Chicago Press. (1967).

Weiner, M., Ed. *State Politics in India*. Princeton, Princeton University Press. (1968).

Weiner, M. 'Ancient Indian Political Theory and Contemporary Indian Politics.' *Orthodoxy, Heterodoxy, and Dissent in India*. S. N. Eisenstadt, D. Shulman and R. Kahane. New York, Mouton. (1984). pp. 111–131.

Wendt, A. 'The Agent-Structure Problem in International Relations Theory.' *International Organization* 41(3). (1987). pp. 335–370.

Wendt, A. 'Anarchy is what States Make of it: The Social Construction of Power Politics.' *International Organization* 46(2). (1992). pp. 391–425.

Wendt, A. 'Collective Identity Formation and the International State.' *The American Political Science Review* 88(2). (1994). pp. 384–396.

Wendt, A. 'Identity and Structural Change in International Politics.' *The Return of Culture and Identity in IR Theory*. Y. Lapid and F. V. Kratochwil. Boulder, Lynne Rienner. (1996). pp. 47–64.

Wildemann, R. *Issues of Intercultural Management between India and Germany*. München, TCW. (2007).

Wittgenstein, L. *Tractatus Logico-Philosophicus (introduction by Bertrand Russell)*, London: Routledge & Kegan Paul. (1974).

Woodcock, G. *Gandhi*. London, Fontana. (1972).

Woodward, B. *Plan of Attack*. London, Pocket Books. (2004).

Worcester, K., S. A. Bermanzohn, et al., Eds. 'A new political science reader.' *Violence and Politics: Globalization's Paradox*. London, Routledge. (2002).

Yeats, W. B. *Michael Robartes and the Dancer*. Churchtown, The Cuala Press. (1920).

Yin, R. K. *Case Study Research: Design and Methods*. Thousand Oaks, Sage. (2003).

Zelikow, P. and C. Rice. *Germany Unified and Europe Transformed: A Study in Statecraft*. Cambridge, Harvard University Press. (1997).

Zimmer, H. R. *Philosophies of India*. Princeton, Princeton University Press. (1969).

Index